2001 was a very exciting year
two new outlets, Newbridge an
the pipeline. We have really s
researching extensively in order to find wineries that are committed to
excellence. It was a year of many air
miles, much listening and tasting. We
firmly believe that our recent additions
to the Group's portfolio are some of the
most inspiring wines in the world.

We would particularly encourage you
to experiment with the wines from the
producers listed below. Each has been
subjected to the most comprehensive
screening to guarantee you a pleasura-
ble and memorable experience. *(Some of the wineries listed below
were not available for review by this book due to their very recent
arrival.)*

T. P. Whelehan TP Whelehan   *David Whelehan* David Whelehan

Australia Angoves • Bethany • Reynolds • St. Halletts •
Tatachilla • Xanadu

Chile Los Boldos • St. Emiliana • Villard

France Chanson • Chateau Arnauld • Chateau Cadet Bon •
Chateau Kirwan • Domaine Bernard • Domaine des Anges •
Gerard Bertrand • Moulin de Gassac

Italy Falesco • Pasetti • Rocca • Travignoli

South Africa Guardian Peak • Rust en Vrede

Spain Abadia Retuerta • Sierra Cantabria

Please try some of our new wines and let us know what you think.
For information on our multi award-winning wines please e-mail us
at info@obriensgroup.ie.

Experience the difference

blackrock • bray • dalkey • donnybrook • dun laoghaire • greystones
glasnevin • malahide • navan rd • navan town • newbridge • rathgar
rathmines • sandymount • stillorgan • templeogue • vevay

EuroCave®

The Wine Guide 2002

The Wine Guide 2002

Edited by
Barbara Boyle & Pat Carroll

A. & A. Farmar

© A. & A. Farmar 2001
© articles by the named contributors 2001

All rights reserved. No text may be reproduced in any medium or storage system
without permission from the publishers. The database of which this book is an
emanation is copyright of A. & A. Farmar Ltd.

British Library Cataloguing in Publication Data
A CIP catalogue record for this book is available from the British Library

ISBN 1-899047-76-X

Published by
A. & A. Farmar
Beech House, 78 Ranelagh Village, Dublin 6
Ireland
Tel: (01) 496 3625 Fax: (01) 497 0107
E-mail: afarmar@iol.ie Web: www.farmarbooks.ie

Editorial director: Anna Farmar
Production director: Tony Farmar

Wine editors: Barbara Boyle & Pat Carroll

Contributions by: Niamh Boylan, Barbara Boyle, Pat Carroll,
Alan Crowley, Katherine Farmar, Sergio Furno

Cover design: Alan O'Dea at Steamdriven
Book design: Brosna Press and Bookworks
Typesetting and layout: Bookworks
Printed and bound by: GraphyCems
Marketing consultant: Carly Ptashnik
Sales: Mullett Fitzpatrick
Distribution: Columba Mercier Distribution

Contents

An Invitation

To Readers

Tell us what you think about this book—especially how you think it could be better, to enable you to get more out of wine. The ten best suggestions will get a free copy of the next edition!

To Importers

We are always happy to welcome new suppliers of interesting wines. If you would like to participate in the next edition, please contact Anna or Tony Farmar at the address below.

A. & A. Farmar
Beech House
78 Ranelagh Village
Dublin 6
Ireland
Tel: (01) 496 3625
Fax: (01) 497 0107
E-mail: afarmar@iol.ie

Introduction

Welcome to the seventh edition of *The Best of Wine in Ireland,* now with a main title bowing to the Japanese custom of making paths where people actually walk. So many people refer to the book as 'The Wine Guide' that we decided to follow the custom.

To celebrate the seventh edition we have added colour and wine labels to the text. Our expert panel tasted 25 per cent more wines than ever before, and the listings reflect this. Regular readers will note that we have reverted to the simple and traditional ordering of wines—by country, colour and price band.

Our wine editors Barbara Boyle and Pat Carroll selected over 1600 wines, out of the 7,000 or more for sale on the Irish market, from the lists of 48 importers. The upper price limit was raised to £30 (apart from Champagne). The wines were selected for blind tasting in consultation with the importers to reflect the best elements in their wine lists, with an eye always to affordability and availability.

The tasting sessions on which the guide is based were conducted in an intense series (three a week) between May and August 2001. Our expert panel recommended over 1,200 wines out of the total tasted for inclusion in the guide. This inclusion rate is similar to that of recent years; however, the panel awarded fewer stars than in previous years, reflecting the increasing sophistication of winebuyers in Ireland.

Some of the wines included this year were also in previous editions, with the same or different vintages. However, every single wine included in the book is *re-tasted* each year. Each of the wines is tasted blind, by two members of our expert tasting panel—tasting first alone and then comparing notes. This is a compromise between the idiosyncrasy of individual tasting (for every palate has its blind spots), while agreeing with Robert Parker that judging wines by committee can penalise wines of individuality and character. Critical to the fairness of the process is the fact that like the International Wine Challenge, all wines are tasted blind, that is, with their labels hidden. This is the only way in which an unbiased judgement can be arrived at.

Each wine was assessed for:
- nose—aroma, intensity, complexity
- taste—balance, structure, extract, complexity, length
- value—price/quality ratio.

This year tasters were encouraged to make their judgements of the quality of the wine without knowing the price, and only then to look up the price and consider the price/quality ratio. Only those wines gaining at least 60 per cent of the available marks were included.

We have indicated the approximate retail price in £ and € of each wine listed. However, wine prices are not fixed, so please regard these bands as guidelines only. At the time of writing no one knows exactly how current wine prices, translated into euro, will look by the middle of 2002. We can be confident that a certain smoothing will occur as new wines and new vintages are delivered. It is unlikely that retailers will sell wines for €12.68 (the exact equivalent of the favourite price break £9.99) for very long.

We would like to thank the members of the tasting panel for their commitment and generosity in giving so freely of their time and experience to evaluate the wines. Their enthusiasm and love for the grape arre constantly rewarding and shine out in the tasting notes. We would also like to thank the importers who support the book year after year by submitting samples and patiently answering our requests for further information. Finally, we would like to thank the management and staff of Findlater's Wine Merchants for the use of their premises for the tastings.

Anna and Tony Farmar
September 2001

How to use this guide

The wines are listed in order of country, colour, price-band and then name (listed in letter by letter format). So to find a good value, everyday white wine from Italy, say, go to the early pages of Italy. If you're looking for a special occasion red wine from Spain go to later pages in the chapter on Spain. If you're looking for a particular wine go to the index. Remember, this is a selection of the best of the wines available in Ireland, it is not a comprehensive list. The new design, with extra information in sidebars, allows you to scan quickly for favourite grapes, suggested food matches or for organic or low-alcohol wines.

The best time to drink a particular wine is always a subjective decision. The recommendations given do not indicate the expected life of a wine but the period over which our tasters thought they would enjoy it most.

The symbols	
✹	*Organic*
£/€	*Value—signifies wines which are exceptionally good value for their style and origin*
✓	*Commended—signifies a wine worthy of extra attention; showing extra quality or character*
★	*1 star—signifies a wine of more than ordinary complexity, showing character and style*
★★	*2 star—signifies an elegant wine showing character and complexity, true to its origins, with balance and subtlety*

3

Wake Up To Wakefield

Australia's most awarded wine-maker

International Wine Challenge, London
Medals Awarded

1999   Seven out of seven
2000   Ten out of ten
2001   Ten out of ten

1998

SHIRAZ
CABERNET

CLARE VALLEY

AUSTRALIA

Year after year, medal after medal

Wines of the year

Four wines emerged from the tastings this year as clear winners in their categories, combining intrinsic excellence with value for money and reasonable availability:

White wine of the year

Faiveley Les Joncs AC Montagny 97

Mature nutty, fruity aromas with lovely complexity on the palate—a rare find these days. Wonderful creamy, buttery, hazelnut, slightly smoky, oaky flavours, with apples and lemons. Great richness, balance and length. *Maxxium*

Price	£13–15/€16.50–19
Grape	Chardonnay
Alc/vol	13%
Food	Monkfish
Drink	2001–4

WHITE WINE OF THE YEAR

Red wine of the year

Peter Lehmann The Barossa Cabernet Sauvignon 98

Attractive introduction on the nose of oak and damsons, which belies a much richer palate of figs, spices and ripe blackcurrants. The palate is beautifully structured, with firm tannins and good acidity backing up the abundant fruit flavours. Rich and lengthy. A sleeping giant that will improve, but drinking beautifully now. Superb. *United Beverages*

Price	£9–11/€11.50–14
Region	Barossa Valley
Grape	Cabernet Sauvignon
Alc/vol	13.5%
Food	Steak
Drink	2001–4

RED WINE OF THE YEAR

Sparkling wine of the year

Bernard Gentil Brut Réserve nv

Would that more Champagnes were as balanced as this one! Lovely complex aromas of warm brioche and honeyed melon with some citrus. The palate is beautifully smooth and integrated, with a creamy texture. Rich and supple, it has a fine mousse, lively acidity and a long, well-rounded finish. It will be delicious for a year or two. *Bubble Brothers*

Price	£25–30/€32–40
Grape	Pinot Noir
Alc/vol	12%
Food	Aperitif, versatile
Drink	2001–2

SPARKLING WINE OF THE YEAR

Best value wine of the year

Bolla DOC Valpolicella Classico 97

Incredible—traditional-style Valpolicella at a very modest price! Complex, tasty, drinkable, yet versatile. Cherries, chocolate, raisins, dates and a hint of rubber mingle on the nose. There's more to come—prune, cherry and dark chocolate flavours are backed by a hint of oak on the palate. Deliciously different—full of flavour and body. *Dillons*

Price	£7–9/€9–11.50
Region	Veneto
Grape	Corvina/Rondinella/Molinara
Alc/vol	12%
Food	Versatile
Drink	2001–2

BEST VALUE WINE OF THE YEAR

The tasting panel

The members of the tasting panel are professionally qualified, with many years' experience of tasting.

Kate Barrett works for Searsons Wine Merchants. Kate has worked in the wine trade for over six years, some of which were spent working and living in France. During her time spent with Wines Direct she travelled and sourced wines in Australia and the US.

Niamh L. Boylan is a food and wine consultant. She lectures for the Wine Development Board and the Restaurants Association of Ireland and is a council member of the Irish Guild of Sommeliers.

Barbara Boyle turned to wine after ten years as a tax and financial consultant. She contributes web and consumer articles to *Wine Ireland*. Barbara gained a distinction in the WSET Diploma.

Liam Campbell was Editor of the 2001 edition of *The Best of Wine in Ireland*, writes the monthly wine column 'Capital Drinks' in *The Dubliner* magazine and is a regular contributor to *Wine Ireland*. Liam also lectures for the Wine Development Board and wine clubs.

Pat Carroll is a food and wine editor. She has lectured for the Wine Development Board and is Secretary of Premier Cru Wine Club.

Tony Cleary, who has worked for over twenty years in the wine trade, is now with Barry & Fitzwilliam, specialising in Central and South-Eastern Europe.

Colm Conaty is a sales representative with TDL.

Tony Condon is a management consultant specialising in strategic and corporate development. He has had a long association with the drinks business and is a former marketing manager of Baileys Irish Cream.

Fiona Conway works with the O'Briens Wine Off Licence Group.

Willie Dardis is Regional Manager for TDL, a member of the Irish Guild of Sommeliers and a member of the WSET Diploma Students' and Graduates' Wine Club.

Martina Delaney has been sommelier at L'Ecrivain restaurant since 1993.

Des Drumm, former Managing Director of Grants of Ireland (Sales) Ltd, has been Managing Director of C&C Wholesale Ltd since 1997. He holds the WSET Diploma (Hons.).

Peter Dunne is a director of Mitchell & Son Wine Merchants.

Gerry Fitzsimons is co-founder of WineOnline. He is a member of the Irish Guild of Sommeliers and a winner of the George O'Malley Tasting Cup.

Sergio Furno has worked with Oddbins in London and was assistant manager with the Crowe SuperValu Off Licence Group. He is now pursuing his wine trade career in France.

Terry Greene owns and runs Vinovate and Winebrief, two independent consultancy services for the trade and the public. He lectures for the Wine Development Board and has judged for the International Wine and Spirit Competition, London.

Catherine Griffith is a wine consultant to Molloy's Liquor Stores and lecturer for the Wine Development Board.

Sarah Grubb entered the wine trade with Oddbins and returned to Ireland in 1997 to work for Wines Direct before moving to Dublin to manage the Findlater Wine Vaults. Currently Sarah is researching food and wine in France and Italy.

Gerry Gunnigan is Wholesale Manager for Mitchell & Son Wine Merchants. He has worked in the wine trade in London as well as working a season in vineyards in Alsace.

Evelyn Jones is the proprietor of The Vintry wine shop, Rathgar, and winner of the Gilbey/NOffLA Dublin Off Licence of the Year Award 2000 and 2001. She is a member of the Champagne Academy and runs wine appreciation courses as well as a wine club.

Jacinta Kennedy, formerly of the Mill Wine Cellar, Maynooth, and Taserra Wine Merchants, is now manager of the Crowe SuperValu Off Licence Group.

Sinead Lewis, formerly of Searsons Wine Merchants and the Wine Development Board, is an independent wine consultant. She won the Maggie McNie Tasting Cup in 1998.

David Lonergan is manager of The Vintry wine shop in Rathgar. He lectures for the Vintry Wine Club, where his particular forte is the Rhône Valley. He is a member of the Champagne Academy.

Canice McCarthy is an off-licence manager for O'Briens Wine Off Licence Group in their Malahide branch. He is a member of the Irish Guild of Sommeliers, teaches wine appreciation and is a wine columnist for the People Group of newspapers.

Cathal McHugh has worked in the wine trade for seven years and is the proprietor of McHugh's Off Licence. He also runs a wine club in Sutton.

Julie Martin is an award-winning sommelier and has represented Ireland; she is ranked Commandeur in the Association Internationale des Maîtres Conseils en Gastronomie Française, has worked at Ashford Castle and Restaurant Patrick Guilbaud, and is Secretary of the Irish branch of the Champagne Academy.

Ben Mason, formerly of Searsons Wine Merchants, is co-owner of the Wicklow Wine Company.

Anne Mullin is co-founder of WineOnline and a council member of the Irish Guild of Sommeliers. She travels extensively to source, taste and buy wines from world suppliers.

Monica Murphy of Febvre is a professional wine and cheese consultant, lecturer and writer.

Ciaran Newman is a Director of Cheers! Take Home and a council member of the Licensed Vintners' Association.

Mary O'Callaghan is Chairperson of the Irish Guild of Sommeliers, wine consultant to the Cheers! Take Home group and the Licensed Vintners' Association and lectures for the Wine Development Board and the College of Marketing, Dublin Institute of Technology.

Maureen O'Hara is brand manager with Findlater Wine Merchants.

Sinead O'Sullivan works for Mitchell & Son Wine Merchants.

Alan O'Toole works for Searsons Wine Merchants.

Carly Ptashnick, formerly with Gleesons Wines & Spirits, now works for the *Irish Farmers' Journal*. She contributes wine articles to *The Big Issues*.

John Quinn owns a management training company, Priority Management, and conducts wine appreciation courses and American wine evenings.

Trudi Rothwell works for Searsons Wine Merchants.

Barry Walsh has been Master Blender at Irish Distillers since 1982. He writes and lectures on wines and spirits in his spare time.

David Whelehan is marketing manager of the O'Briens Wine Off Licence Group.

John Wilson is an independent wine consultant. He has wide experience of the wine trade in Ireland and the UK.

Grape varieties *Pat Carroll*

What determines the character of a wine? The country, the soil and the climate are all very important. And let's not forget the winemaker. But the grape variety is crucial. We all know the names of the most popular varieties—Cabernet Sauvignon, Chardonnay, Shiraz, Sauvignon Blanc—but wine is made from around a thousand European grape varieties. Portugal, for example, has hundreds of grape varieties not found elsewhere, including the infamous Esgana Cão, or 'Dog Strangler'.

Sometimes the name of a grape variety is shown on the label, which makes it simple to identify, but wines are often blends of different varieties. When you buy Valpolicella, you may not realise that it is made from Corvina, Rondinella and Molinara grapes. And up to thirteen varieties may go into red Châteauneuf-du-Pape. The fact that a wine is a blend of different varieties doesn't make it inferior—some of the most expensive wines in the world are blends. Bordeaux clarets, such as Premier Cru Château Margaux, are made from Cabernet Sauvignon, Cabernet Franc, Merlot and Petit Verdot, while sweet French Sauternes is made from a blend of Sémillon, Sauvignon Blanc and Muscadelle.

The table below aims to provide a short guide to some of the most popular grape varieties.

White

Albariño/Alvarinho (NW Spain; NW Portugal)	
Dry, aromatic, lemon/peach aromas, full flavours of citrus and peaches, firm backbone of acidity; can become honeyed with age but usually drunk young	*Rías Baixas wines from Spain; some Portuguese Vinho Verde wines*

Chardonnay (originally from Burgundy, France, but now grown everywhere)	
Chameleon—ranges from very dry, light, minerally, high-acid, citrus-dominated wines from cooler climates to dryish oaked heavyweights full of butterscotch, peaches, melons and pineapples from hotter regions; affinity with oak cask ageing	*Champagne, white Burgundy, including Chablis, Mâcon, Marsannay, Meursault, Montagny, Montrachet, Pouilly-Fuissé and Rully; varietal from Argentina, Bulgaria, California, Chile, New Zealand, South Africa, Australia*

Chenin Blanc/Pineau/Steen (Loire, France; South Africa; California)	
Dry to sweet, pale lemon in youth maturing to pale gold in older sweet wines, honey, wet wool and damp straw flavours, possibly nuts and marmalade in mature sweet wines; high acidity ensures that Loire sweet wines will age for decades	*Dry: Savennières, South African varietals and blends, mass-produced Californian blends* *Dry/medium dry/sweet: Vouvray* *Sweet: Bonnezeaux, Coteaux du Layon, Montlouis, Quarts de Chaume* *Sparkling: Saumur Mousseux*

Cortese (Piedmont, NW Italy)

Dry, crisp wines with fresh acidity, slightly floral, lemony aromas and steely lemon fruit	*Gavi*

Garganega (Veneto, NE Italy)

Dry, aromas of lemon and almonds in the best wines, fresh and fruity; drink very young	*Soave (with Trebbiano—dry), Recioto di Soave (sweet)*

Gewurztraminer/Gewürztraminer (Alsace, France; Germany; Austria; New Zealand; Australia)

Medium dry to sweet, colour can be deep; very characteristic perfumed aromas of lychees, roses and spice, flowery flavour but lacking the acidity of Riesling; classic accompaniment to spicy food	*Try a dry Gewurztraminer from Alsace for pure flavour; available as a varietal from Germany, Austria and the New World*

Macabeo/Viura/Maccabeu (Spain; S France)

Dry, floral aromas, not much acidity, quite fruity; most wines should be drunk young	*Blended in white Rioja, Cava, Rueda, white Côtes du Roussillon*

Malvasia/Malmsey (Sardinia, Friuli, central Italy; Madeira, Portugal)

Ancient grape, making dry to sweet styles, pale lemon (dry) to deep amber (dessert), nuts, cream and apricots, slightly spicy; early drinking or long ageing	*Collio, Isonzo, blended with Trebbiano in Frascati and central Italian whites; sweet wines in Sardinia; Madeira*

Marsanne (Rhône, Languedoc-Roussillon, France; Victoria, Australia)

Dry, deep coloured, full bodied, peach, honeysuckle and almond aromas (melons and mangoes in Australia), quite heavy, usually matured in oak, often blended with Roussanne	*White Coteaux du Tricastin, white Côtes du Rhône, white Crozes-Hermitage, white Hermitage, white St Joseph, St Péray; S French whites; varietal in Australia, e.g. Ch. Tahbilk*

Melon de Bourgogne/Muscadet (Loire, France)

Very dry, light, fresh, crisp, some green apple flavours but often fairly neutral; best examples are 'sur lie' (matured in barrels containing yeast sediment); classic seafood wine	*In ascending order of quality—Muscadet, Muscadet de Sèvre et Maine, Muscadet de Sèvre et Maine Sur Lie*

Müller-Thurgau/Rivaner (Germany)

Usually off-dry to medium-sweet wines, light in colour, low in aroma and acidity; not a quality grape; drink young	*Liebfraumilch, e.g. Black Tower, Blue Nun*

Muscat (Alsace, Rhône, France; Italy; Australia; Greece)

Dry to very sweet, pale lemon (dry) to
deep amber (sweet), marked grape and
musk aromas, scented fruity flavours,
touch of spice, moderate acidity

*Dry: Muscat d'Alsace
Sparkling medium sweet: Asti Spumante
Sweet: vins doux naturels from France,
e.g. Muscat de Beaumes de Venise,
liqueur Muscats from Australia and
Greece*

Palomino (Jerez, Spain; South Africa; Australia; California)

Low acidity, low sugar levels and its
tendency to oxidise make Palomino the
perfect grape for dry, medium or sweet
sherry

*All styles of sherry—Fino, Amontillado,
Oloroso, Palo Cortado*

Parellada (Spain)

Dry, lemon and flower aromas, zesty
acidity, apple fruit; drink very young

*Blended in Spanish sparkling wine Cava
and white Costers del Segre; 100% in
Torres' Viña Sol*

Pinot Blanc/Pinot Bianco/Weissburgunder (Alsace, France; Italy; Germany;
Austria)

Mostly dry, some apple aromas,
almonds in Austria, soft, quite full
bodied, moderate/high acidity; usually
for early drinking

*Alsace varietal, Italian varietal or blend,
e.g. Colli Orientale del Friuli, Collio;
Italian sparkling wine; dry wines from
Pfalz and Baden; sweet and dry wines
from Austria*

Pinot Gris (formerly Tokay d'Alsace)
Pinot Grigio/Ruländer/Grauburgunder (Alsace, France; NE Italy; Germany;
New Zealand)

In Alsace styles range from dry to
sweet, with fairly deep colour and quite
full body, slightly spicy, perfumed
aromas, peach fruit that develops
buttery flavours with age—rich and
spicy wine; drier, lighter, crisper and
not so aromatic in Italy

*Varietal in Alsace; varietal in Italy or part
of the blend in Collio; varietal in Germany
and New Zealand*

Riesling (Germany; Alsace, France; Austria; Australia; New Zealand; USA; South Africa)

Dry to sweet, pale straw with green
hints to deep gold in older sweet
wines, floral and honey aromas when
young, developing petrol-like notes on
ageing; apple or peach flavours in
Europe (depending on sweetness),
limes in New World, piercing acidity,
rich fruit on the palate; can age for
decades

*Made usually as a 100% varietal, from
dry to sweet, in Germany (Mosel-Saar-
Ruwer, Rheingau, Pfalz, Nahe), Alsace,
Austria (Wachau), Australia (Clare Valley,
Eden Valley), New Zealand
(Marlborough), California, Oregon,
Washington State, South Africa*

Roussanne (Rhône, Languedoc-Roussillon, France)

Dry, aromatic, herbal aromas, elegant,
good acidity, often blended with
Marsanne

*White Châteauneuf-du-Pape, white
Coteaux du Tricastin, white Côtes du
Rhône, white Crozes-Hermitage, white
Hermitage, white St Joseph, St Péray;
S French whites*

Sauvignon Blanc (Loire, Bordeaux, France; New Zealand; Chile; California; South Africa)

Dry or sweet, grassy, herbaceous, gooseberries, green apples, even cat's pee aromas, with citrus and green apple flavours, steely acidity; mostly for early drinking	*Sancerre, Pouilly-Fumé, part of the blend in white Bordeaux and Sauternes; varietal from New Zealand (especially Marlborough), Chile, California (oaked), South Africa*

Sémillon/Semillon (Bordeaux, France; Australia; South Africa)

Dry to sweet, light in colour to deep gold, not much aroma when young, perhaps some toast or wax, lowish acidity, but matures to nutty, waxy, honeyed aromas in Australia and honey and marmalade in Sauternes and Barsac wines; citrus and nuts on the palate in drier wines, marmalade and honey in sweet wines; very long-lived wines	*Most important grape in Sauternes, Barsac and white Bordeaux; varietal in the Hunter Valley and Barossa Valley; often blended with Chardonnay or Sauvignon Blanc in Australian mass-market wines; varietal in South Africa*

Torrontés (Argentina)

Dry, with distinctive flowery, Muscat-like fragrant nose, zesty acidity, rich fruit; early drinking	*Blended or varietal from Argentina*

Trebbiano/Ugni Blanc (Italy; SW France)

Dry, light, high acidity, quite neutral flavour, medium body, workaday grape; early drinking	*Found in Trebbiano d'Abruzzo, Trebbiano di Romagna, Orvieto, Frascati, Soave, Lugana, Galestro, VdP des Côtes de Gascogne; base wine for French Cognac and Armagnac*

Verdelho (Madeira, Portugal; Australia)

Fresh, lively, lemony wines of good quality; good ageing potential	*Dry whites from the Douro Valley and Australia; Madeira*

Verdicchio (Marches, central Italy)

Dry, pale straw with a green tinge, crisp, lemony acidity, nutty flavour with a mineral, salty edge, slight bitter almonds finish; drink young, though best can age for five years; good with seafood; semi-sweet and sweet wines also made	*Verdicchio dei Castelli di Jesi, Verdicchio di Matelica (white and sparkling)*

Viognier (Rhône, Languedoc-Roussillon, France; California; South Africa)

Dry, pale straw developing to pale gold, apricot, peach and spring blossom aromas becoming honeyed with maturity, deep, rich palate with apricot and peach flavours, quite high alcohol; drink young, less than eight years old; moderate to low acidity	*Condrieu (vast majority dry, but a few producers make demi-sec wines), Ch. Grillet; can appear in Côte Rôtie; increasingly used in white Côtes du Rhône; vins de pays from Languedoc-Roussillon; varietal in California; interesting wines from South Africa*

Red

Barbera (Piedmont, NW Italy; Victoria, Australia)

Deep ruby, fruity, full bodied, not very tannic; for early drinking	*Barbera d'Alba, Barbera d'Asti, Barbera del Monferrato*

Bonarda (Argentina; N Italy)

Dense, fruity, plummy, full bodied	*Rising star in Argentina; Oltrepò Pavese*

Brunello (Tuscany, central Italy)

Relative of Sangiovese, but with more flavour and body; plums, prunes and spices, fair bit of tannin; ages well	*Brunello di Montalcino*

Cabernet Franc (Bordeaux, Loire, France)

Fragrant, lighter in colour and less tannic than its relative, Cabernet Sauvignon; redcurrant fruit, medium body	*Blended in Bordeaux, playing a more important role on the Right Bank of the Gironde in the St Émilion/Pomerol area; on its own or blended in Loire reds— Saumur-Champigny, Bourgeuil, Chinon, Anjou-Villages*

Cabernet Sauvignon (originally from Bordeaux, France, but now planted world wide)

Deep ruby with a purple tinge, blackcurrants, chocolate, violets, green peppers, cigar-box aromas when mature, firm tannins; capable of very long ageing; good affinity with oak cask maturing	*Blended in Bordeaux clarets, ranging in quality from AC Bordeaux through crus bourgeois to crus classés; on its own or blended in Australia (with Shiraz), California (with Merlot etc.), Chile, Italy (Supertuscans), South Africa, Spain, Romania, Bulgaria—everywhere*

Carignan/Cariñena/Mazuelo (S France (most widely planted grape variety in France), Rioja, Spain; Sardinia, Italy)

Lots of colour, tannin, alcohol and bitterness, but little fruit or aroma; some good examples from old vines in S France, but mostly blended with Cinsault and Grenache	*Part of the blend in many Languedoc-Roussillon wines such as Corbières, Costières de Nîmes, Coteaux du Languedoc, Côtes du Roussillon, Faugères, Fitou, Minervois, St Chinian; Carignano del Sulcis from Sardinia; some Riojas from Spain*

Carmenère (Chile; Bordeaux, France)

Deep ruby, red berry fruit aromas, soft red fruit flavours, hint of chocolate, full bodied, similar to Merlot but less ageing potential	*Now being produced as a varietal in its own right in Chile, but confused with Merlot in Chile for many years (70–90% of Chilean 'Merlot' is Carmenère); permitted ingredient of red Bordeaux but rarely used*

Cinsault/Cinsaut/Hermitage (S France; Lebanon; South Africa)

Pale, soft, light, quite perfumed and fruity; used a lot for rosé in France	*Blended in Languedoc-Roussillon wines such as Corbières, Costières de Nîmes, Côtes du Roussillon, Faugères, St Chinian; blended with Cabernet Sauvignon and Syrah in Ch. Musar (Lebanon); crossed with Pinot Noir in South Africa to produce the Pinotage grape*

Dolcetto (Piedmont, NW Italy)

Deep purple-ruby colour, soft, gentle wine with a touch of liquorice; drink young	*Dolcetto DOCs from Italy, e.g. Dolcetto d'Alba*

Gamay (Beaujolais, Loire, France)

Pale in colour with a bluish tinge, light wine with juicy red fruit aromas; some people find bananas and boiled sweets there too; drink very young	*Beaujolais, Beaujolais crus (Brouilly, Chénas, Chiroubles, Côte de Brouilly, Fleurie, Juliénas, Morgon, Moulin-à-Vent, Regnié, St Amour), Cheverny, St Pourçain*

Grenache/Garnacha/Cannonau (Rhône, S France; Spain; Sardinia, Italy; Australia; California)

Fairly light colour, fruity, juicy, slightly sweet raspberry fruit, lowish tannin and acidity, high alcohol; can be spicy if not overcropped; huge variation in quality	*One of the ingredients in Châteauneuf-du-Pape; S France rosés, vins doux naturels such as Rivesaltes and Banyuls (great with chocolate desserts), Spanish Priorato and Rioja; Cannonau di Sardegna; blended into mass-market wines in Australia and California*

Malbec/Cot (Argentina; Cahors, SW France)

Dark-coloured, ripe, tannic wines with good concentration and blackberry flavour; can be austere, peppery, spicy; wines age well	*Treated properly, capable of great things in Argentinian varietals—similar to Bordeaux in flavour but not as firm in structure; in France, part of the blend in AC Cahors and other wines from the SW*

Merlot (Bordeaux, S/SW France; Italy; California; Washington; South America; Bulgaria; Romania; Australia; New Zealand)

Deep ruby, smooth, plummy, maturing to rich fruit cake flavours—velvety texture, with less colour, tannin and acidity than Cabernet Sauvignon; softer and earlier maturing	*Generic AC Bordeaux, St Émilion, Pomerol, Buzet, Cahors, vins de pays from S France, N Italian Merlots, US varietals or 'Meritage' (a blend of Cabernet Sauvignon, Merlot, Cabernet Franc, Malbec and Petit Verdot), varietal in South America (though much Chilean 'Merlot' is really Carmenère, a Bordeaux variety now little used in France); Bulgarian, Romanian, Australian and New Zealand varietals*

Montepulciano (central Italy, mainly Abruzzo)

Deeply coloured, rich, brambles, cherries, pepper, spice, zesty acidity, firm tannins; best can age well	*Montepulciano d'Abruzzo, Rosso Conero, Biferno, Rosso Piceno (confusingly, Vino Nobile di Montepulciano is made with Sangiovese, not Montepulciano)*

Mourvèdre/Monastrell/Mataro (S Rhône, Languedoc-Roussillon, S France; Spain; Australia; California)

Lots of blackberry fruit, fleshy, high in alcohol and tannin, slightly meaty flavour in youth; blends well with Grenache or Cinsault, giving structure	*Blended in Bandol, Côtes du Rhône, Côtes du Ventoux, Vacqueyras, Costières de Nîmes, Côtes du Roussillon, Faugères, Fitou, Minervois, St Chinian; used in many Spanish DOs, e.g. Alicante, Almansa, Jumilla, Valencia, Yecla; Australian varietals from the Barossa Valley; fashionable in California in the 90s as part of the Rhône Ranger movement to make Rhône-style wines*

Nebbiolo (Piedmont, NW Italy)

Not very deep colour, but powerful truffle, raspberry, liquorice, chocolate and prune aromas—even violets; high acidity, very firm tannins; usually needs long ageing	*Barolo, Barbaresco, Gattinara, Nebbiolo d'Alba, Valtellina*

Negroamaro (Puglia, S Italy)

Deep colour, high alcohol, rich, robust red wines, some of which can age well	*Salice Salentino, Rosso di Cerognola*

Petit Verdot (Bordeaux, France; California)

Rich colour, hint of violets on the nose, concentrated tannic wines with a touch of spice	*Used as a small part of the blend in Bordeaux clarets and Californian Meritage wines*

Petite Sirah (California; South America)

Inky, quite tannic, firm, robust, full-bodied wines	*Unrelated to the Syrah of the Rhône; traditionally blended with Zinfandel in California, now offered as a varietal as well*

Pinot Meunier (Champagne, France; Australia; California)

Gives freshness, fruitiness and crisp acidity to sparkling wines	*Champagne, sparkling wines from Australia and California*

Pinot Noir/Pinot Nero/Spätburgunder (Burgundy, Champagne, Loire, Alsace, France; Germany; Italy; California; Oregon; Australia; New Zealand; South Africa; Romania)

Much lighter in colour and less tannic than, say, Cabernet Sauvignon, quite high acidity, magical sweet aromas of strawberries or cherries, turning to mushrooms, truffles and even farmyards as it ages; velvety texture; long ageing; used in sparkling wines to give body and fruit	*Red Burgundy from basic AC Bourgogne to Grand Cru, blended in Champagne, used in sparkling wines from the New World; red Menetou-Salon, red Sancerre; varietal in Alsace, Germany, Italy, California, Oregon, Australia, New Zealand, South Africa, Romania; best in cool, marginal climates*

Pinotage (South Africa)

South African crossing of Pinot Noir and Cinsault, deep colour, can have good body and juicy berry fruit, but there can be a certain paint-like or 'hospital' aroma (isoamyl acetate) in some wines	*South African varietal*

Sangiovese (central Italy, especially Tuscany; Argentina)

Slightly pale colour, very dry, cherry and possibly farmyard aromas, cherry and plum flavours, high acidity, robust tannins, slightly bitter finish; good for ageing, can be austere in youth	*Part of the blend in Chianti, Carmignano, Vino Nobile di Montepulciano, Torgiano and the Supertuscan Tignanello; varietal in Argentina*

Syrah/Shiraz (Rhône, Languedoc-Roussillon, France; Australia; South Africa; California)

Deep colour, intense blackberries, raspberries, earthy, spicy, pepper, burnt rubber, tannic, rich, needs time to soften	*Hermitage, Crozes-Hermitage, St Joseph, Châteauneuf-du-Pape, vins de pays from Languedoc-Roussillon; on its own or blended with Cabernet Sauvignon in Australia; varietal in South Africa; varietal or Rhône blend in California*

Tannat (SW France; Uruguay)

Very dark, very tannic, raspberry aromas, needs time in bottle; can age well	*Part of the blend in Madiran and Cahors; as a varietal in Uruguay*

Tempranillo/Tinta Roriz (Spain; Portugal)

Deep colour, strawberry and tobacco aromas, low acidity and tannin, good for early drinking or ageing	*Blended in Rioja, Costers del Segre, Navarra, Penedès, Ribera del Duero, Somontano, Valdepeñas; as Tinto Roriz, part of the blend in port; Portuguese red wines*

Touriga Nacional (Portugal; Australia)

Deep colour, mulberry aromas, concentrated fruit, high tannins; in port, very long ageing potential	*Part of the blend in port, Douro and Dão wines; Australian port*

Zinfandel (California)

Varies in style from very dark, alcoholic, bramble-flavoured reds to mass-produced sweetish 'blush' wines; can make excellent reds in the right hands	*Zinfandels in all shades from palest pink to deepest red*

Wine web sites *Barbara Boyle*

This year I have focused on Irish web sites, as these are immediately available to the Irish consumer. Many of these sites are attached to real bricks and mortar businesses and can do very well, as they are extensions of existing businesses with all the recognition that implies. Setting up a completely new business from scratch, on the other hand, is always difficult and the Web poses particular problems. The infinite length and complexity of the 'virtual High Street' make it very difficult to persuade consumers to beat a path to a new site.

Worldwide, the trend has been for rapid consolidation and mergers, not only between web sites but also between web sites and independent bricks and mortar businesses. This is bound to happen in Ireland too, with some sites disappearing and others growing by consolidation. The following are just some of the sites available to Irish consumers at the time of writing.

Off-licence chains
Most large off-licence chains have well-designed web sites. Have a look at bubblebrothers.com, molloys.ie, mitchellandson.com and oddbins.ie.

Also take a look at mccabeswines.ie and obrienswines.ie, which were both under construction or reconstruction at the time of going to print. The Cheers! Take Home group has a web site at cheerstakehome.ie.

Supermarkets
You can buy wine on line from Tesco and Superquinn at tesco.ie and buy4now.ie and both sites are very professional. When it comes to getting wine to your door, they have very reliable and flexible services. Super-valu is developing online shopping at supervaluonline.ie. While you can't yet buy wine from Dunnes Stores at dunnesstores.com you can pick up quite a bit of information on their wines. Pettitts, with a number of stores in Wexford and Wicklow, has a site at pettitts.ie with a small 'World of wine' section.

Independents
A number of independent wine retailers have quite exciting and interesting sites, due in no small part to the interesting wines they have on their shelves. You can travel the country in search of goodies from some of the following sites:
- karwigs.ie (Cork)
- lecaveau.ie (Kilkenny)
- waterfordwinevault.com (Waterford)
- onthegrapevine.ie (Dalkey, Co. Dublin)
- jnwine.com (Nicholsons of Crossgar)
- redmonds.ie (Ranelagh, Dublin 6)
- greenacres.ie (Wexford)

Direct selling and mail order
Companies selling to the consumer directly via mail order or the Web are on the increase; some also sell their wine through the retail or restaurant trades. Wines Direct is a long-established mail-order company with an extensive list of wines at wines-direct.com. Burgundy Direct has also been in business for quite some time and now has a web site, burgundydirect.ie. wineonline.ie and slainteonline.com are successful businesses that have been

developed on the Web. All these sites are easy to navigate, have interesting selections of wines at good prices and deliver quickly and competently. There are a host of other Irish sites with which I am less familiar, including:

- ewine.com
- frontpagewines.com
- wineworks.ie
- onthecase.ie
- merchantwines.com
- winebythecase.net

irelandonwine.com has now closed its web site and is operating as a wholesaler.

The wine importers

Details of importer addresses are given at the back of the book. An increasing number have web sites. While some of these sites are consumer oriented, others are more for business-to-business purposes. If you like a wine from a particular importer and want to find out where it is available or more information on it, their web site is a good place to start. One useful web site is Gilbeys thewineroom.ie, which is intended as an information and educational resource for the consumer, and includes discussion boards and a chat room. The amount of information that you can get and the way it is presented varies widely, but you can pick up useful information on wines and wineries from sites such as grantsofireland.ie, findlaters.com, daltonwines.com, barryfitzwilliam.com and wine-ireland.com (the site of the Spanish wine importer, IberExpo). Companies that have gone down the business-to-business route, which forms such an important part of the future of the Web, include irishdistillers.ie and febvre.ie (whose site is under construction).

Other web sites

There are a small number of wine-related sites that do not fit into other categories but are well worth using. These include a fine wine brokerage site, thewinecentre.ie, and cellars.ie for wine storage and accessories.

Worth a detour also are the web sites of the Wine Development Board, wineboard.com, and the independent wine and spirit retailers' association, noffla.ie. Then there are the magazine sites for wineireland.ie and foodandwine.ie (under construction).

Quite a few wine businesses in Ireland have registered their names as a dot com or dot ie. Whether this is just to protect their name or is evidence of an Internet strategy is not clear. All that is certain is that more sites will come, change and go over the next year.

Web essentials

Some wine sites are so essential that they should be included in everyone's Favourites folder. These are my desert island web sites:

- decanter.com, the web site of *Decanter* magazine
- winespectator.com, the *Wine Spectator* magazine web site
- uvine.com, a growing and really competent, easy-to-use wine auction site
- winesearcher.com, where you can search a wide range of wine merchants worldwide for your desired wine purchase

Note: Inclusion of a web site address is not an endorsement of the products or services offered.

Food and wine *Niamh Boylan*

Sounds simple—food and wine, a natural pairing—yet it is so easy to get bogged down with the vast and often confusing range of wines available as we stand in front of the supermarket or wine shop display. The easy option is the one frequently taken as we rush in and grab a familiar bottle of Château Something-Super.

You know the wine, it's red, rich and oaky, with lots of chewy tannins and tonight's dinner is a Thai chicken curry. How was it for you? Barely OK or, to be really honest, a bit yucky. All those strong tannins and heavy oaking will have overpowered the more subtle flavours of the chicken. Much better to have had an aromatic white such as a New World Gewürztraminer, a Torrontés or, perhaps, a dry Muscat. If red is your thing, stick to something with soft tannins and lots of juicy fruits, such as a Spanish Garnacha.

Food styles and methods of cooking have changed enormously in recent years, along with our lifestyles. Very rich food is no longer as fashionable as it was and many classic dishes are prepared in a lighter way. Buzz words such as 'organic', 'healthy options' and, thankfully, 'wine is good for you' pop up all over the place. As if we needed an excuse! Continuous evolution in cooking means that there are no real rules in modern cuisine. Flexible innovation is the name of the game and modern wines are well suited, being largely made in a forward, food-friendly style. Along with chefs, winemakers are meeting the challenge of their customers' palates.

Modern cuisine encompasses a vast spectrum—Mexican, Pacific Rim, Thai, Middle Eastern and North African. The list is endless. Many different ethnic foods and cooking methods abound to create some fascinating and delicious dishes. So it is a challenge to find a wine to match a particular style of cooking. But what fun you can have tasting and hitting on a great combination.

Modern winemakers are producing lots of zippy, fruit-driven styles and of course some of the most innovative modern cooking comes from New World wine regions. Think of the Napa Valley with their wonderful salad and vegetable combinations. Italian varietal wines are very hip in fashion-conscious California. Last summer I enjoyed a delicious food and wine match at an outdoor lunch in Santa Barbara in a peaceful courtyard restaurant with the gentle background music of a small central fountain (very feng shui). The wine was a local Pinot Grigio Di Bruno, crisp and fruity, which tasted delicious with a simple linguine and clams. Or think of New Zealand, where local chefs cook an exotic range of fish dishes with unusual fruit and herb garnishes, perfectly suited to their vibrant, fruity Sauvignon Blanc and Riesling wines.

The golden rule when matching food and wine is 'a light wine with light dishes, something big and gutsy with rich, hearty food'. The balance and weight of the wine should match the balance and weight of the dish. If some of the extra ingredients appear to conflict with the main ingredient, stick to the dominant one. For instance, in a dish of baked fish with coconut curry and banana relish (believe me, I've had it!)—coconut and banana are dominant, so try an oaky Chardonnay or Marsanne.

A delicate Mosel Riesling would be swamped alongside a rich lobster Thermidor. Instead, try a full-bodied Chardonnay from South Africa. The rich, buttery sauce will balance beautifully with the smooth, creamy flavour of the wine. For light fish and shellfish dishes I suggest Muscadet, Sancerre or Pinot Grigio wines. These all have good clean fruit with refreshing acidity.

Let's not forget fizz in all of this—Spanish Cava really lifts fish and chips and also goes well with smoked fish dishes. Go on, try it!

From young, fruity Dolcettos and Beaujolais to big, brawny Shiraz and Barolo, the choice of red wines is vast. Definitely a cellar full of riches. Simple, soft fruity reds are pretty versatile, but wines with a lot of tannin can really affect the taste of food. Tannic wines need richly flavoured meat dishes, something with plenty of protein such as sirloin steak. Keep your fine Napa Cabernet or Hermitage for a winter game dinner. These wines are certainly too big and complex to drink with a simple grilled chicken or burgers.

Having a hot Indian dish? Why not try a macho red Zinfandel or a South African Pinotage to power along Harley-Davidson style.

Let's consider some of the elements in wine and how they can affect food flavours.

Acidity

Acidity in food needs to be matched by acidity in the wine, otherwise the wine will taste flat and boring. So bear this in mind if a dish includes capers, tomatoes or apples. Sauvignon Blanc, with its natural acidity, is very good with tomato sauces and the chalky acidity of goats' cheese. Portuguese reds have a lot of acidity too and are great with fatty foods such as chorizo or ham. The acidity helps to cut through the fat.

Tannin

This applies to red wines and is a necessary part in the structure and body of a wine. There are different levels of tannin in different wines, ranging from very firm and gripping in Bordeaux reds (particularly young clarets) to soft in many New World Merlots, southern French wines and many Grenache-based wines. Tannin in wine can make salty food taste very bitter. A similar effect happens with food flavoured with chilli, as it increases the perception of tannin. Tannic wines make fish dishes taste unpleasantly metallic. Fruity Pinot Noir reds can be very successful with many fish dishes, particularly rich or oily fish like tuna or salmon.

With spicy food, try something soft and fruity from the southern Rhône or a light New World Merlot. Very tannic young reds are softened by the right dish. Lamb or beef with a lot of protein or creamy cheeses with a high fat content are well suited.

Oak

Oak is a big player in many wines, both red and white. Sometimes it plays a minor role, as in the use of oak chips—but that's another story. Oak softens the harsh tannins in red wine and gives that luscious, smooth creaminess to white wine, particularly Chardonnays. Adding a squeeze of lemon to a dish can make a wine taste less oaky. Oaked wines generally have an added richness, so bear this in mind when matching them with food.

Sweetness

If a dish is sweet, be sure to have a sweet wine with it. The wine should be sweeter than the food, or it will taste sour. Sweetness in wine increases our perception of acidity. Scallops and crab have a certain natural sweetness, so think of a demi-sec Vouvray or one of the many New World Viogniers.

Some of my own favourites from the past year include drinking a 1990 Veuve Clicquot champagne with a Japanese Tepanaki dinner. This was a truly amazing synergy of how two components made for one fantastic experience. Last Christmas I had roast goose memorably partnered with a rich concentrated Aussie Shiraz, Summerfield. It was sensational, a whopper of a wine, a real knife and fork job, well suited to the richness of the goose.

The great thing about this food and wine exercise is that there isn't just one magic formula, but a range of good choices. Be adventurous and experiment—you'll find lots of dream combos, hopefully a few with the 'wow' factor. It's not necessary to spend a lot of money to get something unique and tasty, so spread your tasting wings. Check out our best wine selections and find some new favourites for 2002.

The mystery of vintages

Alan Crowley, Master of Wine

A great part of the mystique of wine is the importance of the vintage, and which are the better or lesser years. Unfortunately, to many consumers the concept of a vintage represents yet another unknown in the wine maze.

Put simply, a vintage is the year in which the grapes were picked and the wine was made. It is therefore an indication of how old the wine is. However, as with other agricultural products, the critical importance of the vintage lies in the variability from year to year of weather conditions during the growing season. In some regions, notably in Europe, the effect is of particular importance on the potential quality of the final wine. Thus, in good vintage years, when there have been sufficient rainy and dry periods, with sufficient sunshine and warm temperatures at the right time, grapes can be produced of a better quality to make a superior wine, as opposed to those in lesser years when the weather is not so right for quality grape production.

The effect of the weather, and hence the reputation of the vintage, is usually more important in wine regions whose climate is more marginal for the growing of grapes. Generally such regions are in Europe—in Germany, in Burgundy and Bordeaux in France, in Spain and Italy. Wine regions with more or less regular weather conditions produce wines where vintages year to year assume less importance. Such wine regions include the New World vineyards of South Africa, California, Australia and Chile. In these cases the vintage serves the consumer simply as a reminder of how old the wine is, and hence when it should be drunk. Of course, even in these regions knowledge of the vintage and wine style is important to ensure the optimum time for drinking the wine.

Because European wines in particular are so dependent for their quality on the weather conditions of any one year, for many wine lovers the vintage is one of the keys to the quality of any particular wine. As such there is a benefit in having vintage knowledge, as it will assist in:

- selecting wines from better years rather than lesser years.
- ensuring a wine which is meant to be drunk young, or is better after a few years ageing, is at the correct age at the time of drinking.

Some wines are best consumed while still young. For example, Muscadet and Valpolicella are best consumed up to three years after their production or vintage as their charm lies in their fresh, youthful character.

On the other hand some wines, while generally not changing much in quality from vintage to vintage, benefit from two to three years' bottle maturation before consumption, for example, Australian Shiraz or Californian Cabernet Sauvignon.

As a very general guide, it can be said that most New World quality red wines benefit from having two to three years' maturation from the date of vintage before consumption, while most New World whites do not benefit from long maturation and are best consumed within three to four years after their vintage.

Identifying which European wines and which vintages have produced wine of superior quality depends more on detailed knowledge of the wine region than on general country classification. This can only be gained by wine education and experience. However, many regions are historically famous for producing fine vintage wines such as Bordeaux, Burgundy, Barolo and Rioja, to name a few.

As a guide to the reputation of each year's vintage since 1985, a quick reference vintage chart is attached. Of course, any vintage chart is only a general guide—the best producers can make a good wine in 'off' years, and in some years a winemaker, or part of a wine region, can experience local problems resulting in quite ordinary or inferior wines in an otherwise good year.

Vintage chart

Each region for each year is given a mark out of ten for its vintage (revised January 2001).

Region	99	98	97	96	95	94	93	92	91	90	89	88	86	Classic Vintages
Bordeaux Red	8	7	7	8	8	6	6	4	4	10	10	9	8	85, 82, 78, 70, 61
Sauternes	8	7	8	8	7	5	5	4	3	10	9	8	9	80
Burgundy Red	8	7	8	7	8	6	7	7	7	10	9	9	7	85, 83, 78
Burgundy White	7	8	8	8	9	6	6	9	5	9	9	8	8	85, 83, 78
Rhone	9	8	7	9	8	7	5	5	7	9	9	8	8	78, 67, 61
Champagne	8	8	8	8	8	5	7	7	6	9	8	8	7	85, 79
Germany	8	7	8	7	8	8	8	7	7	10	8	8	6	76, 75
Spain	7	8	8	8	9	10	4	6	8	9	6	5	6	82, 64
Italy	7	8	8	8	7	7	8	4	5	9	8	7	7	85, 78, 71
Port	6	7	8	8	7	10	–	8	7	–	–	–	–	85, 77, 70, 66, 63
Australia	7	9	7	8	7	8	7	7	8	7	6	7	8	82, 79
California	9	7	6	6	7	8	7	8	9	8	7	7	7	74
South Africa	7	6	8	7	8	7	7	8	8	7	7	7	7	

Storing & drinking wine *Barbara Boyle*

Storage

Most of us don't have a great amount of space to devote to wine storage. But even if you have only a modest collection of wine or keep bottles for a relatively short time, it is worth while giving some thought to where they are kept. When selecting a storage space, there are a few factors to be considered. Bottles should be kept in darkness—light can penetrate even dark green bottles with damaging effects. Remove bottles from cardboard boxes and place them on racks or stack them horizontally on their sides so that the cork is in contact with the liquid. (Champagne, on the other hand, can be stored upright.) Wine should be kept at a constant temperature, ideally at around 11°C and preferably less than 16°C. However, the key point is that the temperature shouldn't fluctuate dramatically. So don't keep wine by the cooker, near radiators or by a back door. Pick the quietest and darkest spot possible. Humidity is also important. If the area is too dry, the corks will dry out and the wine will be spoiled. If you are amongst the lucky few to have a dedicated cellar space, humidity can be measured by a hygrometer. Too much humidity poses a greater risk to labels than to the wine itself. The space should also be free from vibration, noise and smells.

Serving wine

When chilling wine, don't put it into the freezer compartment. If you need to chill a bottle quickly, it's better to immerse it in a bucket of cold water with ice cubes and add salt to speed up the chilling process. Never warm a bottle of red wine by placing it in boiling water.

There is a tradition about letting wine breathe. However, some leading authorities maintain that leaving an opened bottle for a few hours is pointless, since the surface area exposed to the air at the neck of the bottle is too small to make a difference. There is definitely an advantage, however, in decanting wine before drinking—this applies to some white wines as well as young and mature reds. The older and more delicate the wine is, the more quickly it should be consumed after opening; it is often younger wines that benefit more from decanting.

Opened bottles

Once opened, wine will oxidise and start to go off. A Vacu Vin vacuum pump will keep opened wine fresh for a day or two or you can recork the wine and keep it in the fridge (reds and whites). Another option is to use a small decanter to minimise the amount of air the wine comes into contact with.

When and what to drink

Most wines are made for immediate consumption and are best consumed within a year of release. Some wines can be enjoyed when young, but will also benefit from short-term maturation of one to two years. Some wines will keep a little longer. Time allows tannins in red wines to soften and secondary aromas such as leather, smoke or spice may develop to complement the more primary fruit aromas, which may start to fade into the background. Whites can become more savoury and subtly complex than they would have appeared in youth. Then there are the wines that are really quite unapproachable in youth. They need time to mature; the enjoyment of the wine will be enhanced by patience.

Here are some rough guidelines on which wines should be consumed as early as possible and which will benefit from further time in bottle.

Wine storage guide	
Immediately	Most inexpensive wines and table or country wines, reds and whites sold as nouveau or Beaujolais style, most brand-name table wines, most Italian whites, Vinho Verde, Muscadet, rosé, Moscato and Asti, Muscat-based *vin doux naturel*, Fino sherry.
1–2 years	Whites from the Loire, e.g. Sancerre, Pouilly Fumé and Menetou-Salon, Jurançon Sec, basic Chablis, medium-quality Alsace, German Qualitätswein, medium-quality New World Chardonnay, basic white and red AC Bordeaux and AC Bourgogne, Côtes du Rhône, Languedoc and Provence wines, non-reserve DOC and DO wines from Italy and Spain, moderately priced New World red wines, non-vintage Champagne and sparkling wines, LBV port, Oloroso sherry.
2–5 years	Premier and Grand Cru Chablis, German Riesling, top-quality Rhône, Alsace and Bordeaux whites, Loire Chenin Blanc, northern Rhône whites from Marsanne, Roussanne or Viognier, e.g. Condrieu, Cru Bourgeois Bordeaux, Cote d'Or Burgundy reds, Loire reds from Cabernet Franc such as Chinon or Bourgeuil, southern Rhône reds, e.g. Châteauneuf-du-Pape, Portuguese reds from Douro, Bairrada and Dão, SW France reds such as Cahors or Madiran, top-quality southern French reds, Banyuls and Maury, red *vin doux naturel*, medium-quality Sauternes and similar sweet wines, good vintage Champagne.
5+ years	Alsace Grand Cru and Sélection de Grains Nobles, top-quality white Burgundy and most expensive white Bordeaux, top red Burgundy and classed-growth Bordeaux from successful vintages, Barolo and Barbaresco, Brunello, top Chiantis and Supertuscans, Rioja Gran Reserva and best reds from Ribera del Duero, premium New World reds from California, South Africa and Australia, top-quality northern Rhône reds, especially Hermitage, Hunter Valley Semillon, top-quality Sauternes, sweet wines such as Tokaji, great vintage Champagne, vintage port.

Argentina

According to our tastings, Argentina's strength still lies in its red wines, with only a small percentage of whites. All the wines were very consistent, with an excellent price/quality ratio. Most of the reds are made from Malbec, a Bordeaux grape variety, now the most widely planted black grape in Argentina, where it thrives in the warm, dry climate, making spicy, soft, juicy wines. Of course Argentina isn't just about Malbec. Represented in the book are Sangiovese, Tempranillo, Merlot, Syrah and Cabernet Sauvignon. Watch out especially for the Cabernets, which can be structured and powerful. As different grape varieties are tried out in cooler sites and winemaking standards continue to improve, Argentina will be interesting to watch over the next few years.

White

Under £7/Under €9

Finca Flichman Chardonnay 99

Very attractive fresh lemony nose. Slight spritz on the palate, giving way to a distinctive green capsicum and lemon flavour. Crisp acidity gives it zest; it's long and warm and finishes well. Good everyday Chardonnay. *TDL*

Price	**Under £7/Under €9**
Region	**Mendoza**
Grape	**Chardonnay**
Alc/vol	**12.5%** *Food* **Chinese**
Drink	**2001–2**

Picajuan Peak Chardonnay 00

For the price this has a lot to offer. It's a rich golden colour with aromas of apples and vanilla and a touch of pineapple. The palate is quite refined, with flavours of apples and lemons. *Tesco*

Price	**Under £7/Under €9**
Region	**Mendoza**
Grape	**Chardonnay**
Alc/vol	**13%** *Food* **Thai**
Drink	**2001–2**

£7–9/€9–11.50

La Nature Torrontés 00 🍃

Torrontés is an interesting grape originally from Galicia, north-west Spain. This example has fragrant floral and apple aromas and lovely floral and peach flavours. Drink young and well chilled. *Koala Wines*

Price	**£7–9/€9–11.50**
Region	**Famatina Valley**
Grape	**Torrontés**
Alc/vol	**12%** *Food* **Seafood**
Drink	**2001–2**

£9–11/€11.50–14

Alta Vista Chardonnay 00

Elegance from Argentina in this delicious but restrained style of Chardonnay. Apple, pineapple and pear fruit are lifted by subtle use of oak to make this a wine to savour. *Mitchells*

Price	**£9–11/€11.50–14**
Region	**Mendoza**
Grape	**Chardonnay**
Alc/vol	**13.5%** *Food* **Prawns**
Drink	**2001–2**

The final of the Gilbeys/NOffLA Off-Licence of the Year Awards will take place at the RDS in Dublin on Monday 14 January 2002. There are eight awards in total: the top award of *National Off-Licence of the Year*, four Regional Awards (Dublin, Leinster, Connaught/Ulster and Munster) and three *Specialist Awards* (Spirits, Wine, Beer). The 25 finalists will be selected out of the following 50 outlets during Round 2 judging in September 2001:

Berry Bros. & Rudd Ireland Ltd. 4 Harry Street, Dublin 2

Burke & Burke Ltd. (T/a Quinn's Off-Licence) 50 Lower Drumcondra Road, Dublin 9

Byrne's Off-Licence 10 Hill Street, Dundalk, Co. Louth

Callan's Off-Licence 40 Park Street, Dundalk, Co. Louth

Castle Street Off-Licence 4 Upper Castle Street, Tralee, Co. Kerry

Centra Foxford, Co. Mayo

Cheers Take Home Store Orchard Complex, Rathfarnham, Dublin 14

Deveney's Off-Licence 382 South Circular Road, Dublin 8

Egan's Off-Licence 1 Peter Street, Drogheda, Co. Louth

Fahy's Off-Licence Teeling Street, Ballina, Co. Mayo

Galvins Wines & Spirits Claremount, Douglas Road, Cork

Galvins Wines & Spirits Washington Street, Cork

Galvins Wines & Spirits 37 Bandon Road, Cork

Jus de Vine Portmarnock Town Centre, Co. Dublin

Kelly's Off-Licence 25E Malahide Road, Dublin 5

Lonergan Off-Licence O'Connell Street, Clonmel, Co. Tipperary

Mac's Off-Licence Ennis Road, Limerick

Martha's Vineyard Rosemount S.C., Rathfarnham, Dublin 16

McCabe's Off-Licence 51/55 Mount Merrion Avenue, Blackrock, Co. Dublin

McHugh's Off-Licence 57 Kilbarrick Road, Dublin 5

Molloy's Liquor Stores Clonsilla, Dublin 15

Molloy's Liquor Stores Nutgrove S.C.,Rathfarnham, Dublin 14

Molloy's Liquor Stores Village Green, Tallaght, Dublin 24

Molloy's Liquor Stores Santry, Dublin 9

Next Door Main Street, Enfield, Co. Meath

Next Door (Abbey Gate Hotel) Tralee, Co. Kerry

O'Briens Wine Off-Licence 30 Donnybrook Road, Dublin 4

O'Briens Wine Off-Licence 22 Sandymount Green,Dublin 4

O'Briens Wine Off-Licence 1 Main Street, Malahide, Co. Dublin

O'Briens Wine Off-Licence 149 Upper Rathmines Road, Dublin 6W

O'Briens Wine Off-Licence Unit 6, Maple Centre, Navan Road, Dublin 7

O'Briens Wine Off-Licence 2 Lower Kilmacud Road, Stillorgan, Co. Dublin

O'Briens Wine Off-Licence Templeogue Village, Dublin 6W

O'Briens Wine Off-Licence 3-4 Kennedy Road, Navan, Co. Meath

O'Briens Wine Off-Licence Church Road, Greystones, Co. Wicklow

O'Briens Wine Off-Licence Newpark Centre, Newtownpark Avenue, Blackrock, Co. Dublin

O'Briens Wine Off-Licence 169 St. Mobhi Road, Glasnevin, Dublin 9

O'Briens Wine Off-Licence 19 Quinsboro Road, Bray,Co. Wicklow

O'Briens Wine Off-Licence 58 Upper Georges Street, Dun Laoghaire, Co. Dublin

O'Donovan's Wine & Spirits Riversdale S.C.,Cork

O'Donovan's Wine & Spirits Looneys Cross, Bishopstown, Cork

O'Donovan's Wine & Spirits Douglas Village, Douglas, Cork

Portlaois Wine Vault 67 Main Street, Portlaois, Co. Laois

Redmond's of Ranelagh Ranelagh, Dublin 6

Sheils Off-Licence Dorset Street, Dublin 1

The Mill Wine Cellar Mill Street, Maynooth, Co. Kildare

The Ryan Vine Wine Shop & Off-Licence 22 Trimgate Street, Navan, Co. Meath

The Vintry 102 Rathgar Road, Dublin 6

The Wine Centre John Street, Kilkenny

Vineyard Off-Licence 14 Mainguard Street, Galway

NOffLA, the National Off-Licence Association
1–3 Sandford Road, Ranelagh, Dublin 6 Tel: 01 497 9286 Fax: 01 491 0172
Email: awards@noffla.ie Website: www.noffla.ie

Red

Under £7/Under €9

Chimango Tempranillo Malbec nv £/€

Malbec, Argentina's favoured grape, has been partnered with the Spanish Rioja grape Tempranillo—does it work? Certainly seems to. Quite an earthy, vegetal nose with red berry fruit. Easy flavours of mint, vanilla, liquorice and summer fruits on the palate, with a good backbone of tannin and a decent finish. *Tesco*

Price	**Under £7/Under €9**
Region	**Mendoza**
Grape	**Tempranillo/Malbec**
Alc/vol	**12.5%**
Food	**Steak**
Drink	**2001–2**

Etchart Rio de Plata Malbec 99 £/€

Medium bodied and very fruity, lots of cherries and currants on nose and palate. The quantity of fruit makes it a pleasant glass on its own or an affordable mid-week bottle. *Irish Distillers*

Price	**Under £7/Under €9**
Region	**Mendoza**
Grape	**Malbec**
Alc/vol	**12.5%**
Food	**Meaty dishes**
Drink	**2001–2**

Etchart Rio de Plata Merlot 99 £/€

Tangy, ripe stewed plum aromas, with some strawberries and cream in the background. A wine full of red fruit flavours—plums, strawberries, cherries. An easy-drinking wine at a great price. *Irish Distillers*

Price	**Under £7/Under €9**
Region	**Mendoza**
Grape	**Merlot**
Alc/vol	**12.5%**
Food	**Versatile**
Drink	**2001–2**

Finca Flichman Cabernet Sauvignon 98

Well-made wine, with blackcurrant fruit on both nose and palate. Still a little tannic with some earthiness that would be best matched with food. Would suit tomato- or meat-based pasta dishes. *TDL*

Price	**Under £7/Under €9**
Region	**Mendoza**
Grape	**Cabernet Sauvignon**
Alc/vol	**13%**
Food	**Pasta**
Drink	**2001–2**

Finca Flichman Malbec 98 £/€ ✓

Yummy nose of blackcurrants and chocolate. Very tasty, lots of blackberries, cream, spice, chocolate and nuts. A big wine without being over the top. Great value for such flavour. Has loads of punch without being a bruiser. *TDL*

Price	**Under £7/Under €9**
Region	**Mendoza**
Grape	**Malbec**
Alc/vol	**13%**
Food	**Beef**
Drink	**2001–2**

Finca Flichman Syrah 98

Savoury currants and cherries, medium weight, spicy palate. Rich and sombre flavours, a bit sultry for the summer, but you could wrap it around you in the winter by the fire. Pleasant on its own but more suited to food. *TDL*

Price	**Under £7/Under €9**
Region	**Mendoza**
Grape	**Syrah**
Alc/vol	**13%**
Food	**Spicy**
Drink	**2001–2**

Picajuan Peak Sangiovese 00 £/€

An Italian variety from Argentina—a wine with
a difference. Strawberries all the way on the
nose; little bit of cherry as well. Soft, easy-
drinking wine with some structure and warmth.
The strawberry/cherry palate has mellow tannins and a decent finish. Great for a party. *Tesco*

Price	**Under £7/Under €9**
Region	**Mendoza**
Grape	**Sangiovese**
Alc/vol	**12.5%**
Food	**Barbecued chicken**
Drink	**2001–3**

Santa Rosa Estate Malbec 00

A very approachable, easy-drinking Malbec.
The nose is bursting with ripe red fruits—plums,
cherries, strawberries and raspberries. It's followed by a soft, mellow palate of refreshing
plum fruit with a tang of liquorice. *Dillons*

Price	**Under £7/Under €9**
Region	**Mendoza**
Grape	**Malbec**
Alc/vol	**13%**
Food	**Aubergines**
Drink	**2001–2**

TriVento Malbec 99

Smoky aromas, with stewed plums, damsons
and a hint of burnt rubber. Cherries galore on
the palate, with a little spice and mellow tannins. A lovely, rich, ripe style. Quite powerful
and robust, but very fruity. At this price it is an
appealing weekday wine. *Findlaters*

Price	**Under £7/Under €9**
Region	**Mendoza**
Grape	**Malbec**
Alc/vol	**13%**
Food	**Versatile**
Drink	**2001–2**

£7–9/€9–11.50

Alta Vista Tinto 99 £/€

Pronounced, pungent nose of strawberries,
raspberries and cherries. The palate has flavours
of cherries, raspberries and rich dark chocolate.
A wine with nice power and concentration, yet
it's soft and ripe. *Mitchells*

Price	**£7–9/€9–11.50**
Region	**Mendoza**
Grape	**Tempranilla/Malbec**
Alc/vol	**13.5%**
Food	**Picnic**
Drink	**2001–2**

Trapiche Malbec Oak Cask 97

Attractive aromas on the nose—plums, cherries,
raspberries and some spice. Appealing style
with an interesting palate of red fruit, spice, a
hint of rosemary and a floral edge.
United Beverages

Price	**£7–9/€9–11.50**
Region	**Mendoza**
Grape	**Malbec**
Alc/vol	**13.5%**
Food	**Lamb**
Drink	**2001–2**

Viña Amalia Malbec 99

Inky plums and damsons with a background of
new leather. Some liquorice appears on the palate, but thick-skinned black fruits are to the
fore. With its supple tannins and balanced acidity, this is a lovely rich wine with nice power
and concentration that still manages to be quite
refreshing. *Oddbins*

Price	**£7–9/€9–11.50**
Region	**Mendoza**
Grape	**Malbec**
Alc/vol	**13%**
Food	**Roasts**
Drink	**2001–3**

Viña de Santa Isabel Malbec Reserva 99 ✓

Ripe black fruit and liquorice flavours with lots of layers—a powerful kick in this. Quite savoury and serious with reasonable length, tasty and pretty satisfying. Enjoy with rich, spicy food. *Dunnes Stores*

Price	**£7–9/€9–11.50**
Region	**Mendoza**
Grape	**Malbec**
Alc/vol	**12.5%**
Food	**Indian**
Drink	**2001–2**

£9–11/€11.50–14

Altos de Temporada Cabernet Sauvignon Reserve 96 ★

Smashing nose of black cherries, plums and forest fruits with a vegetal hint. A tightly structured palate of mocha, coffee beans, cedar wood and baked fruits is backed by firm tannins and good supporting acidity. *Dunnes Stores*

Price	**£9–11/€11.50–14**
Region	**Mendoza**
Grape	**Cabernet Sauvignon**
Alc/vol	**14%**
Food	**Lamb**
Drink	**2001–3**

Altos de Temporada Reserve Malbec 96

Love those luscious, ripe plummy fruits with lots of chew. A concentrated Malbec that extends its fruity yet savoury flavours over the palate with persistent length. *Dunnes Stores*

Price	**£9–11/€11.50–14**
Region	**Mendoza**
Grape	**Malbec**
Alc/vol	**13.5%**
Food	**Veal**
Drink	**2001–2**

*The **Mendoza** region accounts for more than 70% of Argentina's wine production. Rainfall in the region is very low, averaging 200 mm a year, so the vineyards are irrigated by water that flows down from the Andes.*

Finca Flichman Cabernet Sauvignon Reserva 96

A quality nose, fruity with blackcurrants and hints of spice. Mature and savoury, not jammy on the palate, but lots of fruit. Mellow tannins. The wine has a good structure and a dry finish. *TDL*

Price	**£9–11/€11.50–14**
Region	**Mendoza**
Grape	**Cabernet Sauvignon**
Alc/vol	**13%**
Food	**Italian**
Drink	**2001–2**

Finca Flichman Malbec Reserva 98 ✓

A very appealing, perfumed wine, medium bodied, rounded and structured. Lots of cherry fruit. A complex wine that fills out gradually on the palate. All the well-known charms of Argentinian Malbec, but with that extra style and class. Great on its own or with food. *TDL*

Price	**£9–11/€11.50–14**
Region	**Mendoza**
Grape	**Malbec**
Alc/vol	**13.5%**
Food	**Beef**
Drink	**2001–3**

£11–13/€14–16.50

Humberto Canale Merlot Reserva Valle del Rio Negro 96

A lovely Merlot with a bit of class. It has aromas of plums, cherry preserve, strawberries, blueberries and cream. Some oaky aromas too. All the fruit carries through to the palate to make a rich yet refreshing wine style that combines power and fruit with smoothness. *Febvre*

Price	**£11–13/€14–16.50**
Region	**Patagonia**
Grape	**Merlot**
Alc/vol	**13.5%**
Food	**Lamb**
Drink	**2001–2**

£15–17/€19–22

BCW Weinert Carrascal 96

Cigar box, vanilla, a touch of cinnamon and some earthiness on the nose. Lots of bramble fruit on the palate with warm, spicy length. Definitely a food wine. *Woodford Bourne*

Price	**£15–17/€19–22**
Region	**Mendoza**
Grape	**Malbec/Cab Sauv/ Merlot**
Alc/vol	**13%**
Food	**Versatile**
Drink	**2001–3**

Australia

Australian wines took the world by storm with their oaky Chardonnays and peppery Shirazes. These varieties continue to be very important to the Australian wine industry, representing up to 40 per cent of production. However, because of differences in soil and climate, styles of Shiraz vary from region to region. Try a concentrated blockbuster Barossa Shiraz, which will have a chocolate, vanilla and eucalyptus character. Or taste a more restrained, finely textured, 'sweaty saddle' Hunter Valley Shiraz against a McLaren Vale Shiraz, which will be more voluptuous, with perfume, violets and a plummy character. For Chardonnay, unwooded styles are becoming more popular. They are fresh, zesty and full of pure tropical fruit and citrus flavours. Where oak is used, it seems to be deftly applied, allowing more fruit character to emerge.

Australia, however, is not just about Chardonnay and Shiraz. There are many other grape varieties and every style of wine. In whites, look for Semillon, Verdelho and Riesling. Probably the most interesting whites to emerge this year were the Clare Valley Rieslings. These wines have refreshing acidity and are full of lime flavours. They tend to mature earlier than their European counterparts, developing the unique Riesling petrol aroma. They're often sold in tall, Germanic-style bottles and sealed with a screw cap, but don't be put off by this, as it is a sign of the commitment of some Clare Valley producers to ensuring the freshness of the wine. In reds, there are some great Cabernets, often blended with Shiraz, and a little Pinot Noir and Merlot to try. In terms of regions, Western Australia—especially Margaret River—is producing consistently stunning wines that are worth exploring. In Australian terms, these areas are closest in style to Bordeaux whites and reds.

White

Under £7/Under €9

Angove's Bear Crossing Chardonnay 00 £/€

Nose of ripe apples and a hint of pineapple. Very friendly and approachable—big, broad flavours. Pears, lemons, apples and earthy/waxy tones are followed by sweet oak and a lively acidity. *O'Briens*

Price	**Under £7/Under €9**
Region	**South Australia**
Grape	**Chardonnay**
Alc/vol	**13%**
Food	**Aperitif**
Drink	**2001–2**

Bethany Schrapel Family Vineyards The Manse Semillon Riesling Chardonnay 99

There's a waxy note on the nose here, contributed by the Semillon, along with some pear, melon and pineapple aromas. On the palate there are concentrated tropical summer fruits balanced by crisp acidity. Easy drinking, fresh and lively. *O'Briens*

Price	**Under £7/Under €9**
Region	**Barossa Valley**
Grape	**Sem/Ries/Chard**
Alc/vol	**11.5%**
Food	**Salmon**
Drink	**2001–2**

Cranswick Estate Semillon Chardonnay 99

Pleasant tropical nose yields to bananas, pineapple and a hint of toast in the mouth. With its refreshing acidity, this is an easy-drinking wine that's perfect for informal occasions.
MacCormaic

Price	**Under £7/Under €9**
Region	**Riverina**
Grape	**Sem/Chard**
Alc/vol	**12.5%**
Food	**Picnic**
Drink	**2001–2**

Hills View Vineyards Chardonnay Verdelho 98 £/€

Butterscotch and vanilla nose with greengages. Melon, pineapple and baked apples come through on a big, buttery palate peppered with greenish acidity—a mouthful of Tarte Tatin. *WineOnline*

Price	**Under £7/Under €9**
Region	**South Australia**
Grape	**Chard/Verdelho**
Alc/vol	**13.5%**
Food	**Spicy foods**
Drink	**2001–2**

> **South Eastern Australia** includes the three most important wine states.
> **South Australia**—the Barossa Valley, Clare Valley, Eden Valley, McLaren Vale, Coonawarra, Padthaway, Langhorne Creek, the Adelaide Hills and Plains.
> **Victoria**—Rutherglen, Milawa, Glenrowan, King Valley, the Ovens Valley, the Pyrenees, the Grampians, the Yarra Valley, Mornington Peninsula, Geelong.
> **New South Wales**—the Lower and Upper Hunter valleys, Mudgee, Orange.

Jacob's Creek Chardonnay 00

Fresh, floral nose. Upfront melon fruit along with Granny Smith apple and lime juice flavours following through with mouth-cleansing acidity. Lively spritz. Good quaffing wine. *Irish Distillers*

Price	**Under £7/Under €9**
Region	**SE Australia**
Grape	**Chardonnay**
Alc/vol	**12.5%**
Food	**Fish**
Drink	**2001–2**

Jacob's Creek Dry Riesling 00 £/€

Crisp and fresh with good fruit quality and lots of zest. Apple and pineapple fruit, lemons, limes—even apple drops in a brown paper bag! Lingering flavours. *Irish Distillers*

Price	**Under £7/Under €9**
Region	**SE Australia**
Grape	**Riesling**
Alc/vol	**11%**
Food	**Aperitif**
Drink	**2001–2**

McWilliam's Inheritance Chardonnay Colombard 00

Pineapple and tropical fruit aromas. The same fruit follows through on the palate, which exudes fruitiness. Colombard adds natural acidity to this wine. Decent finish. *TDL*

Price	**Under £7/Under €9**
Region	**SE Australia**
Grape	**Chard/Colombard**
Alc/vol	**13%**
Food	**Pork**
Drink	**2001–3**

Miranda Opal Ridge Semillon Chardonnay 00 £/€

An easy-drinking wine with a nose and palate of melons, honeysuckle and some honeyed citrus notes. Acidity is crisp, making it very refreshing. *Taserra*

Price	**Under £7/Under €9**
Region	**SE Australia**
Grape	**Sem/Chard**
Alc/vol	**12%**
Food	**Aperitif**
Drink	**2001–2**

Miranda Unoaked Chardonnay 00 £/€

Nice example of that still-too-rare beast, the Australian unoaked Chardonnay, especially if you like lots of upfront fruit. Honey and citrus notes on the nose are followed by tropical honeyed citrus fruit and fresh acidity, with good length. *Taserra*

Price	**Under £7/Under €9**
Region	**SE Australia**
Grape	**Chardonnay**
Alc/vol	**13%**
Food	**Chicken**
Drink	**2001–2**

Penfolds Rawson's Retreat Bin 21 Semillon Chardonnay Colombard 99 £/€

Fruity, upfront wine. A great palate—dry, with citrus and honeyed yet nutty and mineral flavours, caramel and fudge, very smooth and juicy. Delicious with food. *Findlaters*

Price	**Under £7/Under €9**
Region	**South Australia**
Grape	**Sem/Chard/Col**
Alc/vol	**12%**
Food	**Fish pie**
Drink	**2001–2**

Seppelt Moyston Unoaked Chardonnay 00 £/€

No oak was used in making this wine, so the tropical fruit and citrus aromas come through cleanly on the perfumed nose. The palate has good depth of lemon, lime, melon and apple fruit with some spice, backed by enough acidity to support the rich fruit. *Dunnes Stores*

Price	**Under £7/Under €9**
Region	**SE Australia**
Grape	**Chardonnay**
Alc/vol	**13%**
Food	**Grilled plaice**
Drink	**2001–2**

Tesco Australian Chardonnay nv £/€

An excellent example of Australia's consistently well-made tasty wines at very good prices. A lovely balance between ripe pears and apples with melon and a little white pepper to lift the flavours. Alcohol and acidity are also kept in balance. The fruit and pepper linger long. *Tesco*

Price	**Under £7/Under €9**
Region	**SE Australia**
Grape	**Chardonnay**
Alc/vol	**13.5%**
Food	**Versatile**
Drink	**2001–2**

Tortoiseshell Bay Semillon Sauvignon 00

A friendly wine—very approachable and easy drinking. Ripe apple/lemon/lime fruit on the palate with a good backbone of acidity, giving it a refreshing quality. Lovely for a hot day in the summer. *Mitchells*

Price	**Under £7/Under €9**
Region	**SE Australia**
Grape	**Sem/Sauv Blanc**
Alc/vol	**12.5%**
Food	**Lunch**
Drink	**2001–2**

£7–9/€9–11.50

Blewitt Springs Semillon 98 £/€

Dry and crisp. A wine of some character and lively acidity. Apple and lemon flavours ring through and the palate finishes long and clean. *WineOnline*

Price	**£7–9/€9–11.50**
Region	**McLaren Vale**
Grape	**Semillon**
Alc/vol	**12.5%**
Food	**Oriental**
Drink	**2001–3**

Brown Brothers Victoria Dry Muscat 99

Huge nose of crushed grape skins, honey and spices—rich and lush. On the palate the acidity is quite marked, checking the big flavours—fruit pastilles and spices. Quite a long finish. *Woodford Bourne*

Price	**£7–9/€9–11.50**
Region	**Victoria**
Grape	**Muscat**
Alc/vol	**12.5%**
Food	**Salads**
Drink	**2001–2**

Ch. Tahbilk Marsanne 98

This unwooded Marsanne is a super wine of its type. Tropical, waxy, orange peel nose and a rather unusual oily, tangy, citrus flavour. Very long finish of tropical fruit flavours. A different taste. *United Beverages*

Price	**£7–9/€9–11.50**
Region	**Victoria**
Grape	**Marsanne**
Alc/vol	**13%**
Food	**Asian**
Drink	**2001–4**

Cranswick Estate Nine Pines Vineyard Unoaked Chardonnay 98

Leafy, slightly floral notes on the nose, with orchard fruit aromas. Not over the top on fruit, but nicely made with good length of clean citrus, melon and yellow apple flavours and well-integrated acidity. *MacCormaic*

Price	**£7–9/€9–11.50**
Region	**Riverina**
Grape	**Chardonnay**
Alc/vol	**13%**
Food	**Salad Niçoise**
Drink	**2001–3**

d'Arenberg The Stump Jump Riesling Marsanne 00

Only the Aussies would think up such a confection of grapes—and it works. Hints of sweet apples and pears on the nose. Ripe red apple fruit flavours with a touch of blackcurrant and decent length. Deliciously different. *Taserra*

Price	**£7–9/€9–11.50**
Region	**McLaren Vale**
Grape	**Riesling/Marsanne**
Alc/vol	**12%**
Food	**Stir fries**
Drink	**2001–2**

Fiddlers Creek Chardonnay 99

One of the new wave of Australian Chardonnays—clean, fresh, fruity and not too much oak. Plenty of body and a tasty finish make this a versatile food wine. *Bacchus*

Price	**£7–9/€9–11.50**
Region	**SE Australia**
Grape	**Chardonnay**
Alc/vol	**14%**
Food	**Versatile**
Drink	**2001–2**

Hardys Nottage Hill Chardonnay 00

Typical OTT Aussie style—fruity and oaky, with melons, mangoes, peaches and cream and other tropical fruits on the palate. The oak rounds it off with a nice buttery vanilla character. *Allied Drinks*

Price	**£7–9/€9–11.50**
Region	**SE Australia**
Grape	**Chardonnay**
Alc/vol	**13%**
Food	**Cod**
Drink	**2001–2**

Hardys Nottage Hill Dry Australian Riesling 99

A good example of Riesling with a pronounced nose and palate of limes and apples with a touch of honeysuckle. Acidity is quite piercing, but, given a little time, the fruit should come to the fore. *Allied Drinks*

Price	**£7–9/€9–11.50**
Region	**SE Australia**
Grape	**Riesling**
Alc/vol	**12.5%**
Food	**Thai**
Drink	**2001–3**

Jindalee Chardonnay 00

This Murray Darling Chardonnay has a complex, honeyed tropical fruit nose, leading into a ripe melon and citrus palate with lively acidity and more than a hint of oak and spice on the palate. *Koala Wines*

Price	**£7–9/€9–11.50**
Region	**Murray Darling**
Grape	**Chardonnay**
Alc/vol	**13.5%**
Food	**Chicken**
Drink	**2001–2**

Knappstein Clare Valley Riesling 00 ★

An excellent wine. Limes, lemon curd and petrol on the nose. The palate has strong fruit characteristics of limes and crisp green apples with fresh lemon twists. Crisp, flavoursome finish. *Oddbins*

Price	**£7–9/€9–11.50**
Region	**Clare Valley**
Grape	**Riesling**
Alc/vol	**12.5%**
Food	**Fish**
Drink	**2001–4**

> *The **Stelvin screw cap** closure is used by a growing number of Riesling producers, particularly in the Clare Valley. Made of a bonded circle of foam and foil that eliminates the chance of spoiling due to cork taint, it has been shown to keep wine fresher and younger, with tighter fruit.*

McGuigan Bin 6000 Verdelho 00

Mouth-watering and lively. The ripe Galia melon and zesty lemon sherbet flavours are deep and concentrated through to the long finish. *Barry & Fitzwilliam*

Price	**£7–9/€9–11.50**
Region	**Hunter Valley**
Grape	**Verdelho**
Alc/vol	**13%**
Food	**Spicy**
Drink	**2001–2**

McGuigan Bin 7000 Chardonnay 99

Lots of character here. Spicy aromas of shortbread, spice, oranges, cloves and a faint hint of wood smoke. The palate is smooth, with smoky, spicy flavours of pralines and cream with peachy undertones. Good long finish too. *Barry & Fitzwilliam*

Price	**£7–9/€9–11.50**
Region	**Hunter Valley**
Grape	**Chardonnay**
Alc/vol	**13%**
Food	**Turkey**
Drink	**2001–2**

McGuigan The Black Label Chardonnay 00

Strikingly rich, spicy nose of nutmeg, minerals and apples. The palate is rich, broad and velvety, with blockbusting cinnamon/apple flavours. This wine is pure pleasure and would go well with lighter fish dishes. *Barry & Fitzwilliam*

Price	**£7–9/€9–11.50**
Region	**SE Australia**
Grape	**Chardonnay**
Alc/vol	**13%**
Food	**Plaice**
Drink	**2001–2**

McWilliam's Hanwood Chardonnay 99 ✓

Aromatic and inviting on the nose. A lovely
example of how oak should be handled.
Delightful vanilla aromas overlaid with toasty
butterscotch are repeated on the palate. Here
you'll also find beautiful tropical fruit—guava,
mango—and lemons. Full and warm with a
long finish. *TDL*

Price	*£7–9/€9–11.50*
Region	SE Australia
Grape	Chardonnay
Alc/vol	14%
Food	Roast pork
Drink	2001–2

Miranda High Country Chardonnay 98

Barrel fermentation in French and American
oak hasn't overpowered this wine—oak is evident on the nose, but there's plenty of citrus,
grapefruit and melon fruit there too. The little
bit of age has served the wine well, as the melon
and citrus flavours have integrated with the
oak, resulting in a complex, spicy palate with
rewarding length. *Taserra*

Price	*£7–9/€9–11.50*
Region	King Valley
Grape	Chardonnay
Alc/vol	13.5%
Food	Pasta
Drink	2001–2

The **Barossa Valley**, where most of the large wine companies have their
headquarters, is the heart of the Australian wine industry. It's particularly
successful with Grenache and Shiraz.

Peter Lehmann The Barossa Semillon 99

Woody, green apple nose, with high acidity and
good green apple flavours. Persistent finish.
Beautifully balanced. *United Beverages*

Price	*£7–9/€9–11.50*
Region	Barossa Valley
Grape	Semillon
Alc/vol	12%
Food	Stir fries
Drink	2001–3

St Hallett Poacher's Blend 00

Apple and citrus fruit on both nose and palate.
Easy-drinking, medium-bodied wine with
uncomplicated fruit flavours and a good line of
acidity running through it. *O'Briens*

Price	*£7–9/€9–11.50*
Region	Barossa Valley
Grape	Chenin Blanc/Sem/ Sauv Blanc/Riesling
Alc/vol	12%
Food	Mussels
Drink	2001–2

Serentos Chardonnay Soft Press 99 £/€

Vanilla, grapefruit and butter nose. A pleasant
mouthful of ripe, concentrated tropical fruits.
Balanced by firm acidity, this wine is very
smooth in the mouth, with zesty lime flavours
and tasty length. *Gleeson*

Price	*£7–9/€9–11.50*
Region	SE Australia
Grape	Chardonnay
Alc/vol	13%
Food	Barbecue
Drink	2001–2

Tesco McLaren Vale Chardonnay 99

Buttery and rich. Aromas of roasted nuts and
mangoes. On the palate there are flavours of
vanilla, pecans, caramel and apples. Try it with
stronger white meat dishes such as barbecued
chicken or roast turkey. *Tesco*

Price	**£7–9/€9–11.50**
Region	**McLaren Vale**
Grape	**Chardonnay**
Alc/vol	**14%**
Food	**White meats**
Drink	**2001–2**

Wakefield Clare Valley Chardonnay 99 ✓

Oak has been deftly used here and is nicely
integrated with the fruit. Melons, limes and
spice on the nose with the same ripe tropical
fruit on the palate. *Koala Wines*

Price	**£7–9/€9–11.50**
Region	**Clare Valley**
Grape	**Chardonnay**
Alc/vol	**14%**
Food	**Grilled chicken**
Drink	**2001–2**

Wakefield Clare Valley Riesling 00

Lime and melons on the palate, with crisp acidity to support the fruit. Nice length too. The
acidity and fruit can stand up to strong flavours.
Koala Wines

Price	**£7–9/€9–11.50**
Region	**Clare Valley**
Grape	**Riesling**
Alc/vol	**13%**
Food	**Asian**
Drink	**2001–3**

Wakefield Promised Land Unwooded Chardonnay 00

Another refugee from oak barrels. There's no
shortage of fruit—fresh, fruity aromas of melons and limes and lovely honeyed citrus and
melon fruit on the palate. Refreshing acidity,
and a limey finish. *Koala Wines*

Price	**£7–9/€9–11.50**
Region	**Clare Valley**
Grape	**Chardonnay**
Alc/vol	**13%**
Food	**Barbecue**
Drink	**2001–2**

Wolf Blass Chardonnay 00

Butter, hazelnut and ripe Ogen melon nose. The
palate has a predominantly oaky flavour, a marzipan background and some fresh pineapple,
but with enough acidity to cut the ripe fruit.
Good, all-round flavours and a lingering finish.
Dillons

Price	**£7–9/€9–11.50**
Region	**South Australia**
Grape	**Chardonnay**
Alc/vol	**13.5%**
Food	**Ham**
Drink	**2001–2**

Wyndham Estate Bin 222 Chardonnay 00

Fruit-driven Aussie Chardonnay with a palate
reminiscent of lemon meringue pie. Ripe tropical flavours with a dash of toasted almonds, but
with a firm backbone of acidity. *Irish Distillers*

Price	**£7–9/€9–11.50**
Region	**SE Australia**
Grape	**Chardonnay**
Alc/vol	**13%**
Food	**Pork**
Drink	**2001–2**

Wyndham Estate Bin 777 Semillon 00

Clean and fresh, quite big in the mouth, with plenty of lemon, grapefruit and green apple flavours. Very much a food wine, it would suit summer salads or grilled lemon chicken.
Irish Distillers

Price	**£7–9/€9–11.50**
Region	**SE Australia**
Grape	**Semillon**
Alc/vol	**11%**
Food	**Versatile**
Drink	**2001–2**

£9–11/€11.50–14

Brown Brothers Victoria Chardonnay 99

Pure citrus nose. The palate opens up to give buttered toast flavours, fresh lemons, very generous alcohol and long length. *Woodford Bourne*

Price	**£9–11/€11.50–14**
Region	**Victoria**
Grape	**Chardonnay**
Alc/vol	**14%**
Food	**Shellfish**
Drink	**2001–3**

Brown Brothers Victoria Verdelho 99

Attractive grapey, citrus aromas. The palate is soft and spicy with a citric edge. Finishes nicely. A versatile food wine. *Woodford Bourne*

Price	**£9–11/€11.50–14**
Region	**Victoria**
Grape	**Verdelho**
Alc/vol	**14%**
Food	**Indian**
Drink	**2001–2**

Western Australia's main regions are Margaret River, the Swan Valley and the Great Southern.

Evans & Tate Two Vineyards Chardonnay 99

A subtle, elegant wine. Quite a soft nose with a herbaceous, gooseberry character. The slightly off-dry palate shows rich tropical fruit and oak with a hint of buttery lemon in the background. Very smooth and balanced with a warm finish.
United Beverages

Price	**£9–11/€11.50–14**
Region	**Margaret River**
Grape	**Chardonnay**
Alc/vol	**14%**
Food	**Trout**
Drink	**2001–2**

Penfolds The Valleys Chardonnay 98

Apple, lemon and butter aromas. Smooth, seductive and silky, with really appetising apple fruit. Plenty of flavour and harmonious length.
Findlaters

Price	**£9–11/€11.50–14**
Region	**Clare Valley/Eden Valley**
Grape	**Chardonnay**
Alc/vol	**13.5%**
Food	**Shellfish**
Drink	**2001–2**

Orange is a new region in New South Wales that produces nutty Chardonnays and high-quality Cabernets and Merlots.

Reynolds Moon Shadow Chardonnay 99

Vanilla and spice leap out of the glass and the generous palate has vanilla, spice, apples, lemons and earthy flavours, well integrated with acidity. For lovers of Australian Chardonnay with stacks of fruit and oak. *O'Briens*

Price	£9–11/€11.50–14
Region	Orange
Grape	Chardonnay
Alc/vol	13%
Food	Spicy
Drink	2001–2

Somerset Hill Unwooded Chardonnay 00

A modern style of Australian Chardonnay, unoaked and balanced with a refreshing streak of acidity. It has lively aromas of citrus, honey and a little spearmint. Very ripe, mouth-watering white-fleshed fruits go on to a creamy ending. *Oddbins*

Price	£9–11/€11.50–14
Region	Great Southern
Grape	Chardonnay
Alc/vol	13%
Food	Thai chicken
Drink	2001–2

Wynns Coonawarra Estate Chardonnay 97 £/€

Lots of ripe tropical fruit on the nose. It's medium bodied with heaps of pineapple, apple and citrus fruit plus spice and vanilla from the oak. *Findlaters*

Price	£9–11/€11.50–14
Region	Coonawarra
Grape	Chardonnay
Alc/vol	13%
Food	Creamy pasta
Drink	2001–2

£11–13/€14–16.50

Capel Vale Sauvignon Blanc Semillon 00

Fresh and zingy young wine, with Sauvignon's cut grass and green pepper dominating on the nose. The Semillon adds weight and the classic Sauvignon characteristics of gooseberry and green pepper fill the palate. *Cassidy*

Price	£11–13/€14–16.50
Region	Western Australia
Grape	Sauv Blanc/Sem
Alc/vol	12.5%
Food	Aperitif
Drink	2001–2

Capel Vale Verdelho 00

A refreshing wine full of crisp fruit flavours. The interesting nose of lemon, melon, freshly cut grass and floral notes is followed by slightly oaky lemons and melons on the palate. *Cassidy*

Price	£11–13/€14–16.50
Region	Western Australia
Grape	Verdelho
Alc/vol	14%
Food	Pasta
Drink	2001–2

Lenswood Vineyards Sauvignon Blanc 99

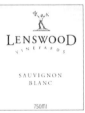

This is a restrained, elegant style. Definitely not run-of-the-mill. Both nose and palate are reminiscent of Granny Smith apples. The bracing acidity is underpinned by a good concentration of fruit. *Wines Direct*

Price	£11–13/€14–16.50
Region	South Australia
Grape	Sauvignon Blanc
Alc/vol	13.5%
Food	Crab
Drink	2001–2

McWilliam's Hunter Valley Chardonnay 99 ★

Remarkably golden colour. Exceptionally buttery, toasty flavours are offset by a slight spritz,
lightening the palate. There's a lovely streak of
lemon/lime and a hint of tropical fruit. With
plenty of ripeness, it's almost Burgundian in
style. Great length—delicious! *TDL*

Price	£11–13/€14–16.50
Region	Hunter Valley
Grape	Chardonnay
Alc/vol	13.5%
Food	Chicken
Drink	2001–2

Aged Hunter Valley Semillon is a unique and classic Australian style. Bottle
aged without any wood treatment, it develops honeyed, buttery, nutty flavours
as it matures. It's generally lower in alcohol than most wines.

McWilliams Mount Pleasant Elizabeth Semillon 94

A lovely complex nose followed by apple and
lemon flavours. Nicely aged and developed,
with some honey notes and a slightly oily texture, it has a long citrus finish. *TDL*

Price	£11–13/€14–16.50
Region	Hunter Valley
Grape	Semillon
Alc/vol	10.5%
Food	Seafood
Drink	2001–6

Nepenthe Lenswood Riesling 00

With a really delicate, subtle character, this
wine is reminiscent of German Rieslings. The
palate moves from floral notes of apple blossom
and honeysuckle flavours and tapers into something a bit more tropical—pineapple. Elegant
and sophisticated, it will develop even more
character as it ages. *Barry & Fitzwilliam*

Price	£11–13/€14–16.50
Region	Adelaide Hills
Grape	Riesling
Alc/vol	13.5%
Food	Japanese
Drink	2001–6

Ninth Island Chardonnay 00

Lively herbaceous nose, which is repeated on
the palate. Very green, gooseberry, herbaceous
character with good body, finesse and length.
Unusually green for an Australian Chardonnay.
Irish Distillers

Price	£11–13/€14–16.50
Region	Tasmania
Grape	Chardonnay
Alc/vol	13%
Food	Salads
Drink	2001–2

Rosemount Estate Show Reserve Chardonnay 99

Grapes were hand picked and fermented in
French oak barrels for this wine. It's a thor-
oughly good example, with care and restraint at
every step—delicious rich (but not blowsy)
fruit, a delicate hand with good French oak,
excellent balance. *Grants*

Price	£11–13/€14–16.50
Region	Hunter Valley
Grape	Chardonnay
Alc/vol	13.5%
Food	Veal
Drink	2001–4

Rothbury Estate Brokenback Semillon 97 ★

An amazing nose, full of nuts, spice, honey, lemons and even some floral notes. The palate combines marked acidity with concentrated citrus fruit, honey and some toastiness. *Cassidy*

Price	£11–13/€14–16.50
Region	Hunter Valley
Grape	Semillon
Alc/vol	11%
Food	Sushi
Drink	2001–6

Scarborough Chardonnay 98

A big wine with plenty of tropical and citrus fruit. Ripe, fruity, perfumed nose with a vanilla backing. The palate has a lovely full mouthfeel. Needs spicy, hearty food. *Wines Direct*

Price	£11–13/€14–16.50
Region	Hunter Valley
Grape	Chardonnay
Alc/vol	13%
Food	Indian
Drink	2001–3

Wolf Blass Presidents Selection Chardonnay 00

Highly aromatic, very sweet pea. Nice upfront tropical fruit flavours, but not overblown. Zesty, with crisp acidity. Mandarin, lemon, lime and green apple fruit. Spritzy and dry with a tasty finish. *Dillons*

Price	£11–13/€14–16.50
Region	South Australia
Grape	Chardonnay
Alc/vol	13%
Food	Seafood
Drink	2001–2

£13–15/€16.50–19.50

Blue Pyrenees Estate Chardonnay 98

This Chardonnay is remarkably fresh and crisp for a wine of this vintage. Made in an oaked style, there are vanilla and citrus aromas on the nose. The peppery lemony/vanilla fruit character is still slightly masked by the oak, but the palate is full, weighty and rich. Long finish. *Bacchus*

Price	£13–15/€16.50–19.50
Region	Victoria
Grape	Chardonnay
Alc/vol	14%
Food	Duck
Drink	2001–3

Brookland Valley Sauvignon Blanc 00

Full bodied but elegant, a fine example of Sauvignon Blanc. Slightly smoky nose of green peppers. Star fruit and limes stir the lively palate into a citrussy and crisp cocktail of flavours. *Oddbins*

Price	£13–15/€16.50–19.50
Region	Western Australia
Grape	Sauvignon Blanc
Alc/vol	13.5%
Food	Shellfish
Drink	2001–2

Cape Mentelle Semillon Sauvignon Blanc 00

Apples on the nose, even a hint of red fruit. Zingy and lively, with fresh acidity, the wine is medium bodied, with a good concentration of summer fruit, lemons, limes, apples and honey. *Findlaters*

Price	£13–15/€16.50–19
Region	Western Australia
Grape	Sem/Sauv Blanc
Alc/vol	13.5%
Food	Fish
Drink	2001–3

41

Geoff Merrill Chardonnay 94

Rich golden colour. Developed nose of butter-scotch and caramel. Pungent palate with oodles of oaky vanilla, but counterbalanced by of lime, ripe pineapple and passion fruit. A big, big wine. *United Beverages*

Price	£13–15/€16.50–19
Region	SE Australia
Grape	Chardonnay
Alc/vol	12.5%
Food	Thai
Drink	2001–2

Nepenthe Lenswood Semillon 99 ★

This Semillon has a marvellous, appetising nose, highly scented with lemons and limes. The palate more than satisfies the promise of the nose, with beautiful buttery, citrussy, toasty flavours with terrific balancing acidity and length. Could be a lovely surprise in five years and should drink well for even longer. *Barry & Fitzwilliam*

Price	£13–15/€16.50–19
Region	Adelaide Hills
Grape	Semillon
Alc/vol	14%
Food	Prawns
Drink	2001–10

£15–17/€19–22

Cape Mentelle Chardonnay 98 ✓

Very flavoursome and delightful. Classic Australian Chardonnay—layers of vanilla, spice, apples, lemons and melon all integrating together beautifully. A very well-made, sophisticated wine with a touch of oak and crisp acidity. A good wine for a special occasion. *Findlaters*

Price	£15–17/€19–22
Region	Margaret River
Grape	Chardonnay
Alc/vol	14%
Food	Salmon
Drink	2001–4

Katnook Estate Chardonnay 97

Rich, characterful bouquet of tropical fruit. Intensely flavoured palate with oaky flavours and a warm high-alcohol backdrop. *Woodford Bourne*

Price	£15–17/€19–22
Region	Coonawarra
Grape	Chardonnay
Alc/vol	13.5%
Food	Pacific Rim
Drink	2001–2

Lenswood Vineyards Chardonnay 98 ✓

From the Adelaide Hills near the town of Lenswood, this is a beautifully crafted wine, full of clean fruit flavours. This is how Australian Chardonnay should be—masses of ripe fruit and good use of oak, with a finish that lingers. *Wines Direct*

Price	£15–17/€19–22
Region	Adelaide Hills
Grape	Chardonnay
Alc/vol	14%
Food	Smoked salmon
Drink	2001–3

£17–20/€22–25

Brookland Valley Chardonnay 97

An elegant wine for a special occasion with buttery notes on the nose and melon and citrus aromas. Melon and tropical fruit flavours have integrated well with the creamy vanilla of the oak, giving a wine that is smooth and multi-layered with a satisfying finish. *Fields*

Price	**£17–20/€22–25**
Region	**Margaret River**
Grape	**Chardonnay**
Alc/vol	**14%**
Food	**Fish**
Drink	**2001–2**

Grosset Polish Hill Riesling 00

Unusual but fascinating nose for a Riesling—spice, red apples and cloves! Ripe red apples again on the palate, along with a clove background. *Wines Direct*

Price	**£17–20/€22–25**
Region	**Clare Valley**
Grape	**Riesling**
Alc/vol	**13%**
Food	**Middle Eastern**
Drink	**2001–6**

£20–25/€25–32

De Bortoli Chardonnay 98

This is a full-blown Australian Chardonnay made with lots of new oak. It has a striking, toasty, biscuity nose with some tropical fruit and a very smooth balance of flavours. Creamy and limy, it has a long, lingering finish. Definitely moreish. *Febvre*

Price	**£20–25/€25–32**
Region	**Yarra Valley**
Grape	**Chardonnay**
Alc/vol	**13.5%**
Food	**Pasta carbonara**
Drink	**2001–3**

Pierro Chardonnay 99

Toasty butterscotch, lemon, melon and mango on the nose. Intensely flavoured palate of butter toffee, bananas, lemon, melons and toast underpinned by lively acidity. Lingering finish. It's still very young and needs time to mature, but it will be worth it. *Wines Direct*

Price	**£20–25/€25–32**
Region	**Western Australia**
Grape	**Chardonnay**
Alc/vol	**14%**
Food	**Seafood**
Drink	**2001–6**

Tyrrell's Vat 1 Hunter Semillon 95 ✓

A totally original Australian style with a classic waxy nose, this aged Semillon is still very fresh. It's a superb example of how well Semillon ages, emerging from its chrysalis into a full-flavoured, limy, peachy wine, yet with a lightness of body that avoids any clumsiness. Long finish. *Maxxium*

Price	**£20–25/€25–32**
Region	**Hunter Valley**
Grape	**Semillon**
Alc/vol	**11.3%**
Food	**Versatile**
Drink	**2001–10**

Tyrrell's Vat 47 Pinot Chardonnay 96 ★

Rich gold colour. A mature butterscotch nose reveals a generous, though not overdone, palate, with predominantly buttery, toasty, hazelnut flavours; nicely creamy. Judiciously balanced, with a long, generous finish. *Maxxium*

Price	**£20–25/€25–32**
Region	**Hunter Valley**
Grape	**Chardonnay**
Alc/vol	**13.5%**
Food	**Pacific Rim**
Drink	**2001–3**

Red

Under £7/Under €9

Cudgee Creek Cabernet Sauvignon 00

An easy-drinking Aussie with jammy black-currant aromas and flavours tempered by spice. Some mocha notes. Tannins are soft and well rounded. *Koala Wines*

Price	**Under £7/Under €9**
Region	**Murray Darling**
Grape	**Cabernet Sauvignon**
Alc/vol	**13.5%**
Food	**Pizza**
Drink	**2001–2**

Drayton's Shiraz Cabernet 99

A smooth, soft, refreshing wine, full of red berry fruit aromas and flavours with leafy herbal and green pepper notes. Perfect at the end of a long day. *Wines Direct*

Price	**Under £7/Under €9**
Region	**South Australia**
Grape	**Shiraz/Cab Sauv**
Alc/vol	**12.5%**
Food	**Takeaway**
Drink	**2001–2**

Geoff Merrill Owen's Estate Grenache Shiraz 98 £/€

Very appealing nose of spice and blackberries. The palate is delicious and rather generous, with its soft roundness, showing oodles of juicy, jammy, peppery fennel/herbal flavours. Lovely finish. *United Beverages*

Price	**Under £7/Under €9**
Region	**SE Australia**
Grape	**Grenache/Shiraz**
Alc/vol	**13.5%**
Food	**Barbecue**
Drink	**2001–2**

Jacob's Creek Cabernet Sauvignon 99

Good nose of juicy black fruit aromas and mint. Soft, ripe tannins and black fruit flavours on the palate; spicy finish. *Irish Distillers*

Price	**Under £7/Under €9**
Region	**SE Australia**
Grape	**Cabernet Sauvignon**
Alc/vol	**13.5%**
Food	**Party**
Drink	**2001–2**

Jacob's Creek Grenache Shiraz 00

Juicy, jammy, bubble-gum aromas on the nose with a hint of fennel. Spicy and full on the palate, with jam, cherries, black fruit and rubber, with an almost burnt dimension. *Irish Distillers*

Price	**Under £7/Under €9**
Region	**SE Australia**
Grape	**Grenache/Shiraz**
Alc/vol	**13.5%**
Food	**Grilled meats**
Drink	**2001–2**

Jacob's Creek Shiraz Cabernet 99 £/€

Black fruits on the nose. Flavours of blackberry jam and peppercorns on the palate are backed by firm tannins. A decent, sit-in-front-of-the-TV wine. *Irish Distillers*

Price	**Under £7/Under €9**
Region	**SE Australia**
Grape	**Shiraz/Cab Sauv**
Alc/vol	**13%**
Food	**Pizza**
Drink	**2001–2**

McWilliam's Inheritance Shiraz Cabernet 00

This is a fruit-driven and very pleasant style. Full of blackcurrants and plums on the nose and palate. Some interesting bitter herbal elements on the finish. *TDL*

Price	**Under £7/Under €9**
Region	**SE Australia**
Grape	**Shiraz/Cab Sauv**
Alc/vol	**12.5%**
Food	**Traditional**
Drink	**2001–3**

Peter Lehmann The Barossa Grenache 00 £/€

Full satisfying flavours of summer fruits (raspberries, cherries), complemented by vegetal nuances, peppery spice and alcohol. Soft, with spicy fruit and a warm, gutsy finish. Buy by the case for parties or barbecues. It won't disappoint. *United Beverages*

Price	**Under £7/Under €9**
Region	**Barossa Valley**
Grape	**Grenache**
Alc/vol	**13.5%**
Food	**Barbecue**
Drink	**2001–2**

Tortoiseshell Bay Mourvèdre Shiraz 00 £/€

Hits all the right spots with its fleshy, supple style, soft tannins, yards of red berry fruits and spicy finish. Would suit a wide range of foods. *Mitchells*

Price	**Under £7/Under €9**
Region	**SE Australia**
Grape	**Mourvèdre/Shiraz**
Alc/vol	**13%**
Food	**Versatile**
Drink	**2001–2**

£7–9/€9–11.50

Angove's Classic Reserve Shiraz 98

Ripe fruit, easy drinking—typical Aussie Shiraz. Red berry fruit flavours and some pepper. It would go well with spicy foods. *O'Briens*

Price	**£7–9/€9–11.50**
Region	**SE Australia**
Grape	**Shiraz**
Alc/vol	**13%**
Food	**Chilli con carne**
Drink	**2001–2**

Baileys North East Victoria Shiraz 98

A big wine with a warm, fruit-driven nose of dark berry fruits, mint and liquorice. Plenty of red fruit flavours aided by softening tannins—ripe plums, chocolate, spice and mint slowly harmonise. Very much a food wine. *Koala Wines*

Price	**£7–9/€9–11.50**
Region	**Victoria**
Grape	**Shiraz**
Alc/vol	**13.5%**
Food	**Ribs, burgers**
Drink	**2001–4**

Bethany Schrapel Family Vineyards Grenache 99 ✓

Tempting nose of summer berries and ground white pepper—but it gets better—the palate is wonderful, very complex, laden with vanilla, juicy raspberries, cherries, pepper, herbs, spices, and well supported by alcohol. Excellent weight and finish. *O'Briens*

Price	£7–9/€9–11.50
Region	Barossa Valley/ McLaren Vale
Grape	Grenache
Alc/vol	14.5%
Food	Mediterranean
Drink	2001–3

*The **98 vintage** is considered to be one of the great vintages in South Australia, New South Wales and Victoria.*

Blewitt Springs Cabernet Sauvignon 98

Perfumed and elegant, eucalyptus and mint aromas. Minty on the palate, too, with sweet cake spice and a touch of star anise. A pretty good all-rounder. *WineOnline*

Price	£7–9/€9–11.50
Region	McLaren Vale/ Langhorne Creek
Grape	Cabernet Sauvignon
Alc/vol	13%
Food	Barbecue
Drink	2001–2

Blewitt Springs Shiraz 99

Typically fruit-driven Aussie Shiraz. Smoky black fruit aromas and juicy black fruits on the palate are backed by ripe tannins. Very easy to drink. *WineOnline*

Price	£7–9/€9–11.50
Region	McLaren Vale
Grape	Shiraz
Alc/vol	13.5%
Food	Beef stir fry
Drink	2001–2

Carlyle Shiraz 98 £/€

A really concentrated, complex vegetal nose. Ripe crushed damson/cherry fruit in the mouth with extra nuances of tar and leather. Very dense, the wine has mellow tannins, pronounced blackcurrant fruit and a long finish. *Gleeson*

Price	£7–9/€9–11.50
Region	Victoria
Grape	Shiraz
Alc/vol	13.5%
Food	Stews
Drink	2001–2

*The **Riverina** produces more white than red varieties, principally Muscat, Semillon and Trebbiano. Reds are made mainly from Shiraz.*

Cranswick Estate Nine Pines Vineyard Shiraz 97

More Rhône than Riverina on the minty, herbal nose, which displays blackcurrant, raspberry, cherry and vanilla aromas. The palate has distinct berry fruit with bracing acidity. *MacCormaic*

Price	£7–9/€9–11.50
Region	Riverina
Grape	Shiraz
Alc/vol	13%
Food	Grilled chops
Drink	2001–3

d'Arenberg The Stump Jump Grenache Shiraz 99 £/€

Black and red fruit aromas on the nose with tar and tobacco. The wine is quite complex, with fruity flavours and crisp acidity. Well-rounded tannins, good structure. *Taserra*

Price	**£7–9/€9–11.50**
Region	**McLaren Vale**
Grape	**Grenache/Shiraz**
Alc/vol	**14.5%**
Food	**Grilled chicken**
Drink	**2001–3**

Deakin Estate Shiraz 00

Gorgeous pure fruit aromas and flavours of blackberries, plums and damsons, with extra dimensions of pepper and cinnamon spice. Very long finish. *Woodford Bourne*

Price	**£7–9/€9–11.50**
Region	**Victoria**
Grape	**Shiraz**
Alc/vol	**13.5%**
Food	**Mediterranean**
Drink	**2001–2**

Fiddlers Creek Shiraz Cabernet 98

Green pepper, cloves and red fruit aromas. Quite a jammy style, but the fruit is ripe with appealing spicy tones. *Bacchus*

Price	**£7–9/€9–11.50**
Region	**SE Australia**
Grape	**Shiraz/Cab Sauv**
Alc/vol	**13%**
Food	**Mediterranean**
Drink	**2001–2**

> *Part of Australia's success is due to the dominance of large companies such as* **Southcorp**, **Hardys** *and* **Orlando Wyndham**. *It also has over a thousand smaller independent wineries, which produce only a quarter of total output.*

Hardys Cabernet Shiraz Merlot 98

Cough sweets and dark red berry fruit on the nose. Flavours of blackcurrants, liquorice, caramel and plums with plenty of white pepper, finishing with an appealing touch of spice. This is a good, gutsy Aussie. *Allied Drinks*

Price	**£7–9/€9–11.50**
Region	**South Australia**
Grape	**Cab Sauv/Shiraz/ Merlot**
Alc/vol	**13.5%**
Food	**Barbecue**
Drink	**2001–3**

Hardys Nottage Hill Cabernet Sauvignon Shiraz 99 £/€

The Aussies have really got a handle on blending these two classic grapes and this is a very tasty example. White pepper and red berry aromas on the nose. Plenty of dark red berry fruit with a softening vanilla edge. An appealing wine with an enjoyable finish. *Allied Drinks*

Price	**£7–9/€9–11.50**
Region	**SE Australia**
Grape	**Cab Sauv/Shiraz**
Alc/vol	**13%**
Food	**Pasta**
Drink	**2001–2**

Shirazes benefit from being opened an hour or two before drinking to allow them to breathe.

Hardys Nottage Hill Shiraz 98 £/€

A rich, strong wine. Mint, spice and black fruit aromas, with bitter cherries. The weighty, powerful palate of dark chocolate, mint and spice has chewy tannins and a slightly bitter twist on the warm finish. *Allied Drinks*

Price	£7–9/€9–11.50
Region	SE Australia
Grape	Shiraz
Alc/vol	14%
Food	Stews
Drink	2001–3

Hardys Stamp of Australia Shiraz Cabernet Sauvignon 00

Ripe, slightly smoky blackberry aromas. Concentrated red summer berry fruit on the palate with some dried fruit flavours and spice. Nice blend of these two grapes, giving soft, fruity flavours with a warm, spicy coat. *Allied Drinks*

Price	£7–9/€9–11.50
Region	SE Australia
Grape	Shiraz/Cab Sauv
Alc/vol	12.5%
Food	Pizza
Drink	2001–2

Hills View Vineyards Cabernet Merlot 99 £/€

Plummy and minty on the nose, the palate is full bodied and fruity, with plums, blackcurrants and some oak. This is a wine that will go well with food, but could easily be drunk by itself. *WineOnline*

Price	£7–9/€9–11.50
Region	Langhorne Creek
Grape	Cabernet/Merlot
Alc/vol	13%
Food	Versatile
Drink	2001–3

Hills View Vineyards Shiraz Cabernet 99 £/€

A wine with lots of fruit and character. Blackcurrant aromas; more blackcurrants and pepper on the palate. Good on its own or with substantial grub. Well rounded. *WineOnline*

Price	£7–9/€9–11.50
Region	Langhorne Creek
Grape	Shiraz/Cab Sauv
Alc/vol	13%
Food	Shepherd's pie
Drink	2001–3

Jindalee Cabernet Sauvignon 00 £/€

Ultra-ripe cassis and sweet vanilla sing out from this medium-bodied red. The palate is packed with the same ripe blackcurrant fruit, backed with oak, which is balanced by mellow tannins and crisp acidity. *Koala Wines*

Price	£7–9/€9–11.50
Region	Murray Darling
Grape	Cabernet Sauvignon
Alc/vol	13.5%
Food	Spicy
Drink	2001–2

Jindalee Merlot 00 £/€

Yum! Cinnamon and nutmeg spice on the nose. Lots of damson fruit on the palate with a hint of chocolate. Easy-drinking wine with yielding tannins but good length. An ideal foil for spiced foods, with its crisp acidity and pure fruit. *Koala Wines*

Price	**£7–9/€9–11.50**
Region	**Murray Darling**
Grape	**Merlot**
Alc/vol	**14%**
Food	**Spicy**
Drink	**2001–2**

Jindalee Shiraz 99 £/€

Spice and plum aromas. The palate is refined, with spicy, faintly woody blackcurrant and dark fruit flavours. Tannins and acidity are well judged and length is good. *Koala Wines*

Price	**£7–9/€9–11.50**
Region	**Murray Darling**
Grape	**Shiraz**
Alc/vol	**14%**
Food	**Roast meats**
Drink	**2001–2**

McGuigan Cabernet Sauvignon Bin 4000 98 £/€

Medley of red and black fruit, spice, chocolate and oak. An initial burst of sweet fruit on the palate is seductive and the balance of fruit, acidity and tannins is excellent. Smooth and spicy with a long, mouth-warming finish. *Barry & Fitzwilliam*

Price	**£7–9/€9–11.50**
Region	**SE Australia**
Grape	**Cabernet Sauvignon**
Alc/vol	**12.5%**
Food	**Lasagne**
Drink	**2001–4**

McGuigan Millennium Shiraz 99 £/€

A powerful wine, youthful but still developing. Nose of spicy chocolate vanilla pudding. Rich, velvety palate of milk chocolate, cinnamon and coffee with layered red fruits. Lots of rich flavours here. *Barry & Fitzwilliam*

Price	**£7–9/€9–11.50**
Region	**SE Australia**
Grape	**Shiraz**
Alc/vol	**13%**
Food	**Beef**
Drink	**2001–3**

McGuigan Oak Matured Bin 3000 Merlot 99 £/€

This is a tasty wine with lots of jammy fruit, ripe tannins and reasonable length. A relaxed, easy-drinking style. *Barry & Fitzwilliam*

Price	**£7–9/€9–11.50**
Region	**SE Australia**
Grape	**Merlot**
Alc/vol	**12.5%**
Food	**Aubergines**
Drink	**2001–2**

McGuigan The Black Label Merlot 00 £/€

This Merlot has rich plums, dates and figs with a chocolate-flavoured, smooth palate. It's very impressive—made in an upfront style for drinking young. *Barry & Fitzwilliam*

Price	**£7–9/€9–11.50**
Region	**SE Australia**
Grape	**Merlot**
Alc/vol	**13.5%**
Food	**Pasta**
Drink	**2001–2**

St Hallett Gamekeeper's Reserve 99

Quite prominent strawberries and black fruits on the nose, some oak, cream and burnt toffee notes in the blackcurrant/peppery palate. *O'Briens*

Price	**£7–9/€9–11.50**
Region	**Barossa Valley**
Grape	**Grenache/ Mourvèdre/Shiraz**
Alc/vol	**14%**
Food	**Versatile**
Drink	**2001–2**

Tatachilla Keystone Grenache Shiraz 99

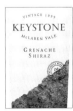

Gorgeously rich and warm, with a creamy palate of plums and spice. Good complexity and a harmonious finish. Roast chicken with garlic would go well with this one. *O'Briens*

Price	**£7–9/€9–11.50**
Region	**McLaren Vale**
Grape	**Grenache/Shiraz**
Alc/vol	**14.5%**
Food	**Poultry**
Drink	**2001–3**

Tyrrell's Old Winery Pinot Noir 00

Lovely elegant nose suggesting vanilla, strawberries and raspberries with savoury hints. Still young, with sweet summer berry and vanilla flavours, but developing herbal, savoury and bacon flavours. *Maxxium*

Price	**£7–9/€9–11.50**
Region	**Hunter Valley/McLaren Vale/Yarra Valley**
Grape	**Pinot Noir**
Alc/vol	**14%**
Food	**Tuna**
Drink	**2001–4**

Wakefield Clare Valley Cabernet Sauvignon 99

This 100% Cabernet, aged in American and French oak barrels, has a minty New World nose, but there are earthy blackcurrants there as well. Good blackcurrant fruit and firm tannins on the palate. *Koala Wines*

Price	**£7–9/€9–11.50**
Region	**Clare Valley**
Grape	**Cabernet Sauvignon**
Alc/vol	**14.5%**
Food	**Barbecue**
Drink	**2001–3**

Wolf Blass Red Label Shiraz Cabernet Sauvignon 99 £/€

A refined, balanced wine. Vanilla, raspberry and peppery aromas lead to a succulent, highly concentrated palate of blackcurrants, black cherries, raspberries, baking spices and vanilla. *Dillons*

Price	**£7–9/€9–11.50**
Region	**South Australia**
Grape	**Shiraz/Cab Sauv**
Alc/vol	**12.5%**
Food	**Roasts**
Drink	**2001–3**

Wyndham Estate Bin 555 Shiraz 99 £/€

A good example of a well-made Aussie Shiraz. Loads of black fruit and spice on the nose and palate. Spicy, earthy, peppery flavours and decent length. *Irish Distillers*

Price	**£7–9/€9–11.50**
Region	**SE Australia**
Grape	**Shiraz**
Alc/vol	**13.5%**
Food	**Indian**
Drink	**2001–2**

Yellow Tail Shiraz 00

Easy-going and very drinkable. Christmas cake aromas, strawberry and ripe plum flavours with a little bit of spice. *Mitchells*

Price	**£7–9/€9–11.50**
Region	**SE Australia**
Grape	**Shiraz**
Alc/vol	**13%**
Food	**Pizza**
Drink	**2001–2**

£9–11/€11.50–14

Bethany Schrapel Family Vineyards Shiraz Cabernet 99

A big, chewy style with chunky rich, ripe black fruits with characteristic Shiraz black pepper on the finish. Versatile and bound to please. *O'Briens*

Price	**£9–11/€11.50–14**
Region	**Barossa Valley**
Grape	**Shiraz/Cab Sauv**
Alc/vol	**13%**
Food	**Versatile**
Drink	**2001–2**

Blue Pyrenees Victoria Cabernet Sauvignon 99

Laid-back style of Australian Cabernet with a ripe, fruity structure. Restrained bouquet of blackcurrants with some herbal notes. Appealing pure loganberry and redcurrant fruit. A crisp all-rounder in the food stakes. *Bacchus*

Price	£9–11/€11.50–14
Region	Victoria
Grape	Cabernet Sauvignon
Alc/vol	14%
Food	Versatile
Drink	2001–2

Brown Brothers King Valley Barbera 99 ★★

A biggie with great fruit and spice. Concentrated chocolate and cherry aromas. Powerful yet elegant palate—bitter cherries and tobacco-like spice, aided by a chocolate vanilla edge. Rounded and well integrated and finishes beautifully. *Woodford Bourne*

Price	£9–11/€11.50–14
Region	King Valley
Grape	Barbera
Alc/vol	14.5%
Food	Antipasto
Drink	2001–4

Brown Brothers Victoria Shiraz 99

A complex wine with a hint of port. Rich Christmas cake fruit on the nose, very concentrated. With integrated oaky vanilla and dark fruit flavours, this is a well-structured wine with a long, silky finish. *Woodford Bourne*

Price	£9–11/€11.50–14
Region	Victoria
Grape	Shiraz
Alc/vol	14.5%
Food	Chinese-style beef
Drink	2001–4

Ch. Tahbilk Cabernet Sauvignon 97

Attractive, mature nose of damsons and spice. The palate is full of ripe autumn fruit, spice and oak. A dinner-party wine to suit a wide variety of meaty dishes. *United Beverages*

Price	£9–11/€11.50–14
Region	Victoria
Grape	Cab Sauv/Cab Franc
Alc/vol	13%
Food	Red meat
Drink	2001–2

Ch. Tahbilk Shiraz 97

Very fruity and extroverted—classic Aussie Shiraz. Strawberry aromas with a hint of pepper and tar. On the palate blackcurrants and strawberry shortcake flavours, damsons and white pepper. It's supported by firm tannins. *United Beverages*

Price	£9–11/€11.50–14
Region	Victoria
Grape	Shiraz
Alc/vol	13.5%
Food	Lasagne
Drink	2001–3

Capel Vale Cabernet Merlot 98 £/€

An Australian take on the traditional Bordeaux blend. It's rich and warm, with the dominant blackcurrant of Cabernet Sauvignon underpinned by smooth Merlot flavours and Cabernet Franc's perfume. Long finish. *Cassidy*

Price	£9–11/€11.50–14
Region	Western Australia
Grape	Cabernet/Merlot/ Cab Franc
Alc/vol	13%
Food	Fillet steak
Drink	2001–3

d'Arenberg d'Arry's Original Shiraz Grenache 99

Spicy, earthy dark fruit flavours, blackcurrants and mint, some softness from the Grenache. Noticeable tannins will soften over the next year. Satisfying wine. *Taserra*

Price	£9–11/€11.50–14
Region	McLaren Vale
Grape	Shiraz/Grenache
Alc/vol	14.5%
Food	Lamb
Drink	2001–3

d'Arenberg The Footbolt Shiraz 99

Some of the Shiraz grapes used for this wine come from vineyards planted at the turn of the century. Old vines make for greater flavour and this Shiraz has abundant blackcurrant and spicy plum fruit on the nose and the palate. Tannins are firmish but nicely integrated and it has a spicy finish. *Taserra*

Price	£9–11/€11.50–14
Region	McLaren Vale
Grape	Shiraz
Alc/vol	14%
Food	Steak
Drink	2001–5

d'Arenberg The High Trellis Cabernet Sauvignon 99

The High Trellis Paddock was called after the way the vines were trained in the 1890s—the first d'Arenberg vines to be grown higher than knee height. Rich blackcurrant flavour with a little mint, gripping tannins and a savoury finish. *Taserra*

Price	£9–11/€11.50–14
Region	South Australia
Grape	Cabernet Sauvignon
Alc/vol	14%
Food	Steak
Drink	2001–3

Evans & Tate Barrique 61 Cabernet Merlot 98

Mature nose of autumn fruits with some developed vegetal aromas. Seriously rich mouthfeel, with plenty of acidity and firm tannins. Flavours are of deep cherry and blackcurrant fruit, still chewy, with a touch of oak and cake spice and a good long peppery finish. *United Beverages*

Price	£9–11/€11.50–14
Region	Margaret River
Grape	Cabernet/Merlot
Alc/vol	14%
Food	Beef Wellington
Drink	2001–3

Ironstone Vineyards Shiraz Grenache 98 ★

Quintessential food wine! The raspberry, strawberry, blackberry and black pepper nose leads into wild berries and loganberries on the palate, where there's a touch of burnt rubber. The peppery Grenache kicks in strongly, married with the berry fruit of the Shiraz. A real winter warmer with a nice wild fruit touch. *Findlaters*

Price	£9–11/€11.50–14
Region	Western Australia
Grape	Shiraz/Grenache
Alc/vol	14.5%
Food	Versatile
Drink	2001–4

Jacob's Creek Reserve Shiraz 98

Ripe autumn fruit of blackberries and damsons on the nose. Rich and powerful palate, revealing liquorice-like fruit with a spicy, inky feel, ripe blackcurrants, mint and sweet vanilla oakiness. Soft wine with supporting firm tannins and balanced acidity. *Irish Distillers*

Price	£9–11/€11.50–14
Region	South Australia
Grape	Shiraz
Alc/vol	13.5%
Food	Versatile
Drink	2001–2

Jamieson's Run Cabernet Shiraz Merlot 98

A very Australian blend of grape varieties. A full-bodied wine with eucalyptus on the nose, the palate has a lot of plum, blueberry and redcurrant fruit with a hint of cream on the finish. A well-rounded wine. *Gilbeys*

Price	£9–11/€11.50–14
Region	Coonawarra
Grape	Cab Sauv/Shiraz/ Merlot
Alc/vol	13%
Food	Traditional
Drink	2001–3

Oxford Landing Limited Release Grenache 98 £/€

Medium-bodied wine full of summer flavours. Dried fruit and mulberries are backed by crisp acidity and a warming alcoholic finish. It goes down easily, but is more serious than it first appears. *Cassidy*

Price	£9–11/€11.50–14
Region	SE Australia
Grape	Grenache
Alc/vol	14.5%
Food	Steak & mushroom pie
Drink	2001–3

Peter Lehmann Clancy's 98 ★ £/€

This unusual blend of grape varieties really works. Rich, inky colour. Nose temptingly full of blackberries, oak and spice. Great depth of fruit on the palate—blackberries, blackcurrants, cherries, spice, tar, black pepper and cedar. Medium acidity, firm tannins, long and developing. Great length. *United Beverages*

Price	£9–11/€11.50–14
Region	Barossa Valley
Grape	Shiraz/Cab Sauv/ Merlot/Cab Franc
Alc/vol	14%
Food	Versatile
Drink	2001–3

Peter Lehmann The Barossa Cabernet Sauvignon 98

Attractive introduction on the nose of oak and damsons, which belies a much richer palate of figs, spices and ripe blackcurrants. The palate is beautifully structured, with firm tannins and good acidity backing up the abundant fruit flavours. Rich and lengthy. A sleeping giant that will improve, but drinking beautifully now. Superb. *United Beverages*

Price	£9–11/€11.50–14
Region	Barossa Valley
Grape	Cabernet Sauvignon
Alc/vol	13.5%
Food	Steak
Drink	2001–4

RED WINE OF THE YEAR

Peter Lehmann The Barossa Shiraz 98 ✓

Ripe, appealing nose of black cherries, squishy raspberries and vanilla. Flavours of caramel-filled gooey chocolates with blueberry, cherry and blackberry pudding on the side. A feast. *United Beverages*

Price	£9–11/€11.50–14
Region	Barossa Valley
Grape	Shiraz
Alc/vol	14%
Food	Beef
Drink	2001–3

Tesco Coonawarra Cabernet Sauvignon 97

Upfront Aussie nose—intense ripe black fruit and cassis aromas. Chewy and chocolatey, the palate has minty black fruit, a full, weighty, velvety mouthfeel and a warm, round finish. *Tesco*

Price	£9–11/€11.50–14
Region	Coonawarra
Grape	Cabernet Sauvignon
Alc/vol	12.5%
Food	Spare ribs
Drink	2001–3

The Potts Family Bleasdale Bremerview Shiraz 99

Lots of rich blackcurrant fruit with a hint of
spice and vanilla giving a deep warm flavour to
the wine. Firm tannins and a long, clean finish.
Oddbins

Price	**£9–11/€11.50–14**
Region	**Langhorne Creek**
Grape	**Shiraz**
Alc/vol	**14.5%**
Food	**Duck**
Drink	**2001–3**

The Potts Family Bleasdale Mulberry Tree Vineyard Cabernet Sauvignon 99 £/€

Seriously dense nose of Christmas pudding, cassis and moist fruit. Complex, big and beefy.
Ripe, spicy fruit flavours on the palate are layered with dark chocolate. Long black pepper
and clove finish. *Oddbins*

Price	**£9–11/€11.50–14**
Region	**Langhorne Creek**
Grape	**Cabernet Sauvignon**
Alc/vol	**14%**
Food	**Casseroles**
Drink	**2001–4**

Wolf Blass South Australia Merlot 99

Heady perfume of plummy fruit. A crowd
pleaser of a wine. Victoria plums and blackberries—juicy, fruity and very ripe. *Dillons*

Price	**£9–11/€11.50–14**
Region	**South Australia**
Grape	**Merlot**
Alc/vol	**13.5%**
Food	**Barbecued lamb**
Drink	**2001–2**

Wolf Blass South Australia Shiraz 99

Intense nose of black fruit, spice, tar, leather
and dark chocolate. Abundant bitter cherry
fruit surrounded by layers of savoury flavours.
Firm tannins, tobacco leaves. Very long finish.
Dillons

Price	**£9–11/€11.50–14**
Region	**South Australia**
Grape	**Shiraz**
Alc/vol	**13.5%**
Food	**Lasagne**
Drink	**2001–2**

Wynns Coonawarra Estate Cabernet Shiraz Merlot 97

Striking aromas of blackcurrants and eucalyptus
with some oaky notes. Outstanding fruit on the
palate—blackcurrants, oak, cream, pepper. A
full wine. Powerful, easy to drink, yet developing in bottle. *Findlaters*

Price	**£9–11/€11.50–14**
Region	**Coonawarra**
Grape	**Cab Sauv/Shir/Merl**
Alc/vol	**13.5%**
Food	**Roast loin of pork**
Drink	**2001–3**

Wynns Coonawarra Estate Shiraz 98 £/€

What you expect an Aussie Shiraz to be! Spice,
vanilla, aniseed, mint and black fruit aromas.
The palate is very big and flavoursome, with
good black fruit and spice intensity—this wine
has plenty of charm, but isn't overpowering.
Findlaters

Price	**£9–11/€11.50–14**
Region	**Coonawarra**
Grape	**Shiraz**
Alc/vol	**13.5%**
Food	**Roast beef**
Drink	**2001–3**

Yaldara Reserve Cabernet Merlot 99

Fruit-packed palate with lots of chocolate and coffee flavours, giving a complex wine with ripe tannins and a very long finish.
Barry & Fitzwilliam

Price	£9–11/€11.50–14
Region	SE Australia
Grape	Cabernet/Merlot
Alc/vol	13.5%
Food	Versatile
Drink	2001–3

Yaldara Reserve Shiraz 99 ★ £/€

This elegant and appealing wine has rich aromas of mint, eucalyptus, black cherries, ripe plums and liquorice essence. The palate is meaty and chewy, with vanilla, sweet Victoria plums, spice, smooth, silky hot chocolate and white pepper, all blending into a warm, rounded finish. *Barry & Fitzwilliam*

Price	£9–11/€11.50–14
Region	SE Australia
Grape	Shiraz
Alc/vol	13.5%
Food	Peppered steak
Drink	2001–4

£11–13/€14–16.50

McGuigan Shareholders Cabernet Merlot 98 £/€

Very concentrated and structured wine. The palate is full of dense black fruit with chocolate and vanilla notes. Tannins are firm and hold the fruit and acidity together. It's an easy-drinking wine but in the grown-up league.
Barry & Fitzwilliam

Price	£11–13/€14–16.50
Region	SE Australia
Grape	Cabernet/Merlot
Alc/vol	13%
Food	Traditional
Drink	2001–3

McGuigan Shareholders Shiraz 98

Ripe plums and blackcurrant on the nose with slightly oaky, earthy, smoked bacon aromas. The palate has rich, layered flavours of plums, chocolate and spice, firm tannins and an attractive, lingering finish. *Barry & Fitzwilliam*

Price	£11–13/€14–16.50
Region	SE Australia
Grape	Shiraz
Alc/vol	13.5%
Food	Meat loaf
Drink	2001–3

Reynolds The Jezebel Cabernet Sauvignon 99

Christmas in a glass—Christmas cake spices, plums, cherries and mint. Rich, intense, concentrated, smoke, tar, liquorice, sweet plummy fruit flavours. Packed with flavour, great structure, a real food wine. *O'Briens*

Price	£11–13/€14–16.50
Region	Orange
Grape	Cabernet Sauvignon
Alc/vol	12.5%
Food	Red meat
Drink	2001–3

Sandalford Mount Barker/Margaret River Cabernet Sauvignon 97

The fruit, tannin and oak are beautifully blended in this wine. It has baked plum and mint aromas and is quite spicy. The soft fruit, gentle tannins and lingering finish make it very easy to drink. *Irish Distillers*

Price	£11–13/€14–16.50
Region	Western Australia
Grape	Cabernet Sauvignon
Alc/vol	13%
Food	Beef
Drink	2001–3

Sandalford Mount Barker/Margaret River Shiraz 97

Nose of blackcurrants, charred wood, vanilla and capsicum. A full-bodied wine, the palate has blackcurrants with lots of nutmeg and black pepper spice. Very lengthy and tasty with plenty of oak evident. *Irish Distillers*

Price	**£11–13/€14–16.50**
Region	**Western Australia**
Grape	**Shiraz**
Alc/vol	**13%**
Food	**Lamb chops**
Drink	**2001–4**

Tatachilla McLaren Vale Cabernet Sauvignon 98

Blackberry nose and blackcurrant fruit pastille flavours. Very tasty, very big, a quality Australian Cabernet, with structure, fruit and punch at an affordable price. *O'Briens*

Price	**£11–13/€14–16.50**
Region	**McLaren Vale**
Grape	**Cabernet Sauvignon**
Alc/vol	**14%**
Food	**Beef**
Drink	**2001–4**

Wolf Blass Presidents Selection Cabernet Sauvignon 98 £/€

Beautiful deep red colour and lovely autumn fruit aromas. Sweet black fruit on the palate, with ripe tannins and a gorgeous spicy finish with plenty of fruit. Tannins are on the firm side, making this a good food wine. *Dillons*

Price	**£11–13/€14–16.50**
Region	**South Australia**
Grape	**Cabernet Sauvignon**
Alc/vol	**14%**
Food	**Steak**
Drink	**2001–3**

Wolf Blass Presidents Selection Shiraz 97 ✓

A big, spicy bouquet with apothecary notes. Muscular and meaty wine, it's full bodied with ripe plum and summer pudding fruits, lots of dark chocolate and moist tobacco leaves. Very long and spicy length. *Dillons*

Price	**£11–13/€14–16.50**
Region	**South Australia**
Grape	**Shiraz**
Alc/vol	**14%**
Food	**Steak**
Drink	**2001–2**

Yalumba Barossa Bush Vine Grenache 99 £/€

A subtle wine—the fruit comes from 70-year-old vines. Attractive juicy summer fruit flavours showing some development. Spicy and mellow. *Cassidy*

Price	**£11–13/€14–16.50**
Region	**Barossa Valley**
Grape	**Grenache**
Alc/vol	**14.5%**
Food	**Moussaka**
Drink	**2001–3**

Yalumba Barossa Cabernet Sauvignon Shiraz 98

Though a bit shy on the nose, this wine really opens up on the palate. Full of summer fruit, blueberry and cherry flavours, it has a delicate floral undertone of violets and a smooth, long, creamy finish from maturation in oak. *Cassidy*

Price	**£11–13/€14–16.50**
Region	**Barossa Valley**
Grape	**Cab Sauv/Shiraz**
Alc/vol	**14%**
Food	**Rare beef**
Drink	**2001–2**

> *Although Australia may seem dominant on our wine shelves, its wine production is only a tenth of French output.*

£13–15/€16.50–19

Bethany Schrapel Family Vineyards Cabernet Merlot 99 ✓

A super wine. Inviting aromas of black fruits and eucalyptus with new oak in the background. Full, fruity wine. Powerful and well structured, the excellent fruit is integrated nicely with the oak and tannins. *O'Briens*

Price	**£13–15/€16.50–19**
Region	**Barossa Valley**
Grape	**Cabernet/Merlot**
Alc/vol	**13%**
Food	**Irish stew**
Drink	**2001–3**

Penfolds Bin 128 Coonawarra Shiraz 97 ✓

Delicious ripe plum and Morello cherry fruit with a spicy cedar box dimension. Full bodied, the wine has great balance between ripe blackcurrants, spice, leather and tar. Hugely lengthy and very tasty. *Findlaters*

Price	**£13–15/€16.50–19**
Region	**Coonawarra**
Grape	**Shiraz**
Alc/vol	**13.5%**
Food	**Veal**
Drink	**2001–6**

Penny's Hill Shiraz 99

Packed with rich blackcurrants and blackberries and nicely balanced between complex fruity and mild oaky flavours. A little tannic now, this wine will continue to develop for the next three to four years. Long, smooth finish. *Oddbins*

Price	**£13–15/€16.50–19**
Region	**McLaren Vale**
Grape	**Shiraz**
Alc/vol	**14.5%**
Food	**Leg of lamb**
Drink	**2001–5**

Riddoch Shiraz 98 ✓

Very pleasing rich style of Aussie Shiraz, yet showing some restraint. Fruity aromas, rich with plums, pepper and smoky bacon. The palate is long, smooth and leathery with chocolate and again lots of fruit—wonderful depth and concentration, with real bite on the finish. *Woodford Bourne*

Price	**£13–15/€16.50–19**
Region	**Coonawarra**
Grape	**Shiraz**
Alc/vol	**13.5%**
Food	**Barbecued steak**
Drink	**2001–4**

> *Coonawarra's fortunes were revived by Wynns in 1951 (previously much of the production went for brandy distillation). Cabernet Sauvignon, grown on the famous terra rossa soils, and Chardonnay are the dominant varieties, followed closely by Shiraz.*

MAKING A GREAT IMPRESSION

HARDYS

'The Cork Wine Merchants'

- Over 500 quality wines
- Quality staff on hand for advice
- 8 shops to choose from
- Full party/function service
- Wine consultancy service available
- Corporate and private tastings arranged
- Direct wine deliveries nationwide arranged
- Wholesale price-list for on-trade available on request
- Wine list available on request
- Wine Club—Douglas and Bishopstown Wine Club

Main Office
Unit 27, St Patrick's Mill Douglas, Cork
Phone: (021) 489 5227/746
Fax: (021) 489 3391
Wine consultant—Gary O'Donovan 086 263 2211

Branches
Douglas (021) 436 3650, Bishopstown (021) 434 3416,
Blackpool (021) 439 8177, Summerhill (021) 450 5444,
Oliver Plunkett St (021) 427 7626
Shandon St (021) 439 9121, Midleton (021) 461 3001,
Riversdale Shopping Centre (021) 461 3792

'We have all the wine in the world'

Robertson's Well Cabernet Sauvignon 98

Vanilla aromas and flavours from oak maturation. A rounded wine, it has a delicate balance
of spice, red berry fruit, acidity and tannin.
Gilbeys

Price	**£13–15/€16.50–19**
Region	**Coonawarra**
Grape	**Cabernet Sauvignon**
Alc/vol	**13%**
Food	**Spaghetti Bolognese**
Drink	**2001–3**

Seppelt Great Western Vineyard Shiraz 96

Big, broad Aussie Shiraz. Lots of aniseed, spice
and vanilla integrating with fruits of the forest,
stewed prunes and plum juice. Upfront and
flavoursome. *Dunnes Stores*

Price	**£13–15/€16.50–19**
Region	**Victoria**
Grape	**Shiraz**
Alc/vol	**14.5%**
Food	**Casseroles**
Drink	**2001–3**

£15–17/€19–22

Blue Pyrenees Estate Reserve 98 ★

A wonderful, complex, earthy nose of smoke,
raisins, vanilla, violets and cloves leads to an
exotic palate of cassis, black cherries and
tobacco. Great length—a class act. *Bacchus*

Price	**£15–17/€19–22**
Region	**Victoria**
Grape	**Cab Sauv/Shiraz/ Merlot**
Alc/vol	**13.5%**
Food	**Roasts**
Drink	**2001–3**

Jim Barry McCrae Wood Shiraz 97 ★

Very appealing and flavoursome. Lovely nose of
mint, spice and black fruit, elegant palate of
rich black fruit, vanilla and a touch of mint.
Excellent finish. *Dunnes Stores*

Price	**£15–17/€19–22**
Region	**Clare Valley**
Grape	**Shiraz**
Alc/vol	**14.5%**
Food	**Lamb**
Drink	**2001–6**

Peel Estate Shiraz 97 ✓

A sophisticated, complex, spicy Shiraz. Matured
in a blend of American and French oak for two
years, the oak comes through on the perfumed
nose. On the palate there are ripe blackcurrants,
plums and pepper. Full flavoured and complex,
it has a splendid finish. *Waterford Wine Vault*

Price	**£15–17/€19–22**
Region	**Western Australia**
Grape	**Shiraz**
Alc/vol	**14.5%**
Food	**Lamb**
Drink	**2002–8**

Pipers Brook Vineyard Pinot Noir 00 ✓

This Pinot Noir, made in cool-climate Tasmania,
has a typical Pinot nose of sweet strawberries
and vanilla. The palate is perfectly judged, displaying strawberry and summer pudding flavours. It's ripe without being cloying and has a
good, positive, alcoholic finish. *Irish Distillers*

Price	**£15–17/€19–22**
Region	**Tasmania**
Grape	**Pinot Noir**
Alc/vol	**13.5%**
Food	**Chicken**
Drink	**2001–3**

Rosemount GSM Grenache Syrah Mourvèdre 98

Delightfully rich blockbuster—the warm, spicy currant flavours are given a smooth vanilla richness from ageing in oak barrels. It's big, with a long, flavoursome finish. A powerful wine, with clean fruit and a smooth, creamy finish. *Grants*

Price	**£15–17/€19–22**
Region	**McLaren Vale**
Grape	**Grenache/Syrah/ Mourvèdre**
Alc/vol	**15%**
Food	**Beef**
Drink	**2001–4**

Stonier Reserve Pinot Noir 98

The nose is pronounced at first, then retreats a little. The flavours on the palate are subtle—softness and restraint are the keynotes in the ripe strawberries and raspberries, the use of oak, the tannins and the alcohol. *Woodford Bourne*

Price	**£15–17/€19–22**
Region	**Mornington Pen.**
Grape	**Pinot Noir**
Alc/vol	**14%**
Food	**Coq au vin**
Drink	**2001–4**

Tyrrell's Vat 8 Shiraz Cabernet 97 ✓

Beautiful aromas of mint and eucalyptus. The palate is packed with layers of rich black fruit with spice and oak. Tannins are firm, giving great grip. Long-lasting finish. *Maxxium*

Price	**£15–17/€19–22**
Region	**Hunter Valley/ Coonawarra**
Grape	**Shiraz/Cab Sauv**
Alc/vol	**13%**
Food	**Lamb**
Drink	**2001–3**

£17–20/€22–25.50

Elderton Barossa Shiraz 98 ✓

Shiraz vines over forty years old are grown in rich alluvial silt and red-brown earth, which gives softness and complexity to the fruit. This wine has lovely aromas of spice, dark fruits and vanilla. The elegant palate is full of blackcurrants, plums and spice. Nice complexity of flavour, fairly assertive tannins and a long finish. One to keep. *Fields*

Price	**£17–20/€22–25**
Region	**Barossa Valley**
Grape	**Shiraz**
Alc/vol	**14.5%**
Food	**Beef**
Drink	**2002–7**

Geoff Merrill Cabernet Sauvignon Reserve 95 ✓

Attractive, complex nose, which is very mature. Eucalyptus dominates the red and black fruit, vanilla and toast. Some vegetal notes. Structure is there—tannins are firm, acidity is crisp and there is plenty of fruit. Strong blackcurrant edge to the long finish. *United Beverages*

Price	**£17–20/€22–25**
Region	**South Australia**
Grape	**Cabernet Sauvignon**
Alc/vol	**13.5%**
Food	**Lamb**
Drink	**2001–3**

Katnook Estate Cabernet Sauvignon 97 ✓

Quite a complex and pronounced nose of broad
beans with lots of savoury gravy. The palate is
full and velvety, with very ripe fruit—violets
and vanilla with ripe squashed blackcurrants/
blackberries and Morello cherries. A delicious
mouthful. *Woodford Bourne*

Price	**£17–20/€22–25**
Region	**Coonawarra**
Grape	**Cabernet Sauvignon**
Alc/vol	**13.5%**
Food	**Rack of lamb**
Drink	**2001–5**

Mary Kathleen Reserve Cabernet Merlot 96 £/€

Ageing beatifully, this powerful wine has
upfront plums, strawberries and herbs on the
nose. Full of summer fruit and bittersweet
cherry flavours. The firm tannic structure and
intense fruit produce a rewarding wine.
Wines Direct

Price	**£17–20/€22–25**
Region	**McLaren Vale**
Grape	**Cabernet/Merlot/ Cab Franc**
Alc/vol	**13.5%**
Food	**Traditional**
Drink	**2001–5**

Nepenthe Lenswood Pinot Noir 99

Perfumed bouquet—crushed strawberries. The
rich, flavoursome palate, though not typical
Pinot Noir, is laden with ripe plums, damsons,
generous cinnamon/pepper and firm tannins.
Barry & Fitzwilliam

Price	**£17–20/€22–25**
Region	**Adelaide Hills**
Grape	**Pinot Noir**
Alc/vol	**14%**
Food	**Poultry**
Drink	**2001–4**

Nepenthe The Fugue 98

With lots of very ripe fruit and plenty of concentration, this Bordeaux blend has super Aussie richness—chocolate, vanilla, blackcurrants
and plums. Made in a definite Bordeaux style,
the tannins are nicely firm and will keep the
wine going. *Barry & Fitzwilliam*

Price	**£17–20/€22–25**
Region	**Adelaide Hills**
Grape	**Cabernet/Merlot/ Cab Franc**
Alc/vol	**13.5%**
Food	**Moroccan**
Drink	**2001–3**

Penfolds Bin 389 Cabernet Shiraz 98

Good nose—minty top notes over blackcurrant
fruit and vanilla. Mouthfeel is rich, contained
within a marked soft tannic structure—stewed
blackberry fruit with strong alcohol support.
Long finish. *Findlaters*

Price	**£17–20/€22–25.50**
Region	**South Australia**
Grape	**Cab Sauv/Shiraz**
Alc/vol	**14.5%**
Food	**Barbecued lamb**
Drink	**2001–5**

St Hallett Old Block Shiraz 96 ✓

This is a big, muscular wine that manages to
have poise and elegance at the same time. Its
baked fruit aromas, with pepper and tar in the
background, are reflected in the plums, cherries
and dark chocolate flavours. Extremely long
finish. *O'Briens*

Price	**£17–20/€22–25.50**
Region	**Barossa Valley**
Grape	**Shiraz**
Alc/vol	**13.5%**
Food	**Versatile**
Drink	**2001–3**

Tatachilla Foundation Shiraz 98 ★

Quite a performance—appealing aromas of
prunes, plums and figs and a terrific palate of
plums, cassis and vanilla. The fruit is opulent
and rich, with velvety tannins and great length.
O'Briens

Price	£17–20/€22–25
Region	McLaren Vale
Grape	Shiraz
Alc/vol	14.5%
Food	Turkey
Drink	2001–4

£20–25/€25–32

d'Arenberg The Dead Arm Shiraz 98

'Dead arm' is a vine disease that causes one half,
or arm, of the vine to die. One side is lifeless and
brittle, but the grapes on the other side are full
of flavour. A spicy, oaky nose leads to more spice
on the palate, with plums, dark fruits and
vanilla. Still quite tannic, this wine has a long
way to go. *Taserra*

Price	£20–25/€25–32
Region	McLaren Vale
Grape	Shiraz
Alc/vol	14.5%
Food	Stir-fried beef
Drink	2002–7

De Bortoli Shiraz 99

Deep, dense, complex nose of blackcurrants,
leather and spice. More blackcurrants on the
palate, but lots of tar, spice, green pepper and
vegetal notes there too. Delicious contrast of
flavour layers. Very chunky with lots of Oxo
cube. Terrific finish. *Febvre*

Price	£20–25/€25–32
Region	Yarra Valley
Grape	Shiraz
Alc/vol	13.5%
Food	Red meat
Drink	2001–4

Peter Lehmann The Barossa Mentor 94 ★

A wonderful, rich, intense wine. Attractive aromas of black fruits, spice and a hint of cedar. On
the palate the wine is rich, round and full, with
great concentration of blackcurrant fruit and
spice. Long finish. A classic wine.
United Beverages

Price	£20–25/€25–32
Region	Barossa Valley
Grape	Cab Sauv/Malbec
Alc/vol	13.5%
Food	Beef
Drink	2001–4

Peter Lehmann The Barossa Mentor 95 ✓

On the nose there are notes of blackcurrant and
cigar box. Strong, lingering black cherry fruits
spread on the palate. This is a wine with a big
tannic structure, plenty of acidity and a firm
finish. Very good indeed. Definitely a food
wine. *United Beverages*

Price	£20–25/€25–32
Region	Barossa Valley
Grape	Cab Sauv/Malbec/ Merlot
Alc/vol	13%
Food	Goulash
Drink	2001–4

£25–30/€32–40

De Bortoli Pinot Noir 97

An expensive bottle, but earning its price tag due to the balance of the wine and the purity of style—no jam here, just pure Pinot character of strawberries, blackberries, spice and cream, helped by some subtle oak. Full flavour and body and great length. Certainly a very big New World Pinot. *Febvre*

Price	**£25–30/€32–40**
Region	**Yarra Valley**
Grape	**Pinot Noir**
Alc/vol	**13%**
Food	**Simple chicken**
Drink	**2001–3**

Peter Lehmann Stonewell Shiraz 95

A big wine with lots of structure and evident tannins. Slightly closed on the nose, but the palate is packed with rich, dark damson and black fruits, combined with cedar and vanilla. Long, structured finish. The deep, complex flavours will have even more depth in one or two years' time. Potential! *Oddbins*

Price	**£25–30/€32–40**
Region	**Barossa Valley**
Grape	**Shiraz**
Alc/vol	**13.5%**
Food	**Fillet steak**
Drink	**2001–10**

Rosemount Estate Balmoral Syrah 98 ★

A few small patches of Shiraz vines up to 100 years old survive in the McLaren Vale, yielding tiny quantities of exquisitely flavoured fruit. Although undeniably expensive, this is a wonderfully fruity wine that attacks the senses from all angles. Enormous dark red fruits, cream, spices, chocolate and damsons with floral undertones on a very, very balanced palate with rich, velvety, ripe tannins and balancing acidity. You could drink it now, but try to keep it for five years. *Grants*

Price	**£25–30/€32–40**
Region	**McLaren Vale**
Grape	**Syrah**
Alc/vol	**14.5%**
Food	**Chargrilled meat**
Drink	**2001–6**

Irish importers of Austrian wine

SEARSONS WINE MERCHANTS
Monkstown Crescent, Blackrock,
County Dublin
Tel: 01-280 0405; *Fax:* 01-280 4771

Contact: Mr Frank Searson,
Managing Director

Freie Weingärtner Wachau
1999 Loibener Riesling Smaragd
1997 Weissenkirchen Achleiten Smaragd
1997 Grüner Veltliner Smaragd
Red:
1997 Azzo Zweigelt Pinot Noir
Weingut Erich & Walter Polz
1997 Grassnitzberg Grauburgunder

BARRY & FITZWILLIAM LTD
Glanmire, Cork
Tel: 021-821555; *Fax:* 021-821604

also at: 50 Dartmouth Square, Dublin 6
Tel: 01-667 1755; *Fax:* 01-660 0479

Contact: Mr Michael Barry;
Mr Tony Cleary

Weinkellerei Lenz Moser, Rohrendorf
SERVUS white
SERVUS red

TERROIRS
103 Morehampton Road, Dublin 4
Tel: 01-667 1311; *Fax:* 01-667 1312

Contact: Mr Seán Gilley;
Ms Françoise Gilley-Traineau

Johanneshof Reinisch, Tattendorf
Johanneshof Reinisch Merlot 1992
(Gold Medal Winner)
Johanneshof Reinisch Cabernet
Reserve 1994
Johanneshof Reinisch Eiswein 1992/4
Johanneshof Reinisch Pinot Blanc 1996/9
Johanneshof Reinisch Pinot Noir
Reserve 1997
Johanneshof Reinisch Pinot Noir
Grand Reserve 1997
Johanneshof Reinisch Dialog 1997
(50% Ch 50% S Bl)
Johanneshof Reinisch Dialog 1999
(50% Ch 20% Wb 30% S Bl)
Johanneshof Reinisch Alter Rebstock 1995
Johanneshof Reinisch St Laurent 1992

**MITCHELL & SON WINE
MERCHANTS LTD**
21 Kildare Street, Dublin 2
Tel: 01-676 0766; *Fax:* 01-661 1509

Contact: Mr Peter B Dunne, Director

Domäne Müller Gutsverwaltung,
Groß St. Florian
2000 Gut am Ottenberg Sauvignon Blanc
1999 Gut am Ottenberg Chardonnay
1998 Gut am Ottenberg Riunterra White
2000 Ried Burgegg, Zweigelt
1997 Gut am Ottenberg Riunterra Red

HENRY J. ARCHER & SONS LTD
Ballymoney, Gorey, Co Wexford
Tel: +353-55-25176; *Fax:* +353-55-25842

Contact: Paul Dubsky

Erzherzog Johann Weine,
Ehrenhausen, Styria
1999 Weissburgunder – Pinot Blanc
1999 Sauvignon Blanc
1999 Pinot Gris, Kabinett
1999 Schilcher
1999 Zweigelt Blau
Johann Kattus Vienna
Alte Reserve Sparkling
1998 Nussberger Rheinriesling

Austria

Austria now has quality laws that are among the strictest in the world. Yields are also kept low—often 50 per cent less than those in neighbouring Germany, which gives the wines plenty of flavour and character.

White wines are made mainly from Riesling, Grüner Veltliner, Weissburgunder (Pinot Blanc) and Sauvignon Blanc, most of which are represented in the book this year. Grüner Veltliner is well worth trying if you're looking for something different, as it has a distinctive spiciness that is very attractive. The Freie Weingärtner featured here comes from the Wachau, one of Austria's most famous white wine regions, where wines achieve great ripeness but maintain crisp acidity.

Though Austria is best known for its dry and sweet white whites, it produces excellent red wine, especially in the Burgenland area. The best-known black grape varieties are Blaufränkisch, St Laurent and Zweigelt, all local grape varieties with distinctive character.

It can be quite difficult to buy Austrian wine, but it's worth asking your local off-licence to stock some, as the wines are different and delicious.

White

£9–11/€11.50–14

Erzherzog Johann Exklusiv Pinot Gris Qualitätswein **99** ✓

A lovely elegant style with lots of ripe melon on the nose and palate. Some apricot flavours too, with a hint of vanilla. Tangy citrus finish. *Henry J. Archer*

Price	**£9–11/€11.50–14**
Region	**Südsteiermark**
Grape	**Pinot Gris**
Alc/vol	**11%**
Food	**Onion tart**
Drink	**2001–2**

Freie Weingärtner Terrassen Thal Wachau Grüner Veltliner Smaragd Qualitätswein **97**

The Wachau region has its own quality rules and Smaragd is the highest grade. Grapes have to be ultra-ripe before picking. This is very different and attractive, with its distinctive spicy nose and palate of ripe, plump orchard fruit. Terrific finish. *Searsons*

Price	**£9–11/€11.50–14**
Region	**Wachau**
Grape	**Grüner Veltliner**
Alc/vol	**13.5%**
Food	**Veal**
Drink	**2001–3**

£11–13/€14–16.50

Nussberger Höhenweg Rheinriesling Kabinett Trocken Qualitätswein **98**

Classic Riesling petrol nose. The zesty palate has green apple and grapefruit flavours, very elegant and typical. *Henry J. Archer*

Price	**£11–13/€14–16.50**
Region	**Vienna**
Grape	**Riesling**
Alc/vol	**12%**
Food	**Stir fries**
Drink	**2001–3**

£15–17/€19–22

Freie Weingärtner Loibner Loibenberg Riesling Smaragd
Qualitätswein **99** ✓

An intriguing nose of crab apples with a floral background. Apples and peaches on the palate, with a deliciously elegant mouthfeel and a long, crisp finish. *Searsons*

Price	**£15–17/€19–22**
Region	**Wachau**
Grape	**Riesling**
Alc/vol	**13%**
Food	**Seafood**
Drink	**2001–5**

£17–20/€25–32

Dom. Müller Riunterra Qualitätswein **98**

A striking peach/apricot nose, complemented by a mineral edge. Outstanding tart flavours, fresh nectarines, with a full flavoursome finish. *Mitchells*

Price	**£17–20/€25–32**
Region	**Styria**
Grape	**Sauv Blanc/Chard**
Alc/vol	**13%**
Food	**Versatile**
Drink	**2001–3**

Red

£20–25/€25–32

Dom. Müller Riunterra Qualitätswein **97**

A blend of Zweigelt and Cabernet Sauvignon with 5% each of St Laurent, Merlot and Cabernet Franc. Intense, spicy nose, with notes of cumin, red fruits and black fruits. Weighty with fresh acidity and firm tannins. Concentrated fruit and lengthy finish. *Mitchells*

Price	**£20–25/€25–32**
Region	**Styria**
Alc/vol	**13%**
Food	**Roast beef**
Drink	**2001–5**

Chile

Chile's winemaking regions span the length of the country. Measured from Santiago, they run 400 km to the north of the city and 650 km to the south. In the past there has been a certain amount of criticism that wines often tasted more or less the same, whatever their region of origin, due to the emphasis on winemaking rather than grape-growing. Now, however, definite differences are emerging.

Although it can be dangerous to generalise, the best whites come from Casablanca in Aconcagua. Until 1982 not a single grape grew in Casablanca, yet this relative newcomer produces fresh and crisp Chardonnay and grassy Sauvignon Blanc. It is also having some success with Pinot Noir.

The best reds are from the Central Valley, the wine region with four of the most famous and familiar of Chile's valleys—Maipo, Rapel, Curicó and Maule. While Maipo is one of the oldest and most established, producing consistently high quality, the Merlots of the Maule Valley are possibly the most highly regarded. The Rapel Valley makes excellent Cabernets, particularly in Cachapoal and Colchagua. Some of the most interesting Carmenère is from the Maule and Rapel.

White

Under £7/Under €9

Andes Peaks Sauvignon Blanc 00

Pleasant, zippy Sauvignon with very attractive pale gold colour. It has fresh acidity and plenty of crisp citrus and melon fruit. Perfect aperitif. *O'Briens*

Price	**Under £7/Under €9**
Region	**Central Valley**
Grape	**Sauvignon Blanc**
Alc/vol	**13%**
Food	**Aperitif**
Drink	**2001–2**

Antu Mapu Sauvignon Blanc 99

A little extra age in a Chilean Sauvignon Blanc always gives it more interest. This one, made by Claudio Barria, is quite gentle, less acidic than many Sauvignons, and, for some, more attractive. It's dry, with balanced acidity and soft fruit, good length and a green apple finish. *Barry & Fitzwilliam*

Price	**Under £7/Under €9**
Region	**Maule Valley**
Grape	**Sauvignon Blanc**
Alc/vol	**13%**
Food	**Goats' cheese**
Drink	**2001–2**

Aresti Family Vineyards Montemar Chardonnay 99 £/€

Very different from the usual run-of-the-mill New World Chardonnay. This has apples and limes but also a green herbaceous edge, with limes and green peppers on the palate. *SuperValu-Centra*

Price	**Under £7/Under €9**
Region	**Curicó Valley**
Grape	**Chardonnay**
Alc/vol	**13%**
Food	**Crab**
Drink	**2001–2**

Aresti Family Vineyards Montemar Sauvignon Blanc 00 £/€ ✓

Intense green flavours on top of ripe, soft, tropical fruit and a very warm feeling in the mouth. Dry, with crisp acidity and a long, clean, dry finish. *SuperValu-Centra*

Price	**Under £7/Under €9**
Region	**Curicó Valley**
Grape	**Sauvignon Blanc**
Alc/vol	**13.5%**
Food	**Seafood**
Drink	**2001–2**

Concha y Toro Gewürztraminer 00 £/€

The tell-tale aromas of lychees, spice and rose petals mark this wine out as a typical Gewürztraminer. On the palate there are more lychees and spice, with some apple. The slightly off-dry style would work well with spicy food. *Findlaters*

Price	**Under £7/Under €9**
Region	**Rapel Valley**
Grape	**Gewürztraminer**
Alc/vol	**13%**
Food	**Oriental**
Drink	**2001–2**

Concha y Toro Sunrise Chardonnay 00

Dry, but with ripe tropical flavours. Lovely smooth feel in the mouth—very mellow, but with a pleasant, long, fruity finish. Nice underlying acidity. *Findlaters*

Price	**Under £7/Under €9**
Region	**Central Valley**
Grape	**Chardonnay**
Alc/vol	**13%**
Food	**Aperitif**
Drink	**2001–2**

Las Casas del Toqui Semillon 00

Delicious dry, crisp Semillon with a waxy greengage nose and lively grapefruit and lemon flavours. A medium-bodied, fruity party wine, juicy and approachable. Dry but not too dry. Perfect for a picnic. *Dunnes Stores*

Price	**Under £7/Under €9**
Region	**Cachapoal Valley**
Grape	**Semillon**
Alc/vol	**13.5%**
Food	**Picnic**
Drink	**2001–2**

San Pedro Sauvignon Blanc 00 £/€ ✓

Citrus flavours abound in this well-structured wine, which was made under the supervision of Jacques Lurton. It's dry and crisp, with a fruity finish. A lovely big mouthful of fresh fruit. *Dunnes Stores*

Price	**Under £7/Under €9**
Region	**Molina**
Grape	**Sauvignon Blanc**
Alc/vol	**12.5%**
Food	**Corn on the cob**
Drink	**2001–2**

Santa Helena Gran Vino Chardonnay 00

Satisfying and pleasing with apple flavours and aromas and a squeeze of lemon. There is a nice bite of acidity and a counterbalancing creaminess. *Greenhills*

Price	**Under £7/Under €9**
Region	**Central Valley**
Grape	**Chardonnay**
Alc/vol	**12.5%**
Food	**Grilled fish**
Drink	**2001–2**

Santa Helena Gran Vino Sauvignon Blanc 00

Sweet pear and grassy aromas mark this delicious smooth wine with its hints of sand and
heat. Dry, it has a nice clean bite and a very
balanced finish with lingering flavours of
lemon and lime. *Greenhills*

Price	**Under £7/Under €9**
Region	**Central Valley**
Grape	**Sauvignon Blanc**
Alc/vol	**12.5%**
Food	**Avocado**
Drink	**2001–2**

Tesco Chilean Chardonnay nv £/€

Typical Chilean Chardonnay style. This wine
has a lot of melon, peach, ripe crispy apple and
vanilla character. For the price, it's a decent
wine that won't disappoint. *Tesco*

Price	**Under £7/Under €9**
Region	**Central Valley**
Grape	**Chardonnay**
Alc/vol	**13%**
Food	**Chicken salad**
Drink	**On purchase**

Undurraga Sauvignon Blanc 00

Attractive, easy-drinking Sauvignon Blanc. On
the nose there is a medley of green fruits balanced by some ripe tropical notes. Good weight
of fruit follows through with lots of flavour and
good length. *United Beverages*

Price	**Under £7/Under €9**
Region	**Lontué Valley**
Grape	**Sauvignon Blanc**
Alc/vol	**12.5%**
Food	**Caesar salad**
Drink	**2001–2**

£7–9/€9–11.50

Carmen Chardonnay 00

Aromatic nose and palate of light, creamy tropical fruit and a hint of vanilla. Peach and apple
flavours are backed by lively acidity and a clean
finish. *Dillons*

Price	**£7–9/€9–11.50**
Region	**Central Valley**
Grape	**Chardonnay**
Alc/vol	**13.5%**
Food	**Risotto**
Drink	**2001–2**

Ch. Los Boldos Chardonnay 00

Strong New World Chardonnay aromas of tropical fruit, with honeydew melon notes and a
hint of smokiness. The wine has a rich mouthfeel, lush and ripe, with spicy oakiness coming
through after the melon/pineapple/pear fruit,
but backed with sufficient supporting acidity.
Lovely clear, dry, fruity finish. *O'Briens*

Price	**£7–9/€9–11.50**
Region	**Requinoa**
Grape	**Chardonnay**
Alc/vol	**13%**
Food	**Barbecued fish**
Drink	**2001–2**

Concha y Toro Casillero del Diablo Chardonnay 00

Pale gold in colour—good weight of fruit on the
palate, with flavours of mango and pineapple
balanced by crisp acidity and a hint of vanilla.
Long finish. *Findlaters*

Price	**£7–9/€9–11.50**
Region	**Aconcagua Valley**
Grape	**Chardonnay**
Alc/vol	**13.5%**
Food	**Picnic**
Drink	**2001–2**

Concha y Toro Casillero del Diablo Sauvignon Blanc 00

Good example of Chilean Sauvignon Blanc. Lots of fresh, fruity, gooseberry flavours with balancing acidity. Fresh and appealing. Try it with *moules marinières* or scallops. *Findlaters*

Price	**£7–9/€9–11.50**
Region	**Central Valley**
Grape	**Sauvignon Blanc**
Alc/vol	**13%**
Food	**Shellfish**
Drink	**2001–2**

Concha y Toro Trio Chardonnay 99

Gentle nose—melony, slight lime touches. Acidity, which is pleasing and quite marked, provides a good backdrop for the fat, buttery fruit flavours with layers of lychees, lemons and limes. Good fruit intensity and dry, spicy, refreshing finish. *Findlaters*

Price	**£7–9/€9–11.50**
Region	**Casablanca**
Grape	**Chardonnay**
Alc/vol	**13%**
Food	**Spicy food**
Drink	**2001–2**

Las Casas del Toqui Chardonnay Grande Réserve 99 £/€

Vanilla, oaky nose. Dry wine with refreshing, lively acidity, laden with mangoes, melons and pears, smoky, buttery, with lots of vanilla/oak flavours. A mouth-filling wine with high alcohol and a long finish. *Dunnes Stores*

Price	**£7–9/€9–11.50**
Region	**Cachapoal Valley**
Grape	**Chardonnay**
Alc/vol	**13.5%**
Food	**Fish**
Drink	**2001–3**

Montes Barrel Fermented Chardonnay Reserve 00

Seventy-five per cent of the grapes for this Chardonnay were fermented in American oak casks, giving it a creamy texture. Satisfying, high-quality wine with abundant melon, peach and citrus fruit, with rich mouthfeel and fair length. *Grants*

Price	**£7–9/€9–11.50**
Region	**Curicó Valley**
Grape	**Chardonnay**
Alc/vol	**13.5%**
Food	**Barbecue**
Drink	**2001–4**

San Pedro Barrel-Fermented Chardonnay Reserva 99

Appealing bouquet—soft and fruity, heaps of butterscotch and toffee. The palate is dry, but opens up to soft, ripe fruit flavours with tropical nuances and pleasant acidity. Good clear length and plenty of flavour. *Dunnes Stores*

Price	**£7–9/€9–11.50**
Region	**Molina**
Grape	**Chardonnay**
Alc/vol	**14%**
Food	**Turkey curry**
Drink	**2001–2**

Santa Carolina Chardonnay Reservado 99

Fruity and juicy with brisk acidity, hints of lime and lemon, even the tart fruitiness of redcurrants. It has fair weightiness in the mouth and a silky texture, showing good balance of fruit and acidity with long length. *TDL*

Price	**£7–9/€9–11.50**
Region	**Maipo Valley**
Grape	**Chardonnay**
Alc/vol	**13%**
Food	**Versatile**
Drink	**2001–3**

Santa Ema Chardonnay 00

Good, zippy grapefruit acidity gives a lovely fresh appeal here. Nothing overblown in this attractive modern-style Chardonnay. Fruit and acidity hold together well; this wine should be matched with spicy dishes. *Mitchells*

Price	**£7–9/€9–11.50**
Region	**Maipo Valley**
Grape	**Chardonnay**
Alc/vol	**13%**
Food	**Indian**
Drink	**2001–2**

Tesco Chilean Chardonnay Reserve 00

Chardonnay from a sunny climate with aromas of ripe melons with a touch of buttery vanilla. The palate is like a pie in a glass—deliciously spicy apple pie and vanilla ice cream flavours with an added peachy touch. Round, velvety mouthfeel. *Tesco*

Price	**£7–9/€9–11.50**
Region	**Central Valley**
Grape	**Chardonnay**
Alc/vol	**12.5%**
Food	**Chicken**
Drink	**2001–2**

Villard Estate Sauvignon Blanc 00

Aromatic nose of lemon, grapefruit, and cut grass. Clean, fresh palate, quite intense, with citrus flavours. One of those versatile Chileans and very smart indeed. Good partner for vegetarian dishes, white meats or fish. *O'Briens*

Price	**£7–9/€9–11.50**
Region	**Casablanca**
Grape	**Sauvignon Blanc**
Alc/vol	**12.5%**
Food	**Versatile**
Drink	**2001–2**

Viña Tarapacá Chardonnay Reserva 99

Lots of ripe tropical fruit on the nose, which follows through on the palate. Mango, pineapple and vanilla flavours and a nice touch of oak go on to a long, pleasant finish with a hint of spice. *Gleeson*

Price	**£7–9/€9–11.50**
Region	**Maipo Valley**
Grape	**Chardonnay**
Alc/vol	**13.5%**
Food	**Roasted peppers**
Drink	**2001–2**

£9–11/€11.50–14

Alto de Terra Andina Chardonnay Reserva 99 ✓

This is a wine with lots of character, not at all a typical New World Chardonnay. The nose may make you think of a sweet wine, but this is dry, with lots of ripe melon and pineapple. Nice subtle use of oak and a flavoursome finish. *Irish Distillers*

Price	**£9–11/€11.50–14**
Region	**Casablanca**
Grape	**Chardonnay**
Alc/vol	**15%**
Food	**Barbecue**
Drink	**2001–3**

Canepa Private Reserve Chardonnay 99

A nose just as Chardonnay should be—buttery and nutty. The palate yields a rounded style of Chardonnay with abundant apple and vanilla fruit and good backing acidity. This wine will blossom in a year or so. *MacCormaic*

Price	**£9–11/€11.50–14**
Region	**Rancagua Valley**
Grape	**Chardonnay**
Alc/vol	**13%**
Food	**Guacamole**
Drink	**2001–3**

Carmen Chardonnay Reserve 98

Upfront ripe apples, tropical fruit, oak and vanilla on the nose and palate, but also soft citrus fruit, peppery melon and peachy vanilla balanced by crisp acidity, giving a long, pleasant finish. *Dillons*

Price	£9–11/€11.50–14
Region	Maipo Valley
Grape	Chardonnay
Alc/vol	13.5%
Food	Smoked haddock
Drink	2001–3

Casas del Bosque Casablanca Valley Chardonnay 99

Apple and vanilla aromas are followed by creamy flavours of baked pears with a smooth vanilla background. Cleanly made Chardonnay and a good wine to have with French onion soup with lots of gooey cheese. *Waterford Wine Vault*

Price	£9–11/€11.50–14
Region	Casablanca
Grape	Chardonnay
Alc/vol	13%
Food	French onion soup
Drink	2001–2

Concha y Toro Marqués de Casa Concha Chardonnay 98

Rich in colour and nose, with subtle aromas of new oak, roses and tropical fruit. On the palate there is stewed tropical fruit, warm pineapple pudding and spicy touches, perhaps cardamom. The wine has a generous mouthfeel, spicy, rich and soft, with fairly muted acidity. Dry, spicy finish. A delicious wine and at its peak. *Findlaters*

Price	£9–11/€11.50–14
Region	Maipo Valley
Grape	Chardonnay
Alc/vol	13.5%
Food	Chicken
Drink	2001–2

Viña Tarapacá Piritas Chardonnay 99 ✓

If you like lots of oak in your Chardonnay, this wine is for you. The deep and intense nose of tropical fruits is enveloped by burnt vanilla aromas. On the palate the wine has ripe tropical fruit with lots of warm toast and vanilla balanced by crisp acidity. The finish is long. *Gleeson*

Price	£9–11/€11.50–14
Region	Maipo Valley
Grape	Chardonnay
Alc/vol	14%
Food	Fish stew
Drink	2001–2

£11–13/€14–16.50

Ch. Los Boldos Chardonnay Vieilles Vignes 99

Smoky vanilla and lemon meringue pie aromas are underpinned on the palate with concentrated fruit and acidity. Subtle use of oak gives a butteriness to the soft, ripe tropical fruit flavours and the backing of acidity gives the wine great structure. The excellent finish is dry and fruity. Super wine. *O'Briens*

Price	£11–13/€14–16.50
Region	Requinoa
Grape	Chardonnay
Alc/vol	13.5%
Food	Versatile
Drink	2001–2

Dallas-Conté Reserve Chardonnay 99

A refined Chardonnay with elegant melon and apple fruit aromas. Interesting palate of cinnamon, vanilla, apple crumble and melons. Smooth finish. Drink it now with fish or let it develop for another year. *Koala Wines*

Price	£11–13/€14–16.50
Region	Casablanca
Grape	Chardonnay
Alc/vol	14.3%
Food	Smoked salmon
Drink	2001–3

£15–17/€19–22

Errázuriz Casablanca Valley Wild Ferment Chardonnay 99

The use of naturally occurring indigenous yeasts has given the wine a lovely dimension on the nose, with toasted nuts and candied fruits coming through. On the palate flavours are equally interesting—Italian florentine biscuits along with nut and marmalade flavours.
Allied Drinks

Price	**£15–17/€19–22**
Region	**Casablanca**
Grape	**Chardonnay**
Alc/vol	**14%**
Food	**Poultry**
Drink	**2001–2**

£20–25/€25–32

Concha y Toro Amelia Chardonnay 97

Delicate nose; complex but restrained, with melon and ripe apple. A hint of oak from the warm toast and vanilla. On the palate the wine is dry, with tropical fruit well integrated with the oak. With its lively acidity, this is a mouth-filling wine that finishes with a slight white pepper and vanilla note. *Findlaters*

Price	**£20–25/€25–32**
Region	**Aconcagua Valley**
Grape	**Chardonnay**
Alc/vol	**13.5%**
Food	**Shellfish**
Drink	**2001–3**

Red

Under £7/Under €9

Andes Peaks Cabernet Sauvignon 00 **£/€**

Blackcurrant and blackberry compote on the nose with some creaminess. Power in the taste—solid-knit, upfront, chocolatey flavours of ripe blackberries and black cherries, mouth-filling with good length and some warmth on the finish. *O'Briens*

Price	**Under £7/Under €9**
Region	**Rapel Valley**
Grape	**Cabernet Sauvignon**
Alc/vol	**12.5%**
Food	**Barbecue**
Drink	**2001–2**

Antu Mapu Cabernet Sauvignon 98

Fresh cherries on the nose with some violets and ripe banana. Quite Beaujolais-like in style. Straightforward and satisfying, with flavours of blackcurrants, dried black fruits and ripe, mellow tannins. A mild, dry wine that could be drunk cool from the fridge. *Barry & Fitzwilliam*

Price	**Under £7/Under €9**
Region	**Maule Valley**
Grape	**Cabernet Sauvignon**
Alc/vol	**12.5%**
Food	**Pizza**
Drink	**2001–2**

Aresti Family Vineyards Montemar Merlot 00 ✓

Easy-drinking Merlot with appealing chocolate aromas. Soft, round flavours reminiscent of the juice of a bowl of fruit, again with dark chocolate overtones. *SuperValu-Centra*

Price	**Under £7/Under €9**
Region	**Curicó Valley**
Grape	**Merlot**
Alc/vol	**13.5%**
Food	**Mexican**
Drink	**2001–2**

Carta Vieja Cabernet Sauvignon Reserve 96

A light style of Cabernet Sauvignon with tobacco leaf, cedar box, blackberry and vanilla aromas. Dark chocolate and blackcurrant/ Morello cherry flavours on the palate, with an inkiness and silkiness that make it very appealing. Medium to full bodied in the mouth with a good spicy finish. *Barry & Fitzwilliam*

Price	Under £7/Under €9
Region	Maule Valley
Grape	Cabernet Sauvignon
Alc/vol	12.5%
Food	Lamb, roasted vegetables
Drink	2001–2

Concha y Toro Sunrise Cabernet Sauvignon 00 ★ £/€

Attractive nose—a hint of eucalyptus with mint and blackcurrant fruit, even a trace of cigar box. Soft, supple tannins, blackcurrant and chocolate flavours, a touch of mint and spice, rounded and balanced, smooth textured. Great length. Super example of good Chilean wine—pure fruit flavours at a reasonable price. *Findlaters*

Price	Under £7/Under €9
Region	Central Valley
Grape	Cabernet Sauvignon
Alc/vol	13%
Food	Traditional roasts
Drink	2001–2

Concha y Toro Sunrise Merlot 00 £/€

Ripe, warm summer raspberry and blackcurrant aromas. The palate is packed with ripe, jammy damson fruit with a hint of chocolate and spice. Behind the fruit are crisp acidity, soft, well-rounded tannins and a pleasant, soft finish. *Findlaters*

Price	Under £7/Under €9
Region	Central Valley
Grape	Merlot
Alc/vol	13%
Food	Shepherd's pie
Drink	2001–2

Concha y Toro Sunrise Pinot Noir 00

Interesting nose, vegetal with a savoury edge. Black fruit, leather and spice on the palate with a herbal bitterness. A crowd pleaser at a barbecue. *Findlaters*

Price	Under £7/Under €9
Region	Central Valley
Grape	Pinot Noir
Alc/vol	13.5%
Food	Barbecued sausages
Drink	2001–2

La Palmeria Cabernet Sauvignon Merlot 98

Quite restrained nose of blackcurrants, old leather and some vegetal aromas. The palate features more blackcurrants with some caramel notes and robust tannins. A reliable stand-by, it's made for pizzas and burgers. *Grants*

Price	Under £7/Under €9
Region	Rapel Valley
Grape	Cabernet/Merlot
Alc/vol	13%
Food	Takeaway
Drink	2001–2

San Pedro Merlot 00 £/€

Youthful light plumminess with a definite touch of mint. On the palate there is a good weight of ripe, soft bramble fruit and some firm tannins, but it's still an easy-drinking wine that doesn't need food. Dry, fruity finish. *Dunnes Stores*

Price	Under £7/Under €9
Region	Molina
Grape	Merlot
Alc/vol	13.5%
Food	Versatile
Drink	2001–2

Santa Carolina Cabernet Sauvignon 99 £/€

Attractive nose of toffee, vanilla and summer pudding fruit leads into a well-integrated, expressive, hot, earthy palate of autumn blackberry fruit, oaky vanilla and ripe, yielding tannins. A gutsy wine with good concentration and a tannic finish. *TDL*

Price	Under £7/Under €9
Region	Lontué Valley
Grape	Cabernet Sauvignon
Alc/vol	13%
Food	Spicy beef
Drink	2001–3

Santa Carolina Merlot 00 £/€

Pleasant nose of homemade strawberry jam and some developed vegetal aromas. Ripe strawberries and autumn fruit, plus an extra dimension of spice on the palate. Soft tannins, juicy fruit and a smooth finish. *TDL*

Price	Under £7/Under €9
Region	Lontué Valley
Grape	Merlot
Alc/vol	13.5%
Food	Cheese
Drink	2001–2

Santa Helena Gran Vino Merlot 00 £/€

Ripe, fruity nose showing a touch of earthiness and a slight hint of eucalyptus. Quite full on the palate, with a meaty, savoury nuance. Nice bistro style, easy-drinking wine. *Greenhills*

Price	Under £7/Under €9
Region	Central Valley
Grape	Merlot
Alc/vol	12.5%
Food	Steak sandwich
Drink	2001–2

Santa Rita 120 Cabernet Sauvignon 99 ★ £/€

The rich, oaky, vanilla nose has pronounced minty, floral and cassis fruit with nutmeg notes. On the velvety palate there are complex flavours of vanilla and earthy blackcurrant fruit, solid and chunky. The nicely judged balance of fruit and tannin gives the wine immediate appeal, making it very drinkable. *Gilbeys*

Price	Under £7/Under €9
Region	Central Valley
Grape	Cabernet Sauvignon
Alc/vol	13.5%
Food	Rare beef
Drink	2001–2

Tesco Chilean Cabernet Sauvignon nv £/€

Upfront, fruity aromas of blackcurrant jam and plums. The wine has medium weight in the mouth, with fresh raspberry fruit and a slight bite on the edge. Smooth finish with decent length. *Tesco*

Price	Under £7/Under €9
Region	Central Valley
Grape	Cabernet Sauvignon
Alc/vol	12.5%
Food	Weekday
Drink	2001–2

£7–9/€9–11.50

Caliterra Merlot 99

Elegant Chilean Merlot nose of spicy plums and blackcurrants. The palate is full of ripe soft summer fruit, blackberries and blackcurrants, aided by a pinch of white pepper. Soft tannins and good backing acidity. Pleasant, flavoursome finish. *Febvre*

Price	£7–9/€9–11.50
Region	Central Valley
Grape	Merlot
Alc/vol	13.5%
Food	Duck
Drink	2001–2

Carmen Cabernet Sauvignon 99

Bramble and toffee nose. Ripe blackberry and
damson fruit on the palate with a hint of pepper. Some herbal tones are also evident. The rich
fruit is backed by fresh acidity and ripe tannins
which gives great structure to the wine. Flavoursome finish. *Dillons*

Price	**£7–9/€9–11.50**
Region	**Central Valley**
Grape	**Cabernet Sauvignon**
Alc/vol	**13.5%**
Food	**Stuffed aubergines**
Drink	**2001–2**

Carmen Merlot 99

Slightly muted nose of green plums, but much
riper plum and blackcurrant fruit on the palate
with crisp acidity and firm tannins. Drinking
well now, this wine has decent length. *Dillons*

Price	**£7–9/€9–11.50**
Region	**Central Valley**
Grape	**Merlot**
Alc/vol	**14%**
Food	**Barbecue**
Drink	**2001–2**

Ch. Los Boldos Cabernet Sauvignon 99

Restrained nose of ripe blackcurrant fruit;
impressively subtle. The palate is soft and gentle—cassis and ripe bramble fruit flavours with
some vanilla. Quite a mouth-filling wine, with
balanced acidity, softening tannins and a fruity,
yet spicy finish. *O'Briens*

Price	**£7–9/€9–11.50**
Region	**Requinoa**
Grape	**Cabernet Sauvignon**
Alc/vol	**13%**
Food	**Roasted vegetables**
Drink	**2001–3**

Ch. Los Boldos Merlot 99

Dark nose with a smoky overlay to a jumble of
dark fruits. Slightly herbaceous, green pepper
flavours on the palate with mashed blackberries. On the finish there is a touch of liquorice
and a lot of soft tannins. *O'Briens*

Price	**£7–9/€9–11.50**
Region	**Requinoa**
Grape	**Merlot**
Alc/vol	**13%**
Food	**Empanadas**
Drink	**2001–3**

Concha y Toro Casillero del Diablo Cabernet Sauvignon 99

Slightly stalky fruit on the nose here, but the
palate has lots of quality—mulberries, ripe
black fruit, firm tannins and a fine, chewy structure. *Findlaters*

Price	**£7–9/€9–11.50**
Region	**Maipo Valley**
Grape	**Cabernet Sauvignon**
Alc/vol	**13.5%**
Food	**Beef stir fry**
Drink	**2001–2**

Concha y Toro Casillero del Diablo Merlot 00

Typical Merlot aromas of plums and blackcurrants with a slight vegetal overtone. Chocolate, mixed spice and damson fruit on the
palate. Crisp acidity, robust tannins and a long,
soft, plummy finish. Good with game or rich
stew. *Findlaters*

Price	**£7–9/€9–11.50**
Region	**Rapel Valley**
Grape	**Merlot**
Alc/vol	**13.5%**
Food	**Stews**
Drink	**2001–2**

Concha y Toro Casillero del Diablo Pinot Noir 99 £/€ ✓

Very expressive nose of red fruit and blackberries with some vegetal hints. Packed with violets and blackberries in the mouth with a huge, tasty finish. An interesting example of Chilean Pinot that would be great with a creamy pasta dish and some fresh Parmigiano cheese. *Findlaters*

Price	£7–9/€9–11.50
Region	Casablanca
Grape	Pinot Noir
Alc/vol	13.5%
Food	Creamy pasta
Drink	2001–3

Concha y Toro Casillero del Diablo Syrah 99

Highly concentrated, inky fruit flavours of home-made blackberry jam with a nutmeg afterthought, which are true to the nose. If you like firm tannins, drink it now, but it will soften and improve in a year. This wine will stand up and stare down the thickest, scariest, meatiest sirloin. *Findlaters*

Price	£7–9/€9–11.50
Region	Rapel Valley
Grape	Syrah
Alc/vol	13.5%
Food	Steak
Drink	2001–2

Concha y Toro Trio Cabernet Sauvignon 99 ★

Concentrated nose of anise, plums and Oxo cubes. Follows through on the palate with stewed fruit, blackcurrants and some hints of tar and rubber. It's chewy and concentrated, with a warm, soft, yet long-lasting finish. *Findlaters*

Price	£7–9/€9–11.50
Region	Maipo Valley
Grape	Cabernet Sauvignon
Alc/vol	13.5%
Food	Beefburgers
Drink	2001–2

Concha y Toro Trio Merlot 98

Blackcurrants, plums and black cherries on the nose. The palate is dry and packed with the same plum and cherry fruit. Fruit, acidity and tannin work well together, making a mouth-filling wine with a harmonious finish of cherry, plum and spice. Flavoursome, juicy, easy-drinking wine. *Findlaters*

Price	£7–9/€9–11.50
Region	Rapel Valley
Grape	Merlot
Alc/vol	13.5%
Food	Roast beef
Drink	2001–2

Errázuriz Estate Curicó Merlot 00 £/€

Strawberry fruit on the nose, but a smoky touch as well. The palate is packed with the same soft strawberry fruits with chocolate and spicy nuances. *Allied Drinks*

Price	£7–9/€9–11.50
Region	Curicó Valley
Grape	Merlot
Alc/vol	13.5%
Food	Duck
Drink	2001–2

Las Casas del Toqui Réserve Cabernet Sauvignon 99 £/€

The nose is soft and approachable—dark plums and ripe blackcurrants—and the richness of the fruit is undeniable. The wine has a strong blackcurranty feel with good tannins and a lovely softness. Big, fruity finish. *Dunnes Stores*

Price	£7–9/€9–11.50
Region	Cachapoal Valley
Grape	Cabernet Sauvignon
Alc/vol	13.5%
Food	Curries
Drink	2001–2

Miguel Torres Santa Digna Cabernet Sauvignon 99 ★

The starting point of Miguel Torres Chilean reds, this wine has perfect balance, with ripe blackcurrant and vanilla flavours and softening tannins. Elegant, stylish, fruity, expressive—superb Chilean Cabernet. *Woodford Bourne*

Price	£7–9/€9–11.50
Region	Curicó Valley
Grape	Cabernet Sauvignon
Alc/vol	13%
Food	Red meat
Drink	2001–2

Porta Reserve Cabernet Sauvignon 99

Striking nose of pencil shavings, spice and smoky vanilla. Fruits of the forest come through on the rich palate, with softening tannins and fresh acidity. Smooth, long-lasting finish. *Taserra*

Price	£7–9/€9–11.50
Region	Aconcagua Valley
Grape	Cabernet Sauvignon
Alc/vol	13%
Food	Meatballs
Drink	2001–3

San Pedro Cabernet Sauvignon Reserva 99

 Attractive aromas of ripe blackcurrants with a minty overtone. Sweet fruit, very ripe blackcurrants, softened with blackberries, dark plums and damsons. Solid tannins hold back the sweetness from being jammy. With its nice touch of oak, this is a rich and robust wine with good length. *Dunnes Stores*

Price	£7–9/€9–11.50
Region	Curicó Valley
Grape	Cabernet Sauvignon
Alc/vol	13.5%
Food	Versatile
Drink	2001–3

Santa Carolina Cabernet Sauvignon Reservado 99

Gentle, minty, herbaceous nose with autumn fruit aromas. Oaky, earthy blackcurrant flavours and a slightly vegetal note. Tannins are soft and the wine has good mouthfeel and a harmonious finish. One to savour on its own or with food. *TDL*

Price	£7–9/€9–11.50
Region	Maipo Valley
Grape	Cabernet Sauvignon
Alc/vol	13.5%
Food	Beef
Drink	2001–2

Santa Carolina Merlot Reservado 99

Accessible, ripe nose with almost overripe blackberry fruit with evident vanilla from the oak. Concentrated palate of blackberries and stewed plums, vanilla and ripe, chewy tannins. Good depth of fruit and structure. *TDL*

Price	£7–9/€9–11.50
Region	Colchagua Valley
Grape	Merlot
Alc/vol	13.5%
Food	Picnic
Drink	2001–2

Santa Ema Cabernet Sauvignon 98

Pronounced nose of cassis and mint underlain with vegetal aromas and stewed fruit—certainly well developed. The mintiness carries through to the palate, which has lush, soft bramble fruit, extraordinarily attractive and smoky. Rich and velvety, with softening tannins and great length. *Mitchells*

Price	£7–9/€9–11.50
Region	Maipo Valley
Grape	Cabernet Sauvignon
Alc/vol	13%
Food	Leg of lamb
Drink	2001–2

Santa Ema Merlot 98

Excellent aromas of ripe blackcurrant fruit. Dry, with balanced acidity and gentle tannins, it's laden with ripe, juicy summer berries on the palate. Drinking well now, with good length and a fruity finish. *Mitchells*

Price	£7–9/€9–11.50
Region	Maipo Valley
Grape	Merlot
Alc/vol	13%
Food	Roast beef
Drink	2001–2

Santa Helena Selección del Directorio Cabernet Sauvignon 99 ✓

Good concentrated blackcurrant nose with a cedarwood/sandalwood background. Hints of spice and cinnamon too. A burst of ripe black-currant fruit expands on the palate with leather, tar and cigar box and goes on to a decent finish. Great balance of sweet fruit, acidity and tannins. *Greenhills*

Price	£7–9/€9–11.50
Region	Central Valley
Grape	Cabernet Sauvignon
Alc/vol	13.5%
Food	Cheddar
Drink	2001–3

Tesco Chilean Cabernet Sauvignon Reserve 00 £/€

Light, pleasant nose of jammy black summer fruits. Velvety, fruity palate—plums, straw-berries and mint. The finish is soft and rounded. A wine to drink on its own or with food. *Tesco*

Price	£7–9/€9–11.50
Region	Curicó Valley
Grape	Cabernet Sauvignon
Alc/vol	13.5%
Food	Indian
Drink	2001–3

Undurraga Cabernet Sauvignon Reserva 98

Amazing frothy nose of fresh blackcurrants and blackcurrant bushes. Comes through less strongly on the palate, but still gives good con-centration at the right price. *United Beverages*

Price	£7–9/€9–11.50
Region	Maipo Valley
Grape	Cabernet Sauvignon
Alc/vol	12.5%
Food	Stuffed peppers
Drink	2001–2

Undurraga Pinot Noir Reserva 99

Chilean Pinot Noir isn't seen very often. This is an all-round pleasant wine—a fruity mouthful of raspberries and cherries, some wood evident, but with soft tannins and a dry, fruity finish. Nicely structured and cleanly made. *United Beverages*

Price	£7–9/€9–11.50
Region	Maipo Valley
Grape	Pinot Noir
Alc/vol	14%
Food	Salami
Drink	2001–3

Villard Estate Cabernet Sauvignon 98 £/€

Touches of black-currant leaves on top of the black-currant fruitiness of the nose. Mixed bramble fruits, blackcurrants and ginger on the palate with a hint of lemon and lime. Still with firm tannins and spicy oak, but good mouthfeel and texture—a persistent finish. *O'Briens*

Price	£7–9/€9–11.50
Region	Maipo Valley
Grape	Cabernet Sauvignon
Alc/vol	13%
Food	Spare ribs
Drink	2001–3

Viña Tarapacá Cabernet Sauvignon Reserva 98 ✓

Good mature style, with a finely balanced structure, soft, inky blackberry fruit and still-evident tannins. Very approachable. Great food wine. *Gleeson*

Price	£7–9/€9–11.50
Region	Maipo Valley
Grape	Cabernet Sauvignon
Alc/vol	13%
Food	Versatile
Drink	2001–3

£9–11/€11.50–14

Alto de Terra Andina Cabernet Sauvignon Reserva 98

Slightly closed typical Cabernet Sauvignon nose—meat, spice and red berry fruit. A complex wine, with hints of smoke underneath the decent weight of blackberry fruit, it has a layer of mushroom/vegetal tones. Very pleasant and elegant. Excellent length. *Irish Distillers*

Price	£9–11/€11.50–14
Region	Cachapoal Valley
Grape	Cabernet Sauvignon
Alc/vol	13%
Food	Gouda
Drink	2001–2

> **Carmenère**, a special variety for Chile, offers something unique. Carmenère was positively identified as such only in 1994 in Chile. Previously thought to be Merlot, it is quite different—often more herbaceous, with green pepper, it can be richer and smoother than Merlot, with less acidity. More and more Carmenère is being seen, sometimes under the name Grande Vidure.

Canepa Private Reserve Carmenère 98

A characteristic of Carmenère on the nose seems to be its quite bittersweet/ripe blueberry fruit, which appears here along with savoury spices. The palate shows a lovely balance of fruit, acids and tannins. Spicy, smoky, fruity flavours—sturdy blueberry fruit and grape skin flavours. Medium-long tangy finish. *MacCormaic*

Price	£9–11/€11.50–14
Region	Colchagua Valley
Grape	Carmenère
Alc/vol	13.5%
Food	Meaty dishes
Drink	2001–2

Carmen Cabernet Sauvignon Reserve 98

Ripe nose of damsons, mulberries and cinnamon. A touch of class on the palate, too—sweet ripe black and red currants, loganberries, blackcurrants—quite concentrated, with the oak knitting well. Still maturing. *Dillons*

Price	£9–11/€11.50–14
Region	Maipo Valley
Grape	Cabernet Sauvignon
Alc/vol	14%
Food	Chargrilled meat
Drink	2001–3

Carmen Grande Vidure Cabernet Sauvignon Reserve 98 ★

Almost purple in colour, this wine has a lovely nose of mint, spice, cigar box and brambles. The complex palate displays intense, ripe fruit—red and black berries, mint and spice, balanced by softening tannins and crisp acidity. Long, tingling, elegant finish. *Dillons*

Price	**£9–11/€11.50–14**
Region	**Maipo Valley**
Grape	**Carmenère/Cab Sauv**
Alc/vol	**13.5%**
Food	**Beef, game**
Drink	**2001–4**

Casa Lapostolle Cabernet Sauvignon 99

Concentrated blackcurrant nose, huge depth of pure fruit on the palate, very gutsy, with mellow tannins and a huge finish. Lovely warm fruits. Drink this one on its own or with food, especially cheese. *United Beverages*

Price	**£9–11/€11.50–14**
Region	**Rapel Valley**
Grape	**Cabernet Sauvignon**
Alc/vol	**13.5%**
Food	**Cheese**
Drink	**2001–3**

Casas del Bosque Cabernet Sauvignon 99 ★

Heady nose of blackberries, mint and eucalyptus. The palate is still youthful, with gripping tannins, but wonderfully concentrated and smooth, with spicy vanilla, mint, chocolate and fruits of the forest. Invigorating, rewarding finish. *Waterford Wine Vault*

Price	**£9–11/€11.50–14**
Region	**Requinoa**
Grape	**Cabernet Sauvignon**
Alc/vol	**13%**
Food	**Szechuan beef**
Drink	**2001–4**

Concha y Toro Marqués de Casa Concha Cabernet Sauvignon 98 £/€ ✓

Green pepper, dark fruit and a little herbiness on the nose, even a slightly meaty character. A big wine, full of complex flavours of figs, blackcurrants, meat, baked prunes and tobacco. *Findlaters*

Price	**£9–11/€11.50–14**
Region	**Maipo Valley**
Grape	**Cabernet Sauvignon**
Alc/vol	**13.5%**
Food	**Lamb**
Drink	**2001–2**

Dallas-Conté Cabernet Sauvignon 99

Reminiscent of Christmas pudding. Fresh blackcurrants on the nose with custard and vanilla whiffs. Some tobacco and cigar box with spicy overtones. Ready to drink now, but will hold for a couple of years. Nice balance between ripe black fruit, firm tannins and a long, spicy, fruity finish. *Koala Wines*

Price	**£9–11/€11.50–14**
Region	**Rapel Valley**
Grape	**Cabernet Sauvignon**
Alc/vol	**13.5%**
Food	**Spicy foods**
Drink	**2001–3**

Dallas-Conté Merlot 98 £/€

Layers of dense, dark chocolate and damson
fruit on the palate with hints of cedar and sweet
vanilla. Generous ripe fruit tamed by a touch of
judicious spiciness. Soft tannins, great finish.
Koala Wines

Price	**£9–11/€11.50–14**
Region	**Rapel Valley**
Grape	**Merlot**
Alc/vol	**13.3%**
Food	**Tuna**
Drink	**2001–3**

Las Casas del Toqui Réserve Prestige Cabernet Sauvignon 98

Attractive aromas of cassis and blackcurrants
with a hint of eucalyptus and green pepper. Big,
soft, mushy fruitiness with edges of blackcurrant and some plumminess in a mouth-filling bonanza. Rich, ripe and robust, it has an
excellent finish and will drink beautifully during 2002. *Dunnes Stores*

Price	**£9–11/€11.50–14**
Region	**Cachapoal Valley**
Grape	**Cabernet Sauvignon**
Alc/vol	**13.5%**
Food	**Lamb chops**
Drink	**2001–2**

Los Robles Carmenère 00

Ripe, intense autumn fruit and overripe strawberry aromas. The palate fruit is much more
brambly, but also reined in by quite tight tannins. Interesting, slightly smoky and spicy flavours. Firm finish with a sweet/sour kick at the
end. A voluptuous wine style. *Papillon*

Price	**£9–11/€11.50–14**
Region	**Curicó Valley**
Grape	**Carmenère**
Alc/vol	**13%**
Food	**Veal**
Drink	**2001–3**

Mont Gras Carmenère Reserva 99

Soft, juicy red berries and black fruits on both
nose and palate. Easy-drinking, fruity wine with
some green peppers and black pepper will slip
down easily with or without food. *Maxxium*

Price	**£9–11/€11.50–14**
Region	**Colchagua Valley**
Grape	**Carmenère**
Alc/vol	**13%**
Food	**Pork**
Drink	**2001–3**

Santa Rita Carmenère Reserva 97

Quite developed aromas—vegetal, spice, backed
up by stewed plums. The plump, complex palate shows leafy autumn fruit, becoming vegetal
but not peaking. Tannins are still quite chewy
and firm. Medium-long finish. *Gilbeys*

Price	**£9–11/€11.50–14**
Region	**Maipo Valley**
Grape	**Carmenère**
Alc/vol	**13.5%**
Food	**Traditional**
Drink	**2001–2**

Santa Rita Merlot Reserva 00

Striking, perfumed, enticing nose—elderflow-
ers, blackberries, oak. The complex, spicy palate
is full of ripe fruit—blackcurrant, apples, elder-
flowers again. Ripe, chewy tannins are to the
fore. White pepper kick on the long finish. A
well-structured wine, with fruit and wood
integrated and tannins balanced against ripe,
elegant fruit. *Gilbeys*

Price	**£9–11/€11.50–14**
Region	**Maipo Valley**
Grape	**Merlot**
Alc/vol	**14%**
Food	**Grilled tuna**
Drink	**2001–2**

Viña Porta Select Reserve Cabernet Sauvignon 98 ✓

What a lovely nose! Plums, blackcurrants, cedar, mint and smoke. The palate shows some complexity as well, with plums, cassis and mint coming through in layer after layer. Tannins are still to the fore, but will mellow over 2002. Impressive finish. *Taserra*

Price	£9–11/€11.50–14
Region	Aconcagua Valley
Grape	Cabernet Sauvignon
Alc/vol	13%
Food	Roast lamb
Drink	2001–3

Viña Tarapacá La Cuesta Cabernet Sauvignon Syrah 99

Earthy aromas of baked plums, cherries, tar and leather, leading to a wine that is rich and complex on the palate. Chewy, weighty mouthfeel of liquorice, spice, baked plums, blackberries and a slight earthiness, giving a dry finish. Warm and balanced, attractive, full, spicy finish. *Gleeson*

Price	£9–11/€11.50–14
Region	Maipo Valley
Grape	Cab Sauv/Syrah
Alc/vol	14%
Food	Lasagne
Drink	2001–2

£11–13/€14–16.50

Caliterra Reserva Cabernet Sauvignon 98 ★

This one has the 'wow' factor. Deep concentration of rich, ripe black fruits and cherries. Luscious, with a warm, silky, elegant structure. Tannins are still firm and need time to soften. Lots of pleasure here. *Febvre*

Price	£11–13/€14–16.50
Region	Maipo Valley
Grape	Cabernet Sauvignon
Alc/vol	13.5%
Food	Versatile
Drink	2001–3

Santa Rita Medalla Real Special Reserve Cabernet Sauvignon 99 £/€ ✓

Broad, rich core of oak, cassis and crumbled earth—an elegant nose. The palate is also rich, with plums, vanilla, dark fruits, oak and earth. Velvety mouthfeel, firm tannins, lovely integration of oak and fruit and a long, long finish. It still needs time to show its best. Great quality at this price. *Gilbeys*

Price	£11–13/€14–16.50
Region	Maipo Valley
Grape	Cabernet Sauvignon
Alc/vol	14.5%
Food	Steak
Drink	2001–3

£13–15/€16.50–19

Errázuriz Don Maximiano Estate Cabernet Sauvignon Reserva 98

A very fruity style, showing the clear, pure flavours of Chilean Cabernet Sauvignon. Masses of blackcurrants on the nose and palate, and more mellow tobacco and vanilla influences. Rounded, gentle tannins and a medium finish. *Allied Drinks*

Price	£13–15/€16.50–19
Region	Aconcagua Valley
Grape	Cabernet Sauvignon
Alc/vol	14%
Food	Salmon steaks
Drink	2001–3

Mont Gras Ninquén Barrel Select Premium Chilean Red 97

Complex aromas of dark berries, tar, leather and liquorice. Ripe Morello cherry fruit and spicy flavours expand in the mouth, leading to a long cherry finish. *Maxxium*

Price	£13–15/€16.50–19
Region	Colchagua Valley
Grape	Cabernet/Merlot
Alc/vol	13.5%
Food	Traditional
Drink	2001–2

Montes Alpha Cabernet Sauvignon 98

Leafy blackcurrant nose, showing a core of concentrated blackcurrant fruit overlain with vanilla. Rich, earthy, dusty bramble and cassis fruit is supported by forceful tannins. The flavours are all nicely integrated, but this wine needs another year to express its true potential. *Grants*

Price	£13–15/€16.50–19
Region	Curicó Valley
Grape	Cabernet Sauvignon
Alc/vol	13.5%
Food	Casseroles
Drink	2002–3

£15–17/€19–22

Miguel Torres Cordillera 99 ★

Intense, rich blackcurrants and plums with a hint of coffee and tar. Lovely velvety feel on the palate. Beautifully made—very concentrated and complex with ripe fruits and a good long finish—the redcurrants linger for ages. A little pricey, but worth it. *Woodford Bourne*

Price	£15–17/€19–22
Region	Curicó Valley
Grape	Cariñena/Syrah/ Merlot
Alc/vol	13.5%
Food	Thai/Chinese
Drink	2001–3

Undurraga Bodega de Familia Cabernet Sauvignon 96

Quite pronounced nose of black fruits with hints of eucalyptus/cedar and earthy, minerally tones. A mature wine with a smoky, dark fruit overtone—a lot there! Underlying tannins are soft but present and fruit flavours are blackberry/blackcurrant jam. Attractive and elegant, it delivers a welcome balance between New World and Old World styles. *United Beverages*

Price	£15–17/€19–22
Region	Maipo Valley
Grape	Cabernet Sauvignon
Alc/vol	12.5%
Food	Traditional
Drink	2001–2

£17–20/€22–25

Casa Lapostolle Cuvée Alexandre Merlot 99

A rich fruit cake of a wine. An intense, aromatic nose of mulberry and spice. On the palate it has a big tannic structure and yields layers of spicy red berry, blackberry and black cherry fruit flavours. Still a little immature, this is a food wine. *United Beverages*

Price	£17–20/€22–25
Region	Colchagua Valley
Grape	Merlot
Alc/vol	14%
Food	Beef
Drink	2001–4

Concha y Toro Terrunyo Carmenère 98 ✓

Opulent nose of cassis, cedar, spicy plums and roasted peppers. Ripe, warm, upfront fruit flavours—herbs, stewed plums, damsons and blackberries with a cedary background. Not powerful—restrained, yet complex. Elegant, rewarding finish. *Findlaters*

Price	**£17–20/€22–25**
Region	**Peumo Valley**
Grape	**Carmenère**
Alc/vol	**13.5%**
Food	**Veal**
Drink	**2001–4**

Miguel Torres Manso de Velasco 97 ★

Huge and dense both on nose and palate. Lovely complex aromas—ripe blackcurrants, vanilla and spices. Velvety mouthfeel and bramble berry flavours with lashings of tar and a steely mineral core. Quite seductive and will age beautifully. The finish goes on and on. *Woodford Bourne*

Price	**£17–20/€22–25**
Region	**Curicó Valley**
Grape	**Cabernet Sauvignon**
Alc/vol	**13.5%**
Food	**Lamb**
Drink	**2001–6**

£20–25/€32–40

Concha y Toro Don Melchior Cabernet Sauvignon 96 ✓

Mint, thyme and eucalyptus aromas. Rich, concentrated palate of mint, cherry and black fruit with a luscious texture, enhanced by vanilla, chocolate and toast. Gripping tannins and a long finish. *Findlaters*

Price	**£25–30/€32–40**
Region	**Maipo Valley**
Grape	**Cabernet Sauvignon**
Alc/vol	**13%**
Food	**Roast lamb**
Drink	**2001–3**

France–Alsace

Alsace wines are nearly always labelled according to the grape variety. This is unusual in France, where most wines are classified according to region. Most commonly seen in Ireland are Pinot Blanc, Riesling, Gewurztraminer and Pinot Gris (formerly called Tokay-Pinot Gris). If these wines have anything in common, it is their distinctive, aromatic perfume and the fact that they match food brilliantly.

What are the differences between them? Pinot Blanc makes early-drinking, light wines with apple and floral flavours. Try to buy the most recent vintage. Riesling makes steely, structured wines that develop beautifully with age. Gewurztraminer is spicy and reminiscent of roses and fresh lychees. While it is often full and voluptuous, some producers, such as Trimbach, make it in a bone-dry style. Pinot Gris tends to be nuttier, smokier and fuller bodied. Different producers can have very different styles, some much drier than others. It pays to find out which producers make styles that appeal to you.

The overall quality of the Alsace whites tasted this year was consistently reliable, sometimes hitting high notes (Zind-Humbrecht and Sipp Mack particularly), but always very good and very dependable.

White

Under £7/Under €9

Thomann AC Alsace Riesling **99** £/€

Pungent, spicy nose, plus apples and boiled sweets. The palate is dry, with crisp green apple flavours and lime cordial carrying through. The finish is long and flavoursome. *Dunnes Stores*

Price	**Under £7/Under €9**
Grape	**Riesling**
Alc/vol	**12%**
Food	**Thai/Chinese**
Drink	**2001–2**

£7–9/€9–11.50

Dietrich Réserve AC Alsace Riesling **99** £/€

Classic Alsace Riesling. A lovely balance between the crisp citrus fruit and moderate alcohol. The wine evolves on the palate to yield a minerally finish with a suggestion of spice. *TDL*

Price	**£7–9/€9–11.50**
Grape	**Riesling**
Alc/vol	**12.5%**
Food	**Seafood**
Drink	**2001–4**

> *Despite its northerly location, **Alsace** is one of the driest and sunniest parts of France. This is mainly due to its situation under the shadow of the Vosges Mountains.*

Dopff & Irion AC Alsace Pinot Blanc **98** £/€

Dopff & Irion make their wines in a dry style. This one is fresh and lively, with good concentration of lemon, lime, pear and apple flavours. Creamy texture, with good body and length. *Bacchus*

Price	**£7–9/€9–11.50**
Grape	**Pinot Blanc**
Alc/vol	**12%**
Food	**Aperitif**
Drink	**2001–2**

Dopff & Irion AC Alsace Riesling 99 £/€

This is a fine example of a youthful Alsace Riesling, with green apples, lemons, limes, melons and a touch of custard. Dry, it has lively acidity and good length. Refreshing and zesty. *Bacchus*

Price	**£7–9/€9–11.50**
Grape	**Riesling**
Alc/vol	**12%**
Food	**Shellfish**
Drink	**2001–2**

Dopff au Moulin AC Alsace Pinot Blanc 99 £/€

Pleasing nose—apples and elderberries. Has real power behind it—both fruit and alcohol. Clean fruit flavours—apples, lemons, limes with some chalk and marked acidity. A stylish wine. *Woodford Bourne*

Price	**£7–9/€9–11.50**
Grape	**Pinot Blanc**
Alc/vol	**12%**
Food	**Onion tart**
Drink	**2001–2**

Hugel Cuvée Les Amours Pinot Blanc de Blancs AC Alsace Pinot Blanc 99 £/€

Pinot Blanc, with its richness, ripeness and lovely plump apple fruit, deserves more popularity. This well-priced example is mouth-watering, its crisp acidity counterbalanced by citrus and apple fruit that lasts right through to the long finish. *Grants*

Price	**£7–9/€9–11.50**
Grape	**Pinot Blanc**
Alc/vol	**12.5%**
Food	**Aperitif**
Drink	**2001–2**

> The term **Vieilles Vignes** (old vines) on a label is a signal of higher quality, as old vines produce fewer but more intensely flavoured and concentrated grapes than younger vines. As the vines age, their roots penetrate deeper into the subsoil and absorb the really interesting minerals and trace elements that produce the extra flavours and aromatics.

Meyer-Fonné Vieilles Vignes AC Alsace Pinot Blanc 99 £/€

Apple and lemon aromas on quite a light nose. Very slightly off-dry, the honeyed, rich palate is full of crisp fruit flavours with a slightly chalky hint. *Le Caveau*

Price	**£7–9/€9–11.50**
Grape	**Pinot Blanc**
Alc/vol	**12.5%**
Food	**Picnic**
Drink	**2001–2**

Sipp Mack AC Alsace Tokay Pinot Blanc 99

Earthy, grassy nose, showing some mineral and floral notes. The wine has a fleshy body of ripe tropical fruit and sweet, ripe melons with green apples and limes in the background. Refreshing acidity and a decent finish. *Mitchells*

Price	**£7–9/€9–11.50**
Grape	**Tokay-Pinot Gris/ Pinot Blanc**
Alc/vol	**12%**
Food	**Fish**
Drink	**2001–2**

Tesco AC Alsace Gewurztraminer 99

Nose of lychees and roses. Full bodied, luscious, slightly off-dry palate with flavours of figs and nuts. It has low acidity, as so often the case with Gewurztraminers. *Tesco*

Price	**£7–9/€9–11.50**
Grape	**Gewurztraminer**
Alc/vol	**13%**
Food	**Spicy food**
Drink	**2001–2**

Thomann AC Alsace Gewurztraminer 99 £/€

Aromatic honeysuckle floral nose. Off-dry style, with intense flavours of violets, honey and spice. Delicious. *Dunnes Stores*

Price	£7–9/€9–11.50
Grape	Gewurztraminer
Alc/vol	13%
Food	Indian
Drink	2001–3

£9–11/€11.50–14

Dietrich Réserve AC Alsace Gewurztraminer 99

This Gewurztraminer is rich and floral on the nose and on the palate, but also has crisp acidity. Good with food, especially lightly spiced Oriental dishes. *TDL*

Price	£9–11/€11.50–14
Grape	Gewurztraminer
Alc/vol	13%
Food	Aperitif/Oriental
Drink	2001–2

Dom. Eugène Meyer AC Alsace Pinot Blanc 98 ✇

Easy-drinking, attractive style. Lots of ripe melon fruit on the nose and refreshingly zesty limes and lemons, with slight mineral notes, on the palate. Nice clean finish. *Mary Pawle Wines*

Price	£9–11/€11.50–14
Grape	Pinot Blanc
Alc/vol	12%
Food	Quiche
Drink	2001–2

Hugel AC Alsace Riesling 98

Alsace Riesling as it should be—clean, crisp and dry, with delicious maturing fruit. Beautifully balanced, its acidity is matched by very clear and expressive apple and citrus fruit and it has the classic ageing Riesling aromas of kerosene/petrol. Long finish. *Grants*

Price	£9–11/€11.50–14
Grape	Riesling
Alc/vol	11.5%
Food	Charcuterie
Drink	2001–3

Mader Muhlforst AC Alsace Riesling 97 £/€

Despite being four years old, this is still a very fresh and lively wine, with a crisp, refreshing backbone of acidity and generous apple and citrus flavours. *Wines Direct*

Price	£9–11/€9–11.50
Grape	Riesling
Alc/vol	12.5%
Food	Pork
Drink	2001–2

Saint-Hippolyte Charles Koehly & Fils AC Alsace Gewurztraminer 99

This is an elegant, balanced and floral wine. Gorgeous nose of lychees, rose petals and spice. The palate is a complex mix of limes, pineapple, lychees, roses—classic Gewurztraminer. Long finish. *Irish Distillers*

Price	£9–11/€11.50–14
Grape	Gewurztraminer
Alc/vol	13.8%
Food	Munster cheese
Drink	2001–2

Trimbach AC Alsace Riesling 98

Crisp, dry Riesling. in a fairly weighty style, with lime cordial and zingy green apple flavours on the full palate. Long finish. *Gilbeys*

Price	£9–11/€11.50–14
Grape	Riesling
Alc/vol	12%
Food	Versatile
Drink	2001–3

£11–13/€14–16.50

Albert Mann Vieilles Vignes AC Alsace Tokay-Pinot Gris 93

A developed wine, yet still classically fresh due
to its wonderful acidity and lovely apple fruit
character. Zesty and fresh on the palate with a
long finish. *MacCormaic*

Price	**£11–13/€14–16.50**
Grape	**Pinot Gris**
Alc/vol	**13%**
Food	**Pâté**
Drink	**2001–2**

Dom. Eugène Meyer AC Alsace Tokay-Pinot Gris 98

Dry, with a mineral character and plump, ripe
apple and melon fruit on the palate. Spicy finish
and versatile at the table. *Bubble Brothers*

Price	**£11–13/€14–16.50**
Grape	**Tokay-Pinot Gris**
Alc/vol	**14%**
Food	**Versatile**
Drink	**2001–2**

Hugel AC Alsace Gewurztraminer 99

Distinctive rose petal and marzipan nose with
sweet, spicy notes. The palate is dry, however,
with concentrated white fruit and almonds,
crisp acidity and a fairly alcoholic finish. *Grants*

Price	**£11–13/€14–16.50**
Grape	**Gewurztraminer**
Alc/vol	**12.5%**
Food	**Smoked salmon, pâté**
Drink	**2001–2**

Sipp Mack Vieille Vigne AC Alsace Gewurztraminer 99

This excellent wine has a lovely perfumed nose
of tropical fruits and lychees. On the palate
there are spicy flavours, soft honey and tropical
fruits. Creamy finish. *Mitchells*

Price	**£11–13/€14–16.50**
Grape	**Gewurztraminer**
Alc/vol	**13.5%**
Food	**Asian**
Drink	**2001–3**

> *Just fifty vineyards on the steep slopes of the Vosges Mountains in Alsace are
> classified as **Grand Cru**. They can offer excellent value, as the jump in quality is
> not reflected proportionally in the price. For example, Rosacker, Steingrubler and
> Schlossberg are Grand Crus. A number of producers, such as Trimbach and
> Hugel, have stayed outside the Grand Cru system. Instead, they promote their
> wines with their own names and sometimes the name of the vineyard the
> grapes are sourced from.*

£13–15/€16.50–19

Albert Mann Grand Cru Schlossberg AC Alsace Riesling 96

Steely, austere, serious Riesling. It has a complex
nose, with developed kerosene aromas along
with honeyed fruit of limes and apples. Bone
dry, this wine is a definite food partner.
MacCormaic

Price	**£13–15/€16.50–19**
Grape	**Riesling**
Alc/vol	**12%**
Food	**Versatile, cheese**
Drink	**2001–3**

Albert Mann Grand Cru Steingrubler
AC Alsace Gewurztraminer **97** ✓

Intense, perfumed nose of lychees, tropical fruit, peaches, apricots and flowers. The palate, which is medium dry, carries a heavy weight of concentrated fruit balanced by crisp acidity. *MacCormaic*

Price	**£13–15/€19–22**
Grape	**Gewurztraminer**
Alc/vol	**13.5%**
Food	**Fruit tart**
Drink	**2001–4**

Sipp Mack Grand Cru Rosacker AC Alsace Riesling **98** ✓

Petrolly notes over the apple and pear aromas. Fresh and zingy, with a rich concentration of lemons, limes and tropical fruit, this is serious wine. Elegant and refreshing, with a zesty acidity. It should mature beautifully. *Mitchells*

Price	**£13–15/€16.50–19**
Grape	**Riesling**
Alc/vol	**13%**
Food	**Salmon**
Drink	**2001–5**

£15–17/€19–22

Dom. Zind-Humbrecht Gueberschwihr AC Alsace Riesling **97**

Fine example of the best of Alsace Riesling. A few years in bottle have given the lemon and lime character the added complexity of paraffin, minerals and some floral nuances. Initial sweet impression, but acidic backbone and a crisp finish. *United Beverages*

Price	**£15–17/€19–22**
Grape	**Riesling**
Alc/vol	**12.5%**
Food	**Pacific Rim**
Drink	**2001–4**

Dom. Zind-Humbrecht Herrenweg de Turckheim
AC Alsace Muscat **97**

Developed blackcurrant leaf nose. The palate is bursting with intense apple fruit, rich yet elegant. The mineral notes are amplified on the very long finish. An unusual and interesting mature Muscat. *United Beverages*

Price	**£15–17/€19–22**
Grape	**Muscat**
Alc/vol	**14%**
Food	**Chicken**
Drink	**2001–3**

Dom. Zind-Humbrecht Turckheim
AC Alsace Gewurztraminer **98** ✓

Gentle perfume of stem ginger, spice, roses and Turkish Delight. Truly delicious Gewurztraminer which impresses with its intense ginger and melon fruit flavours. Rich and spicy, the flavours magnify into the very long finish. *United Beverages*

Price	**£15–17/€19–22**
Grape	**Gewurztraminer**
Alc/vol	**14.5%**
Food	**Peking duck**
Drink	**2001–3**

A WORLD OF TASTES JUST WAITING TO BE DISCOVERED

Febvre is a family owned business, built on a commitment to provide discerning Irish palates with a selection of carefully chosen wines from around the world. We bring you these wines through our close links with grower-producers, both large and small, who share our desire to uphold the traditions of quality and good taste for which family owned vineyards are renowned.

FEBVRE

Febvre & Company Limited, 15-17 Maple Avenue,
Stillorgan Industrial Park, Stillorgan, Co. Dublin.
Tel: (01) 295 9030   Fax: (01) 295 9036   Email: info@febvre.ie

NO-ONE COULD EVER
ACCUSE US OF NAME-DROPPING

£20–25/€25–32

Trimbach Cuvée des Seigneurs de Ribeaupierre
AC Alsace Gewurztraminer **86**

Trimbach is renowned for Gewurztraminer, particularly this cuvée, which can age for 10 to 15 years, gaining pungency and complexity. Beautiful nose—pure wild honey with waxy elements, but subtle. Dry palate, with a good balance of honeyed citrus fruit and acidity. Long finish. *Gilbeys*

Price	**£20–25/€25–32**
Grape	**Gewurztraminer**
Alc/vol	**14%**
Food	**Pork**
Drink	**2001–2**

Trimbach Cuvée Frédéric Emile AC Alsace Riesling **97**

Mature, intense, honeyed nose with a floral perfume. The palate is dry and appetising, with crisp acidity. The palate seems more youthful than the nose. Long, tangy, green apple finish. *Gilbeys*

Price	**£20–25/€25–32**
Grape	**Riesling**
Alc/vol	**13%**
Food	**Goose**
Drink	**2001–3**

France–Bordeaux

Bordeaux produces as much wine as the whole of Australia. With 57 different appellations, there is definite value and affordability at the two most basic levels of the appellation system—AC Bordeaux and AC Bordeaux Supérieur. Over 40 per cent of all wine in Bordeaux falls into these categories and there is a wide choice. Above this level, costs increase and availability can be an issue.

Most Bordeaux wines use a blend of varieties. Whites are blends of Sauvignon Blanc and Sémillon, sometimes with a small amount of Colombard, Ugni Blanc or Muscadelle. The reds are predominantly blends of Cabernet Sauvignon, Merlot and Cabernet Franc. Small amounts of Petit Verdot and Malbec are sometimes added.

Bordeaux is bisected by the River Gironde, which divides the region into the Left Bank and the Right Bank. On the Left Bank of the river are the properties of the Médoc and Haut-Médoc, dominated by Cabernet Sauvignon and giving some of the greatest wines, capable of long ageing. Although Cabernet Sauvignon is king here, Merlot is the most widely planted red variety in the whole Bordeaux region. The Right Bank includes the wines of St Émilion and Pomerol, which are generally based on Merlot and Cabernet Franc. Cabernet Sauvignon gives the wines their tannic structure and unmistakable blackcurrant flavours, whereas Merlot makes supple, plummy wines that develop more quickly. Cabernet Franc adds a raspberry touch.

Crucial to understanding Bordeaux is the significant variation from one year to the next. About a third of the wines listed this year are from the 97 vintage. This was a difficult year all over Bordeaux, with poor weather conditions. This is not to say that the wine is not good, in fact far from it, but it will not live for as long as, say, an equivalent 95 or 96. On the plus side it should be seen as a vintage that is drinking well now. The 98 vintage was exceptional in Pomerol and St Émilion (the Right Bank). It was also a good year elsewhere and the wines of the Médoc and Haut-Médoc (the Left Bank) showed very well in our tastings. Though 99 is not considered to be a great year, expectations are high for 00.

White

> Traditionally, **white Bordeaux** was made from a blend of Sémillon and Sauvignon Blanc. Today the proportion of Sauvignon in the blend is often increased, sometimes to 100%, in which case this is stated on the label. White AC Bordeaux are at their best when they are young and fresh.

Under £7/Under €9

Mitchell's Sauvignon Blanc AC Bordeaux **00**

A good example of an easy-drinking, modern, fresh Bordeaux white—apples, green fruit flavours and balancing crisp acidity. *Mitchells*

Price	**Under £7/Under €9**
Grape	**Sauvignon Blanc**
Alc/vol	**12%**
Food	**Picnic**
Drink	**2001–2**

£7–9/€9–11.50

Marquis de Chasse AC Bordeaux **00**

A complete and pleasing wine, with apple, green pea and gooseberry flavours and a hint of peaches. Fresh, appealing finish. *Bacchus*

Price	**£7–9/€9–11.50**
Grape	**Sauv Blanc/Sémillon**
Alc/vol	**12%**
Food	**Shellfish**
Drink	**2001–2**

Red

*The permitted grapes for **red Bordeaux blends** are Cabernet Sauvignon, Merlot, Cabernet Franc, Petit Verdot and Malbec. In this book wines that are predominantly Merlot are described as **Merlot blend**; wines that are predominantly Cabernet Sauvignon are described as **Cabernet blend**. Wines with roughly equal proportions of each are described as **Cabernet/Merlot**. Where the proportions are not known the wine is described as **Bordeaux blend**.*

Under £7/Under €9

Berrys' Own Selection Good Ordinary Claret
AC Bordeaux **nv**

The nose is very correct for the region—ripe blackberry fruits and green pepper aromas with a herbaceous edge. Fruit on the palate is ripe and sweet, reminiscent of blackcurrant pastilles, and backed by softening tannins. *Fields*

Price	**Under £7/Under €9**
Grape	**Bordeaux blend**
Alc/vol	**12%**
Food	**Weekday**
Drink	**2001–2**

£7–9/€9–11.50

Ch. Briot AC Bordeaux **99**

Red fruit aromas. Blackcurrant flavours and light tannins make this an easy-drinking wine. *Bacchus*

Price	**£7–9/€9–11.50**
Grape	**Cabernet/Merlot**
Alc/vol	**12%**
Food	**Spicy chicken wings**
Drink	**2001–2**

Ch. Cadillac-Branda AC Bordeaux Supérieur **99**

Slightly jammy fruit, but heaps of it—blackcurrants and plums with a slight element of leather. Soft tannins and good length. *Mitchells*

Price	**£7–9/€9–11.50**
Grape	**Cabernet/Merlot**
Alc/vol	**12%**
Food	**Roast pork**
Drink	**2001–2**

Ch. de Rabouchet AC Bordeaux **97**

Blackcurrants and redcurrants on the nose with some unexpected coffee notes. Subtle black fruit flavours linger on the palate. Mellow tannins, medium-long finish. Food wine. *Jenkinson*

Price	**£7–9/€9–11.50**
Grape	**Cabernet/Merlot**
Alc/vol	**12.5%**
Food	**Lamb**
Drink	**2001–3**

Ch. Méaume AC Bordeaux Supérieur 98 £/€

Quite a concentrated claret in a very traditional style with dry tannins. Peppery black fruits stay the distance on the palate. Inky and black, the flavours linger long. *Findlaters*

Price	**£7–9/€9–11.50**
Grape	**Merlot blend**
Alc/vol	**13%**
Food	**Tandoori chicken**
Drink	**2001–3**

Ch. Trocard AC Bordeaux Supérieur 97

Blackcurrant leaves and a slight stalkiness to the mixed fruit aromas on the nose. Good mixed berry fruit extract on a medium-bodied palate with a reasonably long finish. Solid, comforting nourishment. *Le Caveau*

Price	**£7–9/€9–11.50**
Grape	**Merlot blend**
Alc/vol	**12%**
Food	**Cheese soufflé**
Drink	**2001–3**

Ch. Villepreux AC Bordeaux Supérieur 99

Pure blackcurrant nose with a hint of oaky vanilla. Plenty of tannic grip and black fruit flavours, with very good length for the price. *Bacchus*

Price	**£7–9/€9–11.50**
Grape	**Bordeaux blend**
Alc/vol	**12%**
Food	**Traditional**
Drink	**2001–2**

> **AC Bordeaux** *is the generic appellation for white and red wines produced anywhere within the Bordeaux region. They are generally inexpensive and intended for early drinking, two to three years from the vintage. The quicker-maturing Merlot is the dominant grape in the blend. These wines are matured in vats rather than small new oak barrels.*

Michel Lynch AC Bordeaux 98

Nice tasty Bordeaux at a good price. Classic pencil shavings and cassis nose and quite tight flavours of red and black fruits with reinforcing tannins. Medium-long finish.
Barry & Fitzwilliam

Price	**£7–9/€9–11.50**
Grape	**Bordeaux blend**
Alc/vol	**12%**
Food	**Chicken**
Drink	**2001–2**

Mitchell & Son Claret AC Bordeaux Supérieur 98

A smooth, easy-to-drink mouthful of summer fruits, with ripe tannins and reasonable length. It's a perfect example of a basic claret—blackcurrant, pepper, restraint. *Mitchells*

Price	**£7–9/€9–11.50**
Grape	**Cabernet blend**
Alc/vol	**12%**
Food	**Beefburgers**
Drink	**2001–2**

£9–11/€11.50–14

Berrys' Own Selection Médoc AC Médoc nv

Attractive aromas of chocolate, cherries and blackcurrants. Grainy tannins, but a good backing of blackcurrant fruit, chocolate and tar flavours. Real intensity, lingering, slightly alcoholic finish. A delicious wine, rich and robust. *Fields*

Price	**£9–11/€11.50–14**
Grape	**Bordeaux blend**
Alc/vol	**12%**
Food	**Lamb**
Drink	**2001–3**

> **AC Bordeaux Supérieur** *contains at least 0.5% more alcohol than AC Bordeaux, but this should not necessarily be taken to indicate superior quality.*

Ch. Béchereau AC Bordeaux Supérieur 98

This lovely wine offers aromas of summer berry fruits and blackcurrants. Ripe strawberries and blackcurrants on the palate, which is backed by supple tannins and balancing acidity. This is an elegant wine, with a dry, fruity, persistent finish. *MacCormaic*

Price	**£9–11/€11.50–14**
Grape	**Merlot blend**
Alc/vol	**12.5%**
Food	**Roast pork**
Drink	**2001–2**

Ch. de Croignon AC Bordeaux Supérieur 98

Sweet ripe strawberry and blackberry fruit aromas with some mintiness and a vegetal edge. The palate has plenty of mashed strawberry and dark cherry fruit with a twist of spice at the end. Made in a softer style with 100% Merlot, it has mellow tannins and a juicy fruit finish. *Waterford Wine Vault*

Price	**£9–11/€11.50–14**
Grape	**Merlot**
Alc/vol	**12%**
Food	**Shepherd's pie**
Drink	**2001–2**

Ch. Jacquinot AC Bordeaux 98 🌿

An aromatic nose of blackberry and apple pie with a hint of tar and chocolate deepens into a palate of soft and juicy bramble fruit. It's a well-structured wine, with ripe tannins, fresh acidity and a medium finish. *Taserra*

Price	**£9–11/€11.50–14**
Grape	**Bordeaux blend**
Alc/vol	**12%**
Food	**Ratatouille**
Drink	**2001–2**

> **Lussac-St Émilion** *and* **St Georges-St Émilion** *are communes bordering St Émilion and are allowed to use their name on the label along with that of their more famous neighbour.*

Ch. Pichon AC Lussac-St Émilion 98

Pronounced nose of blackberry and damson fruits with a hint of green pepper, spice and vanilla. Well-flavoured palate of very ripe dark cherry and bramble fruits. The ample fruit is supported by supple tannins. *Taserra*

Price	**£9–11/€11.50–14**
Grape	**Bordeaux blend**
Alc/vol	**12.5%**
Food	**Rack of lamb**
Drink	**2001–3**

> *The best* **Côtes de Castillon** *wines, located east of St Émilion, are similar in style to good St Émilion—plummy and velvety.*

Ch. Puy-Landry AC Côtes de Castillon 97

There are meaty, Oxo cube notes among the blackcurrant aromas. Medium bodied, it has blackcurrant and green pepper flavours with an interesting peppery streak. *Wines Direct*

Price	**£9–11/€11.50–14**
Grape	**Merlot blend**
Alc/vol	**12.5%**
Food	**Cheese**
Drink	**2001–3**

Lafleur de Lynch AC Médoc **98**

This Bordeaux sports cedar and black fruit aromas. The palate doesn't disappoint—it has bags of black fruit with some spice in the background. *Dunnes Stores*

Price	**£9–11/€11.50–14**
Grape	**Bordeaux blend**
Alc/vol	12%
Food	**Grilled aubergines**
Drink	2001–3

£11–13/€14–16.50

Ch. Arnauld AC Haut-Médoc **97 £/€ ✓**

Wonderful bouquet with discernible complexity—blackcurrants, a touch of mocha, pepper and cinnamon/cloves. No disappointments on the palate, which has a wonderful extra element of leather and a savoury character. *O'Briens*

Price	**£11–13/€14–16.50**
Grape	**Cabernet/Merlot**
Alc/vol	12.5%
Food	**Versatile**
Drink	2001–2

Ch. Croix de Rambeau AC Lussac-St Émilion **97 £/€**

A rich, classic style with harmony and elegance. Nose of cassis and green peppers. Flavours are mature and elegant, with delicious plum and damson fruit and a certain earthiness. Very well balanced in the acidity/tannin department with a rich mouthfeel, it has gorgeous, lip-smacking length. *Le Caveau*

Price	**£11–13/€14–16.50**
Grape	**Merlot blend**
Alc/vol	12.5%
Food	**Roast beef**
Drink	2001–4

> **Lalande-de-Pomerol**, *beside the commune of Pomerol and the port town of Libourne, is a red AC with a rich plummy style like Pomerol and St Émilion. The emphasis on Merlot in the blend makes for a soft and supple style with less tannin than most red Bordeaux.*

Ch. Haut-Surget AC Lalande-de-Pomerol 97

Young but elegant nose of damsons and black cherries. Concentrated palate—inky, blackcurrant fruit with sweet peppers. Ripe fruit well integrated with oak, chewy tannins, almost full bodied. *Wines Direct*

Price	**£11–13/€14–16.50**
Grape	**Merlot blend**
Alc/vol	**13%**
Food	**Game**
Drink	**2001–3**

> The **Médoc** *was originally named the Bas-Médoc or lower Médoc, but the Bas was dropped many years ago. The land was salt marsh until the mid-17th century, when the Dutch drained the area. The mild and moist maritime climate and the richer soil or sand produce wines less fine than those from the gravel soil of the Haut Médoc. The exception is near where the two ACs meet, where pockets of gravel soil can yield higher-quality wine.*

Ch. Loudenne AC Médoc Cru Bourgeois 97 £/€

Complex nose of violets, blackberries, redcurrants and fruits of the forest. Fruit on the palate is intensely concentrated with Bourneville chocolate and roasted coffee. The gripping tannins and lingering finish show that this wine still has some way to go. *Gilbeys*

Price	**£11–13/€14–16.50**
Grape	**Cabernet/Merlot**
Alc/vol	**12.5%**
Food	**Steak**
Drink	**2001–3**

Ch. Puy Castéra AC Haut-Médoc Cru Bourgeois 97 ✓

Pronounced nose of cassis, forest fruits, cedar and coffee with a touch of meat. The smooth, creamy palate has espresso coffee and ripe dark berries. Deft use of oak. This is a fine claret with plenty of flavour and a rewarding finish. *Wines Direct*

Price	**£11–13/€14–16.50**
Grape	**Cabernet/Merlot**
Alc/vol	**12.5%**
Food	**Lamb**
Drink	**2001–3**

£13–15/€16.50–19

Ch. Beaumont AC Haut-Médoc Cru Bourgeois 97

Elegant, spicy, classic claret. Brambly hedgerow scents with earthy aromas. The palate has a slightly earthy note among the blackcurrant and sweet pepper flavours. Tannins are gentle and it has a strong finish. *O'Briens*

Price	**£13–15/€16.50–19**
Grape	**Cabernet/Merlot**
Alc/vol	**12.5%**
Food	**Roasts**
Drink	**2001–2**

Ch. de Gironville AC Haut-Médoc Cru Bourgeois **96**

Shy initially on the nose—blackcurrants, green peppers—but opens up to a palate of subtle berry fruit flavours, blackcurrants and hints of green peppers, firm but yielding tannins and nice length. *Findlaters*

Price	**£13–15/€16.50–19**
Grape	**Cabernet/Merlot**
Alc/vol	**12.8%**
Food	**Entrecôte steak**
Drink	**2001–5**

> **St Émilion** is on the right bank of the river Dordogne, east of the sister port towns of Bordeaux and Libourne. Merlot is the dominant grape here, as it is quite tolerant of the compact, moisture-retaining clay soils. The juicy wines of the St Émilion district tend to mature more quickly than Cabernet-Sauvignon-based wines of the west bank. St Émilion Grand Cru is a separate AC established in 1955. Estates are assessed for inclusion in the classification every ten years, most recently in 1996, when 68 châteaux qualified.

Ch. de la Cour AC St Émilion Grand Cru **98**

An enticing nose with ripe, plummy fruits and hints of rich, creamy coffee. Well made, but youth still apparent as tannins take a strong position. A lovely, elegant wine with a good chewy texture. *Mitchells*

Price	**£13–15/€16.50–19**
Grape	**Merlot blend**
Alc/vol	**12.5%**
Food	**Truffles**
Drink	**2001–5**

Ch. du Paradis AC St Émilion Grand Cru **98**

Lovely, aromatic, smoky, spicy, plummy nose, elegant but with subtle concentration. The palate has good ripeness, again with some smokiness, set against grainy tannins and an earthy texture. Satisfyingly long finish. *Irish Distillers*

Price	**£13–15/€16.50–19**
Grape	**Merlot blend**
Alc/vol	**12.5%**
Food	**Chicken casserole**
Drink	**2001–4**

Ch. Fourcas Hosten AC Listrac-Médoc **97**

Attractive, rather mature nose of ripe, juicy berries with a hint of nutmeg. The palate is more complex—sweet, ripe damsons, even some prunes and figs, complemented by cedar, tobacco and spice. Drinking well now. *O'Briens*

Price	**£13–15/€16.50–19**
Grape	**Cabernet/Merlot**
Alc/vol	**12.5%**
Food	**Irish stew**
Drink	**2001–2**

Ch. La Rose-Bouquey AC St Émilion **99**

Appealing nose of caramel, redcurrant fruit and spice. The palate has more to offer—leafy autumn fruit, fairly firm tannins, good concentration and a warm finish. Still developing. Classic Old World flavours. *Peter Dalton*

Price	**£13–15/€16.50–19**
Grape	**Merlot blend**
Alc/vol	**12.5%**
Food	**Beef**
Drink	**2001–5**

Ch. Macquin-St Georges AC St Georges-St Émilion **96 £/€**

Bramble, plum and blackcurrant aromas, a little twiggy. Slightly herbaceous nose. The palate has a solid balance of acidity, soft tannins and plum/blackcurrant fruit with a hint of dark chocolate. Very dry finish. *Searsons*

Price	**£13–15/€16.50–19**
Grape	**Bordeaux blend**
Alc/vol	**12.5%**
Food	**Lamb curry**
Drink	**2001–2**

Ch. Magnol AC Haut-Médoc Cru Bourgeois 97

A smooth, rounded wine full of flavour. Lots of red berry fruit with lovely smooth cream and chocolate. The finish is long and satisfying. *Dillons*

Price	**£13–15/€16.50–19**
Grape	**Cabernet/Merlot**
Alc/vol	**12.5%**
Food	**Versatile**
Drink	**2001–3**

Ch. Rozier AC St Émilion Grand Cru 97 £/€

Traditionally made, elegant, complex wine with aromas of ripe plums, black cherries, mulberries and fruit cake. The palate has an earthy character, with excellent black fruit flavours and a touch of smoke and leather. The overall result is a serious, plummy wine. *Wines Direct*

Price	**£13–15/€16.50–19**
Grape	**Merlot blend**
Alc/vol	**12.5%**
Food	**Turkey**
Drink	**2001–5**

Ch. St Ahon AC Haut-Médoc Cru Bourgeois 98 ✓

This classy claret delights the senses. The velvety palate reflects fruits of the forest with raspberry sorbet. Balanced acidity and ripe tannins underpin the fine structure of the wine. *Wine-Online*

Price	**£13–15/€16.50–19**
Grape	**Cabernet blend**
Alc/vol	**12.5%**
Food	**Cheese soufflé**
Drink	**2001–4**

> **Pessac-Léognan** *covers the northern part of the Graves district and many of the finest vineyards, including Ch. Haut-Brion (one of Bordeaux's top five Premier Cru Classés, and the only non-Médoc wine included). The AC was created as recently as 1987.*

£15–17/€19–22

Ch. Brown AC Pessac-Léognan 97

Mature, earthy vegetal nose. Succulent, developed palate with lots of juicy plums, blackberries and cake spice. Wonderfully mature and drinkable. Typical of the 97 vintage—sappy, lightly structured, ripe fruit, but drinking very well now. *O'Briens*

Price	**£15–17/€19–22**
Grape	**Cabernet blend**
Alc/vol	**12.5%**
Food	**Roast lamb**
Drink	**2001–3**

Ch. Franc Lartigue AC St Émilion Grand Cru 98

Powerful aromas—meaty, strong, very defined and intriguing. The soft palate has stacks of dark, stewed plum fruit with a twist of liquorice. A dark, brooding, mouth-filling wine, intense and powerful with a lovely rich finish, it should soften and open out very nicely. *Waterford Wine Vault*

Price	**£15–17/€19–22**
Grape	**Merlot blend**
Alc/vol	**12.5%**
Food	**Fillet of beef**
Drink	**2002–4**

> **Moulis** *is a narrow strip of land 7 miles long and between 300 and 400 metres wide. It produces earlier-drinking wines, which are soft, supple and almost delicate. Ch. Malmaison and Ch. Maucaillou are representative of the high quality of the region.*

Ch. Malmaison Baronne Nadine de Rothschild
AC Moulis Cru Bourgeois **98**

A big, chunky, punchy, modern Bordeaux. Finely structured, lots of class, this is an elegant claret, full of cassis fruit. Drinking beautifully now, but should age gracefully over the next two years. *Mitchells*

Price	**£15–17/€19–22**
Grape	**Cabernet/Merlot**
Alc/vol	**12.5%**
Food	**Roast beef**
Drink	**2001–3**

Ch. Moncets AC Lalande-de-Pomerol **96 £/€**

Wonderful aromas of Christmas cake and sweet black fruit with a touch of meatiness. The palate has striking flavours, a lush mouthfeel and layers of sweet, ripe fruit—blackberries and plums with a touch of liquorice. Tannins are softening and the finish is long. *Searsons*

Price	**£15–17/€19–22**
Grape	**Merlot blend**
Alc/vol	**12.5%**
Food	**Beef**
Drink	**2001–5**

Ch. Rollan de By AC Médoc Cru Bourgeois **97**

Huge nose, very complex, with lots of different aromas—cedar, blackcurrant, spice, even an edge of dark chocolate. Robust tannins don't mask the excellent earthy dark berry fruit, coffee and truffle flavours. Classic, a very good example of Bordeaux. *Wines Direct*

Price	**£15–17/€19–22**
Grape	**Merlot blend**
Alc/vol	**12.5%**
Food	**Lamb**
Drink	**2001–4**

> **St Estèphe** *is the largest and most northerly of the four great commune ACs in the Haut-Médoc district—the other three are Pauillac, St Julien and Margaux. It is the most tannic in style, often unapproachable in youth, and requires more ageing than the others to tame the tannins.*

£17–20/€22–25

Berrys' Own Selection St Estèphe AC St Estèphe **nv**

This wine is made by Ch. Phélan-Ségur for Berry Bros. & Rudd. A jumble of fruits on the aromatic nose—blackcurrants, brambles, scented flowers, eucalyptus and figs. The palate is classic Bordeaux, with concentrated blackcurrant and baked summer fruits, well marshalled by strong (yet soft) tannins and a good edge of acidity. *Fields*

Price	**£17–20/€22–25**
Grape	**Bordeaux blend**
Alc/vol	**12.5%**
Food	**Confit of duck**
Drink	**On purchase**

> **Listrac-Médo**c *produces robust wines, which may be a little hard when young but round out with age. Ch. Clarke was acquired by Baron Edmond de Rothschild in 1973 and is one of the finest of the appellation.*

Ch. Clarke AC Listrac-Médoc Cru Bourgeois 98

Appealing perfume of truffles and pencil shavings. The palate is dry with firm tannins and abundant concentrated blackcurrant fruit with hints of mushroom. This wine will mature and soften over the next two years. *Mitchells*

Price	**£17–20/€22–25**
Grape	**Cabernet/Merlot**
Alc/vol	**13%**
Food	**Steak**
Drink	**2001–4**

---

*Though **Pomerol** has a variety of soil types, its wines have a basic common structure—round and supple, but with real strength and fragrance. They can be drunk young but also age very well. Some of the most famous names from Pomerol include Ch. Beauregard, Ch. Certan-de-May and Ch. Pétrus.*

Ch. des Pelerins AC Pomerol 99 ✓

Aromas of plums and damsons are followed by multi-layered flavours of plums, black fruits and mocha tones. It's ultra-smooth, with a wonderful, lingering, spicy, fruity finish. Fabulous food wine. *Maxxium*

Price	**£17–20/€22–25**
Grape	**Merlot blend**
Alc/vol	**12.5%**
Food	**Goose**
Drink	**2001–4**

Ch. Haut-Nouchet AC Pessac-Léognan 96 ⚘

Inviting nose of warm, spicy blackcurrant fruit. Combination of fruit and vegetal flavours with lots of peppery spices masked by firm tannins. Excellent length. This wine has some way to go, but is already showing its potential. *Peter Dalton*

Price	**£17–20/€22–25**
Grape	**Cabernet blend**
Alc/vol	**12.5%**
Food	**Meat or game casseroles**
Drink	**2001–7**

Ch. Jacques Blanc Cuvée Aliénor
AC St Émilion Grand Cru 98 ⚘

Breeding and class typify this fine St Émilion. It has an earthy nose of blackcurrants and green pepper and a sumptuous palate of rich, concentrated dark berry fruits, dark chocolate and leather, backed by brooding tannins. *Mary Pawle Wines*

Price	**£17–20/€22–25**
Grape	**Merlot blend**
Alc/vol	**12.5%**
Food	**Camembert**
Drink	**2001–4**

Ch. La Commanderie AC St Émilion Grand Cru 97

Upfront, accessible nose—vegetal, plummy. Full, rich palate of chocolate, apple, spice and dark fruits. Long, rewarding finish. Definitely worth the money. Lovely wine. *United Beverages*

Price	**£17–20/€22–25**
Grape	**Merlot blend**
Alc/vol	**13%**
Food	**Roast turkey**
Drink	**2001–3**

Ch. La Couronne AC St Émilion Grand Cru 97

Smoky, blackcurrant aromas with toffee notes. A complex, smoky palate full of plums, tomato and leafy autumnal fruit. This wine has depth and concentration and a long, tannic finish. *TDL*

Price	**£17–20/€22–25**
Grape	**Merlot blend**
Alc/vol	**12.5%**
Food	**Lamb**
Drink	**2001–3**

Ch. Ramage la Batisse AC Haut-Médoc Cru Bourgeois 96

Absorbing, pronounced nose—blackcurrants, fruits of the forest, farmyard, spices. Classic Bordeaux, with subtle elements. A velvety palate, blackcurrant and plum flavours dominating, firm tannins with a lingering finish. Still very young. *Findlaters*

Price	**£17–20/€22–25**
Grape	**Cabernet/Merlot**
Alc/vol	**12.5%**
Food	**Classic French**
Drink	**2001–5**

Ch. Rocher Bellevue Figeac AC St Émilion Grand Cru 97

Fruity, forward and a lovely food wine, this has plenty of St Émilion trademark plum and Christmas cake character on the palate. Tannins are mature and ripe and the wine finishes long and smooth. *Woodford Bourne*

Price	**£17–20/€22–25**
Grape	**Merlot blend**
Alc/vol	**13%**
Food	**Roast lamb**
Drink	**2001–3**

Frank Phélan AC St Estèphe 96 ★

Utterly delicious nose—pencil shavings, cassis and leather. The palate lives up to the promise—rich, smooth, multi-textured with dense black fruit, a hint of liquorice and some coffee nuances. The finish is long, warm and spicy. Tannins are still firm, so this wine definitely needs food. *Barry & Fitzwilliam*

Price	**£17–20/€22–25**
Grape	**Cabernet/Merlot**
Alc/vol	**12.5%**
Food	**Steak**
Drink	**2001–4**

AC Margaux *produces wines of exceptional finesse and elegance, rarely heavy. The most famous châateau in the commune is Ch. Margaux, 1er Cru Classé (First Growth).*

Les Charmes de Kirwan AC Margaux 95 ★

The second wine of Ch. Kirwan, made from younger vines. Huge concentration of ripe summer berries on the nose, as well as blackberries, black cherries, blackcurrants, cedar and polished wood. Very classy. The rich, ripe, robust palate is packed with dense, blackcurrants with a touch of spice at the end. Tannins are firm but not forbidding and the finish is long, with sweet fruit right to the end. *O'Briens*

Price	**£17–20/€22–25**
Grape	**Cabernet/Merlot**
Alc/vol	**12.5%**
Food	**Rack of lamb**
Drink	**2001–5**

£20–25/€25–32

Ch. Coufran AC Haut-Médoc Cru Bourgeois 95

Well-developed blackcurrant and baked plum fruit aromas with a hint of leather and spice. Warm blackberry pie and cream on the palate, mouth-filling texture and layers of baked fruits, chocolate, and ginger. Good savoury finish. *Gilbeys*

Price	**£20–25/€25–32**
Grape	**Merlot blend**
Alc/vol	**12.8%**
Food	**Beef**
Drink	**2001–3**

Ch. d'Angludet AC Margaux Cru Bourgeois 97

This excellent 97 is still in the early stages of development, so the blackcurrant/cherry nose is rather closed. The palate is also still youthful, with a soft, velvety mouthfeel with a basketful of summer fruits, delicately layered with some rose hips, backed by robust tannins that will soften over the next two years. A classic Margaux with lots of promise. *Fields*

Price	**£20–25/€25–32**
Grape	**Cabernet/Merlot**
Alc/vol	**12.5%**
Food	**Roast duck**
Drink	**2001–4**

Ch. de Lamarque AC Haut-Médoc Cru Bourgeois 96

Oaky cassis nose. A dry wine with still-robust tannins and firm black fruit flavours with a hint of vanilla and violets. An excellent food wine. *Woodford Bourne*

Price	**£20–25/€25–32**
Grape	**Cabernet/Merlot**
Alc/vol	**12.5%**
Food	**Versatile**
Drink	**2001–5**

Ch. de Pez AC St Estèphe Cru Bourgeois 97

Still quite closed on the nose. The palate is more generous, with layers of vegetal fruit, nutmeg and leather nuances. Lovely long finish. Still very young and firm. *Searsons*

Price	**£20–25/€25–32**
Grape	**Cabernet blend**
Alc/vol	**12.5%**
Food	**Roast turkey**
Drink	**2002–4**

Ch. Haut-Beauséjour AC St Estèphe Cru Bourgeois 96 £/€

The lush fruit makes for a really appealing wine. Nose of ripe blackberry/mulberry fruit with a touch of mint. Ripe, mouth-filling flavours of a mélange of dark fruits are held in check by fair acidity and plenty of softening tannins. *Searsons*

Price	**£20–25/€25–32**
Grape	**Cabernet blend**
Alc/vol	**12.5%**
Food	**Lamb**
Drink	**2001–2**

Ch. La Tour de Mons AC Margaux Cru Bourgeois 96

Aromas on the nose are still contained, but it promises a lot, with cedary notes and underlying black fruit. Tannins are notable, but don't mask the ripe baked blackcurrant fruits with touches of treacle and chocolate. This elegant wine hasn't yet opened up completely, but it has a wonderful structure. *Gilbeys*

Price	**£20–25/€25–32**
Grape	**Cabernet/Merlot**
Alc/vol	**12.8%**
Food	**Steak**
Drink	**2003–6**

£25–30/€32–40

Ch. Cadet-Bon AC St Émilion Grand Cru **96** ★

Wonderful nose. Powerful, rich blackcurrant
and mulberry fruit with a touch of vegetation.
The palate is laden with lush, mouth-filling,
fruit—plums, damsons, mint and a dash of lemony acidity. The finish is delicious, with intense
plumminess. *O'Briens*

Price	**£25–30/€32–40**
Grape	**Merlot blend**
Alc/vol	**13%**
Food	**Rabbit**
Drink	**2001–4**

> **St Julien** *wines are elegant, with a cedar wood bouquet. The commune is
> located in the heart of the Haut-Médoc district on the left bank of the Gironde,
> home to some of Bordeaux's most serious wines. Cabernet Sauvignon is the
> dominant grape in most of the blends.*

Ch. du Glana AC St Julien Cru Bourgeois **95** ★

Lovely nose of cassis, cigar box and undergrowth. The elegant and subtle palate has a
delicious mélange of black fruits overlain with
cedary tones and hints of vanilla and plums—
complex and multi-dimensional.
Woodford Bourne

Price	**£25–30/€32–40**
Grape	**Cabernet blend**
Alc/vol	**13%**
Food	**Roast beef**
Drink	**2001–5**

> *The 1855 classification of the top red wines of the* **Médoc, Haut Médoc** *and
> the dessert wine* **Sauternes** *was based on the market prices of the wines in that
> year. In the Médoc there are five levels of excellence, ranging from the top
> Premier Cru (First Growth) to Cinquième Cru (Fifth Growth). Apart from the
> promotion of Ch. Mouton-Rothschild from Second to First Growth in 1973,
> the system remains unchanged.*

Ch. du Tertre AC Margaux Grand Cru Classé **97** ✓

Beautiful, elegant, perfumed nose of black fruit
and pencil shavings. The wonderfully soft, rich
palate is full of delicious black fruit flavours
with ripe tannins and just a hint of liquorice.
This is a really accessible wine for drinking now.
Maxxium

Price	**£25–30/€32–40**
Grape	**Cabernet blend**
Alc/vol	**12.5%**
Food	**Steak**
Drink	**2001–3**

Ch. Les Ormes de Pez AC St Estèphe Cru Bourgeois **97** ✓

Lovely leathery notes to the cassis nose. The
palate is full with smooth, smoky blackcurrant
fruit flavours. Tannins are supple, the finish
long, harmonious and subtle. *Maxxium*

Price	**£25–30/€32–40**
Grape	**Cabernet blend**
Alc/vol	**13%**
Food	**Leg of lamb**
Drink	**2001–4**

Ch. Maucaillou AC Moulis Cru Bourgeois 97

Heady perfume. This muscular and sleek Moulis shows claret at its classiest. An explosion of flavour. Mocha coffee paired with ripe black fruit, deep and concentrated, with the stamina to linger on the finish. *Febvre*

Price	**£25–30/€32–40**
Grape	**Cabernet/Merlot**
Alc/vol	**13%**
Food	**Roasts**
Drink	**2001–4**

Ch. Meyney AC St Estèphe Cru Bourgeois 95

The essence of Bordeaux. This is a classic. Rich garnet colour. The nose has blackcurrant fruit and touches of spice and cedar with a hint of leather. Elegant and subtle, with layers of black fruit, green pepper, spices, pepper and smoke. Tannins are still pretty firm. *United Beverages*

Price	**£25–30/€32–40**
Grape	**Cabernet blend**
Alc/vol	**12.5%**
Food	**Versatile**
Drink	**2001–5**

Connétable Talbot AC St Julien 96

Classic farmyard nose with hints of blackcurrant and a touch of smoke. Firm tannins assert themselves on the palate, but the black fruit flavours are strong enough to come through.
United Beverages

Price	**£25–30/€32–40**
Grape	**Cabernet blend**
Alc/vol	**12.7%**
Food	**Casseroles**
Drink	**2001–4**

France–Burgundy

The overall excellent quality of the wines this year reflects the fact that Burgundy has had a run of good vintages since 1995 for both red and white wines. But knowing a good vintage is not the entire answer in Burgundy—it pays to look for a reliable producer as well.

Stars were more or less equally distributed between whites and reds this year, with many wines scoring well. Prices, as always, are high in Burgundy, but that doesn't mean that there aren't any good-value wines around—a number are highlighted as offering exceptional value for money.

The main Burgundian grape varieties of Chardonnay and Pinot Noir are well represented this year, but Aligoté and Gamay also make an appearance. Aligoté makes crisp, dry white wine that is traditionally mixed with blackcurrant liqueur to make Kir. Gamay makes soft, juicy Beaujolais, Beaujolais-Villages and the crus from ten named villages—Fleurie is the most popular one in Ireland, though Régnié and Moulin-à-Vent are favourites as well. And don't forget St Amour for St Valentine's Day!

Chardonnay styles vary from the north to the south of the region. Wines from the cooler region of Chablis are bone dry, with steely acidity and mineral/citrus flavours, while the warmer southern region of the Mâconnais produces rounder, softer wines with fruit leaning more towards apples, peaches and melons.

Burgundy Pinot Noir wines have strawberry and cherry flavours in their youth, developing mature aromas and flavours of game, undergrowth and even a whiff of the farmyard after a few years. Winemakers all over the world try to emulate this style, but rarely achieve the heights that Burgundy Pinot can reach.

Burgundy has a justified reputation for being difficult and expensive. However, our tastings this year showed that there are some truly delicious, reasonably priced wines on the shelves. Why wait?

White

Under £7/Under €9

Chanson Père et Fils AC Mâcon-Villages **98 £/€**

A wine with crowd appeal. Dry, with a generous concentration of delicious tropical fruit and honeyed tones. *O'Briens*

Price	Under £7/Under €9
Grape	Chardonnay
Alc/vol	12.5%
Food	Picnic
Drink	2001–2

£7–9/€9–11.50

Dom. Fribourg AC Bourgogne Aligoté **98**

Lively and refreshing, this wine has flavours of home-made apple jelly with a grating of fresh lime zest. The palate shows very good concentration of lemons, limes and green apples and it has a decent finish. *Le Caveau*

Price	£7–9/€9–11.50
Grape	Aligoté
Alc/vol	12%
Food	Snails
Drink	2001–2

£9–11/€11.50–14

Champy AC Mâcon-Uchizy 98

 Intense bouquet of butter-scotch and ripe melon. Buttery overtones and fruit flavours develop in the mouth. Lengthy, fruity, weighty finish. *Allied Drinks*

Price	**£9–11/€11.50–14**
Grape	**Chardonnay**
Alc/vol	**13%**
Food	**Chinese**
Drink	**2001–2**

Chanson Père et Fils AC Chablis 99

Bone dry, with that lovely flinty, steely charac-ter of a Chablis. Ripe, concentrated fruit with melons and pears. Classic. *O'Briens*

Price	**£9–11/€11.50–14**
Grape	**Chardonnay**
Alc/vol	**12.5%**
Food	**Grilled pork**
Drink	**2001–3**

Dom. André Bonhomme AC Mâcon-Viré 98 £/€ ✓

Delicious! A striking nose of honey, lemon sher-bet and vanilla follows through to a broad, rich palate of apple strudel and vanilla ice cream. Very ripe fruit and a terrific, crisp lemon finish. *Le Caveau*

Price	**£9–11/€11.50–14**
Grape	**Chardonnay**
Alc/vol	**13%**
Food	**Seafood**
Drink	**2001–3**

Dom. Bouchard Père et Fils AC Mâcon-Lugny St Pierre 99

Touch of pear and spearmint on the nose, along with the more typical melon and apple. Invig-oratingly fresh on the palate, backed with ripe apple, pear and melon fruit flavours. *Findlaters*

Price	**£9–11/€11.50–14**
Grape	**Chardonnay**
Alc/vol	**13%**
Food	**Thai-style fish**
Drink	**2001–2**

> *Mâcon* whites, from Burgundy's most southerly wine district, are fast maturing with fairly soft acidity. Made from Chardonnay, they can be labelled AC Mâcon, AC Mâcon-Villages or AC Mâcon plus the name of a specific village such as Uchizy or Viré. Mâcon-Villages wines are made by blending wines from different villages.

Dom. de la Condemine Mâcon-Péronne Le Clou
AC Mâcon-Villages 00 £/€

Intriguing nose of dried apricots with mineral overtones. The palate is zippy and fresh, with red apple and herbal qualities—some grapefruit as well. *Wines Direct*

Price	**£9–11/€11.50–14**
Grape	**Chardonnay**
Alc/vol	**13%**
Food	**Roast chicken**
Drink	**2001–2**

Dom. Saumaize-Michelin Les Crèches AC St Véran 99 ★ £/€

An enticing nose of apricots and wood smoke. Big, expansive palate of spicy, sweet oak, ripe melons and apples with zippy lemon acidity and a savoury bacon-like, flavour. Elegant, com-plex wine with a splendid finish. *Wines Direct*

Price	**£9–11/€11.50–14**
Grape	**Chardonnay**
Alc/vol	**12.8%**
Food	**Fresh salmon**
Drink	**2001–2**

Dom. Séguinot-Bordet AC Chablis **99 £/€**

Slightly honeyed, nutty nose, but fruity too—pears, lemons, limes and melons. Rich, intense melon and pear fruit on the palate, plus that necessary zingy acidity. Great length—crisp, dry, long-lasting. *Wines Direct*

Price	**£9–11/€11.50–14**
Grape	**Chardonnay**
Alc/vol	**12.5%**
Food	**Sole**
Drink	**2001–3**

Duroy Latour AC Chablis **99**

Fresh, subtle and attractive nose. Gorgeous fresh taste of apples with an assertive mineral streak throughout. Lovely balance and finish. *SuperValu-Centra*

Price	**£9–11/€11.50–14**
Grape	**Chardonnay**
Alc/vol	**12.5%**
Food	**Prawns**
Drink	**2001–2**

Jean-Marc Brocard AC Chablis **99**

Wonderful and unusual nose of apples and flowers. Fresh palate enlivened with a touch of spritz. Rounded, buttery mouthfeel and flavour. Subtle yet elegant, with a refreshing finish. *Oddbins*

Price	**£9–11/€11.50–14**
Grape	**Chardonnay**
Alc/vol	**12.5%**
Food	**Poached fish**
Drink	**2001–4**

> **St Véran** *often represents the best value in the whites of the Mâconnais and—when very good—can rival its neighbour Pouilly Fuissé. Wines are soft and mature quickly, so are best drunk young.*

Joseph Drouhin AC St Véran **98**

Quite a faint, waxy nose with delicate aromas of apricots and citrus fruit. The palate shows real finesse, changing from bright citrus and green apple notes to toast, finishing with roasted cashew nuts and minerals. *Gilbeys*

Price	**£9–11/€11.50–14**
Grape	**Chardonnay**
Alc/vol	**13%**
Food	**Versatile**
Drink	**2001–2**

Laroche AC Mâcon-Lugny **00**

Fresh, floral bouquet of a gentle character. Slightly off-dry style. Tropical and citrus fruit flavours with a mouth-watering citrus finish. A clean, fresh wine, light enough to be enjoyed by itself, and also with light dishes. *Allied Drinks*

Price	**£9–11/€11.50–14**
Grape	**Chardonnay**
Alc/vol	**13%**
Food	**Lunch**
Drink	**2001–2**

Louis Latour Les Genièvres AC Mâcon-Lugny **99**

Caramel and a bit of smoke on the nose. Classic Chardonnay—lots of lemons and limes, zippy with fresh apple flavours, velvety texture and a smoky citrus finish. *Gilbeys*

Price	**£9–11/€11.50–14**
Grape	**Chardonnay**
Alc/vol	**13%**
Food	**Roast chicken**
Drink	**2001–3**

Lupé-Cholet AC Mâcon-Lugny 99 £/€

Fruit cocktail and melon aromas follow through on the palate with melon and apple. Easy-drinking, traditional rustic style; a flavoursome finish. *Dillons*

Price	**£9–11/€11.50–14**
Grape	**Chardonnay**
Alc/vol	**13%**
Food	**Salads**
Drink	**2001–2**

Roger Roblot AC Mâcon-Villages 99

Aromas of lemon, citrus and hints of peach. Nicely balanced citrus and apple flavours, zingy mouthfeel and a lovely finish. Good with food. *Peter Dalton*

Price	**£9–11/€11.50–14**
Grape	**Chardonnay**
Alc/vol	**12.5%**
Food	**Versatile**
Drink	**2001–2**

> *Aligoté* is a lesser-known white grape variety grown in Burgundy. While it shares the same broad structure as Chardonnay, it is not as highly regarded. Its very high acidity makes it the ideal base for Kir, a local aperitif, which is made with Aligoté and a little Crème de Cassis.

£11–13/€14–16.50

A. et P. de Villaine AC Bouzeron Aligoté 99

A light nose of waxy apple peel with a faint herbal character. The palate is just slightly off-dry, with crab apple flavours and notes of something green, cut grass perhaps. Light, fresh and zingy with a broad mouthfeel. *Wines Direct*

Price	**£11–13/€14–16.50**
Grape	**Aligoté**
Alc/vol	**12.5%**
Food	**Kir**
Drink	**2001–2**

Barton & Guestier Tradition AC Chablis 98

Crisp and lively with green apple crunch and mouth-watering freshness. Firm backbone of acidity supported by decent weight of fruit. Long, scented, strong finish. Very food friendly. *Dillons*

Price	**£11–13/€14–16.50**
Grape	**Chardonnay**
Alc/vol	**12.5%**
Food	**Sole**
Drink	**2001–2**

Berrys' Reserve White Burgundy AC Bourgogne 98

Striking nose of stewed apples and toffee apples with a slightly floral background. Dry, steely and crisp, this wine has concentrated lemon and lime fruit on the palate. *Fields*

Price	**£11–13/€14–16.50**
Grape	**Chardonnay**
Alc/vol	**12.5%**
Food	**Monkfish**
Drink	**2001–2**

Dom. Bart Chardonnay-Musqué Les Favières
AC Marsannay 99

Rich, developed nose of mangoes and caramel, with a creamy background to the apple, peach and honey flavours. Long, nutty finish. *Wines Direct*

Price	**£11–13/€14–16.50**
Grape	**Chardonnay**
Alc/vol	**13%**
Food	**Lobster**
Drink	**2001–2**

Dom. Joseph et Xavier Garnier AC Chablis 98 ✓

Precise and memorable. Crisp acidity, but lots of honeyed melon and pear fruit to stand up to it. Long, lingering finish—an elegant and delicious wine. *Mitchells*

Price	**£11–13/€14–16.50**
Grape	**Chardonnay**
Alc/vol	**12.5%**
Food	**Veal**
Drink	**2001–3**

Dom. Talmard AC Mâcon-Uchizy 00

Luscious concentration of honeyed tropical fruits in this well-made wine from a ripe vintage. Long, lingering finish. Extremely refreshing. *J. S. Woods*

Price	**£11–13/€14–16.50**
Grape	**Chardonnay**
Alc/vol	**13%**
Food	**Pork**
Drink	**2001–3**

Dom. Vincent Girardin Cuvée St Vincent AC Bourgogne 98

Steely nose with a hint of buttered toast. Dry, with zippy acidity, the palate has zesty apple fruit with a nutty element. This is a delicious wine with layers of fruit and a generous finish. Wonderful food wine. *Le Caveau*

Price	**£11–13/€14–16.50**
Grape	**Chardonnay**
Alc/vol	**13%**
Food	**Versatile**
Drink	**2001–3**

> **Montagny** *is located in the Côte Chalonnaise. The AC is for white wine only, from four villages. The wines usually have a subtle peppery tone from some oak maturation, yet they maintain a fresh crispness and an expression of the soil.*

La Buxynoise AC Montagny 99

An excellent introduction to affordable white Burgundy. Gentle nose, baked apple pie, a touch of cinnamon. Clean, with abundant fruit balanced by crisp lemony acidity. Very flavoursome and persistent length. *Febvre*

Price	**£11–13/€14–16.50**
Grape	**Chardonnay**
Alc/vol	**13%**
Food	**Scallops**
Drink	**2001–3**

Laroche AC Chablis 99

Smoky citrus bouquet. Dry on the palate, with red apple/citrus fruit and buttery undertones. Quite light bodied, a touch of smokiness adds to the appeal. *Allied Drinks*

Price	**£11–13/€14–16.50**
Grape	**Chardonnay**
Alc/vol	**12.5%**
Food	**Seafood**
Drink	**2001–3**

Paul Sapin Cuvée Prestige AC St Véran 99

Green fruit and nettle nose with vanilla notes. Melon and blackcurrant leaf tones with a slight vegetal character give the palate some interesting flavours. Crisp, lengthy and very distinctive. Smoky notes on the finish. *Febvre*

Price	**£11–13/€14–16.50**
Grape	**Chardonnay**
Alc/vol	**13%**
Food	**Shrimps**
Drink	**2001–3**

Roger Roblot AC Petit Chablis **98 £/€**

Bone dry Petit Chablis. Striking, smoky, spicy aromas with citrus fruit, apples and tropical fruit. Good complexity of bready, citrus and apple flavours and pretty good length.
Peter Dalton

Price	**£11–13/€14–16.50**
Grape	**Chardonnay**
Alc/vol	**12.5%**
Food	**Crab**
Drink	**2001–2**

Ropiteau AC Chablis **99**

Typical Chablis green apple nose with butter and citrus notes. Good balance of flavours on the palate, with citrus/apple flavours and tingly, zingy acidity. Lingering finish. *TDL*

Price	**£11–13/€14–16.50**
Grape	**Chardonnay**
Alc/vol	**12.5%**
Food	**Oysters, grilled prawns**
Drink	**2001–3**

Chablis is one of France's classic white wines, characteristically steely and fresh. Made from Chardonnay, much of its character comes from the limestone subsoil with its high content of marine fossils and chalk. AC Chablis, made from grapes grown all over the region, is flinty and minerally with green apple flavours and should be drunk about two to three years from the vintage. The best vineyards are designated Premier Cru or Grand Cru. Premier Cru wines require at least five years' bottle ageing. The wines are more intense and concentrated than AC Chablis, with pure citrus fruit flavours. Grand Cru wines are richer and fuller and should be aged for ten years.

£13–15/€16.50–19

Berrys' Own Selection Chablis AC Chablis **99** ★

Made in traditional Chablis style without oak, the nose shows quite ripe green fruits with hints of honey and flowers. Those green fruits carry on through the palate, which has depth, ripeness and flavour backed by steely acidity. Superb finish. An elegant wine of great quality. *Fields*

Price	**£13–15/€16.50–19**
Grape	**Chardonnay**
Alc/vol	**12.5%**
Food	**Turbot**
Drink	**2001–3**

Rully was the first village appellation in the Côte Chalonnaise or the Région de Mercurey. White Rullys do not have the weight and concentration of their neighbours but have delicacy and elegance. They are one of the best-value white Burgundies.

Dom. Bouchard Père et Fils AC Rully **98**

Subtle aromas of pineapple and cardamom. Intensity of green fruit flavours with enough acidity to keep the wine balanced. Elegant and pleasing, the wine has classic style and a long finish. *Findlaters*

Price	**£13–15/€16.50–19**
Grape	**Chardonnay**
Alc/vol	**13%**
Food	**Clams**
Drink	**2001–2**

Dom. de Chaude Ecuelle AC Chablis 98

Dry, full-bodied wine with quite weighty fruit—lots of ripe pears and an underlying steeliness. Subtle and restrained style, with a very long finish. *J. S. Woods*

Price	**£13–15/€16.50–19**
Grape	**Chardonnay**
Alc/vol	**12.5%**
Food	**Oysters**
Drink	**2001–2**

Dom. du Colombier AC Chablis 99

Interesting, multi-layered nose of minerals, lemons, limes, flowers, bread and honey. Dry, with a lovely balance of zesty green fruit, stewed apples and a touch of lemon zest. Refreshing acidity and a clean finish. *Fields*

Price	**£13–15/€16.50–19**
Grape	**Chardonnay**
Alc/vol	**12.5%**
Food	**Salmon**
Drink	**2001–3**

Dom. du Vieux Château AC Montagny 1er Cru 99 ✓

A very flavoursome and rounded style—ripe apple and melon fruitiness, zesty acidity. Delicate floral nose carries through to the palate. Lovely structure with a touch of spice at the end. Though dry, the wine has an almost honeyed style and some lushness. Excellent. A wine for all seasons. *Febvre*

Price	**£13–15/€16.50–19**
Grape	**Chardonnay**
Alc/vol	**13.5%**
Food	**Versatile**
Drink	**2001–3**

Faiveley Les Joncs AC Montagny 97

WHITE WINE OF THE YEAR

Mature nutty, fruity aromas with lovely complexity on the palate—a rare find these days. Wonderful creamy, buttery, hazelnut, slightly smoky, oaky flavours, with apples and lemons. Great richness, balance and length. *Maxxium*

Price	**£13–15/€16.50–19**
Grape	**Chardonnay**
Alc/vol	**13%**
Food	**Monkfish**
Drink	**2001–4**

Laroche St Martin AC Chablis 99

Stainless steel fermentation results in aromas and flavours of pure Chardonnay fruit. Juicy greengages, nectarines and fresh limes follow on the refreshing palate—this is lean and tasty. There's a herby background of fennel and liquorice to the citrus and pear fruit and typical Chablis steeliness. *Allied Drinks*

Price	**£13–15/€16.50–19**
Grape	**Chardonnay**
Alc/vol	**12.5%**
Food	**Oysters**
Drink	**2001–5**

Pierre Ponnelle AC Chablis 1er Cru Fourchaume 98

A refreshing bite of acidity and ripe apple and melon fruitiness give this wine great appeal. Clean as a whistle on the finish. *Dunnes Stores*

Price	**£13–15/€16.50–19**
Grape	**Chardonnay**
Alc/vol	**13%**
Food	**Seafood**
Drink	**2001–4**

Roger Roblot AC Chablis 98

Inviting bready, citrus aromas. Some smoke comes through on the citrus palate, which has a tasty, persistent finish. The oak doesn't overpower the fruit. Good example of Chablis. *Peter Dalton*

Price	**£13–15/€16.50–19**
Grape	**Chardonnay**
Alc/vol	**12.5%**
Food	**Shellfish**
Drink	**2001–3**

£15–17/€19–22

Dom. Emilian Gillet Quintaine AC Mâcon-Viré 98

Soft, refined nose of peaches, waxy apples, hints of minerals and smoke. The palate is subtle and soft, offering creamy flavours of lemon, apple pie, dried apricots and honey, even some candied peel. Soft, nutty finish. *Wines Direct*

Price	**£15–17/€19–22**
Grape	**Chardonnay**
Alc/vol	**12.8%**
Food	**Veal escalopes**
Drink	**2001–3**

Dom. Long-Depaquit AC Chablis 1er Cru Les Vaillons 98

Aromas are light and fresh with a touch of smokiness. Nice weight of ripe, concentrated apple flavours balanced by lemony acidity and some warmth of spices at the end. Medium-long finish. A pleasing Chablis. *Irish Distillers*

Price	**£15–17/€19–22**
Grape	**Chardonnay**
Alc/vol	**13%**
Food	**Squid**
Drink	**2001–4**

> The vines producing **Pouilly-Fuissé** wines are grown in a number of amphitheatre-like slopes that trap the sun's rays. The resulting wines are amongst the richest in Burgundy.

Ropiteau AC Pouilly-Fuissé 99

Pineapples, tropical fruit, citrus and buttery aromas waft out of the glass. Complex, smoky citrus and apple flavours are supported by balancing acidity. Long finish. *TDL*

Price	**£15–17/€19–22**
Grape	**Chardonnay**
Alc/vol	**12.5%**
Food	**Fish**
Drink	**2001–2**

£17–20/€22–25

Dom. Valette Tradition AC Pouilly-Fuissé 98

A good crisp Pouilly-Fuissé with rich fruit character. The slightly high acidity bodes well for keeping for a couple of years, as there is enough citrus and apple fruit to sustain it. At the moment it needs food—rich, creamy sauces. *Wines Direct*

Price	**£17–20/€22–25**
Grape	**Chardonnay**
Alc/vol	**13.5%**
Food	**Salmon**
Drink	**2001–4**

Jaffelin AC Chablis 1er Cru 98

Distinctive, pungent nose of pears, toast, melons and apples. Dry, with a medley of fruit salad flavours—apples, pears, apricots—and a nutty background. It's underpinned by brisk acidity and finishes wonderfully. *Cassidy*

Price	**£17–20/€22–25**
Grape	**Chardonnay**
Alc/vol	**13%**
Food	**Pork**
Drink	**2001–6**

Louis Latour AC Chablis 1er Cru 98 ★

Striking nose of nuts, honey and exotic fruits. Rich, ripe palate of melons, pears, minerals and some smoky, earthy hints. Long, lingering finish. Classy stuff and a pleasure to drink. *Gilbeys*

Price	**£17–20/€22–25**
Grape	**Chardonnay**
Alc/vol	**13%**
Food	**Seafood platter**
Drink	**2001–3**

Ropiteau AC Chablis 1er Cru Montmains 98

Typical citrus, apple and buttery aromas with some vegetal and smoky notes on the nose. Lovely palate, revealing layers of flavours—the crisp acidity supports concentrated apple and citrus fruit. Lingering finish. Very enjoyable! *TDL*

Price	**£17–20/€22–25**
Grape	**Chardonnay**
Alc/vol	**13%**
Food	**Crab**
Drink	**2001–4**

£20–25/€25–32

Dom. Bouchard Père et Fils AC Beaune 1er Cru 96 ✓

Complex and interesting, with ripe mango fruit and some vegetal aromas and spice. A developing, classic wine with rich, heavyweight fruit flavours of peach, butterscotch and vanilla, showing some spice in the long finish. Luscious. *Findlaters*

Price	**£20–25/€25–32**
Grape	**Chardonnay**
Alc/vol	**13%**
Food	**Cheese**
Drink	**2001–3**

Louis Max AC Chablis 1er Cru Les Vaillons 96

Toasty, honeyed nose of apples, lemons and a bit of tropical fruit. Deep flavours of citrus and apples on the palate, backed by lively acidity and good length. *United Beverages*

Price	**£20–25/€25–32**
Grape	**Chardonnay**
Alc/vol	**12.5%**
Food	**Sole**
Drink	**2001–4**

> **Meursault** is a commune in the Côte de Beaune, the best area for Burgundy whites. Showing another side to the Chardonnay grape, the wines are full bodied, rich, ripe and nutty.

£25–30/€32–40

Ropiteau AC Meursault 97 ★★

A wine to savour. Incredibly rich bouquet with toasty flavours—roasted hazelnuts, toffee apples, oak. The palate has a wonderful balance of fruit, with nuttiness and spicy oak. Honeyed citrus. Fabulous length. Will continue to develop but drinking well now. *TDL*

Price	**£25–30/€32–40**
Grape	**Chardonnay**
Alc/vol	**12.5%**
Food	**Versatile**
Drink	**2001–4**

Red

Dom. de Fontalognier Beaujolais-Lantignié
AC Beaujolais-Villages **00**

Very attractive strawberry jam nose, but more restraint and class on the palate. A lovely, light, fruity style of wine, ideal for the summer. Lots of juicy raspberry fruit with good concentration and a long finish. *River Wines*

Price	**Under £7/Under €9**
Grape	**Gamay**
Alc/vol	**12%**
Food	**Salad**
Drink	**2000–1**

> The **Beaujolais** district is planted with the Gamay grape on granite soil and produces fruity, easy-drinking wines, light in tannin, that mature quickly. A common fermentation method, which suits the Gamay, is carbonic maceration, where the grapes are fermented under a layer of carbon dioxide. This process minimises tannins and makes wine with fresh fruit flavours.

Olivier Ravier AC Beaujolais **00 £/€**

Pleasant, slightly confected nose of ripe mushy strawberries with a hint of demerara. Smooth, gentle palate of strawberries. A very nice example of a fruity wine that is also delicate and refreshing. Could be served slightly chilled. *Oddbins*

Price	**Under £7/Under €9**
Grape	**Gamay**
Alc/vol	**12%**
Food	**Lamb chops**
Drink	**2000–1**

Dom. de Fantalognier AC Régnié **00 £/€**

Lots of juicy summer berry fruits jumping out of the glass. Good depth of flavour but not overly serious—an easy-drinking style for a summer's evening. *River Wines*

Price	**£7–9/€9–11.50**
Grape	**Gamay**
Alc/vol	**12.5%**
Food	**Antipasto**
Drink	**2001–2**

Dom. de la Madone AC Beaujolais-Villages **00**

Interesting nose of spice, smoke and cherries. Tannins are firm, but backed by lots of upfront cherry and raspberry fruit, fruits of the forest and a hint of spice. Savoury and delicious. *Mitchells*

Price	**£7–9/€9–11.50**
Grape	**Gamay**
Alc/vol	**12.5%**
Food	**Salmon**
Drink	**2000–1**

Jean-Claude Regnaudot AC Bourgogne **98**

Pronounced aromas of damsons and plums. Good fruit extract on the palate—cherries and more damsons and plums. Soft and elegant wine, with mellow tannins and persistent length. *Le Caveau*

Price	**£7–9/€9–11.50**
Grape	**Pinot Noir**
Alc/vol	**12%**
Food	**Mushroom-based dishes**
Drink	**2001–2**

Pierre Ponnelle AC Bourgogne Hautes-Côtes-de-Beaune 99

A dry wine with a fairly firm tannic structure, redcurrant and cherry fruit, summer berries and a clean, smooth finish. *Dunnes Stores*

Price	**£7–9/€9–11.50**
Grape	**Pinot Noir**
Alc/vol	**13%**
Food	**Baked ham**
Drink	**2001–2**

AC Bourgogne is the most basic AC in Burgundy, but should not be overlooked. It often offers very good quality and value.

Ropiteau AC Bourgogne 98

Appetising Pinot aromas of strawberries, but with developing vegetal nuances and a slight mineral note. A delicious mouthful with noticeable tannins and jammy cherry fruit. The tartness and acidity mingle well together. Long finish. *TDL*

Price	**£7–9/€9–11.50**
Grape	**Pinot Noir**
Alc/vol	**12.5%**
Food	**Coq au vin**
Drink	**2001–5**

£9–11/€11.50–14

Berrys' Own Selection Red Burgundy AC Bourgogne nv

Complex smoky aromas of spicy cherry, raspberry and cedar. The palate is soft and round, with silky red summer fruit flavours underpinned by gentle tannins. *Fields*

Price	**£9–11/€11.50–14**
Grape	**Pinot Noir**
Alc/vol	**12.5%**
Food	**Guinea fowl**
Drink	**2001–2**

Dom. Bouchard Père et Fils Ch. du Souzy
AC Beaujolais-Villages 99

Good nose of red cherries and plums. Quite a structured style with a refreshsing bite of acidity and black fruit appeal. Lengthy with lots of flavours. *Findlaters*

Price	**£9–11/€11.50–14**
Grape	**Gamay**
Alc/vol	**12.5%**
Food	**Scallops**
Drink	**2000–1**

Dom. de la Madone AC Fleurie 00 £/€

Full-bodied Fleurie with lots of jammy summer fruits. The firm tannins and stylish palate of plum and strawberry fruit go on to a long, lingering finish. *Mitchells*

Price	**£9–11/€11.50–14**
Grape	**Gamay**
Alc/vol	**13%**
Food	**Terrines**
Drink	**2001–3**

Louis Jadot Couvent des Jacobins AC Bourgogne 98

Bramble fruit aromas with a hint of cedar. Typical Pinot Noir flavours of juicy strawberries and redcurrants with a long, fruity finish. The ripe tannins and generous fruit make this a versatile food wine. *Grants*

Price	**£9–11/€11.50–14**
Grape	**Pinot Noir**
Alc/vol	**12.5%**
Food	**Versatile**
Drink	**2001–3**

£11–13/€14–16.50

Caves de Bailly Bourgogne Pinot Noir AC Bourgogne 99

Good introduction to a basic red Burgundy style. Pinot Noir nose of red berries and a slight edge of farmyard. Soft, fruity, easy-drinking with raspberry and cherry flavours. Mild tannins and a good acidic backbone. *Febvre*

Price	**£11–13/€14–16.50**
Grape	**Pinot Noir**
Alc/vol	**13%**
Food	**Mushroom risotto**
Drink	**2001–2**

Coudert Père et Fils Clos de la Roilette AC Fleurie 00

Lush summer fruit aromas. On the palate there is a good balance of complex ripe raspberry/cherry fruit and soft tannins. Excellent summer wine. Serve it slightly chilled with food. *Wines Direct*

Price	**£11–13/€14–16.50**
Grape	**Gamay**
Alc/vol	**13%**
Food	**Pork**
Drink	**2001–2**

Dom. Bouchard Père et Fils AC Fleurie 99 ✓

An excellent example of a Cru Beaujolais style. Layers of red and dark fruit wrapped around spicy flavours with a good tannic grip. The nose has a twiggy note to it, almost fern-like, but with red fruits below. *Findlaters*

Price	**£11–13/€14–16.50**
Grape	**Gamay**
Alc/vol	**13%**
Food	**Salamis**
Drink	**2001–2**

Dom. de Gry-Sablon AC Fleurie 00 ✓

A superior Fleurie with luscious summer berry fruits. Lovely harmony of fruit, tannin and acidity, giving this wine balance and structure. *J. S. Woods*

Price	**£11–13/€14–16.50**
Grape	**Gamay**
Alc/vol	**12.5%**
Food	**Cold meats**
Drink	**2001–3**

Faiveley AC Morgon 99

Typical Beaujolais nose, smacking of clean, ripe raspberries with an underlying mineral nuance. Well-flavoured fruity palate with a little something extra. Long, fruity, vanilla finish. *Maxxium*

Price	**£11–13/€14–16.50**
Grape	**Gamay**
Alc/vol	**12.5%**
Food	**Rare beef**
Drink	**2001–3**

> *Beaune is the centre of the wine trade in Burgundy. Hautes-Côtes-de-Beaune vineyards lie high in the hills behind the town on the slopes of the Montagne de Beaune. It is an area of basic AC wines with no Premier Cru sites. Wines are made from the traditional Burgundian varieties of Pinot Noir, Chardonnay and Aligoté. Wines are red and can offer good regional character and excellent value in a good vintage. As it's harder to ripen grapes at such a high altitude (up to 500 m), poor vintages should be avoided.*

Jaffelin AC Hautes-Côtes-de-Beaune 98

Elegant, complex, earthy nose of coffee and strawberries. Light and easy with a bite of acidity and soft tannins; flavours are of freshly crushed strawberries and cherries. The finish lingers on and on. Great with food. *Cassidy*

Price	**£11–13/€14–16.50**
Grape	**Pinot Noir**
Alc/vol	**13%**
Food	**Versatile**
Drink	**2001–2**

Jean-Paul Brun Terres Dorées AC Moulin-à-Vent **99**

Attractive aromas of freshly picked strawberries. Refreshing acidity, firm tannins and plenty of ripe cherry, redcurrant and loganberry fruit. Lovely wine, with good length. *Wines Direct*

Price	**£11–13/€14–16.50**
Grape	**Gamay**
Alc/vol	**12%**
Food	**Pork**
Drink	**2001–2**

Joseph Drouhin AC Fleurie **00**

Ripe redcurrants on the nose. The palate is laden with soft summer fruits and has a clean, dry, fruity finish. Refreshing and light, it's ideal for summer outdoor drinking. *Gilbeys*

Price	**£11–13/€14–16.50**
Grape	**Gamay**
Alc/vol	**13%**
Food	**Charcuterie**
Drink	**2001–2**

Paul Sapin Cuvée Prestige AC Fleurie **99**

Pronounced nose of red fruits into distinct aromas of spice and dark fruit. Appealing and flavoursome. There is a lengthy, spicy aftertaste. *Febvre*

Price	**£11–13/€14–16.50**
Grape	**Gamay**
Alc/vol	**13%**
Food	**Barbecue**
Drink	**2001–2**

Pierre Ducret Clos Marolle AC Givry 1er Cru **99**

Strawberry jam nose—light but ripe, with some vanilla. Touch of ripe plums, too. Quite substantial fruit on the palate, but the youthful tannins will need time to mellow before the full fruit flavours will emerge. *Wines Direct*

Price	**£11–13/€14–16.50**
Grape	**Pinot Noir**
Alc/vol	**13%**
Food	**Roast pork**
Drink	**2001–3**

£13–15/€16.50–19

Dom. Estienne de Lagrange AC Moulin-à-Vent **97**

Developed Beaujolais style with a mulberry nose. Though quite mature, the wine has an attractive, meaty character with a background of dark fruit and spice. The mouthfeel is full, with a richness of fruit and lightness of tannin that make for a wine drinking well now. *Findlaters*

Price	**£13–15/€16.50–19**
Grape	**Gamay**
Alc/vol	**13%**
Food	**Baked ham**
Drink	**2001–2**

Joseph Roty Cuvée de Pressonier AC Bourgogne **97**

This complex mature wine has subtle aromas of smoky wood and tinned strawberries. The silky palate is full of brambles, black cherries and damsons. Mouth-filling, rich and meaty, with a harmonious finish. Very much a food wine. *Le Caveau*

Price	**£13–15/€16.50–19**
Grape	**Pinot Noir**
Alc/vol	**13%**
Food	**Duck**
Drink	**2001–2**

Côtes de Nuits-Villages *wines come from villages near Nuits-St-Georges with less favourably sited vineyards. They offer a glimpse of the character of their more famous neighbour at a lower price.*

Philippe Rossignol AC Côte de Nuits-Villages 98 £/€

Striking, concentrated nose of smoky black cherries with nut and lavender notes. The robust palate has masses of meaty black cherries with some cedar in the background. A hearty Burgundy, this wine has terrific length. *Le Caveau*

Price	**£13–15/€16.50–19**
Grape	**Pinot Noir**
Alc/vol	**13%**
Food	**Goose**
Drink	**2001–5**

£15–17/€19–22

Champy AC Savigny-lès-Beaune 97

Complex, vegetal nose. Full-bodied, classic style, nicely oaked, showing a layer of vanilla and lots of flavours of summer pudding, stewed cherries, green pepper, leather and tar, all supported by ample tannins and a long finish. Extremely juicy with a silky texture. *Allied Drinks*

Price	**£15–17/€19–22**
Grape	**Pinot Noir**
Alc/vol	**13%**
Food	**Game**
Drink	**2001–4**

Faiveley AC Côtes-de-Beaune-Villages 98 ★

Really perfumed nose! Some hints of coffee and spice as well. Very well put together on the palate, with generous measures of earthiness, ripe plums, ground pepper and cake spice, held together with firm tannins and alcohol. Great length. *Maxxium*

Price	**£15–17/€19–22**
Grape	**Pinot Noir**
Alc/vol	**12.5%**
Food	**Pork steak**
Drink	**2001–3**

Lupé-Cholet AC Fleurie 99

Very spicy with excellent underlying dark fruit flavours. Mixed red and black cherries; light tannin and easy acidity, with a solid finish of lingering scented red fruit and berries. A food-friendly wine. *Dillons*

Price	**£15–17/€19–22**
Grape	**Gamay**
Alc/vol	**13%**
Food	**Cheese**
Drink	**2001–2**

Philippe Rossignol En Tabellion AC Fixin 97 ★

Sweet coffee and strawberry nose. The palate shows concentrated ripe, juicy summer pudding flavours—strawberries, raspberries and blackcurrants—and plenty of chewy tannins. This is classic Burgundy. *Le Caveau*

Price	**£15–17/€19–22**
Grape	**Pinot Noir**
Alc/vol	**13%**
Food	**Versatile**
Drink	**2001–6**

£17–20/€22–25

Dom. Latour AC Aloxe-Corton 96

Both fruity and savoury, with vanilla, redcurrant and strawberry fruit on the appealing nose. The palate shows a good balance of bittersweet fruit and firm tannins. Lingering finish. *Gilbeys*

Price	**£17–20/€22–25**
Grape	**Pinot Noir**
Alc/vol	**13.5%**
Food	**Capon**
Drink	**2001–4**

£20–25/€25–32

Dom. du Clos Frantin AC Gevrey-Chambertin 96 ★

If you haven't experienced 'farmyard' aromas in a wine, you should try this! A whole fruit bowl comes through on the palate (plums, cherries, damsons) complemented by oak and hints of farmyard maturity. The finish is long and most enjoyable. *Irish Distillers*

Price	**£20–25/€25–32**
Grape	**Pinot Noir**
Alc/vol	**13%**
Food	**Coq au vin**
Drink	**2001–5**

*Half-way between Beaune and Dijon, **Nuits-St-Georges** lies in the heartland of Burgundy. As well as the basic AC Nuits-St-Georges appellation, there are over thirty Premier Cru sites, including Les St Georges, Les Vaucrains, Les Cailles and Les Pruliers. Nuits-St-George reds (a tiny amount of white is produced) are firm, fairly tannic, with a minerally backbone and solid fruit flavours. Wines should be aged for three to five years to allow flavours to develop and tannins to soften.*

£25–30/€32–40

Dom. Bouchard Père et Fils AC Gevrey-Chambertin 97 ★

Classic style. Starts with a lift of sweet, soft fruit of the forest aromas and continues with intense fruit flavours of red berries, raspberries and strawberries. The structure is strong, with a real backbone of acidity and rounded tannins behind the rich fruit. Great spicy finish. *Findlaters*

Price	**£25–30/€32–40**
Grape	**Pinot Noir**
Alc/vol	**13%**
Food	**Coq au vin**
Drink	**2001–6**

Dom. Bouchard Père et Fils AC Nuits-St-Georges 98 ★

Sweet-smelling aromas of cherry and red berry fruit. Structured palate with a velvety texture and abundant fruit flavours. Excellent nose with a perfumed mélange of dark and red fruits in perfect balance. Superb and drinking well now. *Findlaters*

Price	**£25–30/€32–40**
Grape	**Pinot Noir**
Alc/vol	**13%**
Food	**Epoisses**
Drink	**2001–3**

Faiveley Clos de la Maréchale
AC Nuits-St-Georges 1er Cru 98 ★★

Appealing bouquet of ripe plums, but the palate is the best part. Coffee, vanilla, plums, strawberries, undergrowth and brambles are plentiful. The wine has a perfect balance of alcohol, fruit and tannin. Really lovely—a treat! *Maxxium*

Price	**£25–30/€32–40**
Grape	**Pinot Noir**
Alc/vol	**13%**
Food	**Duck**
Drink	**2001–5**

Faiveley Les Avaux AC Beaune 1er Cru 93

Quite a farmyardy nose, as expected from a wine of this maturity. On the palate the farmyard flavours are taken over by ripe summer fruits, firm tannins and pepper, giving complexity. Good finish. *Maxxium*

Price	**£25–30/€32–40**
Grape	**Pinot Noir**
Alc/vol	**13%**
Food	**Veal**
Drink	**2001–4**

France–Loire

Our tastings this year reflect the diversity of the Loire. The whites are dominated by Muscadet, Sancerre and Pouilly-Fumé. Muscadet used to be very popular in Ireland, but has been overtaken by the crisp whites of the New World. It's worth another look, as it's an ideal wine for seafood, with its crisp acidity and understated fruit.

Much further east, the two regions of Sancerre and Pouilly-Fumé sit beside each other in the flinty soils of the Central Vineyards. Both wines are made from Sauvignon Blanc in that distinctive gooseberry and nettle style and are very similar, though Pouilly-Fumé can be smoky with some gunflint on the nose.

The red version of Sancerre, made with Pinot Noir, featured in our tastings this year, but most Loire reds, such as Saumur-Champigny and Chinon, are based on Cabernet Franc. These wines are medium bodied, with bright strawberry, raspberry and redcurrant fruit and have typical refreshing Loire acidity.

Sparkling Saumur is very popular in France, where around 12 million bottles are produced each year. It's made with Chenin Blanc, Chardonnay and Sauvignon Blanc in dry and off-dry styles and has a favourable price tag.

Loire sweet wines are unique. The high acidity of Chenin Blanc prevents the wines from being cloying and its wonderful fruit intensifies with age. They have rich fruit, crisp acidity and great longevity and are very reasonably priced. Names to look for are Coteaux du Layon, Quarts de Chaume and Bonnezeaux.

White

Under £7/Under €9

Kiwi Cuvée Sauvignon Blanc VdP du Jardin de la France **00**

Green fruit flavours and aromas mark this fresh, summery wine made by winemakers from New Zealand. It has crisp acidity and good length with a nice fruity finish. *Oddbins*

Price	**Under £7/Under €9**
Grape	**Sauvignon Blanc**
Alc/vol	**12%**
Food	**Picnic**
Drink	**2001–2**

Tesco AC Muscadet de Sèvre et Maine Sur Lie **00**

Lemon, lime, nettles and French bread aromas. The palate has a clean, crisp, zingy grapefruit character with an attractive spritz. Long, clean finish. *Tesco*

Price	**Under £7/Under €9**
Grape	**Melon de Bourgogne**
Alc/vol	**12%**
Food	**Mackerel**
Drink	**2001–2**

£7–9/€9–11.50

Ch. de la Roche Sauvignon Sec AC Touraine **00**

Crisp and fresh style, with a green apple and grapefruit character. The high acidity gives a mouth-watering finish. *Bacchus*

Price	**£7–9/€9–11.50**
Grape	**Sauvignon Blanc**
Alc/vol	**12%**
Food	**Goats' cheese**
Drink	**2001–2**

Muscadet de Sèvre et Maine Sur Lie is made from the Muscadet grape and has a maximum alcohol level—12%. 'Sur lie' ('on the lees') means that the wine has been aged on the sediment left behind after fermentation, which gives it a creamy, yeasty flavour and even perhaps a slight spritz. These wines are made to be drunk young and are traditionally partnered with seafood.

Ch. La Noë AC Muscadet de Sèvre et Maine Sur Lie **00**

Green gold in colour. The nose is clean and fresh with lemon zest aromas and some yeasty nuances. Crisp citrus fruit on the palate with lingering green apple and quince length. Long, clean finish. *Irish Distillers*

Price	**£7–9/€9–11.50**
Grape	**Melon de Bourgogne**
Alc/vol	**12%**
Food	**Seafood**
Drink	**2001–2**

Dom. du Landreau-Villages
AC Muscadet de Sèvre et Maine Sur Lie **99**

A very good example of Muscadet Sur Lie. Light on the palate, crisp and refreshing with gentle hints of fruit and subtle yeast flavours. *Dillons*

Price	**£7–9/€9–11.50**
Grape	**Melon de Bourgogne**
Alc/vol	**12%**
Food	**Shellfish**
Drink	**2001–2**

Guy Bossard AC Muscadet de Sèvre et Maine Sur Lie **00**

Lively and zippy. Granny Smith apples coat the palate, with bready flavours judiciously integrated. Dry, good Muscadet style; it can be drunk on its own or with light fish dishes. *Mary Pawle Wines*

Price	**£7–9/€9–11.50**
Grape	**Melon de Bourgogne**
Alc/vol	**12%**
Food	**Prawns**
Drink	**2001–2**

Sancerre wines, which include some of the finest in the Loire, are made from Sauvignon Blanc. The wines have a distinctly herbaceous taste and tend to be high in acidity. They are best drunk young.

Tesco AC Sancerre **00 £/€**

Pungent aromas of green apples, gooseberries, nettles and a hint of cooked celery follow through to the palate, where flavours are quite concentrated. Acidity is refreshing and the finish is crisp and clean. *Tesco*

Price	**£7–9/€9–11.50**
Grape	**Sauvignon Blanc**
Alc/vol	**12.5%**
Food	**Thai**
Drink	**2001–2**

£9–11/€11.50–14

Dom. Doudeau-Léger AC Sancerre **99**

A pronounced personality. Gooseberries and asparagus on the nose are followed by asparagus and mineral flavours with some green apples. *Wicklow Wine Co.*

Price	**£9–11/€11.50–14**
Grape	**Sauvignon Blanc**
Alc/vol	**12.5%**
Food	**Salads**
Drink	**2001–2**

Dom. du Rouet AC Sancerre 00

Well-made wine with a strong fruit character of green fruit and ripe red apples. The fruit on the palate has a slightly herbaceous quality and there is plenty of sharp, mouth-tingling freshness. *Dunnes Stores*

Price	**£9–11/€11.50–14**
Grape	**Sauvignon Blanc**
Alc/vol	**12.5%**
Food	**Seafood**
Drink	**2001–2**

> *Menetou-Salon, made from Sauvignon Blanc, is not as well known as its neighbour Sancerre, so is often cheaper. It also tends to be slightly more floral. The vineyards are based on the same Kimmeridgian-type subsoil as Chablis, which grows Chardonnay.*

Dom. Henry Pellé Morogues AC Menetou-Salon 00 ✓

Elegant style. Gentle nose of attractive green fruit notes with a blackcurrant leaf tinge. On the palate there is good concentration of green-gage fruit, with some softer fruit as well. Plenty of crisp acidity and a fantastic finish. This is a wine to savour. *Findlaters*

Price	**£9–11/€11.50–14**
Grape	**Sauvignon Blanc**
Alc/vol	**12.5%**
Food	**Aperitif**
Drink	**2001–2**

Marquis de Goulaine Cuvée du Millénaire AC Muscadet de Sèvre et Maine Sur Lie 99 £/€

Most unusual and pleasant Muscadet—powerful aromas of apricots and honey. There is a slight spritz on the palate and some honey notes with apricot, lime zest and bready flavours. Rich and elegant finish. *Gilbeys*

Price	**£9–11/€11.50–14**
Grape	**Melon de Bourgogne**
Alc/vol	**12%**
Food	**Seafood**
Drink	**2001–2**

> *Pouilly-Fumé is made from Sauvignon Blanc grapes grown on chalky, stony and flinty soil. The flint produces characteristic smoky ('fumé'), flinty aromas, hence the name of the appellation.*

£11–13/€14–16.50

Barton & Guestier Tradition AC Pouilly-Fumé 98

Complex, nutty nose with developed mature apple aromas. The palate is restrained and subtle, with layers of green fruit flavours, mineral and smoky dimensions, and refined length. *Dillons*

Price	**£11–13/€14–16.50**
Grape	**Sauvignon Blanc**
Alc/vol	**12.5%**
Food	**Sashimi**
Drink	**2001–2**

Ch. de la Gravelle AC Muscadet de Sèvre et Maine Sur Lie 99

A fresh palate, mingling subtle brioche flavours with green apples. It has more weight of fruit on the palate than many Muscadets. A real touch of class. Nice length too. *Febvre*

Price	**£11–13/€14–16.50**
Grape	**Melon de Bourgogne**
Alc/vol	**12%**
Food	**Mussels**
Drink	**2001–2**

Chatelain AC Pouilly-Fumé **99**

Intense, complex nose of ripe, almost tropical green fruits with minerally, honeyed hints. Crisp and fresh, mouth-watering palate. It manages to fill the palate with green apple, gooseberry and rhubarb flavours, yet maintains subtlety and restraint. *Findlaters*

Price	**£11–13/€14–16.50**
Grape	**Sauvignon Blanc**
Alc/vol	**13%**
Food	**Chicken pie**
Drink	**2001–3**

> **Savennières** *is one of the smallest ACs in the Anjou region of the Loire district. Made from Chenin Blanc grapes, it can take up to seven years to reach maturity.*

Dom. des Baumard Les Sables AC Savennières **98** ★

Definite class and elegance. The fruit is still masked by high acidity—at the moment there are lots of lemons, limes and tart green apples. Lengthy, delicate finish. This wine is capable of ageing well and at its current stage needs to be matched with food—something like sweet shellfish, scallops or lobster. *J. S. Woods*

Price	**£11–13/€14–16.50**
Grape	**Chenin Blanc**
Alc/vol	**12%**
Food	**Seafood**
Drink	**2002–5**

Dom. Masson-Blondelet Thauvenay AC Sancerre **00**

A nice, crisp, fruity wine full of green fruit flavours—lemon, lime and hints of apples and grass. Classic style, with very good mouthfeel, texture and length. *Wines Direct*

Price	**£11–13/€14–16.50**
Grape	**Sauvignon Blanc**
Alc/vol	**12.5%**
Food	**Versatile**
Drink	**2001–3**

Drouet Frères Les Charmes Cuvée Prestige
AC Pouilly-Fumé **00**

Smoky aromas, muted mineral tones and lemon/mandarin notes on the nose. Dry, with lively acidity and a mineral edge to the mandarin flavours. The finish is crisp and refreshing. Tasty and a little quirky—aromatic and quite a ripe style. *Cassidy*

Price	**£11–13/€14–16.50**
Grape	**Sauvignon Blanc**
Alc/vol	**12.5%**
Food	**Trout**
Drink	**2001–3**

Fournier AC Sancerre **99**

Traditional Sauvignon Blanc nose—grassy, green fruits, minerals and a touch of maturity. Traditional in style, but with plentiful ripe gooseberries and green fruits. Terrific finish. *TDL*

Price	**£11–13/€14–16.50**
Grape	**Sauvignon Blanc**
Alc/vol	**12.5%**
Food	**Aperitif**
Drink	**2001–2**

£13–15/€16.50–19

Cuvée de Boisfleury AC Pouilly-Fumé **99**

A lovely, layered nose of minerals, green aromas, rich and inviting. Elegant and classy, with great integration of ripe green fruit flavours, even apple pie. Long, crisp finish. A treat. *Febvre*

Price	**£13–15/€16.50–19**
Grape	**Sauvignon Blanc**
Alc/vol	**12.5%**
Food	**Goats' cheese**
Drink	**2001–3**

Dom. Jean-Paul Balland AC Sancerre **00**

Clean, fresh nose of newly cut grass, garden peas and hints of honey. Bracing acidity underpins the ripe melon and green apple fruit on the palate. Pure varietal tones. Long, structured finish. *Taserra*

Price	**£13–15/€16.50–19**
Grape	**Sauvignon Blanc**
Alc/vol	**12.5%**
Food	**Barbecued fish**
Drink	**2001–2**

Fournier Vieilles Vignes AC Sancerre **99**

A scented nose of green fruits and minerals. Layers of elegant green fruit flavours permeated with mineral notes emerge on the palate, which has balanced acidity and a powerful, spicy finish that lingers. *TDL*

Price	**£13–15/€16.50–19**
Grape	**Sauvignon Blanc**
Alc/vol	**12.5%**
Food	**Smoked trout**
Drink	**2001–2**

Genetin AC Pouilly-Fumé **99**

Gooseberries on the nose and on the palate—rich, luscious fruit balanced by lively acidity. Fresh, lingering aftertaste. *Searsons*

Price	**£13–15/€16.50–19**
Grape	**Sauvignon Blanc**
Alc/vol	**12.5%**
Food	**Salmon**
Drink	**2001–2**

£15–17/€19–22

Comte Lafond AC Sancerre **99**

A lively, refreshing wine with a very interesting nose and a crisp palate. The multi-layered nose has lemon, lime, apples, grass, nettles and a hint of melon and cream. Full of green fruit flavours, this is a wine with piercing acidity but a well-rounded, smooth finish. *Gilbeys*

Price	**£15–17/€19–22**
Grape	**Sauvignon Blanc**
Alc/vol	**12.5%**
Food	**Asparagus quiche**
Drink	**2001–3**

De Ladoucette AC Pouilly-Fumé **99**

A crisp, refreshing wine. Lots of clean, green fruit flavours that gel together well—a great way to tease the tastebuds. Abundant lemon, lime and gooseberry fruit with a smoky background, integrated wood flavours, weighty mouthfeel and very long length. *Gilbeys*

Price	**£15–17/€19–22**
Grape	**Sauvignon Blanc**
Alc/vol	**12.5%**
Food	**Goats' cheese**
Drink	**2001–3**

Dom. Vacheron AC Sancerre **99**

You pay more for a Sauvignon Blanc from Sancerre and this wine shows why. The wine is dry, with crisp acidity—lean and green, with plenty of rewarding, intensely flavoured ripe fruit and a long finish. *Febvre*

Price	**£15–17/€19–22**
Grape	**Sauvignon Blanc**
Alc/vol	**12.5%**
Food	**Sole bonne femme**
Drink	**2001–2**

Fournier La Chaudouillonne Grande Cuvée
AC Sancerre **98** ✓

This is a serious and concentrated wine with excellent structure, weighty mouthfeel and pronounced grassy, gooseberry and citrus fruit. Lively and refreshing. *TDL*

Price	**£15–17/€19–22**
Grape	**Sauvignon Blanc**
Alc/vol	**12.5%**
Food	**Goats' cheese**
Drink	**2001–3**

£17–20/€22–25

Pascal Jolivet Les Caillottes AC Sancerre **00** ✓

Classic, stylish. Subtle nuances on the nose. The crisp, zingy palate is dry, with very ripe fruit, intense grassiness and hints of white pepper. It has a long, classic Sauvignon Blanc finish, grassy and crisp. *Maxxium*

Price	**£17–20/€22–25**
Grape	**Sauvignon Blanc**
Alc/vol	**12.5%**
Food	**Seafood**
Drink	**2001–3**

Red

> *Chinon* is made from the Cabernet Franc grape, which ripens better than Cabernet Sauvignon in this cool northern region. A small amount of Cabernet Sauvignon is grown here too, however, and is sometimes added to Chinon. Wines are light bodied, with raspberry and red fruit flavours and a slightly earthy background.

£9–11/€11.50–14

Dom. du Roncée Clos des Marronniers AC Chinon 99

A deep crimson colour. Medium-bodied style with crisp acidity, it has lots of red berry flavour. A fruity yet savoury style red from a cooler climate. *Dunnes Stores*

Price	**£9–11/€11.50–14**
Grape	**Cabernet Franc**
Alc/vol	**12.5%**
Food	**Poultry**
Drink	**2001–3**

£11–13/€14–16.50

Dom. Filliatreau AC Saumur-Champigny 99

A gentle, light, young red that unfolds gradually on the palate, revealing pure blackberry fruit and lots of curranty character. Very elegant style with a flavoursome finish. *Searsons*

Price	**£11–13/€14–16.50**
Grape	**Cabernet Franc**
Alc/vol	**12.5%**
Food	**Veal**
Drink	**2001–3**

£15–17/€19–22

Couly-Dutheil Clos de l' Echo AC Chinon 96 £/€

Sweet, vegetal aromas of blackcurrants and blackberries with a leathery influence. Quite a bit of power on the palate, with elegant, concentrated strawberry flavours, crisp, balancing acidity and just the right degree of tannin. *Le Caveau*

Price	**£15–17/€19–22**
Grape	**Cabernet Franc**
Alc/vol	**12.5%**
Food	**Duck**
Drink	**2001–3**

Dom. Vacheron AC Sancerre 98

Pleasing nose which opens out gradually—fruit compote, redcurrants, vegetal notes and then clear Pinot fruit on the palate. A Burgundy this good would cost twice the price. *Febvre*

Price	**£15–17/€19–22**
Grape	**Pinot Noir**
Alc/vol	**12.5%**
Food	**Roast poultry**
Drink	**2001–2**

France–Rhône

The Rhône Valley is divided into two broad areas, north and south, with quite different terrains, weather and grape varieties—and they produce very different wines. Northern wines are based mainly on Syrah, which makes dark, tannic wines that traditionally required long ageing. Wines such as Côte Rôtie and Hermitage need several years' bottle ageing, though St Joseph and Crozes-Hermitage are more accessible in youth.

Much softer wines come from the warmer, sunnier southern Rhône. The main grape here is Grenache, which thrives in the baking heat, making approachable wines with earthy, slightly jammy fruit and quite high alcohol. Southern Rhône wines also differ in that they are usually made from a more diverse blend of grape varieties, principally Grenache, Mourvèdre, Cinsault, Carignan and, increasingly, Syrah.

The northern stalwarts of Hermitage, Crozes-Hermitage and St Joseph, several of which were from the outstanding 99 vintage, showed well, with Vidal-Fleury earning a star for their 94 Côte Rôtie.

The majority of reds, however, were from the south, with a terrific showing from Châteauneuf-du-Pape. The tasters found the wines from the fabulous 98 vintage lived up to the hype—wines were powerful and packed with black fruit and spice.

Côtes du Rhône and neighbouring appellations stood out. Wines were approachable and well priced, with firm black fruit flavours and easy tannins. Whites, which are slightly overshadowed by reds, deserve more attention. They are reasonably priced and their peach and melon fruit flavours go well with a variety of foods.

As a region, the Rhône is doing very well, with sales up 29 per cent in the year 1998/9. Both 98 and 99 were excellent vintages and 00 looks promising as well.

White

Under £7/Under €9

Cuvée Orélie VdP des Coteaux de l'Ardèche 00 £/€

Light and charming, with peach, apple and lime fruit and refreshing acidity.
Wicklow Wine Co.

Price	**Under £7/Under €9**
Region	**Southern Rhône**
Grape	**Chard/Sauv Blanc**
Alc/vol	**12%**
Food	**Picnic**
Drink	**2001–2**

> **White Côtes du Rhône** *is usually made from a blend of white grapes—Clairette, Roussanne and Bourboulenc, although it may also be made from other grapes, for example Viognier.*

£7–9/€9–11.50

Alain Jaume AC Côtes du Rhône 99

Apple and apricot flavours, beautifully stylish with bite and flavour. Very versatile and satisfying. Ideal party wine. *Mitchells*

Price	**£7–9/€9–11.50**
Region	**Southern Rhône**
Grape	**Grenache Blanc/ Clairette/Viognier**
Alc/vol	**13%**
Food	**Party**
Drink	**2001–2**

Ch. de Ruth AC Côtes du Rhône 99

Appealing nose of ripe melon, pineapple, dried figs and dried apricots, following through to a nice weighty palate of melon and citrus fruit, with satisfying length and balance. *Dillons*

Price	**£7–9/€9–11.50**
Region	**Southern Rhône**
Grape	**Clairette/Roussanne/ Bourboulenc**
Alc/vol	**13%**
Food	**Chicken pie**
Drink	**2001–3**

Dom. des Anges AC Côtes du Ventoux 00

Easy-drinking, attractive style with apple fruit and a streak of acidity. Satisfying, dry finish. Versatile food wine. *O'Briens*

Price	**£7–9/€9–11.50**
Region	**Southern Rhône**
Grape	**Marsanne/Roussanne/ Bourboulenc/ Grenache Blanc**
Alc/vol	**13.5%**
Food	**Versatile**
Drink	**2001–2**

Dom. Les Terrasses d'Eole AC Côtes du Ventoux 00

Minerals and peach fruit on the nose. Deliciously fresh on the palate with heaps of ripe melon and peach fruit and a lovely peppery finish. *Nectar Wines*

Price	**£7–9/€9–11.50**
Region	**Southern Rhône**
Grape	**Clairette/Bourboulenc/ Grenache Blanc**
Alc/vol	**13%**
Food	**Seafood**
Drink	**2001–2**

La Chasse du Pape AC Côtes du Rhône 00

A good all-round nutty style of Côtes du Rhône with peppery papaya on the palate and warm Mediterranean alcohol. This is a classic food wine with a peachy, floral nose, harmonious and subtle, with lingering flavours of melons and apples. *Dillons*

Price	**£7–9/€9–11.50**
Region	**Southern Rhône**
Grape	**Grenache/Clairette/ Bourboulenc**
Alc/vol	**12.5%**
Food	**Versatile**
Drink	**2001–3**

La Vieille Ferme AC Côtes du Lubéron 00

Right on the edge of the southern Rhône, the Côtes du Lubéron appellation uses a mix of traditional grapes. This blend gives the wine a floral nose, with rose petals to the fore. It has good peachy ripe fruit and fresh acidity on the palate. *Allied Drinks*

Price	**£7–9/€9–11.50**
Region	**Southern Rhône**
Grape	**Grenache Blanc/ Roussanne/Ugni Blanc**
Alc/vol	**12%**
Food	**Poached salmon**
Drink	**2001–2**

£9–11/€11.50–14

Guigal AC Côtes du Rhône 98 £/€

Spicy aromas with some floral hints. The lively palate is dry, with balanced acidity and soft, solid fruit—peaches, apricots, cream and a touch of grass. Spicy end feel.
Barry & Fitzwilliam

Price	**£9–11/€11.50–14**
Region	**Southern Rhône**
Grape	**Bourboulenc/ Roussanne/Viognier/ Grenache Blanc/ Clairette**
Alc/vol	**13%**
Food	**Aperitif**
Drink	**2001–2**

Louis Latour Grand Ardèche Chardonnay
VdP des Coteaux de l'Ardèche **98**

Aged in French oak barrels, which gives a nutty, toffee apple hint to the stewed apple and melon aromas. The palate has fresh, round, nutty, spicy green apple fruit. Crisp and fresh with a good finish. *Gilbeys*

Price	**£9–11/€11.50–14**
Region	**Southern Rhône**
Grape	**Chardonnay**
Alc/vol	**13%**
Food	**Fish**
Drink	**2001–3**

Perrin Réserve AC Côtes du Rhône **99**

Made by the Perrin brothers of Ch. de Beaucastel, one of the foremost Châteauneuf-du-Pape estates, this white Côtes du Rhône is a golden colour with a waxy, spicy nose. The palate is clean and minerally with a rich texture and a long, flavoursome finish. A wine of individuality and some style. *Allied Drinks*

Price	**£9–11/€11.50–14**
Region	**Southern Rhône**
Grape	**Grenache Blanc/ Bourboulenc/ Marsanne/Roussanne/ Viognier**
Alc/vol	**13%**
Food	**Shellfish**
Drink	**2001–2**

£11–13/€14–16.50

Dom. Grand Veneur Blanc de Viognier
AC Côtes du Rhône **99**

Aromas of apricots and nuts are followed by lovely apricot, peach and pear flavours with a touch of spiciness. *Mitchells*

Price	**£11–13/€14–16.50**
Region	**Southern Rhône**
Grape	**Viognier**
Alc/vol	**13%**
Food	**Aperitif**
Drink	**2001–2**

£15–17/€19–22

Bosquet des Papes AC Châteauneuf-du-Pape **98** ✓

Traditional methods and older vines have produced a wine with a mature and developed nose, showing spice, toasted almonds and some strawberry and herbal aromas. The densely textured palate has ripe fruit and spice with well-integrated oak and a long finish. This is a wine for rich food. *Le Caveau*

Price	**£15–17/€19–22**
Region	**Southern Rhône**
Grape	**Grenache Blanc/ Clairette/Bourboulenc**
Alc/vol	**13%**
Food	**Bouillabaisse**
Drink	**2001–3**

Dom. de Nalys AC Châteauneuf-du-Pape **98**

Super, elegant, concentrated nose—slightly nutty and minerally, with fresh, honeyed green fruits and a floral note. The palate is dry and minty with slightly spicy and herbal flavours, with tangy green fruits giving balance. *TDL*

Price	**£15–17/€19–22**
Region	**Southern Rhône**
Grape	**Grenache Blanc blend**
Alc/vol	**13%**
Food	**Paella**
Drink	**2001–3**

Red

Under £7/Under €9

Le Vigneron Ardèchois Cuvée Prestige Merlot
VdP des Coteaux de l'Ardèche **99 £/€ ✓**

Bags of chunky, jammy summer fruit on the nose. Ripe, concentrated, spicy liquorice and baked bramble fruits on the palate. A real winter warmer. Great depth of flavour for the price. *Wicklow Wine Co.*

Price	**Under £7/Under €9**
Region	**Southern Rhône**
Grape	**Merlot**
Alc/vol	**13.5%**
Food	**Spaghetti Bolognese**
Drink	**2001–3**

Le Vigneron Ardèchois Merlot VdP des Coteaux de l'Ardèche **99 £/€**

Great Monday night wine, with wonderful aromas of violets and cherries. Flavours on the palate don't disappoint—cherry, raspberry and loganberry fruits carry right through to a decent finish. *Wicklow Wine Co.*

Price	**Under £7/Under €9**
Region	**Southern Rhône**
Grape	**Merlot**
Alc/vol	**12%**
Food	**Pizza**
Drink	**2001–2**

Côtes du Rhône-Villages wines require lower yields from the vineyard and stipulate a minimum of 12.5% alcohol for reds, compared to higher yields and an 11% minimum for basic **Côtes du Rhône** wines. Villages red wines must contain a maximum of 65% Grenache and a minimum of 25% Syrah, Cinsault and/or Mourvèdre, which are seen as 'improver' grapes. No such restrictions apply to basic Côtes du Rhône reds.

Tesco AC Côtes du Rhône-Villages **00**

Smoky, earthy stewed fruits, yet quite tangy. Stewed fruit comes through again on the juicy, soft palate, but with a nice cut of acidity. Typical Côtes du Rhône at a very reasonable price. *Tesco*

Price	**Under £7/Under €9**
Region	**Southern Rhône**
Grape	**Grenache/Cinsault/ Syrah/Mourvèdre**
Alc/vol	**13%**
Food	**Macaroni cheese**
Drink	**2001–3**

£7–9/€9–11.50

Berrys' Own Selection Côtes du Rhône
AC Côtes du Rhône **99 £/€**

Made by Michel Chapoutier, this plummy, rich wine has aromas of stewed black fruits. The palate has a good concentration of soft ripe fruits in a lovely tangy style. Refreshing, yet rich and smooth in a restrained way. *Fields*

Price	**£7–9/€9–11.50**
Region	**Southern Rhône**
Grape	**Grenache/Syrah**
Alc/vol	**13.5%**
Food	**Versatile**
Drink	**2001–3**

Cave de Rasteau AC Côtes du Rhône **98**

Elegant aromas with a good concentration of ripe summer fruits on the nose. Plenty of flavours on the smooth, round palate of plummy, spicy, figgy fruit. Balanced and weighty style with a tasty finish. *Peter Dalton*

Price	**£7–9/€9–11.50**
Region	**Southern Rhône**
Grape	**Grenache/Cinsault/ Syrah/Mourvèdre**
Alc/vol	**14%**
Food	**Casseroles, Cheddar**
Drink	**2001–2**

> **St Joseph** *is the second-largest AC in the northern Rhône. Up to 10% of the white grape Marsanne may be added to Syrah at the fermentation stage to soften and add perfume to the wine.*

Cave de Tain l'Hermitage Nobles Rives AC St Joseph **99 £/€**

Nose of spice and black fruit. Lots of lively summer fruits, black fruits and spice on the palate. Robuts tannins. Would benefit from decanting. *Dunnes Stores*

Price	**£7–9/€9–11.50**
Region	**Northern Rhône**
Grape	**Syrah (90% min.)**
Alc/vol	**12.5%**
Food	**Steak**
Drink	**2001–2**

Ch. de Bastet Cuvée Ste Nelly AC Côtes du Rhône **00 £/€** 🌾

Fruity red berry nose with a hint of spice. With a bite of tannin that will soften over 2002, it offers a warm, supple palate of rich red fruit flavours and spice. *Mary Pawle Wines*

Price	**£7–9/€9–11.50**
Region	**Southern Rhône**
Grape	**Grenache/Cinsault/ Syrah/Mourvèdre**
Alc/vol	**13%**
Food	**Pasta**
Drink	**2001–3**

Ch. de Ruth AC Côtes du Rhône **98**

Slightly jammy bramble nose and soft damson and summer fruit flavours make for an easy-drinking style. Don't worry too much about a food match—this will drink happily on its own. Savoury finish. *Dillons*

Price	**£7–9/€9–11.50**
Region	**Southern Rhône**
Grape	**Grenache/Cinsault/ Syrah/Mourvèdre**
Alc/vol	**13.5%**
Food	**Versatile**
Drink	**2001–2**

Cuvée de l'Ancêtre, Rot' de Schurchill VdP des Comtés Rhodaniens **99**

This wine has fruit of the forest and strawberry aromas and a palate of brambles and pepper. With its gentle tannins and long finish, it's very easy to drink. *Wicklow Wine Co.*

Price	**£7–9/€9–11.50**
Region	**Southern Rhône**
Grape	**Cabernet/Merlot**
Alc/vol	**12%**
Food	**Traditional**
Drink	**2001–2**

Dom. Les Terrasses d'Eole AC Côtes du Ventoux **00**

Very typical of the southern Rhône, with its spice and black summer fruit flavours. Well-rounded tannins give good structure to this supple, easy-drinking wine. Peppery finish. *Nectar Wines*

Price	**£7–9/€9–11.50**
Region	**Southern Rhône**
Grape	**Grenache/Syrah**
Alc/vol	**13.5%**
Food	**Pork**
Drink	**2001–2**

Gabriel Meffre La Chasse du Pape Réserve
AC Côtes du Rhône **99**

Aromas of raspberries and smoke. Deliciously soft fruit flavours of raspberries and dark cherries with an attractive hit of warm, peppery spice. Finishes nicely. Great with a picnic platter of mixed salami. *Dillons*

Price	**£7–9/€9–11.50**
Region	**Southern Rhône**
Grape	**Syrah/Grenache/ Cinsault**
Alc/vol	**12.5%**
Food	**Salami**
Drink	**2001–3**

Le Vigneron Ardèchois Cuvée Prestige
VdP des Coteaux de l'Ardèche **98**

Attractive red berry and liquorice aromas, even a hint of nuts. The palate has spicy, jammy red berry flavours that go on to a flavoursome finish. *Wicklow Wine Co.*

Price	**£7–9/€9–11.50**
Region	**Southern Rhône**
Grape	**Cabernet/Merlot/ Syrah/Grenache**
Alc/vol	**12%**
Food	**Beefburgers**
Drink	**2001–2**

Louis Bernard AC Côtes du Rhône-Villages **98**

Warm aromas of blueberries and ripe summer fruits. Good weight of red cherry fruit on the palate. Light, easy drinking, with soft tannins. Ideal picnic or lunch wine. *O'Briens*

Price	**£7–9/€9–11.50**
Region	**Southern Rhône**
Grape	**Grenache/Cinsault/ Syrah/Mourvèdre**
Alc/vol	**13%**
Food	**Lunch**
Drink	**2001–2**

Mas de Libian AC Côtes du Rhône **98**

Packs quite a punch from beginning to end. Very attractive, complex nose of wood, spice, leather and blackcurrant. Lashings of spice and very ripe damson fruit on the palate and a big, chewy mouthfeel with vanilla and black pepper. *Nectar Wines*

Price	**£7–9/€9–11.50**
Region	**Southern Rhône**
Grape	**Grenache/Cinsault/ Syrah/Mourvèdre**
Alc/vol	**13%**
Food	**Game, casseroles**
Drink	**2001–2**

Parallèle 45 AC Côtes du Rhône **99 £/€**

Fragrant lily aromas lie behind the jammy blackcurrants and black cherries on the nose. The palate has lovely power and concentration, yet is very smooth—a lovely combination of power and elegance. *Gilbeys*

Price	**£7–9/€9–11.50**
Region	**Southern Rhône**
Grape	**Grenache/Cinsault/ Syrah/Mourvèdre**
Alc/vol	**13%**
Food	**Roast beef, roast pork**
Drink	**2001–2**

Vidal-Fleury AC Côtes du Rhône 98 £/€

Nice complexity on the nose—leather, plums, spice and succulent dried fruits. Black pepper and spice on the palate with some cherry joining the dried fruits. Full and rich but with warm alcohol and a good streak of acidity.
Irish Distillers

Price	**£7–9/€9–11.50**
Region	**Southern Rhône**
Grape	**Grenache/Cinsault/ Syrah/Mourvèdre**
Alc/vol	**12.5%**
Food	**Steak and onions**
Drink	**2001–2**

£9–11/€11.50–14

Alain Jaume AC Vacqueyras 98

Very seductive on the nose with its wafts of coffee, caramel and spice. Equally complex on the palate, but tannins will need some taming.
Mitchells

Price	**£9–11/€11.50–14**
Region	**Southern Rhône**
Grape	**Grenache/Syrah/ Mourvèdre**
Alc/vol	**13%**
Food	**Peppered steak**
Drink	**2001–4**

Cave de Rasteau AC Côtes du Rhône-Villages 99 ✓

Packed with brooding dark fruit and spice. Wonderful rich aromas of ripe autumn fruits, hints of herbs and robust flavours of spice, liquorice and dark cherries with a cedar backdrop. Vibrant, with a flavoursome finish. *Peter Dalton*

Price	**£9–11/€11.50–14**
Region	**Southern Rhône**
Grape	**Grenache/Cinsault/ Syrah/Mourvèdre**
Alc/vol	**14%**
Food	**Bean casserole**
Drink	**2001–3**

Dom. St Gayan AC Côtes du Rhône-Villages Rasteau **98 £/€**

Interesting aromas of roses, red fruits, spices and herbs. The palate is full of rich cherry fruit with a peppery overtone. Good long finish. *Searsons*

Price	**£9–11/€11.50–14**
Region	**Southern Rhône**
Grape	**Grenache/Cinsault/ Syrah/Mourvèdre**
Alc/vol	**14%**
Food	**Cheese**
Drink	**2001–3**

Guigal AC Côtes du Rhône **98**

A very rich nose of ripe black fruit. On the palate there is a good balance of summery dark fruits with a slightly earthy character. Firm tannins and a complex finish. *Barry & Fitzwilliam*

Price	**£9–11/€11.50–14**
Region	**Southern Rhône**
Grape	**Grenache/Cinsault/ Syrah/Mourvèdre**
Alc/vol	**13%**
Food	**Liver and onions**
Drink	**2001–2**

Louis Bernard AC Vacqueyras **98 £/€**

A gorgeous wine, with heavenly aromas of raisined fruit, spice, wood smoke, toffee, leather and vanilla. Just as good on the palate. Masses of rich, ripe plum fruit are layered with spice, giving a long, complex, peppery finish. Very good indeed. *O'Briens*

Price	**£9–11/€11.50–14**
Region	**Southern Rhône**
Grape	**Grenache/Syrah/ Mourvèdre**
Alc/vol	**13%**
Food	**Veal**
Drink	**2001–3**

Perrin Nature AC Côtes du Rhône **99 £/€** 🌱

On the nose there are black fruits, pepper, leather and smoke. The peppery palate has generous plums, cherries and black fruit with leather and smoke elements. Classically French, this is a stylish wine. *Allied Drinks*

Price	**£9–11/€11.50–14**
Region	**Southern Rhône**
Grape	**Grenache/Syrah**
Alc/vol	**13%**
Food	**Versatile**
Drink	**2001–3**

Perrin Réserve AC Côtes du Rhône **99**

This wine is made in a typical Côtes du Rhône style. Fruits of the forest with an earthy influence on the nose follow through on the palate. Lovely winter wine—easy drinking and a good accompaniment to bean or meat casseroles. *Allied Drinks*

Price	**£9–11/€11.50–14**
Region	**Southern Rhône**
Grape	**Grenache/Cinsault/ Syrah/Mourvèdre**
Alc/vol	**13%**
Food	**Meat casserole**
Drink	**2001–2**

Plan Pégau D. du Pégau VdT nv **£/€**

A very user-friendly wine that delivers. Fruity on the nose, with a palate of spicy, smoky raspberry with cranberry undertones. Elegant and very drinkable. *J. S. Woods*

Price	**£9–11/€11.50–14**
Region	**Southern Rhône**
Grape	**Mainly Grenache**
Alc/vol	**12.5%**
Food	**Lasagne, cheese**
Drink	**2001–2**

Verget du Sud AC Côtes du Lubéron 98

Warm, spicy black cherry and blackcurrant fruit, with a bitter cherry aftertaste. Has the structure to improve over the next two years and at this stage will benefit from decanting. *J. S. Woods*

Price	**£9–11/€11.50–14**
Region	**Southern Rhône**
Grape	**Grenache/Syrah/ Mourvèdre**
Alc/vol	**13%**
Food	**Duck confit**
Drink	**2001–4**

Vidal-Fleury AC Vacqueyras 98 ★

Subtle yet concentrated aromas of ripe, spicy cherries and figs. The palate is packed full of ripe black tarry fruit flavours, and yet more cherries. Lovely long finish. One to savour. *Irish Distillers*

Price	**£9–11/€11.50–14**
Region	**Southern Rhône**
Grape	**Grenache/Syrah/ Mourvèdre**
Alc/vol	**12.5%**
Food	**Lamb tagine**
Drink	**2001–3**

£11–13/€14–16.50

Alain Jaume AC St Joseph 99

A good example of a refined Syrah from the northern Rhône, with a flavoursome mouthful of fruits of the forest, blackcurrants, spice, vanilla and chocolate. Firm tannins give it structure. Good wine for red meats. *Mitchells*

Price	**£11–13/€14–16.50**
Region	**Northern Rhône**
Grape	**Syrah (90% min.)**
Alc/vol	**13%**
Food	**Lamb casserole**
Drink	**2002–4**

Ch. du Trignon AC Gigondas 98 £/€

Forceful open style, richly flavoured with spice and black fruit. It has great structure, with crisp acidity and firm tannins, but it's very easy to drink. *River Wines*

Price	**£11–13/€14–16.50**
Region	**Southern Rhône**
Grape	**Grenache/Syrah/ Mourvèdre**
Alc/vol	**14%**
Food	**Rabbit**
Drink	**2001–3**

Chapoutier Les Meysonniers AC Crozes-Hermitage 98

Good Crozes-Hermitage, with typical fruit and style. Some rosemary comes through on the nose along with the blackcurrants and red-currants. The palate is full of lively red berry flavours with a hint of pepper and spice and the finish is long, spicy and oaky. *Grants*

Price	**£11–13/€14–16.50**
Region	**Northern Rhône**
Grape	**Syrah (75% min.)**
Alc/vol	**12.5%**
Food	**Roasts, grills**
Drink	**2001–4**

Dom. Daniel et Denis Alary AC Cairanne 99

A young wine with a bright future. With its spicy, herby nose and damson and prune fla-vours, it's approachable now but will improve for the next year or two. *J. S. Woods*

Price	**£11–13/€14–16.50**
Region	**Southern Rhône**
Grape	**Grenache/Syrah/ Mourvèdre**
Alc/vol	**13.5%**
Food	**Versatile**
Drink	**2001–3**

Dom. des Remizières Cuvée Particulière
AC Crozes-Hermitage **99** ✓

Classic Rhône Syrah aromas of meat, cherries, raspberries and a herbal note. Very good structure—juicy black fruit, undergrowth and mushroomy tones are underpinned by firm, serious tannins and an acid balance. Brilliant food wine. *Wines Direct*

Price	**£11–13/€14–16.50**
Region	**Northern Rhône**
Grape	**Syrah (75% min.)**
Alc/vol	**12.5%**
Food	**Steak**
Drink	**2002–4**

---

*Up to thirteen grape varieties are permitted in the **Châteauneuf-du-Pape** blend (some of them white). The style is full bodied and high in alcohol, 12.5% being the minimum volume permitted.*

Dom. Roger Perrin AC Châteauneuf-du-Pape **99 £/€**

Perfumed and peppery with black berry flavours and firmish tannins, this is a food-friendly wine. Full bodied with a lovely spicy finish. *Dunnes Stores*

Price	**£11–13/€14–16.50**
Region	**Southern Rhône**
Grape	**Châteauneuf varieties**
Alc/vol	**14%**
Food	**Spinach & cheese pie**
Drink	**2001–3**

Gabriel Meffre Laurus AC Crozes-Hermitage **97**

From the fragrant nose of violets and raspberries through the creamy, oaky, strawberry palate and the long finish, this is a lovely wine—full of fruit with excellent structure and balance. *Dillons*

Price	**£11–13/€14–16.50**
Region	**Northern Rhône**
Grape	**Syrah (75% min.)**
Alc/vol	**12.5%**
Food	**Cheese**
Drink	**2001–4**

Jean-Luc Colombo Les Abeilles AC Côtes du Rhône **98**

Lots of rich berry fruits on the nose follow through to the palate with extra spice and a hint of chocolate. Soft, rounded tannins are well integrated with the fruit. Long, pleasant finish. *Woodford Bourne*

Price	**£11–13/€14–16.50**
Region	**Southern Rhône**
Grape	**Grenache/Cinsault/ Syrah/Mourvèdre**
Alc/vol	**13%**
Food	**Stuffed pork**
Drink	**2001–2**

£13–15/€16.50–19

Dom. de la Mordorée AC Lirac **99**

Composed and well blended in a very subtle and appealing style. Good, rounded black cherry flavours mingling with cedar hints and soft cigar box notes. Velvety finish. *J. S. Woods*

Price	**£13–15/€16.50–19**
Region	**Southern Rhône**
Grape	**Grenache/Cinsault/ Mourvèdre/Syrah**
Alc/vol	**13%**
Food	**Moussaka**
Drink	**2001–3**

139

Dom. Jérome Quiot AC Châteauneuf-du-Pape **99**

Aromas of cooked fruit lead to a medley of ripe black fruit flavours on the palate. The finish has a spicy, peppery dimension. Very approachable and ideal with Sunday lunch. *Searsons*

Price	**£13–15/€16.50–19**
Region	**Southern Rhône**
Grape	**Châteauneuf varieties**
Alc/vol	**13.5%**
Food	**Traditional**
Drink	**2001–2**

Dom. St Gayan AC Gigondas **97**

Rich and classy, a heavyweight with luscious fruit flavours—blackcurrants, blackberries—and tobacco. Good acidity. Tannins are still fairly firm and the wine will benefit from decanting. *Searsons*

Price	**£13–15/€16.50–19**
Region	**Southern Rhône**
Grape	**Grenache/Syrah/ Mourvèdre**
Alc/vol	**14%**
Food	**Pork with mushrooms**
Drink	**2001–3**

Gabriel Meffre Laurus AC Gigondas **96**

Intense ripe bramble fruits and some toffee aromas to this weighty, mature wine. Enjoy the rich palate of flavours here—dried fruits, smooth chocolate and coffee beans. The palate is mouth-filling but elegant and the finish is rich. *Dillons*

Price	**£13–15/€16.50–19**
Region	**Southern Rhône**
Grape	**Grenache/Syrah/ Mourvèdre**
Alc/vol	**13%**
Food	**Pheasant**
Drink	**2001–2**

Le Grand Pompée AC St Joseph **99**

A big, juicy, robust wine. Rich, inviting aromas of dark, brooding fruit. Black, juicy berries and chocolate on the palate. Forceful tannins and a medium-long finish. This is a very satisfying, winter-warm, spicy wine. *Gilbeys*

Price	**£13–15/€16.50–19**
Region	**Northern Rhône**
Grape	**Syrah (90% min.)**
Alc/vol	**13%**
Food	**Turkey, ham**
Drink	**2001–4**

Louis Bernard AC Gigondas **98**

Restrained nose. Delicate plum, strawberry and redcurrant fruit flavours on the palate. Deliciously rich, combining power and elegance. One bottle would not be enough! A wonderfully versatile food wine. *O'Briens*

Price	**£13–15/€16.50–19**
Region	**Southern Rhône**
Grape	**Grenache/Syrah/ Mourvèdre**
Alc/vol	**13.5%**
Food	**Versatile**
Drink	**2001–4**

Paul Jaboulet Ainé Pierre Aiguille AC Gigondas **99**

Still needing time to mature, this wine has a nose of port-like raisined fruit with plum, spice and black fruits on the palate. Tannins are still very firm, but this serious wine will reward TLC for a year or two. *Gilbeys*

Price	**£13–15/€16.50–19**
Region	**Southern Rhône**
Grape	**Grenache/Syrah/ Mourvèdre**
Alc/vol	**14.5%**
Food	**Rack of lamb**
Drink	**2001–4**

£15–17/€19–22

Cave de Tain l'Hermitage Nobles Rives AC Hermitage **98** ✓

A powerful wine with rich red berry fruits. Still quite young, it has a great weight of fruit and flavour, filling a broad palate. A classic style. If you like firm, gripping tannins, drink it now, but decant it first. It will continue to soften and improve over the next few years. *Dunnes Stores*

Price	**£15–17/€19–22**
Region	**Northern Rhône**
Grape	**Syrah (85% min.)**
Alc/vol	**13%**
Food	**Rich beef casseroles**
Drink	**2001–4**

Ch. Gigognan Vigne du Dauphin
AC Châteauneuf-du-Pape **98**

From a fantastic vintage, this wine has earthy aromas of blackberries, plums, forest fruits and a touch of yoghurt. The palate is rich and ripe, with inky, blackberry, plum and strawberry fruit with vegetal and leather notes. Super-ripe, with lots of complexity. *Taserra*

Price	**£15–17/€19–22**
Region	**Southern Rhône**
Grape	**Châteauneuf varieties**
Alc/vol	**13.5%**
Food	**Steak in red wine sauce**
Drink	**2001–4**

Dom. de Nalys AC Châteauneuf-du-Pape **98**

This is a wonderful example of the 98 vintage. It has a perfumed, fruity style, with blackberries, pepper and toast. With its sweet, voluptuous fruit, it's too easy to drink—one for the hedonist. *TDL*

Price	**£15–17/€19–22**
Region	**Southern Rhône**
Grape	**Châteauneuf varieties**
Alc/vol	**13.5%**
Food	**Braised beef**
Drink	**2001–3**

Dom. Grand Veneur AC Châteauneuf-du-Pape **98** ✓

Black Forest gâteau in a glass! Very tight flavours that work well together—black cherry and blackcurrant with fig and strawberry. A restrained note of gingerbread spices complements the fruit of this elegant wine. *Mitchells*

Price	**£15–17/€19–22**
Region	**Southern Rhône**
Grape	**Châteauneuf varieties**
Alc/vol	**14%**
Food	**Roast beef**
Drink	**2001–5**

Montirius AC Gigondas **98**

Very elegant and complex aromas of game, meat, Christmas cake and leather. Plum and blackcurrant fruit overlain with pepper, a firm backbone of tannin and wonderful length. Great depth and interest. *Bubble Brothers*

Price	**£15–17/€19–22**
Region	**Southern Rhône**
Grape	**Grenache/Mourvèdre**
Alc/vol	**14%**
Food	**Steak**
Drink	**2001–3**

£17–20/€22–25

Chapoutier La Bernardine AC Châteauneuf-du-Pape **98** **£/€**

A serious wine, with red/black cherry and plum fruit, black pepper and spice. This lovely wine, made in a big, forward style with 100% Grenache, has elegance, class, a wonderful finish and a long life ahead of it. *Grants*

Price	**£17–20/€22–25**
Region	**Southern Rhône**
Grape	**Grenache**
Alc/vol	**14%**
Food	**Game**
Drink	**2001–5**

Dom. du Cayron AC Gigondas **99** ✓

Glorious, smooth wine, densely packed with
black cherry, chocolate, raisins and figs. It has a
wonderfully rich mouthfeel that just seems to
go on and on. Very fine. *J. S. Woods*

Price	**£17–20/€22–25**
Region	**Southern Rhône**
Grape	**Grenache/Syrah/ Mourvèdre**
Alc/vol	**14%**
Food	**Traditional**
Drink	**2001–2**

Dom. Jerôme Quiot Les Combes d'Arnevel
AC Châteauneuf-du-Pape **98**

Nose of spice and bramble fruits, but concentrated Morello cherries, plums and even a hint
of wild strawberries, creamy chocolate and coffee on the palate. Drinking nicely now, the wine
has a flavoursome finish. *Febvre*

Price	**£17–20/€22–25**
Region	**Southern Rhône**
Grape	**Châteauneuf varieties**
Alc/vol	**13.5%**
Food	**Beef casserole with walnuts**
Drink	**2001–3**

Dom. La Roquette AC Châteauneuf-du-Pape **96** ★

If you like big, rich wine that packs an elegant
punch, this fine Châteauneuf-du-Pape is the
wine for you. Intense aromas of blackcurrants
and figs. Complex, earthy, seriously concentrated palate of dates, Oxo, smoke, spice, dark
cherries, damsons, black fruits and figs. Long,
warm finish. *Findlaters*

Price	**£17–20/€22–25**
Region	**Southern Rhône**
Grape	**Châteauneuf varieties**
Alc/vol	**14%**
Food	**Duck**
Drink	**2001–4**

Gabriel Meffre Laurus AC Châteauneuf-du-Pape **97**

Elegant, light, scented nose of strawberries,
toffee and figs. Developing palate of sweet
strawberries, caramel and spice. Smooth and
intriguing finish. An elegant wine of potential.
Dillons

Price	**£17–20/€22–25**
Region	**Southern Rhône**
Grape	**Châteauneuf varieties**
Alc/vol	**14%**
Food	**Steak and kidney pie**
Drink	**2002–4**

£20–25/€25–32

Château-Fortia AC Châteauneuf-du-Pape **98**

Leafy aromas of blackberries and hints of clove.
The palate has heaps of ripe dark fruit, crisp
acidity and firm tannins, and is quite spicy. This
wine is still very young, but can be drunk now,
preferably with food. *Taserra*

Price	**£20–25/€25–32**
Region	**Southern Rhône**
Grape	**Châteauneuf varieties**
Alc/vol	**14%**
Food	**Cassoulet**
Drink	**2001–3**

Dom. du Grand Tinel AC Châteauneuf-du-Pape 98 ★

A heady, spicy nose with forest fruits. Powerful in a refined way, the palate, which reveals itself slowly, has a classic style of blackberry fruit and typical Rhône pepperiness. The pure fruit character of the wine reflects the tremendous vintage of 98. *J. S. Woods*

Price	£20–25/€25–32
Region	Southern Rhône
Grape	Châteauneuf varieties
Alc/vol	14%
Food	Meat casseroles, cheese
Drink	2001–4

Dom. Monpertuis AC Châteauneuf-du-Pape 98

Plenty of aromas of black and dried fruits, warm chocolate, coffee beans and lots of spice. The palate, which will develop further, has inky concentration, with spicy cherry flavours and gripping tannins. Patience—a little wait should reward the buyer. *United Beverages*

Price	£20–25/€25–32
Region	Southern Rhône
Grape	Châteauneuf varieties
Alc/vol	13.8%
Food	Roast duck, Chateaubriand
Drink	2002–4

Paul Jaboulet Aîné Les Cèdres
AC Châteauneuf-du-Pape 98

An opportunity to celebrate the great 98 vintage before it disappears from the shelves. Made in a traditional style with some subtlety, the wine has a lovely fragrance, followed by red fruits and a touch of spice, leather and fruit cake on the palate. *Gilbeys*

Price	£20–25/€25–32
Region	Southern Rhône
Grape	Châteauneuf varieties
Alc/vol	13.5%
Food	Roast goose
Drink	2001–3

Vidal-Fleury AC Côte Rôtie 94 ★

Fragrant aromas of smoky black fruits, plums, pepper and liquorice deepen into flavours of plums, cherries, cinnamon, cloves and lemon peel. Tannins are still quite firm, fruit is plentiful and acidity is crisp. *Irish Distillers*

Price	£20–25/€25–32
Region	Northern Rhône
Grape	Syrah (80% min.)
Alc/vol	13%
Food	Lamb
Drink	2001–3

£25–30/€32–40

Dom. du Pégau Cuvée Réservée
AC Châteauneuf-du-Pape 98 ✓

A massive nose of autumn leaves, baked fruits, cherries and wood smoke. In a big, fleshy style, with gripping tannins and cherry and prune flavours, it's definitely a food wine. Very long finish. *J. S. Woods*

Price	£25–30/€32–40
Region	Southern Rhône
Grape	Châteauneuf varieties
Alc/vol	13.5%
Food	Venison
Drink	2001–3

Guigal Brune et Blonde AC Côte Rôtie 97 ✓

Lovely elegant nose, very perfumed and intense, with notes of blackcurrants, plums and violets. Savoury and satisfying palate, with a concentrated core of sweet cherry and raspberry fruit. Very good length. *Barry & Fitzwilliam*

Price	£25–30/€32–40
Region	Northern Rhône
Grape	Syrah (80% min.)
Alc/vol	13%
Food	Roasts
Drink	2002–6

France–South

The most striking thing about this year's wines from the South of France is the high proportion of commendations for outstanding value. In the case of Languedoc-Roussillon, over half of the red wines listed were commended as giving particularly good quality for the price. Many of the whites were also given value ratings and in two cases were awarded stars as well (Ch. L'Hospitalitet Summum La Clape and Comte Cathare Marsanne-Viognier).

Since the 1970s the Languedoc-Roussillon area, which produces 40 per cent of French wine, has been transformed from an area of dusty co-ops producing huge quantities of *vin ordinaire* into a hotbed of experimentation, with foreign investors and local vignerons alike using modern techniques to produce inexpensive, fruity wines that can compete with the New World. Much of the wine is Vin de Pays or Vin de Table, categories that allow winemakers to escape the straitjacket of Appellation Contrôlée rules, which stipulate traditional grape varieties such as Carignan and Cinsault.

The transformation of the area was achieved by uprooting inferior vines and allowing non-traditional grapes to be used to make Vin de Pays wines. 'Varietal' wines such as Merlot, Cabernet Sauvignon and Chardonnay opened up a new market and investment in the region followed. Vin de Pays d'Oc, one of the best known, comes in a variety of guises, mainly Chardonnay, Viognier, Marsanne, Merlot, Syrah, Grenache, Cabernet Sauvignon and Mourvèdre.

Provence and the South-West are just as interesting. From Provence come herby, spicy, structured wines. The South-West is a large area with a variety of sub-regions. Areas near Bordeaux make wines very similar to those of their better-known neighbour in terms of style and grape varieties—names to look for are Bergerac, Buzet, Cahors, Côtes de Duras, Monbazillac and Pécharmant. Further south, Jurançon wines, which can be dry or sweet, are floral and spicy and Vin de Pays de Côtes de Gascogne whites are fresh and crisp.

White

Under £7/Under €9

Barton & Guestier Chardonnay VdP d'Oc **99**

Fruity, smooth and balanced with an attractive peachy nose. A straightforward, well-made, simple, wine, best drunk within two years of vintage while still vibrant. *Dillons*

Price	**Under £7/Under €9**
Region	**Languedoc-Roussillon**
Grape	**Chardonnay**
Alc/vol	**12.5%**
Food	**Aperitif**
Drink	**2001–2**

Comte Cathare Marsanne-Viognier VdP d'Oc **00** ★ £/€ ⬥

Lovely fruity/floral aromas, with touches of peach and an underlying certain earthiness. Peachy lemon flavours, with a hint of grass and rosebud. Dry, with muted acidity and a good finish. Excellent flavour and quality. *Oddbins*

Price	**Under £7/Under €9**
Region	**Languedoc-Roussillon**
Grape	**Marsanne/Viognier**
Alc/vol	**13%**
Food	**Mild curry**
Drink	**2001–2**

Dom. de la Cessane Marsanne-Viognier VdP d'Oc **99**

An unusual wine for the ABC (Anything But Chardonnay) brigade. The slightly austere stoniness is nicely offset by hints of a more frivolous nature from the creamy, peachy Viognier. *WineOnline*

Price	**Under £7/Under €9**
Region	**Languedoc-Roussillon**
Grape	**Marsanne/Viognier**
Alc/vol	**13%**
Food	**Thai/Chinese**
Drink	**2001–2**

Gros Manseng, originally a Basque grape variety, is used to make dry Jurançon as well as Vin de Pays from South-West France.

Dom. du Rey VdP des Côtes de Gascogne **00** 🌿

Fresh, crisp style with clear floral and citrus aromas. Zesty, juicy fruit flavours, apples, gooseberries and some greenness. A wine to sip on its own or to enhance a fish dish. *Searsons*

Price	**Under £7/Under €9**
Region	**South-West**
Grape	**Colombard/Gros Manseng/Ugni Blanc**
Alc/vol	**11.5%**
Food	**Fish**
Drink	**2001–2**

Dom. du Tariquet VdP des Côtes de Gascogne **00**

A pleasant, crisp, fruity offering, balanced and refreshing. Oodles of character—nettles and blackcurrant leaves on the nose, delicious flavours of green apples and green peppers on the palate. *River Wines*

Price	**Under £7/Under €9**
Region	**South-West**
Grape	**Ugni Blanc/ Colombard**
Alc/vol	**11%**
Food	**Prawn salad**
Drink	**2001–2**

Honoré de Berticot Sauvignon AC Côtes de Duras **00** **£/€** ✓

Wonderful, spicy, fruity nose. Beautifully balanced palate, savoury as well as citrussy. Apples, lemons and vanilla sweetness parade against a peppery backdrop. Excellent Sauvignon, broad, ripe and easy. *Searsons*

Price	**Under £7/Under €9**
Region	**South-West**
Grape	**Sauvignon Blanc**
Alc/vol	**12%**
Food	**Seafood**
Drink	**2001–2**

La Gascogne VdP des Côtes de Gascogne **00**

This is a perfect summer wine, with its pronounced floral nose and delicate hints of primrose. The palate is dry, light and tangy, with tons of ripe apple fruit. Crisp finish. *Le Caveau*

Price	**Under £7/Under €9**
Region	**South-West**
Grape	**Gros Manseng/ Sauvignon Blanc**
Alc/vol	**12%**
Food	**Scallops**
Drink	**2001–2**

Les Étoiles Chardonnay Chenin Blanc VdP d'Oc **nv £/€** 🌿

Fresh floral aromas of rose petals mingled with tropical fruits. Dry, with lovely mouthfeel and ripe, appealing tropical fruit flavours with a slightly honeyed edge. Refreshing and easy drinking. *Tesco*

Price	**Under £7/Under €9**
Region	**Languedoc-Roussillon**
Grape	**Chard/Chenin Blanc**
Alc/vol	**12%**
Food	**Picnic**
Drink	**2001–2**

Michel Laroche South of France Chardonnay VdP d'Oc 00

Lovely buttery nose, typical Chardonnay. A flavoursome palate follows, showing lively lemon and pineapple flavours with rounded acidity. A slight spritz, barely discernible, makes it very lively. Smooth texture. *Allied Drinks*

Price	Under £7/Under €9
Region	Languedoc-Roussillon
Grape	Chardonnay
Alc/vol	13.5%
Food	Grilled chicken
Drink	2001–2

Michel Laroche South of France Terret VdP d'Oc 00 £/€

Light, fresh herbaceous/floral nose; simple yet attractive balanced, flavoursome palate, showing rounded citrus flavours, mainly lemon. A wine with broad appeal. Great for a party, wedding or family get-together. *Allied Drinks*

Price	Under £7/Under €9
Region	Languedoc-Roussillon
Grape	Terret
Alc/vol	12.5%
Food	Party, lunch
Drink	2001–2

Tesco Viognier VdP d'Oc 00 £/€

Beautiful nose of ripe peaches and pear-like fruit with creamy and tropical hints. Very weighty mouthfeel with lots of ripe tropical fruit. Acidity is a bit low, but the peach and tropical fruit flavours on the palate are delicious. *Tesco*

Price	Under £7/Under €9
Region	Languedoc-Roussillon
Grape	Viognier
Alc/vol	12.5%
Food	Chinese
Drink	2001–2

£7–9/€9–11.50

Ch. de Nages AC Costières de Nîmes 99

Refreshing and appealing nose of citrus and pineapple. There is a crispness to the acidity that is nicely counterbalanced by the weight of peach fruit. A wine to match with quite strongly flavoured foods and heavy, chunky fish like turbot. *Findlaters*

Price	£7–9/€9–11.50
Region	Languedoc-Roussillon
Grape	Southern French varieties
Alc/vol	13%
Food	Turbot
Drink	2001–2

Ch. Jolys AC Jurançon Sec 99 £/€

Jurançon wines are distinctively floral and spicy. This example, which is dry, has an elegant, complex nose, slightly honeyed with minerally hints and ripe tropical fruits. It's very pure, with lovely tangy green tropical fruit flavours and a decent finish. *Wines Direct*

Price	£7–9/€9–11.50
Region	South-West
Grape	Gros Manseng/Petit Manseng/Courbu
Alc/vol	13%
Food	Thai/Chinese
Drink	2001–2

Ch. l'Hospitalet Summum La Clape
AC Coteaux du Languedoc 99 ★ £/€

Massive nose—earthy, vanilla, vegetal. Mature and exciting—a Mrs Robinson of a wine! Powerful flavours of lemon, apple and melon with lots of toast. A really interesting and fascinating wine. *Oddbins*

Price	£7–9/€9–11.50
Region	Languedoc-Roussillon
Grape	Bourboulenc/Rolle/ Grenache Blanc/ Roussanne
Alc/vol	12.5%
Food	White meats
Drink	2001–3

Dom. de Terre Megere Viognier VdP d'Oc **99 £/€**

Very complex on the nose, honeyed and floral
with buttery, nutty hints and intense tropical
fruits. Dry, weighty palate, with honeyed tropical
fruit; creamy and ripe with a long finish. A
serious white wine. *Wines Direct*

Price	**£7–9/€9–11.50**
Region	**Languedoc-Roussillon**
Grape	**Viognier**
Alc/vol	**13%**
Food	**Thai/Chinese**
Drink	**2001–2**

Dom. Fontenelles Viognier VdP d'Oc **00**

Heady, perfumed bouquet. The palate is equally
intriguing, with complex flavours of peaches
and cream, citrus, black pepper, spice and some
green herbaceousness. Well-integrated, rich
wine with character. *Bubble Brothers*

Price	**£7–9/€9–11.50**
Region	**Languedoc-Roussillon**
Grape	**Viognier**
Alc/vol	**13%**
Food	**Fusion**
Drink	**2001–2**

Laroche L Chardonnay VdP d'Oc **00**

This wine has an unusual pinkish tinge and a
very minerally palate, with a rich, almost oily
texture, good firm acidity and a finish of tropical
fruit and butter. Cleanly made, all-purpose
Chardonnay. *Allied Drinks*

Price	**£7–9/€9–11.50**
Region	**Languedoc-Roussillon**
Grape	**Chardonnay**
Alc/vol	**13.5%**
Food	**Versatile**
Drink	**2001–2**

Mas de Chambert Picpoul de Pinet
AC Coteaux du Languedoc **99**

Plenty of layers of flavour in this smooth, silky
wine. Made with an unusual grape variety,
Picpoul, it has flavours of lemon, apple and
melon and is showing some richness and development. *Bubble Brothers*

Price	**£7–9/€9–11.50**
Region	**Languedoc-Roussillon**
Grape	**Picpoul**
Alc/vol	**13%**
Food	**Chicken**
Drink	**2001–2**

Michel Picard Chardonnay VdP d'Oc **99**

Buttery, citrus, apple and pineapple aromas lead
to pleasing buttery, citrus and floral complexity
on the palate. Fruity, aromatic, consumer-
friendly wine. *TDL*

Price	**£7–9/€9–11.50**
Region	**Languedoc-Roussillon**
Grape	**Chardonnay**
Alc/vol	**13%**
Food	**Fish**
Drink	**2001–2**

£9–11/€11.50–14

Ch. de Navailles AC Jurançon Sec **99** ✓

A very typical, bone dry, austere and citrussy
Jurançon. It's challenging, but repays on the
finish. Refreshing, with concentrated fruit flavours
of apples and citrus, it holds together
really well. *Searsons*

Price	**£9–11/€11.50–14**
Region	**South-West**
Grape	**Gros Manseng**
Alc/vol	**13.5%**
Food	**Quiche**
Drink	**2001–3**

Dom. de Brau Chardonnay VdP d'Oc **99** ♨

Upfront ripe fruit, offering baked apple, peach and spice flavours. For early drinking, this is a good example of a rounded southern French Chardonnay. *On the Case*	*Price* **£9–11/€11.50–14**
	Region **Languedoc-Roussillon**
	Grape **Chardonnay**
	Alc/vol **13%**
	Food **Guacamole**
	Drink **2001–2**

Red

> **Red wines** from Languedoc-Roussillon, such as Corbières, Costières de Nîmes, Coteaux du Languedoc, Côtes du Roussillon, Fitou, Minervois and St Chinian are made from a blend of southern French varieties, among them Carignan, Grenache, Cinsault, Mourvèdre, Syrah, Maccabeu Blanc and Lladoner Pelut.

Under £7/Under €9

Dom. Coste AC Coteaux du Languedoc **99 £/€**

Fruits of the forest and ripe autumnal fruit aromas with a little pepper. Ripe, warm flavours of damsons and spicy plums are supported by firm tannins and fairly crisp acidity. *Dunnes Stores*	*Price* **Under £7/Under €9**
	Region **Languedoc-Roussillon**
	Grape **Syrah**
	Alc/vol **12.5%**
	Food **Red meats**
	Drink **2001–3**

Dom. de Limbardie VdP des Coteaux de Murviel **99 £/€**

Pronounced aromas of blackcurrant, pepper and oak. Great concentration and body, with rich black summer berry fruit. The tannins have a little way to go. A wine with enough character to stand up to food with strong flavours. *Findlaters*	*Price* **Under £7/Under €9**
	Region **Languedoc-Roussillon**
	Grape **Merlot/Cab Sauv**
	Alc/vol **12.5%**
	Food **Pasta with meatballs**
	Drink **2001–2**

Dom. de Montplaisir Merlot VdP d'Oc **99 £/€** ✓

Good entry-level Merlot. Great colour, pronounced plummy nose and a ripe, fruity finish. Excellent quality at a great price.
SuperValu-Centra

Price	**Under £7/Under €9**
Region	**Languedoc-Roussillon**
Grape	**Merlot**
Alc/vol	**12.5%**
Food	**Pizza**
Drink	**2001–2**

Dom. Lalaurie Cuvée des Marie-Cèdres VdP d'Oc **98 £/€**

Slightly earthy, vegetal nose of dark summer fruits, showing the heat of its origins. Good concentration of soft summer fruits with a slight bitter cherry aftertaste. Excellent length.
River Wines

Price	**Under £7/Under €9**
Region	**Languedoc-Roussillon**
Grape	**Merlot/Cab Sauv/Syrah**
Alc/vol	**12%**
Food	**Barbecue**
Drink	**2001–2**

Dom. Saint-Julien Merlot VdP d'Oc **99 £/€**

An honest Merlot with enticing aromas of earthy, autumnal, plummy fruit. Flavours of plums, peppers and spice with a touch of vanilla. *Molloys*

Price	**Under £7/Under €9**
Region	**Languedoc-Roussillon**
Grape	**Merlot**
Alc/vol	**13%**
Food	**Fried chicken**
Drink	**2001–3**

> *The vineyards of **Languedoc-Roussillon** lie to the west of the Rhône's marshy Camargue delta, and together they produce more wine than Australia. The good consistent Mediterranean climate ensures ripe fruit, especially in the superb 98 vintage. There are many bargains to be had in this region.*

Gabiam AC Coteaux du Languedoc **98 £/€** ✓

Huge concentration of aromas—black fruit and herbal, perfumed undertones. Packs lots of black fruit, liquorice and dark cherry flavours into each mouthful. Tannins are still firm, but the ripe fruit makes the wine accessible now.
Dunnes Stores

Price	**Under £7/Under €9**
Region	**Languedoc-Roussillon**
Grape	**Southern French varieties**
Alc/vol	**12%**
Food	**Lamb**
Drink	**2001–3**

Merlot de Campuget VdP du Gard **99**

Aromas of plums and red berry fruits. The palate has plenty of character, with fruits of the forest and spice. Tannins are soft and rounded and the wine has a minty finish. *River Wines*

Price	**Under £7/Under €9**
Region	**Languedoc-Roussillon**
Grape	**Merlot**
Alc/vol	**12.5%**
Food	**Traditional**
Drink	**2001–2**

Michel Laroche South of France Grenache VdP d'Oc **00 £/€**

Light, easy drinking, with a fine balance of strawberry fruit and tannin with a hint of sweet vanilla. Very quaffable! *Allied Drinks*

Price	**Under £7/Under €9**
Region	**Languedoc-Roussillon**
Grape	**Grenache**
Alc/vol	**13%**
Food	**Grilled red meats**
Drink	**2001–2**

Mosaïque Syrah VdP d'Oc **99 £/€**

Pleasant fruity red wine with nicely balanced flavours. Lots of syrah character on the nose, tasty summer fruit on the palate, with a hint of spice. Soft tannins. *Oddbins*

Price	**Under £7/Under €9**
Region	**Languedoc-Roussillon**
Grape	**Syrah**
Alc/vol	**12.5%**
Food	**Pasta**
Drink	**2001–2**

Réserve de la Garrigue AC Corbières **99 £/€**

Plum and damson aromas. Soft, easy-drinking wine with some rich flavours. Black fruit, damsons and a hint of Christmas cake, full and rich. An excellent wine. *Mitchells*

Price	**Under £7/Under €9**
Region	**Languedoc-Roussillon**
Grape	**Carignan/Grenache/ Cinsault**
Alc/vol	**12%**
Food	**Steak pie**
Drink	**2001–3**

Vignes de Paul Valmont Syrah VdP d'Oc **99 £/€**

Aromas and flavours of blackberry and pepper with a nice bite and long, smooth tobacco length. Firm and full on the palate. Even better with food. *Molloys*

Price	**Under £7/Under €9**
Region	**Languedoc-Roussillon**
Grape	**Syrah**
Alc/vol	**12%**
Food	**Beefburgers**
Drink	**2001–2**

£7–9/€9–11.50

Ch. de Gourgazaud Réserve AC Minervois La Livinière **98 £/€**

Robust, earthy wine, showing plenty of complexity and depth. Spicy vanilla, summer fruits and pepper intermingle on the palate. Satisfying, complex length. Still developing. *Dunnes Stores*

Price	**£7–9/€9–11.50**
Region	**Languedoc-Roussillon**
Grape	**Southern French varieties**
Alc/vol	**13%**
Food	**Chicken in red wine**
Drink	**2001–3**

Ch. de l'Amarine Cuvée des Bernis AC Costières de Nîmes **98**

A warm Mediterranean climate and ripe fruit are evident in this lovely wine. Warm, earthy flavours mingle with ripe plums, ending with a final burst of mint. *River Wines*

Price	**£7–9/€9–11.50**
Region	**Languedoc-Roussillon**
Grape	**Southern French varieties**
Alc/vol	**13%**
Food	**Mediterranean**
Drink	**2001–3**

Ch. des Ganfards AC Bergerac **99**

This easy-drinking wine has aromas of mixed berries and flavours of dark fruits. The palate has character and structure with a slight earthiness. *Waterford Wine Vault*

Price	**£7–9/€9–11.50**
Region	**South-West**
Grape	**Merlot/Cab Franc/ Cab Sauv**
Alc/vol	**12.5%**
Food	**Meat**
Drink	**2001–2**

Ch. La Baronne Montagne d'Alaric AC Corbières 98 £/€

A ray of sunshine from the south—big, gutsy, concentrated and powerful. Very satisfying, with plenty of red and black fruits, full and ripe, with a touch of vanilla and spice. *Wines Direct*

Price	**£7–9/€9–11.50**
Region	**Languedoc-Roussillon**
Grape	**Carignan/Grenache/ Mourvèdre**
Alc/vol	**13%**
Food	**Baked ham**
Drink	**2001–2**

Ch. La Condamine Cuvée Tradition AC Corbières 99

A good example of Corbières—very rich, with soft Christmas cake flavours, fruit of the forest and spice. Nicely balanced tannins and fruit. A terrific, full, rich finish. *J. S. Woods*

Price	**£7–9/€9–11.50**
Region	**Languedoc-Roussillon**
Grape	**Carignan/Grenache/ Cinsault**
Alc/vol	**12.5%**
Food	**Roasts**
Drink	**2001–3**

Comté de Mérinville AC Minervois 97 £/€

Lovely nose with pronounced, upfront black-currant and blackberry aromas. There is plenty of black fruit to the fore on the palate. Tannins are pretty robust. Full bodied, it will go well with full-flavoured foods. *Bubble Brothers*

Price	**£7–9/€9–11.50**
Region	**Languedoc-Roussillon**
Grape	**Mainly Syrah**
Alc/vol	**12%**
Food	**Rich casseroles**
Drink	**2001–3**

Dom. Borie de Maurel Esprit d'Automne
AC Minervois 00 £/€

An easy-drinking wine. The palate has rich blackcurrant fruit with a background of roast peppers and a hint of leather or liquorice. Soft, well-rounded tannins. Good long finish. *Oddbins*

Price	**£7–9/€9–11.50**
Region	**Languedoc-Roussillon**
Grape	**Southern French varieties**
Alc/vol	**13%**
Food	**Cheese**
Drink	**2001–2**

Dom. Clavel Les Garrigues Terroir de la Mejanelle
AC Coteaux du Languedoc 99

Ripe, juicy, concentrated wine with attitude! A rich, stewed black fruit nose. The tannins are firm but the the fruit comes through in the finish—rich, ripe blackcurrants. *Wines Direct*

Price	**£7–9/€9–11.50**
Region	**Languedoc-Roussillon**
Grape	**Southern French varieties**
Alc/vol	**14%**
Food	**Mediterranean**
Drink	**2001–2**

Dom. de Bisconte AC Côtes du Roussillon 99

Medium bodied with soft, sweet red berry fruit aromas. Cherry jam flavours on the palate with a touch of cinnamon, finishing with lovely length. *Searsons*

Price	**£7–9/€9–11.50**
Region	**Languedoc-Roussillon**
Grape	**Southern French varieties**
Alc/vol	**12%**
Food	**Lamb chops**
Drink	**2001–2**

Dom. des Chênes Les Grands-mères
AC Côtes du Roussillon-Villages **98 £/€**

Appealing, rich nose of blackcurrant. The palate has a good grip of tannins that call for food and sticky blackcurrant fruit flavours with a touch of vanilla and crisp acidity. Decent, ripe, crunchy stuff. *Wines Direct*

Price	**£7–9/€9–11.50**
Region	**Languedoc-Roussillon**
Grape	**Grenache/Carignan/ Syrah/Mourvèdre**
Alc/vol	**13.6%**
Food	**Versatile**
Drink	**2001–2**

Dom. du Grand Crès AC Corbières **99 £/€**

Grippy, peppery, dry, but very drinkable. A food wine. You won't find a Bordeaux at this price to touch it. Still young, but has a lot going on— complex flavours of chocolate, plum, blackcurrants and vanilla. Great finish. *Wines Direct*

Price	**£7–9/€9–11.50**
Region	**Languedoc-Roussillon**
Grape	**Carignan/Grenache/ Cinsault**
Alc/vol	**13%**
Food	**Rich casseroles**
Drink	**2001–2**

Dom. du Pech AC Buzet **97**

Redcurrant and wild strawberry aromas with some herbaceous notes and concentrated flavours. A very enjoyable fruity wine, perfect for informal mealsa. *River Wines*

Price	**£7–9/€9–11.50**
Region	**South-West**
Grape	**Merlot/Cab Sauv/ Cab Franc**
Alc/vol	**12.5%**
Food	**Bistro**
Drink	**2001–2**

Laroche L Pinot Noir VdP de l'Île de Beauté **00**

Nose of plum jam with a mineral edge, vegetal and spicy. Generous red berry fruit with balanced acidity and mouth-coating tannins. Similar to Burgundy in style. *Allied Drinks*

Price	**£7–9/€9–11.50**
Region	**Corsica**
Grape	**Pinot Noir**
Alc/vol	**12%**
Food	**Pork**
Drink	**2001–4**

Mansenoble VdP des Coteaux de Miramont **99 £/€**

A very appealing nose—blackcurrants and eucalyptus. Beautifully made and balanced, the palate provides abundant blackcurrant fruit and pepper flavours, a rounded mouthfeel and a satisfying finish. *Bubble Brothers*

Price	**£7–9/€9–11.50**
Region	**Languedoc-Roussillon**
Grape	**Merlot/Carignan**
Alc/vol	**12.5%**
Food	**Traditional**
Drink	**2001–3**

Michel Picard Syrah VdP d'Oc **99 £/€**

Hot and sultry, a savoury example of the serious style of varietal wine coming from this region. It has spicy pepper, blackberry and cream aromas and pure Syrah fruit on the palate. *TDL*

Price	**£7–9/€9–11.50**
Region	**Languedoc-Roussillon**
Grape	**Syrah**
Alc/vol	**12.5%**
Food	**Rabbit or beef**
Drink	**2001–2**

Moulin de Gassac Albaran VdP de l'Hérault **98**

Quite an oaky nose, but strawberries, cherries and blackcurrants come through. More black fruits and strawberries appear on the palate, which has good spice and a long finish. Nicely made. Good with food but also on its own. *O'Briens*

Price	**£7–9/€9–11.50**
Region	**Languedoc-Roussillon**
Grape	**Cab Sauv/Syrah/ Mourvèdre**
Alc/vol	**12.5%**
Food	**Cheese**
Drink	**2001–2**

£9–11/€11.50–14

Balmont de Cahors AC Cahors **98**

Big, assertive, structured wine. On the nose there are damson, plum and meat aromas. Concentrated black fruit flavours are backed by chewy tannins on the palate. *Bubble Brothers*

Price	**£9–11/€11.50–14**
Region	**South-West**
Grape	**Malbec**
Alc/vol	**12.5%**
Food	**Roasts**
Drink	**2001–3**

Ch. de Biran AC Pécharmant **97**

Soft red fruit flavours—plums, cherries, redcurrants. An interesting wine with more going for it than basic fruit. Relatively complex, it's for the enthusiast on a budget. *River Wines*

Price	**£9–11/€11.50–14**
Region	**South-West**
Grape	**Cab Sauv/Cab Franc/ Merlot/Malbec**
Alc/vol	**12.5%**
Food	**Traditional**
Drink	**2001–2**

Ch. de Gueyze AC Buzet **92**

It has taken a long time to reach this maturity, but this wine still has time left. Vegetal, mature nose of compost, rhubarb and spice. Mature palate with dried fruit flavours. A good opportunity to taste a wine with some age. *WineOnline*

Price	**£9–11/€11.50–14**
Region	**South-West**
Grape	**Merlot/Cab Sauv/ Cab Franc**
Alc/vol	**12.5%**
Food	**Roast beef**
Drink	**2001–2**

Ch. du Cèdre AC Cahors **98**

There's a hint of aniseed among the dark fruit aromas. Good black fruit concentration on the palate, gripping tannins and good length. This wine has an excellent jam structure and will mature and soften. *Le Caveau*

Price	**£9–11/€11.50–14**
Region	**South-West**
Grape	**Malbec/Merlot/ Tannat/Jurançon Noir**
Alc/vol	**12.5%**
Food	**Steak**
Drink	**2002–5**

Ch. La Voulte-Gasparets Cuvée Réservée
AC Corbières **96** **£/€**

Concentrated fruit of soft strawberries and raspberries with some prunes and a spicy kick. This is a style that improves with maturity. A rewarding finish. *Searsons*

Price	**£9–11/€11.50–14**
Region	**Languedoc-Roussillon**
Grape	**Carignan/Grenache/ Cinsault**
Alc/vol	**12.5%**
Food	**Beef, duck**
Drink	**2001–2**

Ch. Les Pins AC Côtes du Roussillon-Villages **98**

Fabulous aromas of plums and damsons. Great follow-through of jammy forest fruits, spice, liquorice and a lovely, clear, minty finish. Still maturing. *River Wines*

Price	**£9–11/€11.50–14**
Region	**Languedoc-Roussillon**
Grape	**Southern French varieties**
Alc/vol	**13%**
Food	**Steak**
Drink	**2001–3**

Dom. Bassac Cabernet Sauvignon
VdP des Côtes de Thongue **99** 🍃

A slightly oaky edge to this wine, which is in typical Cabernet style. Mint, black cherry, leather and tar flavours abound in an elegant Old World style. *On the Case*

Price	**£9–11/€11.50–14**
Region	**Languedoc-Roussillon**
Grape	**Cabernet Sauvignon**
Alc/vol	**13%**
Food	**Barbecue**
Drink	**2001–3**

Dom. de Brau Cuvée Exquise AC Cabardès **99** 🍃

Big and broad with a nice mouthfeel of sweet black cherries and strawberry/raspberry compote. A spicy backbone of tannin holds the wine together. *On the Case*

Price	**£9–11/€11.50–14**
Region	**Languedoc-Roussillon**
Grape	**Merlot/Grenache/ Syrah/Cab Sauv**
Alc/vol	**13%**
Food	**Traditional**
Drink	**2001–3**

Dom. de Roumanille AC Fitou **96**

Great summer flavours. A very serious and foodie style of Fitou. Lots and lots of liquorice on both nose and palate, with elements of prune and currant fruit alongside dates and walnuts. Nice softness with age. *Febvre*

Price	**£9–11/€11.50–14**
Region	**Languedoc-Roussillon**
Grape	**Southern French varieties**
Alc/vol	**12.5%**
Food	**Pork**
Drink	**2001–2**

La Cuvée Mythique VdP d'Oc **98**

Warm summer mouthfeel on the palate, with soft, ripe cherry and black fruit, firm tannins and bracing acidity. Some spice and dark chocolate lurking in the depths. *Searsons*

Price	**£9–11/€11.50–14**
Region	**Languedoc-Roussillon**
Grape	**Grenache/Cinsault/ Mourvèdre**
Alc/vol	**12.5%**
Food	**Casseroles, cheese**
Drink	**2001–3**

£11–13/€14–16.50

Ch. Bouscassé AC Madiran 95 £/€

Dense nose of leather and black fruits with a creamy influence. The palate has good cherry fruit and mouth-drying tannins. A robust style. *Le Caveau*

Price	**£11–13/€14–16.50**
Region	**South-West**
Grape	**Tannat**
Alc/vol	**12.5%**
Food	**Roast lamb**
Drink	**2002–5**

Ch. de Mérinville AC Minervois 99 £/€ ✓

This is a serious, full-bodied wine with great concentration and character. Creamy black-currant, summer fruit and pepper aromas continue through to the palate. *Bubble Brothers*

Price	**£11–13/€14–16.50**
Region	**Languedoc-Roussillon**
Grape	**Southern French varieties**
Alc/vol	**13%**
Food	**Versatile**
Drink	**2001–4**

Ch. St Martin de la Garrigue Bronzinelle
AC Coteaux du Languedoc 99 £/€

Youthful aromas of ripe brambles and cherry cake with some spice. On the palate there are warm red fruits with a touch of spice and white pepper. Ripe, rich and big, still developing. *J. S. Woods*

Price	**£11–13/€14–16.50**
Region	**Languedoc-Roussillon**
Grape	**Southern French varieties**
Alc/vol	**13%**
Food	**Steak pie**
Drink	**2001–4**

> The **98 vintage** was wonderful in Languedoc-Roussillon, with beautiful weather all through the harvest and a dry wind—perfect for the vines. Red wines benefited most—the best have an impressive tannic structure that is not at all harsh, and are bursting with ripe fruit.

Dom. Rimbert Le Mas au Schiste AC St Chinian 98

So many different lovely flavours and scents. Mushroom, liquorice and blackberry aromas are followed by a complex, flavoursome palate. A serious wine from a great vintage. *Bubble Brothers*

Price	**£11–13/€14–16.50**
Region	**Languedoc-Roussillon**
Grape	**Southern French varieties**
Alc/vol	**14%**
Food	**Red meat**
Drink	**2001–4**

La Bastide Blanche AC Bandol 93 £/€

This impressive wine has a developed nose of black fruits and vanilla and a silky, smooth palate of black fruits and black pepper, very mellow. Some tobacco notes. A wine of character—classic Provence style. Deliciously different. *MacCormaic*

Price	**£11–13/€14–16.50**
Region	**Provence**
Grape	**Mourvèdre/ Grenache/Cinsault**
Alc/vol	**13%**
Food	**Sunday lunch**
Drink	**2001–2**

£13–15/€16.50–19

Ch. Dalmeran AC Les Baux de Provence **97 £/€**

A blockbuster, with mint, aniseed, baked black fruits and spice. A mature wine, it has good body and structure and will drink well over the next year. *Wicklow Wine Co.*

Price	**£13–15/€16.50–19**
Region	**Provence**
Grape	**Grenache/Cab Sauv/ Syrah**
Alc/vol	**13.5%**
Food	**Beef**
Drink	**2001–2**

£15–17/€19–22

Ch. Pradeaux AC Bandol **97**

Bandol gives a range of flavours unlike anywhere else in France. A seriously structured wine from the Mediterranean displaying lots of walnuts and dates alongside the spice of Mourvèdre. *Bubble Brothers*

Price	**£15–17/€19–22**
Region	**Provence**
Grape	**Mourvèdre/ Grenache/Cinsault**
Alc/vol	**13%**
Food	**Casseroles**
Drink	**2001–3**

Cuvée Henri Serres AC Corbières **98**

Mint and fruit of the forest aromas. On the palate summer fruits and spice intermingled with cherries are supported by firm tannins and a decent finish. *Searsons*

Price	**£15–17/€19–22**
Region	**Languedoc-Roussillon**
Grape	**Carignan/Grenache/ Cinsault**
Alc/vol	**12.5%**
Food	**Game**
Drink	**2001–4**

£17–20/€22–25

Ch. Étienne des Lauzes Cuvée Yneka AC St Chinian **98 ✓**

A great winter warmer with distinctive gingerbread aromas. A burst of spicy, rich fruits of the forest and pepper on the palate. Full of flavour and with a finish of great character, its firm tannins provide enough backbone to enable the wine to age well. *Searsons*

Price	**£17–20/€22–25**
Region	**Languedoc-Roussillon**
Grape	**Southern French varieties**
Alc/vol	**12.5%**
Food	**Rack of lamb**
Drink	**2001–3**

£20–25/€25–32

Baron'Arques VdP de la Haute Vallée de l'Aude **98**

This wine could well challenge a Bordeaux. On the nose there are notes of black fruits, spice and pepper. A youthful wine, it has layers of fruit and vegetal flavours that are still masked by firm tannins. *Findlaters*

Price	**£20–25/€25–32**
Region	**Languedoc-Roussillon**
Grape	**Cabernet/Merlot/ Cab Franc**
Alc/vol	**13%**
Food	**Roast turkey**
Drink	**2001–5**

Germany

One of Germany's advantages as a wine country is the Riesling grape variety, which features strongly in the wines listed this year. As Riesling makes a name for itself in the New World, especially in countries such as Australia, more attention may turn to its native homeland. Though Riesling comes in a number of different styles and from a variety of regions, it is one of those grape varieties that always tastes of itself. In Germany, styles from the Mosel-Saar-Ruwer are lighter and more delicate, while wines from further south are fuller and spicier. It's versatile as well, spanning the whole range of tastes, from bone dry to ultra sweet.

Included this year are red wines made from grape varieties Dornfelder and Pinot Noir. Dornfelder is unique to Germany. Developed as a variety that would suit Germany's cooler climate, it has deep colour with appetising fruit and can be aged in wood and bottle with good results.

It can be difficult to convince people who grew up drinking Liebfraumilch to try German wine again. But there is a new generation of wine drinkers willing to try the drier wines. Some export-focused producers have simplified their wine labels, for example Bend in the River and Carl Erhard. With drier styles of wine, simpler labelling, a great affinity with food and alcohol levels on the low side, could Germany claim back some of its lost market share?

White

Rivaner is another name for Müller-Thurgau. It is one of the most widely planted grape varieties in Germany.

Under £7/Under €9

Bend in the River Rivaner Riesling QbA 99

Floral, spicy aromas, with apples and limes. Dry, with pleasant ripe fruit flavours, a hint of spice and clean, fresh length—very appealing. *Findlaters*

Price	Under £7/Under €9
Region	Rheinhessen
Grape	Rivaner/Riesling
Alc/vol	11.5%
Food	Picnic
Drink	2001–2

Riesling Hochgewächs means that the wine is made from 100% Riesling grapes that have reached a higher level of ripeness than the minimum set for the region.

Ewald Friederich Erben Riesling Hochgewächs Trocken Merler Fettgarten QbA 99

The nose has soft petrol notes, honeysuckle, dried apricot and floral aromas. The palate is tart and crisp, with gooseberry and green apple flavours with a fairly long finish that tapers into floral notes. *Molloys*

Price	Under £7/Under €9
Region	Mosel-Saar-Ruwer
Grape	Riesling
Alc/vol	11.5%
Food	Versatile
Drink	2001–3

£7–9/€9–11.50

Carl Ehrhard Riesling Trocken QbA **00**

Light, fresh, intense nose, with youthful apple aromas and some mango fruit in the background. The palate is off-dry, with crisp acidity backed up by cooking apple fruit. It's pleasant and refreshing and surprisingly substantial in the mouth. Clean and refreshing finish.
Karwig Wines

Price	**£7–9/€9–11.50**
Region	**Rheingau**
Grape	**Riesling**
Alc/vol	**12%**
Food	**Fish**
Drink	**2001–3**

> **Trocken** *on a label means that the wine is dry, while* **halbtrocken** *is half dry and made in a sweeter style.*

Dürkheimer Schenkenböhl Spätburgunder Weissherbst Halbtrocken QbA **99**

Unusually, this white wine is made from a black grape. Fresh, promising nose of honeyed apple with a melon garnish. The off-dry palate shows more apple and lemon meringue pie character. Supple and smooth. *Karwig Wines*

Price	**£7–9/€9–11.50**
Region	**Pfalz**
Grape	**Spätburgunder (Pinot Noir)**
Alc/vol	**12%**
Food	**Oriental**
Drink	**2001–2**

> **QbA** *(Qualitätswein bestimmter Anbaugebiete) means 'quality wine from a specified region'. Regions of importance in Germany include Mosel-Saar-Ruwer, Rheingau, Rheinhessen, Nahe and Pfalz. QbA wines may be made trocken or halbtrocken.*

Louis Guntrum Niersteiner Rivaner Trocken QbA **99**

Light, fresh nose—ripe apple skins and grassy, herbaceous notes. Delicacy, too, with some floral characteristics. The youthful palate is dry, with apple fruit, lemon and crisp acidity. Texture and mouthfeel are light and fresh. Good fruit and low alcohol. *Waterford Wine Vault*

Price	**£7–9/€9–11.50**
Region	**Rheinhessen**
Grape	**Rivaner**
Alc/vol	**10%**
Food	**Aperitif**
Drink	**2001–2**

Winzer Von Erbach Riesling Classic QbA **00**

Ripe apple and honey aromas on the nose hint at petrolly characteristics to come. Quite a floral palate, with a hint of honeycomb and wax. The palate is dry. Acidity is crisp and the wine has a fullish texture. *Karwig Wines*

Price	**£7–9/€9–11.50**
Region	**Rheingau**
Grape	**Riesling**
Alc/vol	**12%**
Food	**Seafood**
Drink	**2001–3**

£9–11/€11.50–14

Dr Wagner Saarburger Rausch Riesling Halbtrocken QbA 98 ✓

Classic German Riesling. Ripe, waxy, honeyed, petrolly aromas on the fresh, clean nose. The off-dry palate has crisp acidity and good solid concentration of overripe apple and citrus fruit, even a hint of orange. Crisp, clean finish. *Karwig Wines*

Price	£9–11/€11.50–14
Region	Mosel-Saar-Ruwer
Grape	Riesling
Alc/vol	10%
Food	Thai/Chinese
Drink	2001–3

> **QmP** *(Qualitätswein mit Prädikat) means a 'quality wine with special attributes'. There are six levels of QmP in order of increasing ripeness of the grapes—Kabinett, Spätlese, Auslese, Beerenauslese, Trockenbeerenauslese and Eiswein. Kabinett, Spätlese and Auslese may be trocken (dry) or halbtrocken (half-dry). The other styles are always sweet.*

Weingut Schumacher Weissburgunder QmP 99

Very dry. The pungent nose has aromas of smoke and minerals. Attractive apple and citrus fruit on the palate with lovely crisp acidity. Long, spicy finish. *Mitchells*

Price	£9–11/€11.50–14
Region	Pfalz
Grape	Weissburgunder (Pinot Blanc)
Alc/vol	12%
Food	Versatile
Drink	2001–2

£11–13/€14–16.50

Carl Ehrhard Riesling Spätlese Trocken QmP 00 ✓

A very 'happening', round, ripe nose—perfume, Turkish Delight, honey, marmalade—an explosion of aromas. The palate, which is much drier than the nose suggests, has crisp acidity, tart apple, citrus and a hint of sweetness at the end. *Karwig Wines*

Price	£11–13/€14–16.50
Region	Rheingau
Grape	Riesling
Alc/vol	12.5%
Food	Chinese
Drink	2001–4

£13–15/€16.50–19

Dr Wagner Ockfener Bockstein Riesling Spätlese QmP 97 ✓

Quite developed, gentle nose, very elegant, with aromas of kerosene, slate, peaches and roses. Medium sweet on the palate, it has lovely balanced acidity and honeyed marmalade/apricot fruit. *Karwig Wines*

Price	£13–15/€16.50–19
Region	Mosel-Saar-Ruwer
Grape	Riesling
Alc/vol	7.5%
Food	Blue cheese
Drink	2001–4

> **Kabinett**, *the lightest style of QmP, is made from ripe grapes picked at the normal harvest time.* **Spätlese** *is made from late-harvested (therefore riper) grapes.* **Auslese**, *made from selected bunches of very ripe grapes, is more likely to be found in a sweet style, but can make rich and powerful dry wines.*

Kreuznacher Narrenkappe Grauer Burgunder Auslese Trocken QmP 99

Unusual and ideal if you're looking for something different. Very attractive on the nose with its waxy, honeyed fruit. The distinctly peppery palate has stewed apple flavours and fairly crisp acidity. Persistent length. *The Wine Seller*

Price	£13–15/€16.50–19
Region	Nahe
Grape	Grauburgunder (Pinot Gris)
Alc/vol	13.5%
Food	Ravioli
Drink	2001–2

£15–17/€19–22

Reichsgraf von Kesselstatt Riesling Spätlese QmP 99

Quite a muted nose with some apple and citrus aromas. Slightly sweet in style, it has firm acidity and rich, rounded fruit flavours. The palate is complex, with a good balance of fruit, sweetness and acidity. The wine finishes long, with piquant flavours of apples. *Searsons*

Price	£15–17/€19–22
Region	Mosel-Saar-Ruwer
Grape	Riesling
Alc/vol	8.5%
Food	Dessert
Drink	2001–5

Red

£7–9/€9–11.50

Wingverein Forst Dornfelder QbA 99

Interesting nose of strawberries with a stony, mineral-like quality. The ripe palate has stacks of soft, fruity strawberries. Easy-drinking, soft, ripe, fruity style of wine that should have wide appeal. *Karwig Wines*

Price	£7–9/€9–11.50
Region	Pfalz
Grape	Dornfelder
Alc/vol	12%
Food	Picnic
Drink	2001–2

£11–13/€14–16.50

Guldentaler Schlosskapelle Dornfelder QbA 00

A good example of a well-made Dornfelder. Ripe cherry fruit with a hint of plums. An agreeable, fruity wine, ready for drinking now.
The Wine Seller

Price	£11–13/€14–16.50
Region	Nahe
Grape	Dornfelder
Alc/vol	11.5%
Food	Beef
Drink	2001–2

Kreuznacher Hofgarten Spätburgunder Trocken QbA 99

If you are looking for a typical, well-made Spätburgunder, this would fit the bill. On the nose and palate it has strawberries with a pleasant hint of cherries. *The Wine Seller*

Price	£11–13/€14–16.50
Region	Nahe
Grape	Spätburgunder (Pinot Noir)
Alc/vol	12.5%
Food	Ham
Drink	2001–2

> **Tafelwein** means 'table wine'. The grapes may be grown anywhere in Germany. Depending on the producer, it can be very good or very basic.

£13–15/€16.50–19

Carl Ehrhard Spätburgunder Rüdesheimer
Tafelwein **98 £/€**

Delicate spring flower aromas with a slight tang of lime. The elegant palate explodes with complex, lasting flavours. A lovely summer wine for the seasoned red wine drinker who likes some complexity. *Karwig Wines*

Price	**£13–15/€16.50–19**
Region	**Rheingau**
Grape	**Spätburgunder (Pinot Noir)**
Alc/vol	**13%**
Food	**Frankfurters**
Drink	**2001–2**

Greece

There are more than three hundred grape varieties indigenous to Greece. The wines included this year are predominantly from these successful native varieties, which is a testimony to Greece's belief in itself. Both reds and whites are very distinctive, not the blockbusters one might expect from a hot country. Many of the wines are quite light in style, with high acidity and tannins, and call out for food. While international varieties such as Cabernet Sauvignon, Merlot, Chardonnay and Sauvignon Blanc are being grown and sold as single varietals, they are just as likely to be found in blends with Greek varieties.

White

Under £7/Under €9

Santorini AO de Qualité Supérieure 99

Gooseberry and Granny Smith apple bouquet, quite aromatic. Made in a very expressive, modern style, it's medium dry, with sweet, honeyed nectarine, lemon and apple fruit on the palate with a touch of white pepper spice and lively, fresh acidity. *Irish Distillers*

Price	**Under £7/Under €9**
Region	**Santorini**
Grape	**Assyrtiko**
Alc/vol	**13%**
Food	**Fried fish**
Drink	**2001–2**

> **Assyrtiko** *is one of Greece's finest white grape varieties, grown mainly on Santorini and other Cycladic islands. Drought resistant and very adaptable, it achieves ripeness without losing acidity and is capable of ageing.*

£9–11/€11.50–14

Sigalas Santorini Oia Barrel Fermented VQPRD 00 ✿

A very different wine. The nose offers toast, fleshy tropical fruit and apple aromas with some vanilla from the oak barrels. The honeyed palate has a slight spritz, red apple and lime flavours, perfect acidity and a fresh finish. *Oddbins*

Price	**£9–11/€11.50–14**
Region	**Santorini**
Grape	**Assyrtiko**
Alc/vol	**13%**
Food	**Greek meze**
Drink	**2001–2**

Red

Under £7/Under €9

Achaia Clauss Topikos Oenos Cabernet Sauvignon St George VdP du Peloponnese 98

Attractive aromas of damson, vanilla and cinnamon. The palate has lots of good chewy fruit, bitter chocolate notes and a peppery twist, with refreshing acidity and softening tannins. *Taserra*

Price	**Under £7/Under €9**
Region	**Peloponnese**
Grape	**Cab Sauv/Aghiorghitiko (St George)**
Alc/vol	**12%**
Food	**Lamb with fennel**
Drink	**2001–2**

> **St George** (Aghiorghitiko), is the second most widely planted black grape variety in Greece. Generally very fruity with good body and intensity, it blends well with Cabernet Sauvignon. **Xynomavro** ('acid black') is Greece's most respected grape variety. It lives up to its name, producing deeply coloured, tannic, fresh wines that can age into relatively complex maturity.

Boutari Naoussa AO de Qualité Supérieure **98**

Baked autumnal fruit and brambles on the nose. Very dry and tannic but easy to drink, with plummy, spicy flavours and good length. A food wine. *Irish Distillers*

Price	**Under £7/Under €9**
Region	**Macedonia**
Grape	**Xynomavro**
Alc/vol	**11.5%**
Food	**Hummus**
Drink	**2001–2**

Tsantalis Nemea AO de Qualité Supérieure **97**

Quite a light style. Spice, cherries and wood on the nose. Chewy on the palate with a herbal aftertaste and a taut finish conjuring up the bitterness of aubergines. Just the thing to cut through Greek food. Try it slightly chilled. *Dunnes Stores*

Price	**Under £7/Under €9**
Region	**Nemea**
Grape	**Aghiorghitiko (St George)**
Alc/vol	**12%**
Food	**Moussaka**
Drink	**2001–2**

£7–9/€9–11.50

Achaia Clauss Cava Clauss VdT **nv**

Slightly spirity, hot-climate nose of dried fruits. Quite an unusual wine with hot rubber and dried fig, date and raisin fruit. A very warm wine that will bring you straight to the heart of Greece. *Taserra*

Price	**£7–9/€9–11.50**
Region	**Patras**
Alc/vol	**12%**
Food	**Greek salad**
Drink	**2001–2**

Achaia Clauss Ch. Clauss VdP des Côtes de Petroto **97**

Perfumed, lavender-like nose with dark cassis fruit, cherries and fruit gums. The soft and supple palate shows plenty of summer berry fruit, mellow tannins and a medium finish. Certainly different—fruit and perfume together. Chill it lightly and have it with a big platter of ham and salami with feta cheese salad. *Taserra*

Price	**£7–9/€9–11.50**
Region	**Petroto**
Alc/vol	**12%**
Food	**Cold meats**
Drink	**2001–2**

Agiorgitiko Boutari AO de Qualité Supérieure **98**

A pale ruby colour with cherry aromas. The palate has real bite, with flavours of red summer fruits backed by some liquorice and cherry flavours. *Irish Distillers*

Price	**£7–9/€9–11.50**
Region	**Nemea**
Grape	**Aghiorghitiko (St George)**
Alc/vol	**11.5%**
Food	**Salmon**
Drink	**2001–2**

Tsantalis Rapsani Epilegmeno AO de Qualité Supérieure 95

Made in a traditional style, this wine shows some development with slightly stewed and tarry aromas. Richer on the palate with good grip, it's fruity but also earthy, with raspberry and cherry flavours and some treacle. *Dunnes Stores*

Price	**£7–9/€9–11.50**
Region	**Rapsani**
Alc/vol	**12.5%**
Food	**Kebabs**
Drink	**2001–2**

Hungary

White

Under £7/Under €9

Chapel Hill South Balaton Irsai Olivér 99

An intense, aromatic bouquet with honeyed spice, pepper, apples, lychee and rose-petal notes. The palate, which is still fresh, is bursting with apples and currants. An unusual wine, light bodied and very fruity. *Barry & Fitzwilliam*

Price	**Under £7/Under €9**
Region	**Balaton**
Grape	**Irsai Olivér**
Alc/vol	**11.5%**
Food	**Creamy dishes**
Drink	**2001–2**

The symbols	
🌱	*Organic*
£/€	**Value**—*signifies wines which are exceptionally good value for their style and origin*
✓	**Commended**—*signifies a wine worthy of extra attention; showing extra quality or character*
★	**1 star**—*signifies a wine of more than ordinary complexity, showing character and style*
★★	**2 star**—*signifies an elegant wine showing character and complexity, true to its origins, with balance and subtlety*

Italy

Italy's performance this year was outstanding, with numerous value awards and several stars. Apart from the high fliers, however, the tasters found that wines were of consistently good quality with remarkably few disappointments.

The most important regions were Piedmont and Tuscany. From Piedmont a range of interesting wines belied the reputation Italy has for nondescript whites, with two table wines made from Muscat and Viognier winning stars. Gavi wines, made from Cortese, were fresh and lively with plenty of nutty fruit and lemon/lime zestiness. The wines of Barolo, Barbaresco and Langhe showed concentrated fruit, fresh acidity and all the ingredients required to make a perfect food wine.

Tuscan wines, based on the Sangiovese grape, were mainly from the excellent 97 and 98 vintages. Tasters found spicy, complex wines layered with cherry, damson and chocolate flavours, all drinking well now. Most Tuscan wines were Chiantis, but look out for the Indicazione Geografica Tipica (IGT) Toscana wines for something slightly different from Chianti. These wines can contain non-Italian varieties such as Cabernet Sauvignon or Merlot, though they may be blended with Sangiovese or indeed made with 100 per cent Sangiovese.

Amarone della Valpolicella from the Veneto is an ultra-rich wine made from dried grapes, so its earthy, figgy, autumn fruit flavours are very concentrated. It is an excellent wine to have with food, but some people prefer to drink it after a meal as a digestif.

Puglia, home of Salice Salentino, continues to produce inexpensive reds that are full of fruit and character. Other wines worth seeking out are Montepulciano d'Abruzzo, with its vibrant red fruit, and Pinot Grigio from Trentino-Alto Adige, a light, fruity wine with zippy acidity.

The quality of Italian wines is higher than it has ever been. With over five hundred different classifications to choose from, there's a wine for every taste and every pocket.

White

Under £7/Under €9

Alasia Dry Muscat VdT 00 ★ £/€

A delicious, light, dry wine with pronounced nutty, fragrant aromas backed with some steeliness. Ripe fruit flavours—stewed apples, gooseberries—flowers, nuts and spice with good length and a lovely refreshing finish. A wine of great character. *Findlaters*

Price	**Under £7/Under €9**
Region	**Piedmont**
Grape	**Muscat**
Alc/vol	**12%**
Food	**Crab cakes**
Drink	**2001–2**

Araldica Cortese DOC Piemonte 00

Light, easy-drinking wine with melon and pear fruit. Pleasant floral and citrus flavours, refreshing acidity and a clean finish.
Findlaters

Price	**Under £7/Under €9**
Region	**Piedmont**
Grape	**Cortese**
Alc/vol	**11.5%**
Food	**Aperitif**
Drink	**2001–2**

> The Latium or Lazio region surrounding Rome is white wine country. This is
> home to **Frascati**—pale, fresh, crisp wines. The more characterful Frascatis have
> a higher proportion of the flavoursome and nutty Malvasia than the neutral
> Trebbiano (Ugni Blanc).

Fontana Candida DOC Frascati 99

Dry wine with a lovely weight of nutty fruit, interesting floral and spicy flavours. It has a fresh zingy quality. Nicely balanced, with crisply and zippy acidity. Dry finish. *Dillons*

Price	**Under £7/Under €9**
Region	**Latium**
Grape	**Malvasia del Lazio/ Malvasia di Candia**
Alc/vol	**12%**
Food	**Creamy pasta**
Drink	**2001–2**

S. Orsola DOCG Gavi 00

Aromatic nose with a hint of petrol. Dry, this wine has refreshing acidity and a good weight of stewed apples with hints of lemon and lime peel on the palate. Zesty finish. *Gleeson*

Price	**Under £7/Under €9**
Region	**Piedmont**
Grape	**Cortese**
Alc/vol	**11.5%**
Food	**Chicken**
Drink	**2001–2**

> **Classico** on an Italian wine label indicates that the wine's source is the
> heartland of the original centre of a DOC quality region, making the most
> typical styles of wine.

Tenuta Le Velette Rasenna Amabile
DOC Orvieto Classico 00 £/€

Striking nose of lime and a little petrol! The palate is soft and medium dry with rich fruit; again the petrol notes come through along with some raisiny touches. A good example of off-dry ('amabile') Orvieto at a great price. *Oddbins*

Price	**Under £7/Under €9**
Region	**Umbria**
Grape	**Trebbiano**
Alc/vol	**12.5%**
Food	**Aperitif**
Drink	**2001–2**

Tenuta Le Velette Secco DOC Orvieto Classico 00 £/€

A nice example of dry Orvieto. Appealing nose—hints of pear with floral notes (honeysuckle). Refreshing acidity supports a lime twist to the intense, soft, almost fragrant, fruit. The finish is clean and very slightly nutty. *Oddbins*

Price	**Under £7/Under €9**
Region	**Umbria**
Grape	**Trebbiano**
Alc/vol	**12.5%**
Food	**Picnic**
Drink	**2001–2**

Tesco DOC Frascati Superiore 00 £/€

Aromatic, nutty aromas. A dry wine with lively acidity, very crisp and fresh with toasted nutty flavours and a dry finish. Very easy to drink, with or without food. *Tesco*

Price	**Under £7/Under €9**
Region	**Latium**
Grape	**Malvasia/Trebbiano**
Alc/vol	**12%**
Food	**Antipasto**
Drink	**2001–2**

£7–9/€9–11.50

Balera Cortese DOC Piemonte **00 £/€**

Soft fruit aromas—peach and apricot notes.
Dry, with citrus fruit flavours and a nice spicy
edge to the long finish, which has a touch of
lime. The oak is well integrated. *Oddbins*

Price	**£7–9/€9–11.50**
Region	**Piedmont**
Grape	**Cortese**
Alc/vol	**13%**
Food	**Pork chops**
Drink	**2001–2**

Betilli Michele Pinot Grigio DOC Lison-Pramaggiore **00 £/€** ❧

Simple but appealing nose of almonds with floral notes. This is a good example of Pinot Grigio,
with its slightly nutty, savoury flavours marry-
ing with fresh lemons. Attractively vibrant.
On the Case

Price	**£7–9/€9–11.50**
Region	**Veneto**
Grape	**Pinot Grigio**
Alc/vol	**12%**
Food	**Fish**
Drink	**2001–2**

Cantina di San Gimignano
DOCG Vernaccia di San Gimignano **00**

Lemon, apple and melon aromas, which
become zesty and refreshing on tasting, packed
with limes and with a nice mouthfeel. Quite a
full-flavoured wine, it has good length.
Select Wines

Price	**£7–9/€9–11.50**
Region	**Tuscany**
Grape	**Vernaccia**
Alc/vol	**12.5%**
Food	**Aperitif**
Drink	**2001–3**

Grigio della Luna Pinot Grigio DOC Valdadige **00 £/€**

Attractive, steely melon and pear aromas with
some earthiness. Good fruit extract on the palate, dry, zippy acidity, balanced with scented
fruit delivery—soft stewed apple flavours with a
touch of nectarine and lime zest. Delicious,
with a crisp, dry finish. *TDL*

Price	**£7–9/€9–11.50**
Region	**Trentino-Alto Adige**
Grape	**Pinot Grigio**
Alc/vol	**12%**
Food	**Crab**
Drink	**2001–2**

> **IGT** *(Indicazione Geografica Tipica) is a new quality category in Italy. Designed
> to encourage better-quality wines, the producer is allowed to specify the region,
> as in French Vins de Pays. IGT encourages experimentation with non-traditional
> winemaking practices and non-Italian grape varieties.*

Marchesi de' Frescobaldi/Robert Mondavi Danzante
Pinot Grigio IGT delle Venezie **00**

Pleasant, gentle nose—nut, apple and melon
aromas with a hint of elderflower. Deliciously
crisp, with soft stewed apple flavours on the
palate and a lovely dry, fruity finish.
Allied Drinks

Price	**£7–9/€9–11.50**
Region	**Veneto**
Grape	**Pinot Grigio**
Alc/vol	**12%**
Food	**Seafood**
Drink	**2001–2**

Zenato San Benedetto DOC Lugana 00 £/€

Appealing citrus aromas. Very rich and satisfying palate with terrific flavours of tart lemon, melon, rich pepperiness and herbal/green flavours. Good spicy finish. *Searsons*

Price	**£7–9/€9–11.50**
Grape	**Trebbiano di Lugana**
Alc/vol	**13%**
Food	**Prawns**
Drink	**2001–3**

£9–11/€11.50–14

Alasia Sorilaria DOC Roero Arneis 99 ✓

Pronounced, piquant aromas of the sea (salty) with a steel quality. The refreshing acidity is supported by lots of ripe apricot fruit. Complex, nutty, bready flavours linger on the long, fruity finish—lovely. *Findlaters*

Price	**£9–11/€11.50–14**
Region	**Piedmont**
Grape	**Arneis**
Alc/vol	**14%**
Food	**Versatile**
Drink	**2001–2**

Cà del Frati DOC Lugana 99

Pronounced aromas of nuts. A developed nose, with excellent ripe, sweet fruit and almond flavours. Delicious, zingy wine with good complexity of flavour and a lovely, persistent, steely finish. *Findlaters*

Price	**£9–11/€11.50–14**
Region	**Lombardy/Veneto**
Grape	**Trebbiano di Lugana**
Alc/vol	**12.5%**
Food	**Chinese**
Drink	**2001–3**

Castello di Pomino DOC Pomino 99

Lovely fresh, lemon-scented bouquet. Super zesty flavours of lemon, with a minerally, rounded, almost oily, mouthfeel. Crisp, clean wine, very well proportioned. *Allied Drinks*

Price	**£9–11/€11.50–14**
Region	**Tuscany**
Grape	**Chard/Pinot Bianco**
Alc/vol	**12%**
Food	**Fish**
Drink	**2001–2**

Colli di Catone DOC Frascati Superiore 99

Aromatic, spicy, nutty, yeasty aromas. Delicious dry wine with refreshing acidity and excellent nutty fruit. Refreshing and full of flavour, with a dry, crisp finish. *Febvre*

Price	**£9–11/€11.50–14**
Region	**Latium**
Grape	**Malvasia del Lazio/ Malvasia di Candia**
Alc/vol	**12%**
Food	**Ravioli**
Drink	**2001–2**

Eisacktaler Gewürztraminer della Valle Isarco
DOC Alto Adige **00**

A fine example made with a light touch. There is abundant ripe melon and orchard fruit on the nose. The same fruit comes through on the palate, which has a smooth fruity finish. *Select Wines*

Price	**£9–11/€11.50–14**
Region	**Trentino-Alto Adige**
Grape	**Gewürztraminer**
Alc/vol	**13.5%**
Food	**Thai/Chinese**
Drink	**2001–3**

Kettmeir Pinot Grigio DOC Alto Adige **99**
This wine has a lot of character. The smoky aromas on the nose range from green apples to melons with some smokiness. The palate is rich and satisfying, with apple, pear and nut flavours. *Select Wines*

Price	**£9–11/€11.50–14**
Region	**Trentino-Alto Adige**
Grape	**Pinot Grigio**
Alc/vol	**12%**
Food	**Pork**
Drink	**2001–2**

Le Moie DOC Verdicchio dei Castelli di Jesi Classico Superiore **99**
Pronounced apple fruit aromas with a touch of nuttiness. Lively acidity, a palate of concentrated citrus and gooseberry fruit with a little saltiness, a refreshing finish and excellent length all add up to a tasty wine. *Select Wines*

Price	**£9–11/€11.50–14**
Region	**Marches**
Grape	**Verdicchio**
Alc/vol	**12.5%**
Food	**Salmon**
Drink	**2001–2**

Regaleali IGT Sicilia **00**

Fragrant aromas of lime and lemongrass with nutty overtones. Dry, with zippy acidity and concentrated ripe sweet pears, melons and limes. Fruity finish and good length. *Select Wines*

Price	**£9–11/€11.50–14**
Region	**Sicily**
Grape	**Inzolia/Catarratto**
Alc/vol	**12%**
Food	**Crab salad**
Drink	**2001–2**

> ***Superiore*** *denotes that a wine has an extra degree of alcohol and a year's additional ageing. The category overlaps with Riserva.*

Sagramoso DOC Soave Superiore **00**
A good example of Soave, full of fruit. The nose is light, clean and rather delicate. On the palate good acidity supports a tangy, fruity wine that has citrus notes with a tight, intense core of nectarine fruit and a touch of nuttiness on the finish. Very decent indeed. *Woodford Bourne*

Price	**£9–11/€11.50–14**
Region	**Veneto**
Grape	**Garganega**
Alc/vol	**12%**
Food	**Aperitif, picnic**
Drink	**2001–2**

Santa Margherita Pinot Grigio DOC Valdadige 00

A zingy, spritzy wine with ripe apple and honey-suckle aromas. The palate has quite strong flavours of apple fruits with a mineral quality and lively acidity. *Select Wines*

Price	**£9–11/€11.50–14**
Region	**Trentino-Alto Adige**
Grape	**Pinot Grigio**
Alc/vol	**12%**
Food	**Thai**
Drink	**2001–2**

Stefano Farina DOCG Gavi 00

With its bright lemon colour and alluring nose of apricots, this wine is fresh and inviting. Concentrated apricot fruit on the palate, zippy acidity and a great finish. Super food wine.
J. S. Woods

Price	**£9–11/€11.50–14**
Region	**Piedmont**
Grape	**Cortese**
Alc/vol	**11.5%**
Food	**Grilled hake**
Drink	**2001–2**

Tenuta San Vita Verdiglio VdT 98

Mature nose of ripe apple and pear. Cox apple flavours dominate the palate, with some tangy lemon and hazelnut in the background. *Mary Pawle Wines*

Price	**£9–11/€11.50–14**
Region	**Tuscany**
Grape	**Verdicchio**
Alc/vol	**12.5%**
Food	**Roast chicken**
Drink	**2001–2**

Zenato Colombara DOC Soave Classico 00

Very attractive fresh nose with honey and floral notes. A slightly off-dry palate of assertive ripe apple flavours gives the wine universal appeal.
Searsons

Price	**£9–11/€11.50–14**
Region	**Veneto**
Grape	**Garganega/Trebbiano**
Alc/vol	**12%**
Food	**Aperitif or picnic**
Drink	**2001–2**

£11–13/€14–16.50

Cabanon Pinot Grigio DOC Oltrepò Pavese 00

Rich, appealing nose of white fleshy fruits, with shades of wine gums or tinned fruit. Rich, complex palate with more fleshy fruit and some creaminess. *Papillon*

Price	**£11–13/€14–16.50**
Region	**Lombardy**
Grape	**Pinot Grigio**
Alc/vol	**13%**
Food	**Aperitif**
Drink	**2001–2**

Michele Chiarlo DOCG Gavi 00 **£/€**

Nice citrus nose of lemons and limes; some nuts too. Dry, the wine has balanced acidity and is laden with concentrated lemony/Granny Smith apple fruit, giving a rounded mouthfeel. A delicious wine with a dry, fruity finish and flavours that linger on and on. *Taserra*

Price	**£11–13/€14–16.50**
Region	**Piedmont**
Grape	**Cortese**
Alc/vol	**12%**
Food	**Scallops**
Drink	**2001–2**

£13–15/€16.50–19

Marchesi di Barolo Gavi di Gavi DOCG Gavi 00

Though almost water-white in colour, the flavours are strong, oozing with steely, minerally
qualities and counterbalanced by sheer lime
zestiness. It packs a mouthful of creamy, nutty
flavours that go on and on. *Select Wines*

Price	**£13–15/€16.50–19**
Region	**Piedmont**
Grape	**Cortese**
Alc/vol	**12%**
Food	**Aperitif**
Drink	**2001–2**

£20–25/€25–32

Ascheri Podere di Montalupa VdT 98 ★

Subtle aromas of almonds and nuts. Young and
fresh, it has intense spicy, floral and citrus flavours and excellent length. Laden with ripe,
juicy fruits of pears and melons, this is a well-
rounded, complex wine with a lovely mouthfeel and refreshing acidity. *Findlaters*

Price	**£20–25/€25–32**
Region	**Piedmont**
Grape	**Viognier**
Alc/vol	**13%**
Food	**Crab claws**
Drink	**2001–2**

Red

> **Montepulciano** is both a grape and a town. The Montepulciano grape (not to
> be confused with the wine of the same name) is one of Italy's finest-quality
> grapes, grown mainly in Abruzzo. The village of Montepulciano is in Tuscany,
> south of Siena. Vino Nobile de Montepulciano is made from Sangiovese.

Under £7/Under €9

Barone di Poderj DOC Montepulciano d'Abruzzo 98 £/€

A very good wine at the price—structure with
spice and good pure red fruit flavours with a
hint of oak. Great midweek supper bottle.
WineOnline

Price	**Under £7/Under €9**
Region	**Abruzzo**
Grape	**Montepulciano**
Alc/vol	**12%**
Food	**Pizza**
Drink	**2001–2**

Mediterraneum DOC Montepulciano d'Abruzzo 98 £/€

Appealing nose of burnt blackberries, rubber
and liquorice. The palate is full of red berry
flavours with a chewy backbone and a satisfying
finish. *Findlaters*

Price	**Under £7/Under €9**
Region	**Abruzzo**
Grape	**Montepulciano**
Alc/vol	**12%**
Food	**Steak**
Drink	**2001–2**

San Fortunato IGT Umbria 99 £/€

Mature nose of plums and damsons. Interesting
mixed bag of flavours, including juicy plums, a
hint of leather and spice, yet with gentle tannins. *Dunnes Stores*

Price	**Under £7/Under €9**
Region	**Umbria**
Grape	**Sangiovese/Merlot**
Alc/vol	**12%**
Food	**Party**
Drink	**2001–2**

Terra Viva VdT **nv** **£/€** 🌿

Pleasant bramble jam nose and a decent palate of berry fruits and spice with a chewy tannin bite. A lovely all-rounder at a soft price. It has delicious cherry flavours. *Tesco*

Price	**Under £7/Under €9**
Alc/vol	**13%**
Food	**Tomata pasta**
Drink	**2001–3**

£7–9/€9–11.50

Alasia DOC Barbera d'Asti Superiore **98** ★ **£/€**

Cherry and plum aromas, tea roses, vanilla, herbs and espresso—what a mix! Superb, elegant palate of cherry pie, vanilla ice cream, plums and spice. So Italian. Charming wine with a beautiful finish. *Findlaters*

Price	**£7–9/€9–11.50**
Region	**Piedmont**
Grape	**Barbera**
Alc/vol	**13.5%**
Food	**Pot-roasted lamb**
Drink	**2001–2**

Alasia DOC Dolcetto d'Asti **99**

Nice summer aromas of cherries and strawberries. Lots of crisp, juicy young fruit in this one, which is bursting with flavour—summer fruit, hints of cinnamon and nuts, lemony acidity and soft tannins. *Findlaters*

Price	**£7–9/€9–11.50**
Region	**Piedmont**
Grape	**Dolcetto**
Alc/vol	**12.5%**
Food	**Pepperoni pizza**
Drink	**2001–2**

Beni di Batasiolo DOC Langhe **98** **£/€**

Lovely meaty wine. From the alpine strawberries and summer berries with a hint of nutmeg on the nose to the luscious, intense coffee/chocolate mousse and berry fruit on the palate, this wine has super fruit. Easy and supple, it's like a basketful of wild mountain fruit coated with smooth dark chocolate. *Barry & Fitzwilliam*

Price	**£7–9/€9–11.50**
Region	**Piedmont**
Grape	**Nebbiolo**
Alc/vol	**13%**
Food	**Casserole**
Drink	**2001–2**

Bolla DOC Valpolicella Classico **97**

Incredible—traditional-style Valpolicella at a very modest price! Complex, tasty, drinkable, yet versatile. Cherries, chocolate, raisins, dates and a hint of rubber mingle on the nose. There's more to come—prune, cherry and dark chocolate flavours are backed by a hint of oak on the palate. Deliciously different—full of flavour and body. *Dillons*

Price	**£7–9/€9–11.50**
Region	**Veneto**
Grape	**Corvina/Rondinella/Molinara**
Alc/vol	**12%**
Food	**Versatile**
Drink	**2001–2**

BEST VALUE WINE OF THE YEAR

Riserva on a label means that the wine has been aged in cask and/or bottle and has a higher alcoholic strength.

Candido DOC Salice Salentino Riserva 97

Cherry fruit aromas with some chocolate and vanilla. Spicy palate—plum tart and creamy chocolate—with a warm, appetising finish. This is such an attractive drink—everyday Italian wine that will suit everyone. *Findlaters*

Price	£7–9/€9–11.50
Region	Puglia
Grape	Negroamaro/ Malvasia Nera
Alc/vol	13.5%
Food	Salami
Drink	2001–3

Conti Serristori DOCG Chianti 99 £/€

A fruity nose with black cherries, raspberries, almonds and a hint of cream. Delicious, easy-drinking Chianti, full of cherries, raspberries and redcurrants. Tannins are still quite firm. *Dillons*

Price	£7–9/€9–11.50
Region	Tuscany
Grape	Sangiovese/Canaiolo
Alc/vol	12%
Food	Creamy pasta
Drink	2001–3

Elorina Villa Dorata DOC Eloro Rosso 98 £/€

Hot-climate, spirity nose of wild forest fruits with herbaceous tones. Damson flavours and more herbaceous notes on the palate, which finishes well. Punchy—lots of Sicilian sunshine helped to make this unique. *Findlaters*

Price	£7–9/€9–11.50
Region	Sicily
Grape	Nero d'Avola
Alc/vol	12.5%
Food	Pepperoni pizza
Drink	2001–2

Fabiano Cabernet Sauvignon IGT Veneto 98 ★

Pepper and cherries on the nose. Delicious glassful of ripe red and black berries with a finely balanced streak of cherry-like acidity. Clean finish. A real food wine. *WineOnline*

Price	£7–9/€9–11.50
Region	Veneto
Grape	Cabernet Sauvignon
Alc/vol	12.5%
Food	Versatile
Drink	2001–3

Fabiano Pinot Nero IGT Provincia di Pavia 98

A pleasant, approachable wine with a brambly, spicy nose. Fruity flavours on the palate with hints of liquorice coming through to give a clean, dry finish. *WineOnline*

Price	£7–9/€9–11.50
Region	Lombardy
Grape	Pinot Nero
Alc/vol	12.5%
Food	Spaghetti Bolognese
Drink	2001–2

Leone de Castris DOC Copertino 98 ✓

Plums, raspberries and vanilla aromas. With quite a minerally quality to the palate and marked acidity, this is an intensely fruity, spicy, characterful wine with a bittersweet twist at the end. *Select Wines*

Price	£7–9/€9–11.50
Region	Puglia
Grape	Negroamaro/ Malvasia Nera
Alc/vol	13%
Food	Beefburgers
Drink	2001–3

Marchesi de' Frescobaldi Rèmole IGT Toscana 99

Dark fruit aromas—loganberries, cherries, even some dried fruits. The soft palate of red fruits and blackcurrants develops into a typically Italian mouthfeel of cherries.
Allied Drinks

Price	**£7–9/€9–11.50**
Region	**Tuscany**
Grape	**Sangiovese/Cab Sauv**
Alc/vol	**12%**
Food	**Pizza**
Drink	**2001–3**

Masseria del Conte DOC Salice Salentino Riserva nv £/€

Oodles of blackcurrant, spice and oak aromas develop even further on tasting. The palate has rich, concentrated damson and spice flavours with warming alcohol. *Dunnes Stores*

Price	**£7–9/€9–11.50**
Region	**Puglia**
Grape	**Negroamaro/ Malvasia Nera**
Alc/vol	**13%**
Food	**Bruschetta**
Drink	**2001–3**

Rocca DOC Leverano Riserva 97

Very aromatic—intense, inky loganberries, rose petals and wild rosemary. Plummy back cherries on the crisp, juicy palate with some rustic, leathery undertones. Warm, long, alcoholic finish. *O'Briens*

Price	**£7–9/€9–11.50**
Region	**Puglia**
Grape	**Negroamaro/ Malvasia Nera**
Alc/vol	**13%**
Food	**Pasta**
Drink	**2001–2**

Tabarin DOC Barbera d'Asti 00

A brooding, dark wine that gives a satisfying warm glow. The spicy nose of plums, liquorice and star anise is followed by a soft palate of smoky, dark, intense blackcurrant pastille fruit flavours and medium length. *Oddbins*

Price	**£7–9/€9–11.50**
Region	**Piedmont**
Grape	**Barbera**
Alc/vol	**13%**
Food	**Versatile**
Drink	**2001–3**

Tesco DOCG Chianti Classico Riserva 98 £/€

Sour cherries, wild strawberries and violet aromas. The palate is dry, mingling cherry and damson fruit with some herbaceous notes. The wine has robust body, crisp lemony acidity and quite gripping tannins that should mellow. *Tesco*

Price	**£7–9/€9–11.50**
Region	**Tuscany**
Grape	**Sangiovese**
Alc/vol	**13%**
Food	**Pork chops**
Drink	**2001–2**

Zenato DOC Valpolicella Classico Superiore 98

Delightful wine, with its lovely Latin character of bitter chocolate, cherry fruit and biting acidity. A modern style of wine. Flavours are smooth and nicely integrated. Easy drinking and cheerful. *Searsons*

Price	**£7–9/€9–11.50**
Region	**Veneto**
Grape	**Corvina/Rondinella**
Alc/vol	**12.5%**
Food	**Barbecued sausages**
Drink	**2001–2**

£9–11/€11.50–14

Alasia Nebbiolo DOC Langhe **97**

Nice sweet chocolate and mint aromas to this well-made example of Nebbiolo. Delicious depth of fruity flavours—chocolate, maraschino cherries, star anise and mint flow smoothly to a crisp cherry-stone finish. *Findlaters*

Price	**£9–11/€11.50–14**
Region	**Piedmont**
Grape	**Nebbiolo**
Alc/vol	**14%**
Food	**Cannelloni**
Drink	**2001–3**

Alasia Rive DOC Barbera d'Asti **99** ★

A very fine Barbera, big, balanced and very elegant. Complex aromas of black cherries, plums, dates and strawberries. Wonderful weight on the palate of powerful dark cherry fruit with figs, raisins and espresso. Firmish tannins and an intriguing finish. This has great style and panache. *Findlaters*

Price	**£9–11/€11.50–14**
Region	**Piedmont**
Grape	**Barbera**
Alc/vol	**14%**
Food	**Venison casserole**
Drink	**2001–3**

Brusco dei Barbi IGT Toscana **99**

Immediately appealing, very fruity, yet very Italian. Lots of structure, lots of blackberry, cinnamon and cherry fruit, savoury yet juicy. Complex yet approachable. Firm tannins. Lovely wine, but still young. One to watch over the next year. *Select Wines*

Price	**£9–11/€11.50–14**
Region	**Tuscany**
Grape	**Sangiovese**
Alc/vol	**13%**
Food	**Roast pork**
Drink	**2001–3**

Carpineto Dogajolo IGT Toscano **99 £/€**

Quite a closed nose, but some aromas of forest fruits. This wine is still very young, with a tight tannic structure overlying juicy black fruit, cassis, tobacco and liquorice. *Taserra*

Price	**£9–11/€11.50–14**
Region	**Tuscany**
Grape	**Sangiovese/Cab Sauv**
Alc/vol	**12.5%**
Food	**Steak**
Drink	**2001–3**

Cesari Mara Vino di Ripasso
DOC Valpolicella Classico Superiore **98 £/€**

Great example of how good Valpolicella can be. The nose is full of cherry, raspberry, strawberry, redcurrant and plum fruits with a hint of oak. Intense, silky, lush palate of cherries and autumn fruits and a touch of mint. *TDL*

Price	**£9–11/€11.50–14**
Region	**Veneto**
Grape	**Corvina/Rondinella**
Alc/vol	**13%**
Food	**Mushroom quiche**
Drink	**2001–2**

Fazi-Battaglia DOC Rosso Conero **99**

A really lively, fruity wine with delicious concentrated cherry and fig flavours. Fragrant and floral, it has zingy lemony length and a fine tangy mouthfeel. *Select Wines*

Price	**£9–11/€11.50–14**
Region	**Marches**
Grape	**Montepulciano/ Sangiovese**
Alc/vol	**12%**
Food	**Antipasto**
Drink	**2001–3**

Il Tarocco DOCG Chianti Classico **98**

Intense aromas of cherries, damsons, mulberries, warm spices and mocha. The palate is dark and inky, with more black cherries and damsons. The rich yet refreshing mouthfeel goes on to a lingering finish. Made for food. *Oddbins*

Price	**£9–11/€11.50–14**
Region	**Tuscany**
Grape	**Sangiovese/Cannaiolo**
Alc/vol	**12.5%**
Food	**Rack of lamb, pizza**
Drink	**2001–3**

Kettmeir Tridentum DOC Teroldego Rotaliano **00**

Fragrant nose of berries and violets. The palate is chock-a-block with blackberry, loganberry and cherry fruit with a dash of espresso. Crisp acidity and a pleasantly bitter aftertaste. Unusual and very enjoyable wine. *Select Wines*

Price	**£9–11/€11.50–14**
Region	**Trentino-Alto Adige**
Grape	**Teroldego**
Alc/vol	**12%**
Food	**Prosciutto**
Drink	**2001–2**

Marchesi di Barolo Ruvei DOC Barbera d'Alba **99**

A little smoky on the nose, this Barbera has lots of typical dark berry and cherry-stone flavours, some elements of nuts and oaky vanilla with a long, tasty finish. *Select Wines*

Price	**£9–11/€11.50–14**
Region	**Piedmont**
Grape	**Barbera**
Alc/vol	**13.5%**
Food	**Italian meatballs**
Drink	**2001–3**

Masi Campofiorin Ripasso IGT Rosso del Veronese **97**

Vibrant, racy nose of redcurrants, cherries, vanilla and plums. Lots of character on the palate, too, with delicious juicy red and black fruits and zippy acidity. There's a hint of bitter cherries on the finish. Very delicious and refreshing style. *Grants*

Price	**£9–11/€11.50–14**
Region	**Veneto**
Grape	**Corvina/Rondinella/ Molinara**
Alc/vol	**13%**
Food	**Antipasto, pasta**
Drink	**2001–2**

Melini Isassi DOCG Chianti Classico **98 £/€**

Chiantis are getting better and better. This one has all those lovely alpine strawberry and cherry flavours, crisp acidity and soft, well-rounded tannins. There is a fine lemon peel twist on the long, clean finish. *Gilbeys*

Price	**£9–11/€11.50–14**
Region	**Tuscany**
Grape	**Sangiovese/Canaiolo**
Alc/vol	**12%**
Food	**Parmesan cheese**
Drink	**2001–3**

Michele Chiarlo DOC Barbera d'Asti **97**

Cherry and damson aromas are followed by masses of ripe, luscious cherries, dark chocolate and spice flavours with an ample mouthfeel, supple tannins and a medium-long finish. *Taserra*

Price	**£9–11/€11.50–14**
Region	**Piedmont**
Grape	**Barbera**
Alc/vol	**13%**
Food	**Macaroni cheese**
Drink	**2001–3**

Regaleali Rosso Tasca d'Almerita IGT Sicilia 99 £/€

A combination of aromas and flavours. Herbs and cherries on the nose are transformed into ripe cherries, bubble-gum and a hint of rubber on the palate, but with vibrant Italian acidity to keep it fresh. *Select Wines*

Price	**£9–11/€11.50–14**
Region	**Sicily**
Grape	**Nero d'Avola/ Perricone**
Alc/vol	**13%**
Food	**Rich casseroles**
Drink	**2001–3**

San Giovanni DOCG Chianti Classico Riserva 97 ★

Aromatic nose of cherries, mulberries, dark chocolate, cinnamon and spice. The fruit is every bit as rich on the palate, with wonderful layers of ripe, luscious cherry/damson fruit with some espresso lurking behind. With a good bite of acidity backed by velvety tannins and a long finish, this wine has all its elements in sync. *Dunnes Stores*

Price	**£9–11/€11.50–14**
Region	**Tuscany**
Grape	**Mainly Sangiovese**
Alc/vol	**13%**
Food	**Charcuterie**
Drink	**2001–3**

Stefano Farina Il Brumaio DOC Langhe 98 ★ £/€

A great all-rounder, with lots of juicy black cherry fruit and an attractive wild game and mushroom character. Really crisp, this wine cries out for some tasty food. *J. S. Woods*

Price	**£9–11/€11.50–14**
Region	**Piedmont**
Grape	**Nebbiolo**
Alc/vol	**12%**
Food	**Roast pheasant**
Drink	**2001–3**

Versato Santa Margherita IGT Veneto Merlot 99

Definitely Merlot but oh so Italian, with more acidity than you usually get with Merlot. Supple and easy drinking, with delicate cherry fruit and oaky characteristics. *Select Wines*

Price	**£9–11/€11.50–14**
Region	**Veneto**
Grape	**Merlot**
Alc/vol	**12.5%**
Food	**Italian sausage**
Drink	**2001–2**

Zaccagnini DOC Montepulciano d'Abruzzo 99 £/€

Bursting with ripe forest fruits and a delicious creamy dark chocolate layer, this is a smashing Italian. Really versatile, it will drink happily with many different foods. *Searsons*

Price	**£9–11/€11.50–14**
Region	**Abruzzo**
Grape	**Montepulciano**
Alc/vol	**12.5%**
Food	**Versatile**
Drink	**2001–3**

£11–13/€14–16.50

Castello di Farnetella DOCG Chianti Colli Senesi 98

Spicy, dark fruit aromas. This wine has typical Chianti flavours of cherries, tea leaves and wild berries, with a long, lingering cherry-stone finish. *J. S. Woods*

Price	**£11–13/€14–16.50**
Region	**Tuscany**
Grape	**Mainly Sangiovese**
Alc/vol	**13%**
Food	**Mushroom risotto**
Drink	**2001–2**

Coltibuono Roberto Stucchi DOCG Chianti Classico 99 £/€

Beautiful Chianti, with its ripe blackberry/toasted almond aromas and hint of rubber. Very intense palate of ripe black cherries, almonds and a touch of oak, with a round, full mouthfeel and a smooth finish. Like all Italian reds, needs food. *Findlaters*

Price	**£11–13/€14–16.50**
Region	**Tuscany**
Grape	**Mainly Sangiovese**
Alc/vol	**13%**
Food	**Chicken casserole**
Drink	**2001–3**

La Gavina Cabernet Sauvignon IGT Toscana 97

Almost inky in colour, there is a whopping concentration of fruit and complexity on the nose—spice, red fruit, pepper, herbs. Spicy damson and plum fruit flavours emerge victorious over robust tannins. *Dunnes Stores*

Price	**£11–13/€14–16.50**
Region	**Tuscany**
Grape	**Cabernet Sauvignon**
Alc/vol	**13%**
Food	**Roast goose with chestnuts**
Drink	**2001–3**

Lamole di Lamole DOCG Chianti Classico 98

Plenty of ripe, sweetish cherry and plum fruit, with some intriguing dark roasted coffee flavours and spicy tones. Tannins are mellow but still evident, making this a perfect food wine. *Select Wines*

Price	**£11–13/€14–16.50**
Region	**Tuscany**
Grape	**Mainly Sangiovese**
Alc/vol	**12.5%**
Food	**Braised beef**
Drink	**2001–3**

Le Canne DOC Bardolino Classico Superiore 98

Very drinkable, with a substantial acid/tannin structure supporting sweet cherry and strawberry fruit. An expensive example, but approachable and fruity. If you've never tried a Bardolino but want to give it a shot, buy this one. *Febvre*

Price	**£11–13/€14–16.50**
Region	**Veneto**
Grape	**Corvina/Rondinella/ Molinara**
Alc/vol	**12%**
Food	**Cannelloni**
Drink	**2001–2**

Leone de Castris DOC Salice Salentino Riserva 98

A tad more finesse here than the average. A smooth, almost velvety palate encapsulates oak, ripe figs, damsons and harmonious pepper, cloves and cinnamon. This wine will seriously impress your friends. *Select Wines*

Price	**£11–13/€14–16.50**
Region	**Puglia**
Grape	**Negroamaro/ Malvasia Nera**
Alc/vol	**13.5%**
Food	**Roast lamb**
Drink	**2001–3**

Marchesi de' Frescobaldi Nipozzano
DOCG Chianti Rufina Riserva **97**

Elegance. Finesse. Style. An expressive, mature nose of wild strawberries, Morello cherries, chocolate and coffee. Fruit is just as rich and concentrated on the palate, which displays inky depths of black cherries, plums and cassis with enlivening acidity. *Allied Drinks*

Price	**£11–13/€14–16.50**
Region	**Tuscany**
Grape	**Mainly Sangiovese**
Alc/vol	**12.5%**
Food	**Chicken cacciatore**
Drink	**2001–4**

Marchesi di Barolo Madonna di Como
DOC Dolcetto d'Alba **00**

This is a rich, concentrated Dolcetto, with aromas of violets and a slight hint of burnt rubber. Tons of ripe, dark damson and cherry fruit on the palate. *Select Wines*

Price	**£11–13/€14–16.50**
Region	**Piedmont**
Grape	**Dolcetto**
Alc/vol	**13%**
Food	**Beef carpaccio**
Drink	**2001–2**

Michele Chiarlo DOC Dolcetto d'Alba **98**

This shows what a classic Dolcetto can be. The nose has quite minerally, leathery loganberry and raspberry fruit, while the palate reveals complex layers of cherries, red fruit, zippy acidity and a terrific savoury finish. *Taserra*

Price	**£11–13/€14–16.50**
Region	**Piedmont**
Grape	**Dolcetto**
Alc/vol	**12%**
Food	**Mediterranean vegetable casserole**
Drink	**2001–3**

Michele Chiarlo Airone DOC Monferrato **98**

Soft, pleasant nose of cherries, cranberries and youthful berries. Abundant fruit on the palate—raspberries, sun-dried tomatoes, smoky hints. There's a nice balance of tasty fruit, mouthwatering acidity and velvety tannins. *Taserra*

Price	**£11–13/€14–16.50**
Region	**Piedmont**
Grape	**Grignolino**
Alc/vol	**13%**
Food	**Salami**
Drink	**2001–3**

Montegradella Santá Sofiá
DOC Valpolicella Classico Superiore **97**

An unusual nose of liquorice with red peppers. On the palate there are big, plump, bursting black cherries balanced with lovely fresh acidity. *Select Wines*

Price	**£11–13/€14–16.50**
Region	**Veneto**
Grape	**Corvina/Rondinella/ Molinara**
Alc/vol	**12.5%**
Food	**Tuna**
Drink	**2001–2**

Villa Antinori DOCG Chianti Classico Riserva **97**

There is lots of life in this rich Chianti from the spectacular 97 vintage. Gorgeous now, with rich tobacco and chocolate flavours and a slight medicinal edge, but another year should reveal even more palate pleasure. *Grants*

Price	**£11–13/€14–16.50**
Region	**Tuscany**
Grape	**Mainly Sangiovese**
Alc/vol	**13%**
Food	**Spaghetti with pesto**
Drink	**2001–2**

MOËT & CHANDON
Fondé en 1743

Nederburg

Barton & Guestier
La passion du vin depuis 1725

LUPÉ-CHOLET

I.L. RUFFINO

CONTI SERRISTORI

BLUE NUN®

WOLF BLASS WINES

FOUNDED IN 1850
CARMEN

SANDEMAN
EST 1790

AD VINUM

BOLLA

MATEUS®
PRODUCED AND BOTTLED IN PORTUGAL

PRODUCE OF SPAIN
Señorío de los Llanos

SANTA ROSA
ESTATE
Mendoza   Argentina

Fetzer.

FONTANA CANDIDA

MONTECILLO

EDWARD DILLON
Distributors of
International Brands
of
Wines & Spirits
& COMPANY LIMITED

Fine wines from Edward Dillon & Co. Ltd.

Vistarenni Vigneto Assolo DOCG Chianti Classico 97

A lovely example from Assolo, a single vineyard. Lots of crisp damson and cherry fruit,
with good inky depth of flavour and a long,
spicy finish. *Select Wines*

Price	**£11–13/€14–16.50**
Region	**Tuscany**
Grape	**Sangiovese**
Alc/vol	**12.5%**
Food	**Lasagne**
Drink	**2001–3**

Zenato Ripassa DOC Valpolicella Superiore 98

Black stone fruit aromas and flavours. The palate has a dash of spice for interest and the finish
is pleasing. With terrific length, a dependable,
solid Italian red. *Searsons*

Price	**£11–13/€14–16.50**
Region	**Veneto**
Grape	**Corvina/Rondinella/ Molinara**
Alc/vol	**13%**
Food	**Lamb chops**
Drink	**2001–2**

£13–15/€16.50–19

Cesari Mitico Merlot IGT delle Venezie 97

Beautiful bouquet of cherries and pencil shavings. Lovely ripe cherry and blackberry fruit,
quite like a serious Valpolicella Classico. Lively,
elegant and fruity wine. *TDL*

Price	**£13–15/€16.50–19**
Region	**Veneto**
Grape	**Merlot**
Alc/vol	**13%**
Food	**Baked ham**
Drink	**2001–2**

Fassati Pasiteo DOCG Vino Nobile di Montepulciano 97

Smoky, spicy aromas with lots of dark fruit. The
plum fruit on the palate is very concentrated
with elements of spice and coffee. Long, spicy,
complex finish. *Select Wines*

Price	**£13–15/€16.50–19**
Region	**Tuscany**
Grape	**Prugnolo/Canaiolo/ Mammolo**
Alc/vol	**13%**
Food	**Roasts**
Drink	**2001–3**

La Botte No. 18 Cuore di Vino Selezione Cabanon
DOC Oltrepò Pavese 98 🦋

This wine has a gamy nose of Oxo cubes mixed
with the fruitier aromas of cherries and summer
berries. The mature palate has deep, leathery,
meaty flavours of soft plums and cherries. This
wine is well put together, with supple tannins,
balanced acidity and medium-long length.
Papillon

Price	**£13–15/€16.50–19**
Region	**Lombardy**
Grape	**Cab Sauv/Cab Franc/ Bonarda/Barbera**
Alc/vol	**13%**
Food	**Lasagne**
Drink	**2001–3**

Lamole di Lamole Barrique DOCG Chianti Classico 98 ✓

A sophisticated, elegant Chianti, this has lots to
offer, with its mature fruits and warm, spicy
flavours, but still with that great classic twist of
cherry-stone acidity in the long finish.
Select Wines

Price	**£13–15/€16.50–19**
Region	**Tuscany**
Grape	**Mainly Sangiovese**
Alc/vol	**12.5%**
Food	**Game**
Drink	**2001–3**

Masi Toar IGT Rosso del Veronese 97

Restrained nose of green leaf tones, raisins and fruit cake. The palate is more expressive, with soft blackberry jam and cherry compote flavours. Quite complex with a firm backbone of acidity, supple tannins and a persistent finish. *Grants*

Price	**£13–15/€16.50–19**
Region	**Veneto**
Grape	**Corvina/ Rondinella/ Oseleta**
Alc/vol	**12.5%**
Food	**Versatile**
Drink	**2001–2**

Sante Lancerio DOCG Vino Nobile di Montepulciano 96

Red fruit and mocha aromas. Rich dark chocolate palate with black cherries, a hint of vanilla and firm tannins to give the wine good grip. Long, clean finish. Smooth and chewy at the same time, this is a good food choice. *Gilbeys*

Price	**£13–15/€16.50–19**
Region	**Tuscany**
Grape	**Sangiovese/Canaiolo**
Alc/vol	**13%**
Food	**Rib of beef**
Drink	**2001–3**

£15–17/€19–22

Bolla DOC Amarone della Valpolicella Classico 95 £/€ ✓

A fine example of the savoury yet sweet flavours of Amarone. Great concentration. A full-bodied, powerful wine, packed with earthy, interesting flavours—chocolate, cherries, leather, even some walnuts. Enjoy this with substantial dishes. *Dillons*

Price	**£15–17/€19–22**
Region	**Veneto**
Grape	**Corvina/Rondinella/ Molinara**
Alc/vol	**14%**
Food	**Game casserole**
Drink	**2001–3**

Castelli di Pomino DOC Pomino 97 ✓

A rich ruby colour, this wine has a terrific perfume of damsons, black cherries, black berries, ink, spice and fruit cake. Very appealing fruit on the palate—cherries, almonds, plums, with a brisk streak of acidity and a refreshingly crisp finish. *Allied Drinks*

Price	**£15–17/€19–22**
Region	**Tuscany**
Grape	**Mainly Sangiovese**
Alc/vol	**12.5%**
Food	**Game**
Drink	**2001–4**

£17–20/€22–25

Castello Banfi DOC Rosso di Montalcino 98

Lovely earthy aromas of cherries, spice, liquorice and blackberries. A solid, well-made wine, full of interesting, rich flavours that reflect the nose. *Febvre*

Price	**£17–20/€22–25**
Region	**Tuscany**
Grape	**Sangiovese**
Alc/vol	**12.5%**
Food	**Rich, spicy dishes**
Drink	**2001–3**

Fabiano DOC Amarone della Valpolicella Classico 95

Big, concentrated and rich, with five years' age at an affordable price. A serious Amarone. A good introduction to this style of wine, full of earthy, oaky, cherry, strawberry jam and leather flavours, with robust tannins and a strong finish. *WineOnline*

Price	**£17–20/€22–25**
Region	**Veneto**
Grape	**Corvina/Rondinella/ Molinara**
Alc/vol	**14%**
Food	**Magret of duck**
Drink	**2001–3**

Leone de Castris Donna Lisa
DOC Salice Salentino Riserva 96 £/€

A complex nose lives up to its promise! Rich, inky, intense damsons and autumn fruits carry the weight of alcohol and oak effortlessly on the palate. This wine will age gracefully. *Select Wines*

Price	**£17–20/€22–25**
Region	**Puglia**
Grape	**Negroamaro**
Alc/vol	**13%**
Food	**Turkey**
Drink	**2002–5**

Masi Costasera DOC Amarone della Valpolicella Classico 97 ✓

Ripe and varied aromas of plums, raisins, espresso and a touch of coconut. The elegant but powerful palate yields figs, dates, dried fruits, plums, strawberries, mocha, creamy dark chocolate and softening vanilla tannins. This is a generous, flavour-packed wine—big and powerful, but with stylish elegance. *Grants*

Price	**£17–20/€22–25**
Region	**Veneto**
Grape	**Corvina/Rondinella/ Molinara**
Alc/vol	**15%**
Food	**Roast meats**
Drink	**2001–3**

£20–25/€25–32

Beni di Batasiolo DOCG Barolo 96

A very fine and elegant bouquet precedes flavours of rose water, wild strawberries and fruits of the forest. With its crisp balancing acidity, firm tannins and long finish, this is an excellent example of the potential of the Nebbiolo grape. Serious stuff, so keep the food simple.
Barry & Fitzwilliam

Price	**£20–25/€25–32**
Region	**Piedmont**
Grape	**Nebbiolo**
Alc/vol	**13.5%**
Food	**Venison**
Drink	**2002–6**

Bersano Niwasco DOCG Barolo 97 ★

There are so many luscious rich flavours packed into this wine. Dark cherry fruits on the nose with plum and vanilla aromas. Elegant and breathtakingly balanced flavours of dark cherry, plum, spice, liquorice and chocolate/vanilla essences. Matures beautifully to a long and elegant finish. *Maxxium*

Price	**£20–25/€25–32**
Region	**Piedmont**
Grape	**Nebbiolo**
Alc/vol	**13.5%**
Food	**Game casserole**
Drink	**2002–6**

Boscaini Marano DOC Amarone della Valpolicella Classico **97**

A fabulous example of classic Amarone. Heady aromas of redcurrants, raspberries, cherries, damp earth, autumnal fruits and oak. The silky palate is multi-layered—autumnal fruits, cinnamon, liquorice, mocha, bitter chocolate. *Febvre*

Price	**£20–25/€25–32**
Region	**Veneto**
Grape	**Corvina/Rondinella/ Molinara**
Alc/vol	**15%**
Food	**Risotto**
Drink	**2001–4**

Carpineto DOCG Chianti Classico Riserva **97** ★

Very elegant nose—black cherries, spice, vanilla, chocolate and pepper. The palate also delivers, with layers of spice, black fruit and chocolate balanced by lively acidity. These are flavours to be savoured slowly, right through to the long, smooth finish. Outstanding example of the great 97 vintage in Tuscany. *Taserra*

Price	**£20–25/€25–32**
Region	**Tuscany**
Grape	**Mainly Sangiovese**
Alc/vol	**13%**
Food	**Roast duck**
Drink	**2001–4**

Carpineto DOCG Vino Nobile di Montepulciano Riserva **96** ✓

Rich, concentrated nose. The palate is layered with rich, ripe blackcurrant, damson and cherry fruit with a hint of cigar box and vanilla. Tannins are quite chewy. This fabulous, intense wine has class and style. *Taserra*

Price	**£20–25/€25–32**
Region	**Tuscany**
Grape	**Sangiovese/Canaiolo Nero**
Alc/vol	**13%**
Food	**Steak**
Drink	**2001–4**

Castello di Brolio DOCG Chianti Classico **97**

This is a big, serious Chianti with a lot of character. It has an appealing nose of black cherries, dark forest fruits and lead pencils. The earthy palate is thick and viscous, with black cherries, damsons, stony fruit and forceful tannins. Long, rich finish. *Cassidy*

Price	**£20–25/€25–32**
Region	**Tuscany**
Grape	**Mainly Sangiovese**
Alc/vol	**13.5%**
Food	**Venison casserole with grilled polenta**
Drink	**2001–4**

Cesari DOC Amarone della Valpolicella Classico **95**

Striking aromas of autumnal fruits, cherries and farmyards. Deliciously intense wine, ripe, silky autumn fruits, cinnamon, Christmas pudding flavours. Great backbone of acidity and tannin. Warming. *TDL*

Price	**£20–25/€25–32**
Region	**Veneto**
Grape	**Corvina/Rondinella/ Molinara**
Alc/vol	**14%**
Food	**Meat casserole**
Drink	**2001–3**

Mantico Bersano DOCG Barbaresco **97** ✓

This Barbaresco shows promise, but needs some time to soften. Forceful tannins mask the emerging fruit and chocolate/liquorice flavours. It's starting to come into balance and will keep for some years yet. Finishes to a smooth and powerful length. *Maxxium*

Price	**£20–25/€25–32**
Region	**Piedmont**
Grape	**Nebbiolo**
Alc/vol	**13.5%**
Food	**Pasta with meat sauce**
Drink	**2002–5**

Mastroberardino Radici DOCG Taurasi 96 ✓

Showing classic maturity, this wine is complex yet very drinkable at this stage, with violets, roses, plums and spice intermingling beautifully. Elegant and satisfying. *Select Wines*

Price	**£20–25/€25–32**
Region	**Campania**
Grape	**Aglianico**
Alc/vol	**13%**
Food	**Loin of pork**
Drink	**2002–5**

Tenuta Trerose Riserva
DOCG Vino Nobile di Montepulciano 95 ✓

Appealing, rich aromas of truffles, chocolate and coffee beans. Savoury and tangy, with fine ripe cherry and liquorice flavours, this is an elegant example of a Vino Nobile. *Searsons*

Price	**£20–25/€25–32**
Region	**Tuscany**
Grape	**Sangiovese/Canaiolo**
Alc/vol	**14%**
Food	**Aubergine parmigiana**
Drink	**2001–2**

Zenato DOC Amarone della Valpolicella Classico 97 ★

Heavenly! Beautiful stewed fruits with a sweet raspberry kick. The complex nose shows liquorice, sultanas, hazelnuts—a stunner. There are lashings of cherry fruit on the palate, along with caramel and toffee flavours. Miraculously there is enough acidity to leave the wine moreish. *Searsons*

Price	**£20–25/€25–32**
Region	**Veneto**
Grape	**Corvina/Rondinella/ Molinara**
Alc/vol	**14.5%**
Food	**Cheese**
Drink	**2001–6**

£25–30/€32–40

Patriglione IGT Rosso del Salento 94 ★

An amazing southern beauty with great richness of flavour. Big, opulent aromas of raisins and milk chocolate lead to a robust and powerful palate of raisins, blackcurrants, spice, chocolate, vanilla and ripe cherries. It's holding its age well, is beautifully balanced and yet still has a bite. Classic finish. Pricey, but wonderful example of winemaking at the highest level. *Woodford Bourne*

Price	**£25–30/€32–40**
Region	**Puglia**
Grape	**Mainly Negroamaro**
Alc/vol	**14.5%**
Food	**Pepper steak**
Drink	**2001–3**

Stefano Farina DOCG Barolo 97 ✓

Beautiful tempting nose of sweet fruit, with vegetal overtones. The flavours are typically Barolo—intense, dark, chewy black fruit, figs and liquorice, and an intriguing layer of rich espresso coffee and violets. *J. S. Woods*

Price	**£25–30/€32–40**
Region	**Piedmont**
Grape	**Nebbiolo**
Alc/vol	**13.5%**
Food	**Beef in red wine**
Drink	**2002–5**

Lebanon

Red

£15–17/€19–22

Ch. Musar Gaston Hochar 94 ✓

Gaston Hochar trained in France and is still influenced by French winemaking techniques, but this wine is made in a very individual style. It has a big, rubbery, fruity nose of plums, strawberries, figs and vanilla. A little Rhône-like, the palate is big and slightly vegetal, with integrated, lasting, textured layers of strawberries, vanilla and figs. The fig flavours give an almost port-like feel. With its elegant, rich (and quite alcoholic) finish, it's something different and very true to its origins. *Grants*

Price	**£15–17/€19–22**
Region	**Bekaa Valley**
Grape	**Cab Sauv/Cinsault**
Alc/vol	**14%**
Food	**Lamb kebabs**
Drink	**2001–3**

New Zealand

New Zealand and Australia are often found side by side on wine shelves, but they are far apart in terms of wine styles. The difference is easy to explain—New Zealand is a thousand miles from Australia and has a cool maritime climate. New Zealand is very successful at producing white wines (about 80 per cent of production) and makes wonderful Sauvignon Blanc, whereas Australia struggles with this variety. While aromatic and pungent Sauvignon Blancs have made New Zealand's name, it also produces some great Riesling and Chardonnay. This year a star goes to a white wine made from Pinot Gris. The standard of red wines using Pinot Noir, Cabernet Sauvignon and Cabernet blends has risen dramatically over the last few years. Merlot, considered a rising star, is found on its own and in blends, especially with Cabernet Sauvignon.

White

£7–9/€9–11.50

Babich Riesling 00

A floral and honeyed nose, yet the palate is quite different, with a fresh, crisp and clean mouthful of apple and citrus fruit backed by wonderful acidity. The whole thing works perfectly. *Gleeson*

Price	**£7–9/€9–11.50**
Region	**Marlborough**
Grape	**Riesling**
Alc/vol	**12%**
Food	**Chinese**
Drink	**2001–2**

Stoneleigh Vineyards Chardonnay 99

Restrained apple and lime aromas. Juicy and mouth-watering citrus and apple fruit on the palate with a long, classy finish. *Irish Distillers*

Price	**£7–9/€9–11.50**
Region	**Marlborough**
Grape	**Chardonnay**
Alc/vol	**14%**
Food	**Whitebait**
Drink	**2001–2**

Stoneleigh Vineyards Sauvignon Blanc 00

A hugely concentrated Sauvignon Blanc on both nose and palate. Ripe gooseberry notes are the order of the day with asparagus and grassiness. Spicy, spiky finish. Strong Sauvignon flavour with a lot of punch. *Irish Distillers*

Price	**£7–9/€9–11.50**
Region	**Marlborough**
Grape	**Sauvignon Blanc**
Alc/vol	**13.5%**
Food	**Fish**
Drink	**2001–2**

Villa Maria Private Bin Marlborough Riesling 00

New World Riesling with a tropical fruit nose and fruit-centred palate of pineapple, guava, honeydew melon, apple and lime. The finish is satisfying, ending in fruity notes with a hint of honey. *Allied Drinks*

Price	**£7–9/€9–11.50**
Region	**Marlborough**
Grape	**Riesling**
Alc/vol	**12.5%**
Food	**Thai**
Drink	**2001–3**

£9–11/€11.50–14

Babich Winemaker's Reserve Gewürztraminer 00 £/€

Pungent nose of spice, pepper, apples and citrus. Definitely a food wine, with concentrated apple and citrus fruit on the palate. Fruit, acidity and alcohol combine to give a nice balance and mouthfeel. *Gleeson*

Price	**£9–11/€11.50–14**
Region	**Hawkes Bay**
Grape	**Gewürztraminer**
Alc/vol	**14%**
Food	**Gently spiced Asian**
Drink	**2001–2**

Babich Winemaker's Reserve Sauvignon Blanc 00 ✓

Vibrant, aromatic Kiwi nose of mangetout, lime peel and blackcurrant leaves. Delicious tangy citrus fruits, with buckets of rich flavours. Very classy. *Gleeson*

Price	**£9–11/€11.50–14**
Region	**Marlborough**
Grape	**Sauvignon Blanc**
Alc/vol	**13.5%**
Food	**Seafood chowder**
Drink	**2001–3**

Esk Valley Chenin Blanc 98

Aromas of fragrant spring flowers with a lovely nutty background. Ripe green apples, lanolin, spice and all things nice on the palate, with a touch of honey. Beautifully integrated, rich mouthfeel. Very ripe style. *Findlaters*

Price	**£9–11/€11.50–14**
Region	**Hawkes Bay**
Grape	**Chenin Blanc**
Alc/vol	**13%**
Food	**Monkfish**
Drink	**2001–2**

> The **Marlborough** region of the South Island is synonymous with Sauvignon Blanc, but Pinot Noir, Chardonnay and Riesling also do very well. Montana planted the first vines in Marlborough in the early 1970s and it is now the largest wine region in New Zealand.

Montana Reserve Vineyard Selection Sauvignon Blanc 00

This is a lively, easy-drinking wine full of lots of crisp citrus and gooseberry flavours. Well structured and balanced with excellent length, it's a great way to start off a meal or cool down on a hot summer's day. *Grants*

Price	**£9–11/€11.50–14**
Region	**Marlborough**
Grape	**Sauvignon Blanc**
Alc/vol	**13.5%**
Food	**Aperitif, picnic**
Drink	**2001–2**

> Although **Sauvignon Blanc** established New Zealand's reputation, it is second to **Chardonnay** in terms of total plantings.

£11–13/€14–16.50

Goldwater Dog Point Sauvignon Blanc 00

Mouth-wateringly attractive and typical New Zealand Sauvignon nose—gooseberries and green summer meadow grass. It's like chewing a stalk of grass on a country walk. Everything is upbeat and it all holds together, the bracing acidity matching the intensity of the fruit. Dry, aromatic, subtle—grown-ups' wine. *Taserra*

Price	**£11–13/€14–16.50**
Region	**Marlborough**
Grape	**Sauvignon Blanc**
Alc/vol	**14%**
Food	**Pork stir fry with coriander and garlic**
Drink	**2001–2**

Huia Pinot Gris 00 ★

A sensational nose of limes, gooseberries and pears. Wonderfully balanced, with lots of flavour on the palate—honeysuckle, violets and green apple fruit—crisp acidity and a smooth finish. A beautiful wine. *Searsons*

Price	**£11–13/€14–16.50**
Region	**Marlborough**
Grape	**Pinot Gris**
Alc/vol	**13%**
Food	**Pork, quiche**
Drink	**2001–3**

Rieslings from New Zealand are typically dry, delicately perfumed and elegant. Quite full bodied, the wines have rich honey and peachy fruit flavours with a degree of complexity.

Huia Riesling 99

Perfumed nose together with aromas of limes and apples. On the palate there is a refreshing burst of more limes and apples, with lively acidity and a solid backing of alcohol. *Searsons*

Price	**£11–13/€14–16.50**
Region	**Marlborough**
Grape	**Riesling**
Alc/vol	**12.5%**
Food	**Fusion**
Drink	**2001–3**

Huia Sauvignon Blanc 00

Inviting, grassy Sauvignon nose. Deliciously fruity, offering ripe gooseberry and passion fruit flavours held together with zippy lemony acidity. Very long finish. *Searsons*

Price	**£11–13/€14–16.50**
Region	**Marlborough**
Grape	**Sauvignon Blanc**
Alc/vol	**13%**
Food	**Crab cakes**
Drink	**2001–2**

Hunter's Sauvignon Blanc 00

Very refreshing and enjoyable. An excellent example of New World Sauvignon, showing concentrated, zesty citrus fruit on the palate. Fresh and crisp, it has lovely mouthfeel and an excellent finish. *Gilbeys*

Price	**£11–13/€14–16.50**
Region	**Marlborough**
Grape	**Sauvignon Blanc**
Alc/vol	**13%**
Food	**Salmon**
Drink	**2001–2**

Lawson's Dry Hills Gewürztraminer 00

A smoky and appealing example of a grape variety not generally associated with New Zealand. Ginger spice and apples on the nose. The typical lychee flavour comes through on the palate, smooth and pure, yet subtle. *Febvre*

Price	**£11–13/€14–16.50**
Region	**Marlborough**
Grape	**Gewürztraminer**
Alc/vol	**14.5%**
Food	**Chinese**
Drink	**2001–2**

Lawson's Dry Hills Riesling 99 £/€

Apple, honey and pineapple aromas with some petrol tones on the nose. A full style of Riesling, with layers of limes, apples and pineapples on the palate. This is an interesting, appealing wine with upfront New World fruit but an Old World texture. *Febvre*

Price	**£11–13/€14–16.50**
Region	**Marlborough**
Grape	**Riesling**
Alc/vol	**12.5%**
Food	**Squid**
Drink	**2001–2**

Matariki Sauvignon Blanc Reserve 99

Classic New Zealand Sauvignon Blanc with the telltale green and gooseberry flavours but with the richness associated with New Zealand. The acidity has the expected crispness. *Bacchus*

Price	**£11–13/€14–16.50**
Region	**Hawkes Bay**
Grape	**Sauvignon Blanc**
Alc/vol	**13%**
Food	**Fish, Thai**
Drink	**2001–2**

Wairau River Sauvignon Blanc 00 ✓

Attractive green fruit/gooseberry nose. On the palate it is intense, with zingy acidity and layers of generous green fruit compote with a touch of vanilla. Classy winemaking. *TDL*

Price	**£11–13/€14–16.50**
Region	**Marlborough**
Grape	**Sauvignon Blanc**
Alc/vol	**13%**
Food	**Deep-fried squid**
Drink	**2001–2**

£13–15/€16.50–19

Matariki Hawkes Bay Chardonnay 99

Rich, elegant, smoky aromas. The palate has a smooth, delicious, creamy mouthfeel with apple, white fruits and nuts. *Bacchus*

Price	**£13–15/€16.50–19**
Region	**Hawkes Bay**
Grape	**Chardonnay**
Alc/vol	**12.5%**
Food	**Seafood**
Drink	**2001–3**

£15–17/€19–22

Wairau River Sauvignon Blanc Reserve 99

This is a beautifully made wine with crisp acidity and excellent green fruit flavours, nicely balanced with a soothing oak finish. The well-integrated wood flavours give a degree of complexity. *TDL*

Price	**£15–17/€19–22**
Region	**Marlborough**
Grape	**Sauvignon Blanc**
Alc/vol	**13%**
Food	**Dim sum dumplings**
Drink	**2001–2**

*New Zealand produces wonderful **Sauvignon Blancs**—some would maintain the best in the world. While the grapes ripen well in the heat-retaining volcanic soil, they never lose their aromatic, vegetal, nettle-like character. Flavours of green pea pod, asparagus and gooseberries are typical, but with an uncommon intensity and focus, and always with crisp, zesty acidity. The more serious wines have a chalky, minerally quality to add interest. Most are best within two years of the vintage.*

£17–20/€22–25

Cloudy Bay Sauvignon Blanc 00

Greenish tinge. An aromatic nose of asparagus, mangetout, lemon and gooseberry. With its great youthful intensity, this is a classy Sauvignon Blanc with great citrus fruit concentration. Still quite young, it will develop. *Findlaters*

Price	**£17–20/€22–25**
Region	**Marlborough**
Grape	**Sauvignon Blanc**
Alc/vol	**13.5%**
Food	**Seafood**
Drink	**2001–3**

£20–25/€25–32

Cloudy Bay Chardonnay 99

Very fragrant, pronounced, creamy, buttery nose. It's dry on the palate, but with sweet pineapple/mango/avocado fruit and buttery vanilla beautifully integrated with the oak. Flavour-packed and tasty—for a special occasion. *Findlaters*

Price	**£20–25/€25–32**
Region	**Marlborough**
Grape	**Chardonnay**
Alc/vol	**14.5%**
Food	**John Dory**
Drink	**2001–3**

Red

> **Montana** *is by far the largest producer in New Zealand, estimated to make around 50% of all its wine.*

£9–11/€11.50–14

Montana Reserve Merlot 99 ✓

Very definitely New World in style, with concentrated aromas of spice and cassis. The richly flavoured palate has heaps of fruit—brambles, plums, blackcurrants, spice and vanilla. Full-bodied wine with excellent texture. Long finish. *Grants*

Price	**£9–11/€11.50–14**
Region	**Marlborough**
Grape	**Merlot**
Alc/vol	**13%**
Food	**Tuna, salsa**
Drink	**2001–4**

£11–13/€14–16.50

Babich Winemaker's Reserve Pinot Noir 98

Inky, mushroomy aromas followed by strawberries and burnt crème caramel on the palate. A relatively complex yet affordable bottle with weight and elegance. *Gleeson*

Price	**£11–13/€14–16.50**
Region	**Marlborough**
Grape	**Pinot Noir**
Alc/vol	**13%**
Food	**Poultry**
Drink	**2001–2**

> *Plantings of* **Pinot Noir** *are increasing and have outstripped Cabernet Sauvignon. It has a great future in New Zealand and is also very important for its sparkling wine industry.*

Hunter's Pinot Noir 99

From one of the best New Zealand estates, this Pinot Noir is a new introduction to Ireland. Wild strawberry, brambly nose, little bit earthy, some jamminess. Full and substantial—raspberry and loganberry fruit, quite forceful, with gripping tannins that will settle. *Gilbeys*

Price	**£11–13/€14–16.50**
Region	**Marlborough**
Grape	**Pinot Noir**
Alc/vol	**13.5%**
Food	**Rabbit**
Drink	**2001–2**

> **Hawkes Bay** *is one of New Zealand's oldest wine regions and is situated on the warmer North Island. The best Cabernets and Cabernet blends are made here as well as whites from Chardonnay.*

Villa Maria Private Bin Cabernet Sauvignon Merlot 99

This is a classic example of the new wave of Kiwi reds using cool-climate techniques. Light in body, with marked acidity, but the fruit shows through, giving a wine that is elegant rather than powerful. Tannins are soft. Minty notes marry happily on the palate with green peppers and redcurrants. *Allied Drinks*

Price	**£11–13/€14–16.50**
Region	**Hawkes Bay**
Grape	**Cabernet/Merlot**
Alc/vol	**12.5%**
Food	**Stews**
Drink	**2001–3**

£15–17/€19–22

Lawson's Dry Hills Pinot Noir 99 £/€

Striking aromas of strawberry, cream, spice and rhubarb, with some vegetal notes. A currant y, strawberry, spicy palate shows complexity. Not, perhaps, as serious as Burgundy, but the price compares well. Enjoy on its own or with subtle, spicy foods. *Febvre*

Price	**£15–17/€19–22**
Region	**Marlborough**
Grape	**Pinot Noir**
Alc/vol	**13.5%**
Food	**Oriental, duck**
Drink	**2001–3**

Matariki Anthology 98

Classic New World style of a Cabernet Sauvignon blend. Intense cassis nose with hints of vanilla. Some green pepper showing through too. On the palate there is a good concentration of black fruit flavours with marked acidity and well-integrated oak flavours. *Bacchus*

Price	**£15–17/€19–22**
Region	**Hawkes Bay**
Grape	**Cabernet/Merlot**
Alc/vol	**12.5%**
Food	**Lamb with garlic**
Drink	**2001–3**

Portugal

Portugal is one of the most unexplored wine regions for most Irish wine drinkers. While its whites are generally underachievers, Portugal's strength most definitely lies in its reds, where it can produce wines of very high quality. Several areas are worth exploring, from the Douro in the north to the more southerly Alentejo. Most Portuguese wines are made from its wealth of indigenous varieties; it has not followed the international Cabernet Sauvignon/Chardonnay brigade. Touriga Nacional, which is widely planted in the Douro and most of the other regions, can compete with any top international variety. It is also the main quality grape in the production of port, together with Tinta Barroca and Tinta Roriz (the Tempranillo of Spain). In Bairrada there is the Baga grape and further south, in the Ribatejo and Alentejo, there are Periquita and Trincadeira. In general, the red wines of Portugal are very traditional, deeply coloured, concentrated and tannic and are often at their best after some time in bottle.

White

£7–9/€9–11.50

Albis VR Terras do Sado **97**

Light, luscious, crisp and clean. Floral and grapey aromas are followed by a palate of apple and citrus fruit, all very light and subtle. Still fresh despite the vintage. *Gilbeys*

Price	**£7–9/€9–11.50**
Region	**Terras do Sado**
Grape	**Arinto/Malvasia/ Moscatel**
Alc/vol	**12%**
Food	**Mussels**
Drink	**2001–2**

Red

Under £7/Under €9

Caves Bonifácio VdM **nv**

Ripe jammy fruits, soft tannins and an old world earthiness make this an easy-drinking, uncomplicated style. *Peter Dalton*

Price	**Under £7/Under €9**
Region	**Ribatejo**
Alc/vol	**12%**
Food	**Takeaway**
Drink	**2001–2**

Dom Teodósio Terra das Fragas DOC Douro **96**

A firm, sturdy wine, full of cherry and strawberry fruit flavours with a hint of pepper. Refreshing acidity. Earthy and rustic style. *WineOnline*

Price	**Under £7/Under €9**
Region	**Douro**
Grape	**Touriga Nacional/ Tiata Roriz**
Alc/vol	**12%**
Food	**Ham**
Drink	**2001–2**

Dom Teodósio Vinhas da Faia DOC Bairrada 96 £/€

A fruity, easy-drinking wine. It has a sappy, crisp attack that enlivens the palate and follows through with bramble fruit. Tannins are pushy, but not aggressively so. Good everyday Bairrada. *WineOnline*

Price	**Under £7/Under €9**
Region	**Bairrada**
Grape	**Mainly Baga**
Alc/vol	**12%**
Food	**Barbecued meat**
Drink	**2001–3**

Monte das Änforas VR Regional Alentejano 99

A fine wine at an easy price and versatile with food too. It's fresh and lively, with black cherry and blackcurrant flavours. Made in a traditional style, it's ideal for easy everyday drinking. *SuperValu-Centra*

Price	**Under £7/Under €9**
Region	**Alentejo**
Grape	**Periquita/Trincadeira Preta**
Alc/vol	**13%**
Food	**Caldo verde, pork**
Drink	**2001–2**

> **IPR** *(Indicação de Proveniência Regulamentada) is the quality category just below DOC and indicates that promotion to full DOC quality wine status may not be far away. VQPRD often appears on the labels of such wines.*
>
> **VR** *(Vinho Regional) is a classification of table wine akin to France's Vin de Pays, where regional character is permitted to flex its muscles by experimentation.*
>
> **VdM** *(Vinho de Mesa) is the Portuguese designation for table wines.*

£7–9/€9–11.50

Dom Teodósio Almargem VQPRD Palmela 96

A soft red, with fresh black fruit, full of flavour. Tannins and acidity are mellow and integrated. Subtle in style but not dilute. *WineOnline*

Price	**£7–9/€9–11.50**
Region	**Palmela**
Grape	**Castelão Francês/ Periquita**
Alc/vol	**12.5%**
Food	**Chicken, barbecue**
Drink	**2001–2**

J. M. da Fonseca Terras Altas DOC Dão 95

A generous wine with gorgeous brooding dark plum and cherry flavours and an intriguing smoky layer—think of a good turf fire. It holds its years very well, with lots of structure matched by the black fruit. *Gilbeys*

Price	**£7–9/€9–11.50**
Region	**Dão**
Grape	**Alforcheiro/Bastardo/ Touriga Nacional**
Alc/vol	**12%**
Food	**Beef burgers**
Drink	**2001–2**

£9–11/€11.50–14

Duas Quintas DOC Douro 97

Rich black cherry and plum aromas and flavours, with spice and pepper on the palate. This
is a super wine and very representative of how
good light Douro wines can be. *Searsons*

Price	**£9–11/€11.50–14**
Region	**Douro**
Grape	**Tinta Roriz/Touriga Nacional**
Alc/vol	**12.5%**
Food	**Pork**
Drink	**2001–2**

Palha-Canas VR Regional Estremadura 00

Made in a modern style—super-ripe, juicy,
fruity flavours (blueberries, mulberries, cherries,
vanilla) help tame the tannins. Long finish.
Good now, but will be even better after two
years. *Searsons*

Price	**£9–11/€11.50–14**
Region	**Estremadura**
Grape	**Periquita/Camarate/ Touriga Nacional**
Alc/vol	**13%**
Food	**Spare ribs**
Drink	**2001–4**

Vinhos Sogrape Duque de Viseu DOC Dão 97

A lovely ripe and juicy Dão with a mature and
complex nose of strawberries, earth and leather.
The palate follows through with redcurrant and
blackberry fruit. An elegant wine with no hard
edges. *Febvre*

Price	**£9–11/€11.50–14**
Region	**Dão**
Grape	**Touriga Nacional/ Tinta Roriz**
Alc/vol	**13%**
Food	**Versatile**
Drink	**2001–2**

£17–20/€22–25

Unilar Vinho Tinto Reserva 77 ★ £/€

What a joy to pour a glass of this gracious and
elegant wine—like fine Burgundy. The wonderful nose of roses, red and black currants, Christmas pudding and cigar box is matched by the
Burgundian palate, with the savoury and vegetal aromas showing age and development. This
is elegance personified with everything beautifully balanced. *Peter Dalton*

Price	**£17–20/€22–25**
Region	**Palmela**
Alc/vol	**12.5%**
Food	**Simple chicken**
Drink	**2001–2**

Romania

Our selection of Romanian wines reflects what's best in the country—inexpensive, soft, easy-drinking wines made from the international grape varieties Chardonnay, Cabernet Sauvignon, Merlot and Pinot Noir. The Dealul Mare ('big hill') region is one of the best areas in the country for red wines. The other region represented here, Murfatlar, is famous for its late-harvest wines, but makes dry whites like the Chardonnay listed as well. (Chardonnay has been planted in the area since 1907.)

Quality in Romania is still patchy, but is improving with input from international wine consultants and international investors such as Prahova Winecellars, which has UK backing.

White

£7–9/€9–11.50

Murfatlar Vineyards Barrel Fermented Chardonnay 97

Old World wine in a New World style created by Romanian winemakers and Australian wine consultant Graham Dixon. The nose is influenced by wood, with vanilla, toast and butter aromas, but the oak treatment still allows the apple, lemon and mango fruit to come through on the palate. Soft, supple and mouth-filling, it has a medium-long finish. *Barry & Fitzwilliam*

Price	£7–9/€9–11.50
Grape	Chardonnay
Alc/vol	12%
Food	Mild curries, picnic
Drink	2001–2

Red

Eagle Valley Merlot 99

Soft plum and strawberry aromas. Mellow tannins and stewed fruits on the palate with some coffee tones. Plenty of soft, plummy fruit here with a pleasing grip of lively acidity. Simple and easy drinking. *Febvre*

Price	**Under £7/Under €9**
Grape	**Merlot**
Alc/vol	**12%**
Food	**Ravioli**
Drink	**2001–2**

Eagle Valley Pinot Noir 00

Strawberry and summer fruit aromas. On the soft palate juicy strawberry pastille fruit characterises this delightfully simple, fruity wine. A modern, commercial style of Pinot Noir. *Febvre*

Price	**Under £7/Under €9**
Grape	**Pinot Noir**
Alc/vol	**12%**
Food	**Pizza**
Drink	**2001–2**

Prahova Winecellars Cabernet Sauvignon 99 £/€

Wild berries mixed with gamy aromas. The palate is dry, with pronounced cedary berry fruit flavours. Tannins are still quite firm, but will soften. *Barry & Fitzwilliam*

Price	**Under £7/Under €9**
Grape	**Cabernet Sauvignon**
Alc/vol	**14%**
Food	**Versatile**
Drink	**2001–3**

Prahova Winecellars Special Reserve Pinot Noir 98

Bright ruby colour. Raspberry, black cherry and loganberry nose. Nice concentration on this one, with lots of crisp cherry and loganberry fruit and lively acidity. Uncomplicated.
Barry & Fitzwilliam

Price	**Under £7/Under €9**
Grape	**Pinot Noir**
Alc/vol	**12%**
Food	**Traditional**
Drink	**2001–2**

Rovit Winery Special Reserve Cabernet Sauvignon 98

Some minty, herbaceous notes come through the blackcurrant and cherry aromas. Cool Cabernet—it has real forest fruit flavours. Tannins are still fairly firm. *Barry & Fitzwilliam*

Price	**Under £7/Under €9**
Grape	**Cabernet Sauvignon**
Alc/vol	**12.5%**
Food	**Cheese-based dishes**
Drink	**2001–3**

Sahateni Vineyards Merlot Reserve 98 £/€

Aromas of cherries, plums and summer berries. Still some firm tannins on the palate, but there is plenty of damson fruit there too. Brisk acidity and satisfactory length. *Barry & Fitzwilliam*

Price	**£7–9/€9–11.50**
Grape	**Merlot**
Alc/vol	**13%**
Food	**Bangers and mash**
Drink	**2001–2**

South Africa

South Africa is an exciting wine region that is still actively defining its wine styles. It has a commitment to pushing out boundaries, a task undertaken with such energy and confidence that it seems it cannot fail—political considerations aside. Some clear trends are emerging, which are reflected in this year's tastings.

There are some very interesting red wines from a blend of grape varieties collectively referred to as a 'Cape blend'. While some Cape blends are combinations of the classic Bordeaux varieties (Cabernet Sauvignon, Merlot, Cabernet Franc, Petit Verdot and Malbec), expect to see the addition of other varieties to create a distinctly South African style—Barbera, Tinta Barroca, Shiraz, Tempranillo, Grenache or Mourvèdre. There is some debate over whether Pinotage, South Africa's indigenous variety, should be included. Some Cape blends to try include Rust en Vrede Estate Wine, Simonsig Tiara, Guardian Peak Trinity, Warwick Estate Trilogy and Kanonkop Paul Sauer.

The 'Old World' belief in blending is inspired as much by the New World as the old, with Cabernet/Shiraz and Chenin/Chardonnay blends to rival the Australians and Californians and some unique blends such as Merlot/Shiraz. South Africa also produces reds from single varieties, principally Cabernet Sauvignon, Pinotage and Shiraz. The Shiraz vines first planted in Australia were allegedly brought from South Africa. While Shiraz has been in South Africa for a long time, it is only now beginning to appear in Ireland. South African Shiraz has a smoky, concentrated style with lots of complexity; the wines often need time in bottle.

Chardonnay and Sauvignon Blanc continue to produce good results. Many winemakers are moving away from Chenin Blanc or use it for their simplest blends. However, some producers are very committed to this variety and are increasing production of high-quality Chenin, using lower yields and experimenting with sweet and well as dry styles.

White

Under £7/Under €9

Arniston Bay Chenin Blanc Chardonnay 00

Floral on the nose, with some apple and damp wool notes. Soft palate of ripe, sweet melon and apple fruit. Easy drinking. *Findlaters*

Price	**Under £7/Under €9**
Region	**Western Cape**
Grape	**Chenin Blanc/Chard**
Alc/vol	**13%**
Food	**Party**
Drink	**2001–2**

Clos Malverne Sauvignon Blanc 00

Lots of fresh, juicy fruit here—it's a wine with plenty of flavour. With asparagus and pea pod on the palate, it's deliciously crisp. *Dunnes Stores*

Price	**Under £7/Under €9**
Region	**Stellenbosch**
Grape	**Sauvignon Blanc**
Alc/vol	**13.5%**
Food	**Thai**
Drink	**2001–2**

199

Danie de Wet Chardonnay Sur Lie 01

A refreshing, unoaked wine with real bite, this
has crisp green apple and green pepper flavours
with a touch of spice. It's clean, fresh and
appealing—perfect chilled in a heat wave.
Oddbins

Price	**Under £7/Under €9**
Region	**Robertson**
Grape	**Chardonnay**
Alc/vol	**13.5%**
Food	**Chicken**
Drink	**2001–3**

KWV Chenin Blanc 00

Assertive nose of grapefruit, peaches and citrus.
Hint of wool. Good balance of fruit and acidity
on the tangy palate of grapefruit and spice.
Clean, crisp finish. *TDL*

Price	**Under £7/Under €9**
Region	**Western Cape**
Grape	**Chenin Blanc**
Alc/vol	**12.5%**
Food	**Grilled sardines**
Drink	**2001–2**

Lutzville Most Westerly Chenin Blanc 00

Ripe, tangy aromas, with citrus and ripe pineapple. The palate shows a bit of character,
with fragrant apples and citrus. Easy-drinking,
appealing, slightly off-dry style. *Mitchells*

Price	**Under £7/Under €9**
Region	**Olifants River**
Grape	**Chenin Blanc**
Alc/vol	**12.5%**
Food	**Aperitif**
Drink	**2001–2**

Robert's Rock Chenin Blanc Chardonnay 00

Buttery nose of apples, peaches and citrus.
Quite a zingy palate of citrus and apple flavours.
Fruity, well-made wine. *TDL*

Price	**Under £7/Under €9**
Region	**Western Cape**
Grape	**Chenin Blanc/Chard**
Alc/vol	**12.5%**
Food	**Chinese**
Drink	**2001–2**

> **Chenin Blanc** is the most widely planted white variety in South Africa, with
> approximately 24% of the vineyard area.

Ryland's Grove Chenin Blanc 00

Kym Milne is the winemaking consultant for
this straightforward, crisp, clean Chenin Blanc
with apple fruit and a spicy, oaky note from
barrel fermentation. Its refreshing acidity whets
the appetite for more. *Tesco*

Price	**Under £7/Under €9**
Region	**Stellenbosch**
Grape	**Chenin Blanc**
Alc/vol	**14%**
Food	**Goats' cheese**
Drink	**2001–2**

£7–9/€9–11.50

Blue White Irina von Holdt Chenin Blanc 98

Concentrated lemon and honey aromas. Good
rich flavours—stewed apples, honey and pears
and a nice weighty mouthfeel. Excellent example of Chenin Blanc with a very fine finish.
Barry & Fitzwilliam

Price	**£7–9/€9–11.50**
Region	**Stellenbosch**
Grape	**Chenin Blanc**
Alc/vol	**14%**
Food	**Creamy chicken**
Drink	**2001–2**

Bon Courage Chardonnay Prestige Cuvée 00

Enticing nose of melon, tropical fruit and lemon with a vanilla backing from the oak treatment. More soothing vanilla on the palate, with lemon, green fruit, apples and melons. *Gleeson*

Price	**£7–9/€9–11.50**
Region	**Robertson**
Grape	**Chardonnay**
Alc/vol	**12.5%**
Food	**Aperitif, picnic**
Drink	**2001–2**

Simonsig Estate Chardonnay 98

This is the epitome of highly oaked wine. At first the oak is very dominant on the palate, with kiwi/passion fruit flavours behind, but a super richness of tropical fruit follows through, very smooth and balanced with quite a warm, long finish. *United Beverages*

Price	**£7–9/€9–11.50**
Region	**Stellenbosch**
Grape	**Chardonnay**
Alc/vol	**13%**
Food	**Pacific Rim, Thai**
Drink	**2001–3**

Villiera Chenin Blanc 00

Villiera makes top-quality Chenin and is a consistently fine producer. This 00 vintage has honey and apples on the nose, crisp, creamy mouthfeel and very good ripe peach fruit. With its perfect balance of honey and citrus acidity, it gives images of flowers, nectar and fruit. Clean, long finish. *Grants*

Price	**£7–9/€9–11.50**
Region	**Paarl**
Grape	**Chenin Blanc**
Alc/vol	**14%**
Food	**Curry**
Drink	**2001–2**

£9–11/€11.50–14

Biesjes Craal Durbanville Hills Sauvignon Blanc 99

Durbanville is from an expanding wine region north of Cape Town, this wine has a powerful nose of vegetation, nettles and gooseberry leaf. Very full-bodied style of Sauvignon, with its mouth-filling gooseberry/lime fruit and crisp acidity. Long, dry finish. *Febvre*

Price	**£9–11/€11.50–14**
Region	**Durbanville**
Grape	**Sauvignon Blanc**
Alc/vol	**13%**
Food	**Asparagus, shellfish**
Drink	**2001–3**

Fleur du Cap Chardonnay 00

An easy-drinking, fruity wine. Ripe pineapples on the nose, with lemons, melons and vanilla aromas from oak ageing. This is typical New World Chardonnay in a buttery, tropical fruit style, but it's not overdone. *Febvre*

Price	**£9–11/€11.50–14**
Region	**Coastal Region**
Grape	**Chardonnay**
Alc/vol	**13.5%**
Food	**Caesar salad**
Drink	**2001–2**

Glen Carlou Chardonnay 00

An oaked Chardonnay with nutty vanilla aromas and toasty flavours. With very good length and balance, this has all the elements—concentrated apple and citrus fruit, acidity and depth of flavour. *Oddbins*

Price	**£9–11/€11.50–14**
Region	**Paarl**
Grape	**Chardonnay**
Alc/vol	**13.5%**
Food	**Tuna**
Drink	**2001–2**

Stellenbosch has it all—excellent quality and every style of wine. Simonsberg and Helderberg are areas within Stellenbosch that may also be seen on labels.

Kanu Limited Release Wooded Chenin Blanc 00

Pronounced nose of ripe apples. Full-bodied and creamy with apple pie flavours on the dry palate. It has great elegance and length. *Papillon*

Price	£9–11/€11.50–14
Region	**Stellenbosch**
Grape	**Chenin Blanc**
Alc/vol	**14.5%**
Food	**Seafood**
Drink	**2001–3**

Klein Constantia Chardonnay 98 ✓

Honest Chardonnay. A complete wine with good varietal character and superb balance of fruit and acidity. The luscious melon and peach fruit is juicy and appetising, but with a delicate mouthfeel and long length. *Gilbeys*

Price	£9–11/€11.50–14
Region	**Constantia**
Grape	**Chardonnay**
Alc/vol	**13.5%**
Food	**Pasta carbonara**
Drink	**2001–3**

WO means Wine of Origin. On South African labels it certifies the wine's area of origin, grape variety and vintage.

Thandi Chardonnay 99

Hard to believe this is Chardonnay—it doesn't scream varietal character. High in alcohol and acidity, it has a smoky nose. On the palate it's minty and flinty, with clear, fresh fruit that lasts on the smooth finish. *Findlaters*

Price	£9–11/€11.50–14
Region	**Coastal Region**
Grape	**Chardonnay**
Alc/vol	**13.5%**
Food	**Veal**
Drink	**2001–2**

Wildekrans Sauvignon Blanc 00 ★ £/€

Classic New World Sauvignon Blanc—big, but with a nice degree of elegance thrown in. Almost pungent nose of nettles and grass. It's crisp, clean and fresh, with buckets of fruit, hints of sweetness and a grassy intensity. Long, off-dry finish. *Barry & Fitzwilliam*

Price	£9–11/€11.50–14
Region	**Walker Bay**
Grape	**Sauvignon Blanc**
Alc/vol	**12%**
Food	**Oriental**
Drink	**2001–3**

£11–13/€14–16.50

Groot Constantia Sauvignon Blanc 00

Ripe style of Sauvignon Blanc, with understated aromas and flavours. The nose is a touch honeyed behind a gentle herbaceousness. The palate displays rich green fruit with a peppery spiciness, going on to a vanilla finish. Appealing balance of fruit and acidity. Long finish. *Irish Distillers*

Price	£11–13/€14–16.50
Region	**Constantia**
Grape	**Sauvignon Blanc**
Alc/vol	**14.5%**
Food	**Aperitif**
Drink	**2001–2**

£13–15/€16.50–19

Jordan Chardonnay 99

Perfumed, ripe, almost tropical fruits on the nose, with oaky/vanilla nuances. Big oaky palate competing with very ripe tropical fruit flavours and generous alcohol. *Maxxium*

Price	**£13–15/€16.50–19**
Region	**Stellenbosch**
Grape	**Chardonnay**
Alc/vol	**14%**
Food	**Chinese prawns**
Drink	**2001–3**

Plaisir de Merle Chardonnay 97

This is a lovely wine. Lively lemon, melon and vanilla flavours with a slight touch of honey are accompanied by crisp acidity and the smoothing effect of oak. *Dillons*

Price	**£13–15/€16.50–19**
Region	**Paarl**
Grape	**Chardonnay**
Alc/vol	**13.5%**
Food	**Chicken**
Drink	**2001–2**

> **Robertson** *has traditionally produced white wines, especially Chardonnay, but is starting to show some interesting results with reds.*

£15–17/€19–22

Oude Weltevrede Chardonnay 00

Clearly made with great care to strike the right balance, this is a wooded style, beautifully integrated with fruit flavours of apples and pears. A wine showing quite a lot of power and concentration. *Taserra*

Price	**£15–17/€19–22**
Region	**Robertson**
Grape	**Chardonnay**
Alc/vol	**13.5%**
Food	**Turkey**
Drink	**2001–4**

Rustenberg Stellenbosch Chardonnay 99

Toasted bread and butter, lemons, pineapple and vanilla on the nose. Oaky palate with lots of pineapple cube and lemon flavours and a long finish. *Woodford Bourne*

Price	**£15–17/€19–22**
Region	**Stellenbosch**
Grape	**Chardonnay**
Alc/vol	**13.5%**
Food	**Smoked chicken with pasta**
Drink	**2001–3**

Steenberg Catharina 00

This Sauvignon/Semillon blend, which is named after the founder of the estate, has a wonderful herbaceous bouquet. The unusual spritz enhances a refreshing, well-rounded palate of baked gooseberry crumble and green pepper flavours. A big, ripe wine. *Papillon*

Price	**£15–17/€19–22**
Region	**Constantia**
Grape	**Sauv Blanc/Semillon**
Alc/vol	**13.5%**
Food	**Baked goat's cheese**
Drink	**2001–3**

Red

> **Ruby Cabernet** *originated in California from a crossing of Cabernet Sauvignon with Carignan. It was created with the aim of producing Cabernet-style wines.*

Under £7/Under €9

Arniston Bay Ruby Cabernet Merlot 00

A good concentration of ripe, warm berry fruit flavours promised on the nose. The same berry fruit and black cherry flavours are delivered on the palate, combined with soft tannins.
Findlaters

Price	Under £7/Under €9
Region	Western Cape
Grape	Ruby Cab/Merlot
Alc/vol	13%
Food	Beefburgers
Drink	2001–2

Clos Malverne Cabernet Sauvignon Shiraz 99 £/€

Restrained peppery nose, with cherry and raspberry flavours on the palate. Lovely, straightforward red wine, ideal for relaxing with.
Dunnes Stores

Price	Under £7/Under €9
Region	Stellenbosch
Grape	Cab Sauv/Shiraz
Alc/vol	13.5%
Food	Party
Drink	2001–2

Long Mountain Merlot Shiraz 00 £/€

Ripe black fruit aromas and flavours, with some spice on the palate. Excellent party wine, easy-drinking style, gentle tannins but with plenty of very ripe and clean fruit. Australian-like. Decent length and concentration. *Irish Distillers*

Price	Under £7/Under €9
Region	Western Cape
Grape	Merlot/Shiraz
Alc/vol	13%
Food	Pizza
Drink	2001–2

Long Mountain Pinotage 99

A round, fruity, medium-bodied, early-drinking red. Ripe fruit with quite a bit of black cherry and plum flavour. An introductory Pinotage that won't break the bank. *Irish Distillers*

Price	Under £7/Under €9
Region	Western Cape
Grape	Pinotage
Alc/vol	12.5%
Food	Chicken pie
Drink	2001–2

Nederburg Cabernet Sauvignon Shiraz 97

A South African take on a popular Aussie blend of grape varieties. Quite a classy and stylish wine, with good blackcurrant flavours and some cedar and mint. Satisfyingly long finish.
Dillons

Price	Under £7/Under €9
Region	Western Cape
Grape	Cab Sauv/Shiraz
Alc/vol	13%
Food	Kebabs
Drink	2001–2

Nederburg Pinotage 99

Fairly traditional in style, with some medicinal notes behind the black fruits on the nose—the famous Elastoplast aroma. A tasty wine, however, with plenty of blackcurrant and plum flavours and a long, fruity finish. *Dillons*

Price	**Under £7/Under €9**
Region	**Western Cape**
Grape	**Pinotage**
Alc/vol	**13%**
Food	**Meat stews**
Drink	**2001–2**

Oude Kaap Cabernet Sauvignon Merlot 00

This wine has a very appealing character, revealing the personality of both grapes, Cabernet Sauvignon's blackcurrant fruit with tobacco and mint and Merlot's soft plumminess, yet attaining harmony on the palate. *Dunnes Stores*

Price	**Under £7/Under €9**
Region	**Western Cape**
Grape	**Cabernet/Merlot**
Alc/vol	**13%**
Food	**Cold roast beef**
Drink	**2001–2**

Vaughan Johnson's Good Everyday Cape Red nv

Soft, fruity and accessible, with tangy, chunky raspberry fruit, quite full-bodied, this is a crowd pleaser for a party. Perfect for outdoor drinking in the summer. *Papillon*

Price	**Under £7/Under €9**
Region	**Western Cape**
Grape	**Mainly Tinta Barocca**
Alc/vol	**13%**
Food	**Party, picnic**
Drink	**2001–2**

Vaughan Johnson's Sunday Best nv

Ripe, jammy fruit with some plum and pepper on the palate and soft tannins tailor-made for a Sunday roast. It would, however, make a good all-round party wine. Pizza or spare ribs would do nicely, but it's tailor made for a Sunday roast. *Papillon*

Price	**Under £7/Under €9**
Region	**Western Cape**
Grape	**Merlot/Shiraz**
Alc/vol	**13%**
Food	**Versatile**
Drink	**2001–2**

£7–9/€9–11.50

Bon Courage Cabernet Sauvignon Shiraz 99

Deeply coloured, this is a gutsy wine in a rich style, with blackcurrant/black cherry fruit and a charred smokiness. A good midweek supper bottle. *Gleeson*

Price	**£7–9/€9–11.50**
Region	**Robertson**
Grape	**Cab Sauv/Shiraz**
Alc/vol	**13%**
Food	**Pizza**
Drink	**2001–2**

> **Coastal Region** is a term indicating that the grapes have been sourced from one or more of a number of regions—it includes Swartland, Tulbagh, Paarl and Stellenbosch and the wards of Constantia and Durbanville.

Fairview Pinotage 99 £/€

Classic aroma of bandages, quite concentrated. A lovely, juicy and mouth-filling Pinotage made in a modern style. Ripe and full of blackberry flavours. *United Beverages*

Price	£7–9/€9–11.50
Region	Coastal Region
Grape	Pinotage
Alc/vol	13.5%
Food	Kebabs
Drink	2001–2

Guardian Peak Cabernet Sauvignon Syrah 98

Blackcurrant, mint and vanilla aromas. There's a bit of complexity on the palate, with firm tannins providing structure for ripe fruits of the forest, blackcurrant and blackberry with a really nice vanilla kick. A typical mintiness and some pepper and spice. *O'Briens*

Price	£7–9/€9–11.50
Region	Stellenbosch
Grape	Cab Sauv/Syrah/ Tinta Barocca
Alc/vol	12.5%
Food	Traditional
Drink	2001–2

Guardian Peak Trinity 99 £/€

Delightful and different! The Portuguese grape Tinta Barocca certainly adds character to this blend, lending perhaps the appealing, slightly vegetal aromas and reinforcing the ripe berry fruit flavours. Elegant and stylish, with plums and blackcurrant fruit flavours, mellow and rich. Very enjoyable. *O'Briens*

Price	£7–9/€9–11.50
Region	Stellenbosch
Grape	Cabernet/Merlot/ Tinta Barocca
Alc/vol	13%
Food	Roast lamb
Drink	2001–3

> Both **KWV** and **Nederburg**, two of the biggest South African wine companies, are based in the town of Paarl.

KWV Cabernet Sauvignon 97 £/€ ✓

Lovely spicy blackcurrant nose with soft tannins and good pure fruit with a spicy edge. A fresh, fruity mouthful with a clean, pleasant finish. Plenty of character in this tasty wine. *TDL*

Price	£7–9/€9–11.50
Region	Western Cape
Grape	Cabernet Sauvignon
Alc/vol	13%
Food	Barbecued steak
Drink	2001–2

KWV Pinotage 99

The nose is slightly muted, but shows smoky black fruit. There follows a virtual assault on the tastebuds that the nose does not prepare you for. A whack of musky perfumed fruit, red berries and wood. Savoury, concentrated—must have food. *TDL*

Price	£7–9/€9–11.50
Region	Western Cape
Grape	Pinotage
Alc/vol	13.5%
Food	Spicy food
Drink	2001–3

£9–11/€11.50–14

Backsberg Estate Merlot 98

Minty, plummy nose with a background of
burnt sugar and rubber. The sweet, ripe fruit on
the palate is reminiscent of wild herbs and eucalyptus, with coffee, vanilla and prune flavours.
It's an intriguing, fruity, minty Merlot. *Papillon*

Price	**£9–11/€11.50–14**
Region	**Paarl**
Grape	**Merlot**
Alc/vol	**13%**
Food	**North African**
Drink	**2001–2**

Beaumont Pinotage 98

Ripe damson fruit on the nose. Flavours are of
rich, sweet, ripe fruits—cherries and plums—
with a lick of dark chocolate. This Pinotage
would suit picnic food—cold meats and pies.
Cheese too. *Fields*

Price	**£9–11/€11.50–14**
Region	**Walker Bay**
Grape	**Pinotage**
Alc/vol	**13%**
Food	**Versatile**
Drink	**2001–2**

Bellingham Shiraz 00

Cedar and vanilla notes on the nose with concentrated ripe blackberry fruit. The palate is
packed with sweet blackcurrant fruit and
smoky, rich flavours held together with firm
tannins and balancing acidity. *Cassidy*

Price	**£9–11/€11.50–14**
Region	**Coastal Region**
Grape	**Shiraz**
Alc/vol	**13.5%**
Food	**Duck, barbecue**
Drink	**2001–3**

Brampton Cabernet Sauvignon Merlot 99 ✓

The prestigious Rustenberg estate makes the
Brampton range as a second label. This is a
serious wine. The Cabernet Sauvignon gives a
sombre red berry nuance to the plummy Merlot
on the palate. *Woodford Bourne*

Price	**£9–11/€11.50–14**
Region	**Stellenbosch**
Grape	**Cabernet/Merlot**
Alc/vol	**13.5%**
Food	**Beef stir fry**
Drink	**2001–3**

Fairview Shiraz 98 ✓

Black cherries on the nose are followed by perfectly blended spice and black cherry flavours
with thick dark chocolate. The ripe fruit is supported by firm tannins. *United Beverages*

Price	**£9–11/€11.50–14**
Region	**Coastal Region**
Grape	**Shiraz**
Alc/vol	**14%**
Food	**Lamb**
Drink	**2001–3**

Fleur du Cap Shiraz 97

Perfumed nose of blackberries and white pepper. The palate has pure, smoky blackberries
and cream cheese with a hint of green pepper.
Tannins are fairly robust. Similar in style to
Coonawarra Shiraz. *Febvre*

Price	**£9–11/€11.50–14**
Region	**Coastal Region**
Grape	**Shiraz**
Alc/vol	**12.5%**
Food	**Grilled meats**
Drink	**2001–3**

The **Western Cape** covers a vast area and includes all the main wine-producing regions in South Africa.

KWV Shiraz 99

Delicious, smooth, fruity and quite full bodied
with creamy vanilla; an underlying silkiness is
backed by a certain smokiness. Oozing blackberries. *TDL*

Price	**£9–11/€11.50–14**
Region	**Western Cape**
Grape	**Shiraz**
Alc/vol	**13%**
Food	**Versatile**
Drink	**2001–2**

L'Avenir Cabernet Sauvignon 97

A cross between the New World and the Old
World. Lots of ripe blackcurrant flavours, yet
restraint, with layers of complexity and quite
firm tannins. Good food match. *Dunnes Stores*

Price	**£9–11/€11.50–14**
Region	**Stellenbosch**
Grape	**Cabernet Sauvignon**
Alc/vol	**13.5%**
Food	**Veal**
Drink	**2001–3**

Simonsig Estate Shiraz 98

An elegant Shiraz—a complex nose of smoke,
ground coffee and black cherries opens into a
palate of slightly bitter plum, wood smoke and
dark chocolatey undertones. The firm tannins
give the wine a strong backbone. Perfect food
partner. *United Beverages*

Price	**£9–11/€11.50–14**
Region	**Stellenbosch**
Grape	**Shiraz**
Alc/vol	**13.5%**
Food	**Lamb chops**
Drink	**2001–2**

> **Pinotage**, *a grape unique to South Africa, is a crossing of Cinsault with Pinot Noir developed by Professor Perold in 1925 at Stellenbosch University. The wine styles vary from flamboyantly ripe with a paint-like pungency to rich, deeply coloured with a wild fruitiness but always with an underlying smouldering volcanic smokiness. The wines have a curious tendency to mature into a toffee and marshmallow softness. Lower yields, shorter fermentations and no irrigation have made definite improvements in the quality of Pinotage.*

£11–13/€14–16.50

Durbanville Hills Pinotage 99

Pinotage in the modern style—blackberries,
ripe plums, spice and vanilla aromas and real
fruit quality on the palate. Blackcurrants, spice
and plum flavours are complemented by the
vanilla oakiness. Great length. *Febvre*

Price	**£11–13/€14–16.50**
Region	**Durbanville**
Grape	**Pinotage**
Alc/vol	**13.5%**
Food	**Steak**
Drink	**2001–3**

Durbanville Hills Shiraz 99

Toasty oak and black fruit aromas. A serious
style of wine, with blackcurrant fruit and nicely
integrated oak. Good structure without being
overpowering. *Febvre*

Price	**£11–13/€14–16.50**
Region	**Durbanville**
Grape	**Shiraz**
Alc/vol	**13.5%**
Food	**Versatile**
Drink	**2001–2**

Fleur du Cap Pinotage 98

A pronounced, rich and intense nose, almost port-like. Immediately appealing pure fruit palate of damsons and bananas, with ample, but not overpowering, tannins. Good length and lovely use of oak. *Febvre*

Price	**£11–13/€14–16.50**
Region	**Coastal Region**
Grape	**Pinotage**
Alc/vol	**13.5%**
Food	**Spare ribs**
Drink	**2001–2**

Graham Beck Shiraz 99

Spicy, rich chocolate, liquorice and black fruit nose. Great extract of dense, dark fruits on the spicy palate. Powerful but elegant, with firm tannins, the fruit-packed finish lingers on and on. A big wine. *Cassidy*

Price	**£11–13/€14–16.50**
Region	**Coastal Region**
Grape	**Shiraz**
Alc/vol	**13.5%**
Food	**Duck**
Drink	**2001–4**

> **Constantia**, *just south of Cape Town, is the oldest and one of the higher-quality regions.*

Groot Constantia Pinotage 95 £/€

Plum and blackberry flavours with some vegetal characteristics on the nose, with a layered palate of plums, black cherries, spice and cream. Approachable and appealing, this wine shows how Pinotage can develop complexity and character with age. *Irish Distillers*

Price	**£11–13/€14–16.50**
Region	**Constantia**
Grape	**Pinotage**
Alc/vol	**12.5%**
Food	**Spicy or chargrilled meats**
Drink	**2001–2**

Springfield Cabernet Sauvignon 98

There's a bit of mint on the nose, but mainly very ripe blackcurrants. The luscious palate has a creamy texture and stacks of black fruit, strawberry and redcurrant flavours. *Papillon*

Price	**£11–13/€14–16.50**
Region	**Robertson**
Grape	**Cabernet Sauvignon**
Alc/vol	**13%**
Food	**Steak**
Drink	**2001–3**

Thandi Cabernet Sauvignon 97

Smooth and minty with an abundance of blackcurrant fruit flavours—a fine example of a wine drinking well now. It has reached the stage where fruit flavours dominate all the other elements of tannin, acidity and alcohol, resulting in a harmonious wine with a long finish. *Findlaters*

Price	**£11–13/€14–16.50**
Region	**Coastal Region**
Grape	**Cabernet Sauvignon**
Alc/vol	**12.5%**
Food	**Rack of lamb**
Drink	**2001–2**

Wildekrans Pinotage 99 £/€

This barrique-aged Pinotage is a lovely example of polished and refined Pinotage without any rustic edges. Summer pudding fruits with great depth of flavour, juicy and mouth-watering. Long finish. Plenty of acidity, so it will go with most foods. *Barry & Fitzwilliam*

Price	**£11–13/€14–16.50**
Region	**Walker Bay**
Grape	**Pinotage**
Alc/vol	**14%**
Food	**Versatile**
Drink	**2001–2**

£13–15/€16.50–19

Jordan Merlot 99

Delicious, deep black fruit flavours, ripe tannic
structure. Silky and rich, with quite a punch at
the end. Oak is an important feature. Not for
wimps! *Maxxium*

Price	**£13–15/€16.50–19**
Region	**Stellenbosch**
Grape	**Merlot**
Alc/vol	**13.5%**
Food	**Spicy foodr**
Drink	**2001–4**

Plaisir de Merle Cabernet Sauvignon 96 £/€

A very tasty number, displaying the benefits of
a little ageing, but still with a good way to go.
Complex but approachable, very drinkable with
lots of blackberry fruit. Bordeaux style. *Dillons*

Price	**£13–15/€16.50–19**
Region	**Paarl**
Grape	**Cabernet Sauvignon**
Alc/vol	**13%**
Food	**Turkey**
Drink	**2001–3**

Rust en Vrede Cabernet Sauvignon 97

Very subtle style, so the nose takes a while to
open out into blackcurrant, damson and spicy
aromas. Arrays of ripe berry fruit dominate, but
are well supported by the integrated tannins
and balancing acidity. *O'Briens*

Price	**£13–15/€16.50–19**
Region	**Stellenbosch**
Grape	**Cabernet Sauvignon**
Alc/vol	**13%**
Food	**Veal**
Drink	**2001–2**

Simonsig Estate Tiara 97

A classic Bordeaux blend, taking its inspiration
from the same region. Elegant and refined.
Classy bramble berries with a cedary influence.
Delicious and memorable. *United Beverages*

Price	**£13–15/€16.50–19**
Region	**Stellenbosch**
Grape	**Cab Sauv/Merl/Cab Franc/Petit Verdot**
Alc/vol	**13%**
Food	**Lamb**
Drink	**2001–3**

Warwick Estate Pinotage 97

Quite pronounced, unusual aromas of blackcurrants, beetroot and baked sweet potatoes.
Flavours of violets and soft plummy fruits with
an earthy touch and a dry finish. A very solid
wine with balanced acidity and firm tannins.
Needs food. *Searsons*

Price	**£13–15/€16.50–19**
Region	**Stellenbosch**
Grape	**Pinotage**
Alc/vol	**12.5%**
Food	**Roast pork**
Drink	**2001–5**

£15–17/€19–22

Steenberg Catharina 98

Rich toffee aromas on the nose along with
plums and mint. The palate is layered with rich,
deep Christmas pudding flavours with vanilla
and sweet black fruit. Long, clean finish.
Papillon

Price	**£15–17/€19–22**
Region	**Constantia**
Grape	**Merlot/Cab Sauv**
Alc/vol	**13.5%**
Food	**Ham**
Drink	**2001–2**

> Close to the ocean, **Walker Bay** produces some of the most elegant wines from Pinot Noir and Chardonnay.

£17–20/€22–25

Hamilton Russell Vineyards Pinot Noir 99 ✓

Hamilton Russell is at the forefront of Pinot Noir production in South Africa. The blackberry and apple nose goes on to full, ripe autumnal and strawberry fruit on the palate, balanced by firm tannins. Vanilla/oak flavours are beautifully integrated and the acidity is fresh. All in all, it's a rich, ripe wine with a finish that lingers on and on. *Gilbeys*

Price	**£17–20/€22–25**
Region	**Walker Bay**
Grape	**Pinot Noir**
Alc/vol	**13.5%**
Food	**Poultry**
Drink	**2001–4**

Kanonkop Cabernet Sauvignon 97 ✓

This elegant and concentrated wine has a minty, almost port-like nose and rich, ripe blackcurrant fruit and minty flavours, well-integrated tannins and a creamy, long finish. Restrained and classic. *Findlaters*

Price	**£17–20/€22–25**
Region	**Stellenbosch**
Grape	**Cabernet Sauvignon**
Alc/vol	**13.5%**
Food	**Game**
Drink	**2001–4**

Kanonkop Paul Sauer 97

Rich and minty, hints of smoke and tobacco, with sweet blackcurrant fruit and smoky oak vanilla coming through. Extremely long finish. Classy, elegant and pretty fantastic. *Findlaters*

Price	**£17–20/€22–25**
Region	**Stellenbosch**
Grape	**Cabernet/Merlot/ Cab Franc**
Alc/vol	**14%**
Food	**Leg of lamb**
Drink	**2001–4**

Kanonkop Pinotage 99 ✓

Pronounced bittersweet aromas of mixed summer berries, stewed black fruits and vanilla. Excellent weight of ripe huckleberries, stewed cherries/black fruits and a touch of vanilla. The firm but well-structured tannins will soften over the next year or two. *Findlaters*

Price	**£17–20/€22–25**
Region	**Stellenbosch**
Grape	**Pinotage**
Alc/vol	**13.5%**
Food	**Steak**
Drink	**2001–4**

Rust en Vrede Estate Wine 98 ★

A deep, dark and concentrated wine. On the nose there are complex layers of blackcurrant, fennel, mint, chocolate and tobacco. The palate is just as interesting, mingling blackcurrant fruit, mint, bitter chocolate, tobacco, creamy oak vanilla and slightly hot spices, yet still managing to be restrained. Lingers on the palate. A competitor for Bordeaux. *O'Briens*

Price	**£17–20/€22–25**
Region	**Stellenbosch**
Grape	**Cab Sauv/Shiraz/ Merlot**
Alc/vol	**13%**
Food	**Beef tournedos**
Drink	**2001–3**

Warwick Estate Trilogy 97

Typifies South Africa's strength in the market-
place, a great example of where Old and New
World meet. The nose is quite herbal, with some
fennel. On the palate the integration of fruit,
tannins, acidity and alcohol is superb. The
blackcurrant fruit is obvious, but very elegant.
Searsons

Price	**£17–20/€22–25**
Region	**Stellenbosch**
Grape	**Cabernet/Merlot/ Cab Franc**
Alc/vol	**12.5%**
Food	**Roast beef**
Drink	**2001–2**

£20–25/€25–32

Hartenberg Shiraz 95

After 12 months in American oak, this wine has
emerged with spicy, plummy, ripe and concentrated aromas. Big, gamy flavours follow
through on the palate, where you'll also find
black olives, smoky bacon and more dark fruit.
It has firm tannins and a long finish. *Fields*

Price	**£20–25/€25–32**
Region	**Stellenbosch**
Grape	**Shiraz**
Alc/vol	**13%**
Food	**Red meats**
Drink	**2001–3**

Spain

The Spanish wines included this year come from Penedès, Calatayud, Costers del Segre, Navarra, Ribera del Duero, Rioja and a variety of lesser-known regions such as Toro and Jumilla.

Although Spain's reputation has traditionally been for red wine, the white wines show how much progress has been made in the past few years. No longer oxidised, they are vibrant, fruity and crisp, showing just how modern winemaking techniques have transformed Spanish wine. Chardonnay and Sauvignon Blanc make an appearance, but most of the white wines are made from the Spanish varieties Verdejo, Viura and Albariño. An example of how flexible the Spanish approach is can be seen in DO Rueda wines, which can combine native grapes Verdejo and Viura with the French variety Sauvignon Blanc.

Red wines are mostly made from Spanish varieties Tempranillo and Garnacha, but quite a few are blended with Cabernet Sauvignon, showing how keen the Spanish are to experiment with international grape varieties, especially in the Penedès region. Spanish winemakers are determined not to be hidebound by tradition and many have invested in state-of-the-art wineries. This forward-looking approach and meticulous attention to detail show concrete results in the wines of regions such as Ribera del Duero, Navarra, Jumilla and Valdepeñas, which offer young wines with ripe, juicy fruit as well as more serious oak-aged examples.

What does all this experimentation mean for Rioja? Some Rioja producers have moved away from the traditional method of long ageing and are making much fresher and fruitier wines. But traditional-style Rioja is still being made by many producers such as Marqués de Murrieta, though even this conservative bodega now produces a younger Rioja, Colección 2100.

White

Under £7/Under €9

Basa DO Rueda **00**

Strong, slightly herbaceous nose of nettles, blackcurrant leaves and some floral notes. Medium bodied, with strong underpinning acidity, fairly full gooseberry flavour and a spicy finish. Decent, fairly blocky style where Sauvignon character dominates. *Approach Trade*

Price	**Under £7/Under €9**
Region	**Rueda**
Grape	**Verdejo/Sauvignon Blanc/Viura**
Alc/vol	**12.5%**
Food	**Paella**
Drink	**2001–2**

Delgado Estate Blanco DO Cariñena

Crisp young wine with delicious fruit and floral flavours. Very easy on the palate and the wallet. *TDL*

Price	**Under £7/Under €9**
Region	**Cariñena**
Grape	**Macabeo**
Alc/vol	**12.5%**
Food	**Stir fries**
Drink	**2001–2**

La Cuvée des Vendangeurs VdM 00 £/€

This is a soft, fruity easy-drinking wine. On the nose there are attractive notes of ripe pear and Cox apple. The palate is soft and ripe with a slight spritz. *Approach Trade*

Price	**Under £7/Under €9**
Grape	**Viura**
Alc/vol	**12%**
Food	**Chinese, takeaway**
Drink	**2001–2**

> **Penedès**, south-west of Barcelona, was the first area in Spain to experiment with international grape varieties such as Chardonnay, Riesling, Gewürz-traminer and Sauvignon Blanc. Miguel Torres introduced these varieties in 1966 and pioneered modern methods such as stainless steel fermentation. Penedès produces red, white, rosado (rosé) and Cava wines.

Loxarel Muscat Chardonnay Xarel-lo DO Penedès 00

Very fresh and crisp with lots of juicy apple and lemon flavours, just the thing to wake up a jaded palate and great at the start of a meal. This should suit the ABC brigade with its blend of Muscat and the native Spanish Xarel-lo to add interest. *Molloys*

Price	**Under £7/Under €9**
Region	**Penedès**
Grape	**Muscat/Chardonnay/ Xarel-lo**
Alc/vol	**12.5%**
Food	**Fish**
Drink	**2001–2**

£7–9/€9–11.50

Can Vendrell de la Codina Chardonnay Xarel-lo
DO Penedès 00 £/€ 🌿

Attractive, uncomplicated style. Ripe apples, green pepper and a lemon and mineral quality on the palate. The Xarel-lo's contribution gives it a lift. *Mary Pawle Wines*

Price	**£7–9/€9–11.50**
Region	**Penedès**
Grape	**Chardonnay/Xarel-lo**
Alc/vol	**12%**
Food	**Salmon**
Drink	**2001–2**

Con Class Vendimia Excepcional DO Rueda 00

Good concentration of lemon and lime aromas with some gooseberry notes from the Sauvignon Blanc. There are more gooseberries on the palate, giving soft fruit flavours with a nice balance of fruit, alcohol and acidity. Lovely finish. *Searsons*

Price	**£7–9/€9–11.50**
Region	**Rueda**
Grape	**Verdejo/Sauv Blanc**
Alc/vol	**12.5%**
Food	**Smoked chicken**
Drink	**2001–3**

Mantel Blanco Sauvignon Blanc DO Rueda 00

A refreshing wine with classic Sauvignon Blanc characteristics. Lovely ripe gooseberries and balancing crisp, lemony acidity go on to a delicious fruity finish. *Approach Trade*

Price	**£7–9/€9–11.50**
Region	**Rueda**
Grape	**Sauvignon Blanc**
Alc/vol	**12.5%**
Food	**Asparagus**
Drink	**2001–2**

Mantel Blanco Verdejo Sauvignon Blanc DO Rueda **00**

An attractive wine. On the nose there are citrus notes with hints of pear. The palate has good weight and concentration, with zingy acidity and attractive green fruit flavours. Quite a traditional style. *Approach Trade*

Price	**£7–9/€9–11.50**
Region	**Rueda**
Grape	**Verdejo/Sauv Blanc**
Alc/vol	**12.5%**
Food	**Gazpacho**
Drink	**2001–2**

Marqués de Riscal DO Rueda **99**

Definite tropical and citrus fruit on the nose, even some grapefruit. There is an attractive vibrant acidity running through this wine, with floral, honey and grapefruit flavours lasting on the palate. *Findlaters*

Price	**£7–9/€9–11.50**
Region	**Rueda**
Grape	**Verdejo/Sauv Blanc**
Alc/vol	**12.5%**
Food	**Mussels**
Drink	**2001–2**

Marqués de Riscal Sauvignon DO Rueda **00** ✓

Nose is soft and muted, but refined—lanolin notes with a touch of lime, gooseberry and vanilla. Crisp green fruit is balanced by a slight creaminess and some mangoes and greengages. Easy-drinking wine with a touch of class. *Findlaters*

Price	**£7–9/€9–11.50**
Region	**Rueda**
Grape	**Sauvignon Blanc**
Alc/vol	**12.5%**
Food	**Tapas**
Drink	**2001–2**

Masia Sagué Blanc de Blancs DO Penedès **00**

Spicy tones, zingy, crisp apple fruit flavours and a twist of lemon combine to produce an interestingly complex wine with character and style. *Nectar Wines*

Price	**£7–9/€9–11.50**
Region	**Penedès**
Alc/vol	**11.5%**
Food	**Cod**
Drink	**2001–2**

Monopole Blanco Seco DOC Rioja **99 £/€**

Dry and refreshing with hints of almond on the nose and the palate. Lots of nutty character and traditional elements, but still fresh and balanced. Unusually different and an interesting wine for wine lovers. *Findlaters*

Price	**£7–9/€9–11.50**
Region	**Rioja**
Grape	**Viura/Malvasia**
Alc/vol	**12.5%**
Food	**Onion tart**
Drink	**2001–2**

Petit Caus DO Penedès **00**

This interesting grape blend is slightly smoky and minerally, but in a crisp, refreshing, citrus style. *Approach Trade*

Price	**£7–9/€9–11.50**
Region	**Penedès**
Grape	**Xarel-lo/Macabeo/ Chardonnay**
Alc/vol	**11.5%**
Food	**Seafood**
Drink	**2001–2**

£9–11/€11.50–14

Txakoli Xarmant VdM 00 £/€

This wine is very spritzy. On the nose there are citrus, pear and peach aromas. Lively and fresh on the palate. With its zippy acidity, it's a good aperitif. *Approach Trade*

Price	**£9–11/€11.50–14**
Region	**Txacoli**
Grape	**Hondarrabi Zuri**
Alc/vol	**11.5%**
Food	**Aperitif, tapas**
Drink	**2001–2**

£11–13/€14–16.50

Abadia San Campio Albariño DO Rías Baixas 00

Intense, vibrant nose, with a hint of tropical fruit and citrus. A good concentration of pear and citrus fruit on the palate is underpinned by crisp acidity. Nice mouthfeel and an excellent finish. *IberExpo*

Price	**£11–13/€14–16.50**
Region	**Rías Baixas**
Grape	**Albariño**
Alc/vol	**12%**
Food	**Crab**
Drink	**2001–4**

Marqués de Murrieta Ygay Capellania Reserva DOC Rioja 95

A traditional wine, complex and interesting. Nutty, woody, coconut aromas lead to a palate smothered in a layer of toasty coconut oak with lots of flavours of apples, nuts, figs and currants. *Gilbeys*

Price	**£11–13/€14–16.50**
Region	**Rioja**
Grape	**Viura/Malvasia/ Garnacha Blanca**
Alc/vol	**12.5%**
Food	**Chicken korma**
Drink	**2001–2**

Martín Códax Albariño DO Rías Baixas 00

Enticing nose of peach, spice and honeysuckle. On the palate it's very lively due to its high acidity, which gives the wine a wonderful freshness and vibrancy. A fruit cocktail of flavours carries through to a refreshing finish. *Approach Trade*

Price	**£11–13/€14–16.50**
Region	**Rías Baixas**
Grape	**Albariño**
Alc/vol	**12%**
Food	**Aperitif, Indian**
Drink	**2001–2**

£13–15/€16.50–19

Lagar de Cervera Albariño DO Rías Baixas 00

A wine made in a modern, fresh and zesty style with aromas and flavours of apples and citrus and long length—very pleasing. The Spaniards love it with seafood. *Woodford Bourne*

Price	**£13–15/€16.50–19**
Region	**Rías Baixas**
Grape	**Albariño**
Alc/vol	**12%**
Food	**Seafood**
Drink	**2001–2**

Terras Gauda O Rosal DO Rías Baixas 00

Citrus fruits on the nose with a slight hint of toast—quite complex. Fresh, fruity and with good concentration, this wine shows an attractive balance between citrus fruit and acidity. It has freshness and character, and a crisp, dry finish. *IberExpo*

Price	**£13–15/€16.50–19**
Region	**Rías Baixas**
Grape	**Mainly Albariño**
Alc/vol	**12%**
Food	**Aperitif, crab**
Drink	**2001–3**

£25–30/€32–40

Can Ràfols dels Caus Vinya La Calma DO Penedès 98

Lovely waxy, lanolin, apple and honey aromas. Full and lengthy flavours of ripe apples ageing beautifully and starting to develop honeyed and waxy characteristics. Displays real quality, with a matching price tag. *Approach Trade*

Price	**£25–30/€32–40**
Region	**Penedès**
Grape	**Chenin Blanc**
Alc/vol	**13%**
Food	**Creamy fish dishes**
Drink	**2001–3**

Red

Tempranillo, the Rioja grape, is grown widely in Spain. Its synonyms include Tinto Fino, Tinta del País, Cencibel, Ull de Llebre and Tinta de Toro. It has strawberry aromas, low acidity and low tannin, which make it suitable for early drinking and for ageing.

Under £7/Under €9

Berberana Dragon Tempranillo VdlT de Castilla 99

Fresh, fruity, jammy nose—strawberries and soft plummy fruit with a touch of rose petals. Flavours follow through very much on the soft, fruity palate, which has medium length. A good quaffer. *Tesco*

Price	**Under £7/Under €9**
Region	**Castilla**
Grape	**Tempranillo**
Alc/vol	**12.5%**
Food	**Midweek supper**
Drink	**2001–2**

Navarra is one of the most innovative wine areas in Spain. Using modern methods and equipment, it produces juicy red wines with lots of fruit as well as oak-aged mature wines.

Clos de Argenzon DO Navarra 00

This wine shows good, tight flavours and an honest bit of character on the palate—tar, raspberry gâteau and the tiniest hint of spice. *Approach Trade*

Price	**Under £7/Under €9**
Region	**Navarra**
Grape	**Garnacha/Tempranillo**
Alc/vol	**12%**
Food	**Chicken wings**
Drink	**2001–2**

Garnacha, the French Grenache from the southern Rhône makes wines with a lightish colour, high alcohol and raspberry fruit.

Cruz de Piedra Garnacha DO Calatayud 99 £/€

Strawberry and pepper aromas. Upfront flavoursome blackcurrant fruit and herbs, with some tannin to give it structure. Still developing and needs food to stand up to the tannins. *Dunnes Stores*

Price	**Under £7/Under €9**
Region	**Calatayud**
Grape	**Garnacha**
Alc/vol	**14%**
Food	**Tapas, barbecue**
Drink	**2001–3**

Delgado Estate Tinto Cariñena DO Cariñena £/€

Strawberry/boiled sweet aromas. Tasty wine with some weight displaying plenty of dark red jammy fruit with a gentle supporting structure of soft tannins. A nice, easy-drinking, soft red. *TDL*

Price	**Under £7/Under €9**
Region	**Cariñena**
Grape	**Cariñena**
Alc/vol	**12.5%**
Food	**Supper**
Drink	**2001–2**

Don Darias Tempranillo VdlT de Castilla 99 £/€

Tasty sweet blackberry aromas and flavours plus a dash of pepper. Light-bodied, but full of flavour and easy drinking. *Gilbeys*

Price	**Under £7/Under €9**
Region	**Castilla**
Grape	**Tempranillo**
Alc/vol	**12.5%**
Food	**Chorizo, tapas**
Drink	**2001–2**

La Cuvée des Vendangeurs VdM 00 £/€

Fruity and savoury with red pepper and plum flavours; easy lunchtime drinking at an attractive price. *Approach Trade*

Price	**Under £7/Under €9**
Region	
Grape	**Tempranillo**
Alc/vol	**12%**
Food	**Stuffed red peppers**
Drink	**2001–2**

Marqués de Chivé Reserva DO Utiel-Requena 95 £/€

Bit of character on the nose—blackberries, raspberries, loganberries and vanilla. Nice velvety feel in the mouth, with concentrated cranberry and black fruit flavours. This is a foodie wine with lots of fruity acidity. *Tesco*

Price	**Under £7/Under €9**
Region	**Utiel-Requena**
Alc/vol	**12.5%**
Food	**Bacon and cabbage**
Drink	**2001–2**

Marqués de Chivé Tempranillo DO Utiel-Requena nv £/€

Strawberry jam nose. Bowls of ripe summer fruit flavours. A lovely, uncomplicated, juicy wine. *Tesco*

Price	**Under £7/Under €9**
Region	**Utiel-Requena**
Grape	**Tempranillo**
Alc/vol	**12.5%**
Food	**Chorizo**
Drink	**2001–2**

Red **Riojas** are made from Tempranillo, Garnacha, Mazuelo and Graciano (and sometimes Cabernet Sauvignon) and are traditionally aged in wooden barrels, giving creamy, soft wines with strawberry and vanilla aromas from the oak barrels. Whites are made from Viura, Malvasia Riojana and Garnacha Blanca grapes. Traditional-style whites are dark in colour, oak aged and creamy; newer-style white Riojas are crisp and fresh.

Preferido Tempranillo DOC Rioja **99**

Deliciously fruity with strawberry and vanilla flavours and rounded tannins. A wine for all seasons and an exciting example of modern Rioja. *Bacchus*

Price	**Under £7/Under €9**
Region	**Rioja**
Grape	**Rioja varieties**
Alc/vol	**12.5%**
Food	**Versatile**
Drink	**2001–3**

The term **Crianza** on a label means that red wines are aged in barrel and bottle for two years, whites for one year. **Reserva** red wines are aged in cask and bottle for three years, whites for two years. **Gran Reservas** are made only in especially good vintages. Reds are aged for a minimum of five years, whites for four.

Señorio de los Llanos Crianza DO Valdepeñas **97 £/€**

An, easy, fruity Crianza. A barbecue quaffer with good tannins and acidity and a pleasant, light, fruity finish of redcurrants and cherries. Not over-oaked. *Dillons*

Price	**Under £7/Under €9**
Region	**Valdepeñas**
Grape	**Tempranillo**
Alc/vol	**12.5%**
Food	**Barbecue**
Drink	**2001–2**

Vega Ibor Crianza DO Valdepeñas 98

Good bistro wine with its jammy nose of peppery strawberries. It's quite spicy on the palate
with a streak of astringency. *Approach Trade*

Price	**Under £7/Under €9**
Region	**Valdepeñas**
Grape	**Tempranillo**
Alc/vol	**13%**
Food	**Omelettes, red peppers**
Drink	**2001–2**

£7–9/€9–11.50

A. L. Monastrell DO Alicante 00 £/€

An interesting nose with tea leaves and earthy
aromas. Still young, with cherries, strawberries
and a touch of prunes on the palate, it's quite
tannic. A big, rustic, warm wine. *Approach Trade*

Price	**£7–9/€9–11.50**
Region	**Alicante**
Grape	**Monastrell**
Alc/vol	**14%**
Food	**Stews**
Drink	**2001–2**

Chivite Gran Feudo Crianza DO Navarra 97

A complex nose of cedary black fruits with spicy,
earthy hints. Juicy fruit oozing blackberries and
cream on the palate with soft tannins underneath. Alcohol well balanced alongside fruit
and structure. *TDL*

Price	**£7–9/€9–11.50**
Region	**Navarra**
Grape	**Cabernet Sauvignon**
Alc/vol	**12.5%**
Food	**Lamb**
Drink	**2001–3**

Coto de Hayas Reserva DO Campo de Borja 95

Pronounced aromas of ripe, jammy bramble
fruit with hints of old cigar box. Spicy, fruity
wine, with good flavour complexity, firm tannins and quite a long finish. *Gleeson*

Price	**£7–9/€9–11.50**
Region	**Campo de Borja**
Grape	**Garnacha**
Alc/vol	**13.5%**
Food	**Sausages**
Drink	**2001–2**

De Muller Viña Solimar DO Tarragona 97 £/€ ✓

Still plenty of life in this 97 wine. Spice and
green peppers on the nose and bags of cherry
fruit. Soft on the palate, it has sweet oak and a
slightly toasted finish. *Approach Trade*

Price	**£7–9/€9–11.50**
Region	**Tarragona**
Grape	**Tempranillo**
Alc/vol	**12.5%**
Food	**Veal**
Drink	**2001–3**

Dehesa Gago DO Toro 99

Striking bubble-gum and black wine gum nose.
Very spicy palate, with raspberry jam and more
wine gums. Long, tasty finish. Still a youthful
wine, it will benefit from being opened in
advance and drunk with food. *Approach Trade*

Price	**£7–9/€9–11.50**
Region	**Toro**
Grape	**Tempranillo**
Alc/vol	**13.5%**
Food	**Mushroom-based dishes**
Drink	**2001–3**

Marqués de Aragon Old Vine Garnacha DO Calatayud **00**

Wonderful jammy fruit aromas with a touch of spice. The palate oozes plenty of spice with lots of plummy fruit rounded off by gentle tannins. *Searsons*

Price	**£7–9/€9–11.50**
Region	**Calatayud**
Grape	**Garnacha**
Alc/vol	**13.5%**
Food	**Pepperoni pizza**
Drink	**2001–3**

Marqués de Valcarlos Crianza DO Navarra **97**

A gentle wine with smooth red fruit and warm, spicy flavours—blackcurrants, vanilla and pepper. The Cabernet Sauvignon definitely adds a bit of body to this delicious wine. *Gilbeys*

Price	**£7–9/€9–11.50**
Region	**Navarra**
Grape	**Tempranillo/Cab Sauv**
Alc/vol	**12.5%**
Food	**Red peppers**
Drink	**2001–2**

Palacio de la Vega Merlot Crianza DO Navarra **97**

Intense and perfumed bouquet of ripe blackberries, plums and spice with a smoky background. A good Merlot, with the richness of the fruit shining through—plums and spice backed by a solid structure of ripe tannin and balancing acidity. A summer pudding of a wine. *Irish Distillers*

Price	**£7–9/€9–11.50**
Region	**Navarra**
Grape	**Merlot**
Alc/vol	**13%**
Food	**Barbecue**
Drink	**2001–2**

Preferido de las Viñas Viejas DOC Rioja **98**

Concentrated style with sweet berry fruit to the fore. Soft, balancing tannins, spicy oak and a lengthy sweet finish make it very appealing. *Bacchus*

Price	**£7–9/€9–11.50**
Region	**Rioja**
Grape	**Tempranillo/Graciano**
Alc/vol	**12.5%**
Food	**Mediterranean**
Drink	**2001–2**

Quaderna Via DO Navarra **98** 🌱

Like opening a jar of blackcurrant jam—pure, rich blackcurrant fruit, a little spice and vanilla, long length. All in all, what one expects from Navarra—fruity, modern, cleanly made wine that always delivers quality. *Gleeson*

Price	**£7–9/€9–11.50**
Region	**Navarra**
Alc/vol	**13%**
Food	**Beefburgers**
Drink	**2001–3**

Riscal Tempranillo VdM Castilla y Leon **99 £/€**

A soft, fruity, easy-drinking red. On the nose there are some juicy, spicy redcurrant and blackcurrant notes. More spicy red fruits appear on the palate, with balancing acidity to keep the wine fresh. *Findlaters*

Price	**£7–9/€9–11.50**
Region	**Castilla y Leon**
Grape	**Tempranillo**
Alc/vol	**13%**
Food	**Kebabs**
Drink	**2001–2**

Señorio de los Llanos Gran Reserva DO Valdepeñas 94 ★ £/€

Very fine wine for the price, showing nice aged development, especially with a lot happening on the palate—smoke, brambles, pepper, tobacco, leather and cherry fruit. This wine shows all that is best about Spain when it performs—delicious, decadent fruit nicely balanced with acidity. *Dillons*

Price	£7–9/€9–11.50
Region	Valdepeñas
Grape	Tempranillo
Alc/vol	12.5%
Food	Stir-fried beef
Drink	2001–2

Señorio de los Llanos Reserva DO Valdepeñas 96

A developed, light, mellow style, with cherry and tea flavours, smoky and a little leathery. A very worthy, fruity, complex wine showing careful clean winemaking without losing regional typicity. A juicy, savoury, spicy offering. *Dillons*

Price	£7–9/€9–11.50
Region	Valdepeñas
Grape	Tempranillo
Alc/vol	12.5%
Food	Squid
Drink	2001–2

Vega Sauco DO Toro 99

Fine example of modern Spanish winemaking. Still a little tannic, but with plenty of cherry and blackcurrant fruit on the palate, making it an excellent food wine. *Approach Trade*

Price	£7–9/€9–11.50
Region	Toro
Grape	Tempranillo
Alc/vol	13.5%
Food	Paella
Drink	2001–3

Viña 105 DO Cigales 99

Vibrant and fruity. Summer fruit aromas, maybe even bakewell tart. The wine is well structured, with lively acidity and robust tannins, but flavours of strawberries and spice are undimmed. *Approach Trade*

Price	£7–9/€9–11.50
Region	Cigales
Grape	Tempranillo/Garnacha
Alc/vol	13%
Food	Shepherd's pie
Drink	2001–2

Viña Mara Reserva DOC Rioja 96

Soft, stewed red fruit aromas—redcurrants, strawberries and blackberries. Smooth palate of summer pudding fruit with a good streak of acidity. Reserva wine at a less than Reserva price, this is a good introduction to the style of Rioja. *Tesco*

Price	£7–9/€9–11.50
Region	Rioja
Grape	Rioja varieties
Alc/vol	12.5%
Food	Vegetarian or meat casseroles
Drink	2001–2

Viña Mater Tempranillo Reserva DO Terra Alta 96 £/€ ✓

A taste of Spain. This mature wine shows depth and character. The very ripe strawberry, cherry and liquorice fruit is restrained by firm tannins. *Approach Trade*

Price	£7–9/€9–11.50
Region	Terra Alta
Grape	Tempranillo
Alc/vol	12.5%
Food	Poultry
Drink	2001–4

£9–11/€11.50–14

Albet i Noya Lignum DO Penedès 98

Ripe fruits marry nicely with soft, smoky spices. Rich, round and supple, this is a generous mouthful with lots of juicy fruit and a long finish. *Mary Pawle Wines*

Price	**£9–11/€11.50–14**
Region	**Penedès**
Grape	**Garnacha/Cariñena/ Cabernet Sauvignon**
Alc/vol	**13.5%**
Food	**Versatile**
Drink	**2001–4**

Beronia Tempranillo DOC Rioja 98 £/€

Typical Rioja—toasty, smooth and warm with elegant spice and coffee. It's a fine brooding wine with terrific length. *Barry & Fitzwilliam*

Price	**£9–11/€11.50–14**
Region	**Rioja**
Grape	**Rioja varieties**
Alc/vol	**13%**
Food	**Roasts**
Drink	**2001–3**

Bodegas Emilio Moro Finca Resalso DO Ribera del Duero 99

Super nose of baked blackcurrant fruit aromas with hints of chocolate, tar and treacle. Nicely balanced flavours—an abundance of blackcurrant fruit with oaky tones in the background. A complex wine, full of unusual flavours, all well integrated. *Approach Trade*

Price	**£9–11/€11.50–14**
Region	**Ribera del Duero**
Grape	**Tempranillo**
Alc/vol	**13%**
Food	**Barbecued or grilled chicken**
Drink	**2001–6**

223

Camparron Crianza DO Toro 98

Concentrated baked blackcurrant fruit aromas with hints of old wood. Excellent balance of oak and dark fruity flavours, giving good flavour complexity. Still young, needing some time to allow the ripe fruit to come to the fore. Well made, with persistent length. *IberExpo*

Price	£9–11/€11.50–14
Region	Toro
Grape	Tempranillo
Alc/vol	13.5%
Food	Game
Drink	2001–3

Campillo Crianza DOC Rioja 96

Game, truffles and undergrowth are the aromas of this big, chewy Rioja with its intense, concentrated flavours of dried fruit and nuts. Definitely a food wine, it will soften and develop over the next few years. *Barry & Fitzwilliam*

Price	£9–11/€11.50–14
Region	Rioja
Grape	Rioja varieties
Alc/vol	13%
Food	Lamb chops
Drink	2001–4

Castell del Remei Gotim Bru DO Costers del Segre 98

Upfront fruity style balanced by a refreshing kick of acidity. With its blackberry and plum fruit, it would make a great food partner. *Searsons*

Price	£9–11/€11.50–14
Region	Penedès
Grape	Tempranillo/Merlot/ Cabernet Sauvignon
Alc/vol	12.5%
Food	Vegetable couscous
Drink	2001–3

Chivite Gran Feudo Reserva DO Navarra 96

A good example of the quality of Navarra wines, combining the weight of Spanish fruit with Cabernet Sauvignon and Merlot. Strong aromas of sweet, spicy currant-like fruit and hints of earth. Soft on the palate, with plenty of ripe, plummy currant and cherry fruit. Very tasty. *TDL*

Price	£9–11/€11.50–14
Region	Navarra
Grape	Tempranillo/Cabernet Sauvignon/Merlot
Alc/vol	12.5%
Food	Chorizo, pasta
Drink	2001–2

Faustino Reserva DOC Rioja 96 £/€

A Rioja in the traditional mould. Strong figgy nose with some stewed fruit. It has concentrated dried fruits—raisins, dates, figs—on the palate with overtones of chocolate and coffee. Tannins are quite chewy. *Gilbeys*

Price	£9–11/€11.50–14
Region	Rioja
Grape	Rioja varieties
Alc/vol	13%
Food	Lamb
Drink	2001–2

Gazur DO Ribera del Duero 99

Plum and bramble fruit on the nose. Spicy, with ripe, baked blackcurrant fruit, very rich and robust, it's quite high in alcohol and has fairly fierce tannins. The palate has complexity and good length. This is a big wine, one to put away for a year to let the tannins soften. *Approach Trade*

Price	£9–11/€11.50–14
Region	Ribera del Duero
Grape	Tempranillo
Alc/vol	13.5%
Food	Mature hard cheeses
Drink	2002–3

Guelbenzu Azul DO Navarra 99

A stylish wine with intense fruity character of
plums and damsons balanced by a firm tannic
structure and spicy oak. This vintage has more
dominant Tempranillo character but with a
good bite from the Cabernet. *Searsons*

Price	**£9–11/€11.50–14**
Region	**Navarra**
Grape	**Tempranillo/Cabernet Sauvignon/Merlot**
Alc/vol	**13%**
Food	**Chicken kebabs**
Drink	**2001–2**

Herencia Remondo Crianza DOC Rioja 97

Warm, spicy bramble fruit aromas. Spice again
on the palate, as well as baked juicy summer
fruits. Made in the traditional style, this is a
nicely complex wine, with layers of flavour.
IberExpo

Price	**£9–11/€11.50–14**
Region	**Ribera del Duero**
Grape	**Tempranillo/ Garnacha/Graciano/ Mazuelo**
Alc/vol	**13%**
Food	**Steak**
Drink	**2001–4**

L'Agnet DO Priorat 99

Pronounced aromas of baked summer fruits and
vanilla. Lovely balance of acidity, chewy tannin
and big, rich, ripe blackcurrant fruit. A complex
wine, still quite young, with a long, creamy
finish. *Approach Trade*

Price	**£9–11/€11.50–14**
Region	**Rioja**
Grape	**Cariñena/Garnacha**
Alc/vol	**13.8%**
Food	**Duck**
Drink	**2001–4**

Manuel de Cabanyes Crianza DO Penedès 97

A fine example of good Penedès. Big mouthful
of rich, peppery fruit. Good length with fruity,
oaky finish. Still tannic but will age nicely.
Worth decanting before drinking. *Nectar Wines*

Price	**£9–11/€11.50–14**
Region	**Penedès**
Grape	**Tempranillo/Cabernet Sauvignon/Merlot**
Alc/vol	**13%**
Food	**North African**
Drink	**2001–3**

Marqués de Murrieta Colección 2100 Tempranillo DOC Rioja 99 ✓

A lovely example of a modern-style Rioja. The
concentrated nose has aromas of blackcurrants,
redcurrants and vanilla. The smoky palate has
plenty of dark fruits, but there are hints of
roasted chestnuts as well. A young wine with a
firm tannic structure. *Gilbeys*

Price	**£9–11/€11.50–14**
Region	**Rioja**
Grape	**Rioja varieties**
Alc/vol	**13%**
Food	**Lamb**
Drink	**2001–3**

Raïmat Abadia DO Costers del Segre 98 ✓

This blend works well, though the mint and
blackcurrant aromas are pure Cabernet. The
palate is wonderful—mint, blackcurrant jelly,
plums and vanilla. A harmonious and well-
structured wine with a warming, lengthy finish.
Grants

Price	**£9–11/€11.50–14**
Region	**Costers del Segre**
Grape	**Cabernet Sauvignon/ Tempranillo**
Alc/vol	**13%**
Food	**Stews**
Drink	**2001–3**

Raïmat Cabernet Sauvignon DO Costers del Segre **97** ✓

Inviting, complex, earthy aromas—liquorice, spice, a little bit of rubber, some vanilla. The palate is chewy and spicy, helped by some rich chocolate, custard and vanilla with a liquorice edge. The fruit on the palate is quite sweet and lasts into the harmonious finish. *Grants*

Price	**£9–11/€11.50–14**
Region	**Costers del Segre**
Grape	**Cabernet/Merlot**
Alc/vol	**13%**
Food	**Roast lamb**
Drink	**2001–2**

Ramirez de la Piscina Crianza DOC Rioja **98**

A very popular traditional style. Concentrated nose, redcurrants, spices and vanilla. The wine is medium bodied, with evident tannins and some complex aged flavours of black fruit and spices. Long-lasting finish. *IberExpo*

Price	**£9–11/€11.50–14**
Region	**Rioja**
Grape	**Rioja varieties**
Alc/vol	**13%**
Food	**Hummus**
Drink	**2001–2**

Vega Sauco Crianza DO Toro **97**

This is a big, highly structured wine. Earthy, full nose with bramble fruits and toast. Terroir very much in evidence, with the palate showing huge tannins and high acidity. Long finish. Ideal for hearty food. *Approach Trade*

Price	**£9–11/€11.50–14**
Region	**Toro**
Grape	**Tempranillo**
Alc/vol	**13%**
Food	**Spicy foods**
Drink	**2001–4**

Viña Herminia Crianza DOC Rioja **98**

Typical Rioja characteristics with good concentration of cherry and strawberry flavours. A lengthy finish of sweet berry fruit wrapped around spicy oak. *Bacchus*

Price	**£9–11/€11.50–14**
Region	**Rioja**
Grape	**Tempranillo/Garnacha**
Alc/vol	**12.5%**
Food	**Pork**
Drink	**2001–4**

Viña Hermosa Crianza DOC Rioja **98**

New-style Rioja. Perfumed, fruity nose of redcurrants with a hint of leather and damp earth. The palate is vibrant due to its high acidity, with firm tannins and persistent length.
Approach Trade

Price	**£9–11/€11.50–14**
Region	**Rioja**
Grape	**Rioja varieties**
Alc/vol	**12.5%**
Food	**Casseroles**
Drink	**2001–4**

Viña Salceda DOC Rioja **95**

A wine with considerable character on both nose and palate. Classy, serious, complex nose—tons of cedar, spice and ripe red fruit. Lovely palate of soft tannins with plenty of sweet, ripe red fruit and vanilla hints from the oak. Textbook Rioja. *TDL*

Price	**£9–11/€11.50–14**
Region	**Rioja**
Grape	**Rioja varieties**
Alc/vol	**12.5%**
Food	**Lamb**
Drink	**2001–2**

£11–13/€14–16.50

Marqués de Murrieta Ygay Reserva DOC Rioja **97**

Cedar and fig notes among the strawberry and blackcurrant aromas. There is a sweetness to the black fruit on the harmonious palate, which also has notes of leather and Madeira cake. Splendid finish. *Gilbeys*

Price	**£11–13/€14–16.50**
Region	**Rioja**
Grape	**Rioja varieties**
Alc/vol	**13%**
Food	**Rabbit**
Drink	**2001–5**

Marqués de Riscal Elciego (Álava) Reserva DOC Rioja **97**

On the nose there are brambles, a hint of cedar, plums, spice and soft red berries. Plums again on the palate, plus spice and toast, with robust tannins and balancing acidity. Long finish. *Findlaters*

Price	**£11–13/€14–16.50**
Region	**Rioja**
Grape	**Rioja varieties**
Alc/vol	**13%**
Food	**Casserole**
Drink	**2001–2**

Palacio de Muruzabal Cosecha Particular DO Navarra **97**

Wonderful rich nose of pure blackcurrants. Quite complex, spicy dark fruit flavours, balanced acidity and excellent weight of rich bramble fruit well integrated with vanilla flavours from the oak. Long finish. Well-made wine, elegant, soft and velvety. *Approach Trade*

Price	**£11–13/€14–16.50**
Region	**Navarra**
Grape	**Cabernet Sauvignon/ Merlot/Tempranillo**
Alc/vol	**13%**
Food	**Steak**
Drink	**2001–2**

Paternina Gran Reserva DOC Rioja **93**

Supple and smooth, this classic Rioja slips down like silk. With its vanilla and strawberry aromas, soft, creamy red fruits and velvety texture, it's a fine example of mature Rioja. *Barry & Fitzwilliam*

Price	**£11–13/€14–16.50**
Region	**Rioja**
Grape	**Rioja varieties**
Alc/vol	**12.5%**
Food	**Pork**
Drink	**2001–2**

René Barbier Cabernet Sauvignon Cosecha DO Penedès **96**

Earthy, quite vegetal aromas. Plenty of blackcurrant fruit, truffle and espresso flavours. A powerful wine, this is Spain's answer to Bordeaux—it could compete with many a Cru Bourgeois. *Febvre*

Price	**£11–13/€14–16.50**
Region	**Penedès**
Grape	**Cabernet Sauvignon**
Alc/vol	**13%**
Food	**Versatile**
Drink	**2001–2**

Tinto Arroyo Crianza DO Ribera del Duero **96**

Strong, earthy nose with complex, concentrated red and black fruits and spice. The palate has a big tannic structure and high acidity. Some more toasty flavours support the berry fruit. Long finish. Made in the traditional style with plenty of oak. *IberExpo*

Price	**£11–13/€14–16.50**
Region	**Ribera del Duero**
Grape	**Tempranillo**
Alc/vol	**13%**
Food	**Sardines**
Drink	**2001–4**

Vega Sauco Reserva DO Toro **96**

A perfect wine for the traditionalist, this is a very earthy style with hints of mushrooms, farmyards and spicy, vegetal notes that evolve to reveal plum and spice flavours. Good strong structure of fruit and gripping tannins; long finish. *Approach Trade*

Price	**£11–13/€14–16.50**
Region	**Toro**
Grape	**Tempranillo**
Alc/vol	**13%**
Food	**Stews**
Drink	**2001–4**

Vera de Estenas Reserva DO Utiel-Requena **95**

Aged aromas of baked autumn fruits, nutmeg, cedar, prunes and nuts. Still quite tannic, the palate has sweet blackberry and raspberry fruit with some smokiness. *IberExpo*

Price	**£11–13/€14–16.50**
Region	**Utiel-Requena**
Grape	**Cab Sauv/Tempranillo**
Alc/vol	**12%**
Food	**Steak**
Drink	**2001–2**

Viña Herminia Reserva DOC Rioja **95** ✓

Beautiful style, with plenty of creamy oak and concentrated berry fruit. Lengthy, complex and with great structure, it has firm tannins and a long finish. *Bacchus*

Price	**£11–13/€14–16.50**
Region	**Rioja**
Grape	**Tempranillo/ Garnacha/Graciano**
Alc/vol	**13%**
Food	**Risotto**
Drink	**2001–3**

Viña Urubi Classico DOC Rioja **99** 🌿

Rich, soft, plummy style of Rioja. More reminiscent of Australia than Spain. A soft, fruity wine, with cherry aromas and cherry/plum flavours, it will provide easy drinking on its own or with food. *Mary Pawle Wines*

Price	**£11–13/€14–16.50**
Region	**Rioja**
Grape	**Rioja varieties**
Alc/vol	**12.5%**
Food	**Lamb**
Drink	**2001–2**

£13–15/€16.50–19

Bodegas Franco-Españolas Rioja Bordon Gran Reserva DOC Rioja **93**

A light but alluring wine with its own classic Rioja style. Soft, spicy fruit aromas. Dry and oaky, with ripe, concentrated fruit and good length. *Jenkinson*

Price	**£13–15/€16.50–19**
Region	**Rioja**
Grape	**Tempranillo/Mazuelo/ Graciano**
Alc/vol	**12.5%**
Food	**Cold meats**
Drink	**2001–2**

Chivite Colección 125 Reserva DO Navarra **94**

Very complex nose, with chocolate and coffee aromas, ripe cherries and plums. Good extract on the palate—ripe black fruit with hints of spice and earth. Initially slightly withdrawn, it fills out to a wine of character on the palate. A wine for food and winter. *TDL*

Price	**£13–15/€16.50–19**
Region	**Navarra**
Grape	**Tempranillo/Garnacha**
Alc/vol	**13%**
Food	**Beef**
Drink	**2001–2**

Rioja Bordón

Simply the best traditional Rioja,
from the Bodegas Franco-Españolas
available from all good wine shops
Imported by Jenkinson Wines
97 Butterfield Park, Rathfarnham, Dublin 14
Tel/Fax: + 353 1 493 3480

Igneus DO Priorat **99** ✓ ◖

Intensely aromatic blackcurrant aromas on the
nose, lush and silky on the palate. It's elegant,
with masses of ripe black fruit, sweet nutmeg,
liquorice, cedar, blackberries and vanilla. Tannins are youthful so it should be put away for a
while. A food wine that will stand up to strong
flavours. *Mary Pawle Wines*

Price	**£13–15/€16.50–19**
Region	**Priorat**
Grape	**Garnacha/Cariñena/ Cabernet Sauvignon**
Alc/vol	**14%**
Food	**Spicy foods**
Drink	**2001–4**

Lanzaga DOC Rioja **98** ✓

This wine will win many friends. Rich and concentrated, it has aromas of vanilla, spice and
mulberries. The rich, velvety palate has concentrated mulberry fruit with spice and toast. Firm
structure with robust tannins and good length.
Elegant. A fine example of new-style Rioja.
Approach Trade

Price	**£13–15/€16.50–19**
Region	**Rioja**
Grape	**Rioja varieties**
Alc/vol	**13.5%**
Food	**Barbecued chicken**
Drink	**2001–3**

Montecillo Crianza DOC Rioja **97**

Deliciously concentrated wine with intense flavours of pure black fruit, liquorice and nutmeg.
Ripe tannins, long finish. Super food wine. A
very Spanish style, drinking nicely now. *Dillons*

Price	**£13–15/€16.50–19**
Region	**Rioja**
Grape	**Rioja varieties**
Alc/vol	**13%**
Food	**Poultry, game**
Drink	**2001–2**

£15–17/€19–22

Albet i Noya Collecció Cabernet Sauvignon
DO Penedès **98** ✓ ◖

A big wine, still youthful but full of complex
flavours. Oak is an important element in this
wine, giving it a silky texture and creaminess.
There are also lashings of rich, ripe blackberry
fruit. *Mary Pawle Wines*

Price	**£15–17/€19–22**
Region	**Penedès**
Grape	**Cabernet Sauvignon**
Alc/vol	**14%**
Food	**Beef**
Drink	**2001–3**

Albet i Noya Collecció Syrah DO Penedès **98** ◖

A fruit-driven Old World Shiraz in the New
World style. Quite delicate and flavoursome,
the palate offers concentrated fruits of the forest, spice, vanilla and aniseed and a long-lasting
finish. The tannins behind the fruit will ensure
that this wine will continue to evolve.
Mary Pawle Wines

Price	**£15–17/€19–22**
Region	**Penedès**
Grape	**Syrah**
Alc/vol	**13%**
Food	**Stews**
Drink	**2001–4**

Albet i Noya Collecció Tempranillo DO Penedès **98** 🌿

Appealing aromas of leather, blueberries and smoke. Plenty of spicy damson fruit and tobacco, with lovely balancing acidity, firm tannins and a lasting finish. *Mary Pawle Wines*

Price	**£15–17/€19–22**
Region	**Penedès**
Grape	**Tempranillo**
Alc/vol	**13.5%**
Food	**Versatile**
Drink	**2001–3**

---

*Although **Ribera del Duero** has been a DO region only since 1982, it is now producing some of Spain's finest wines, making dark, elegant reds from Tempranillo, the Rioja grape. Such quality of fruit is due to the high altitude of the vineyards, which are cooler than the plains below.*

Arzuaga Crianza DO Ribera del Duero **97** ★

Silk-textured red with all the elements in the right places. Flavoursome, with creamy, oaky vanilla and rich, concentrated, ripe dark berry fruits. Harmonious finish. Elegant and stylish. *Searsons*

Price	**£15–17/€19–22**
Region	**Ribera del Duero**
Grape	**Tempranillo/Cab Sauv**
Alc/vol	**13.5%**
Food	**Roasts**
Drink	**2001–3**

Condado de Haza DO Ribera del Duero **98** ✓

Classic Spanish style—meaty with underlying dark fruit flavours of dark berries and plums. Lengthy, robust and very satisfying. *Searsons*

Price	**£15–17/€19–22**
Region	**Ribera del Duero**
Grape	**Tempranillo**
Alc/vol	**13%**
Food	**Steak**
Drink	**2001–4**

Emilio Moro Crianza DO Ribera del Duero **98**

The fragrant, creamy nose of strawberries and blackberries deepens into delicious, delicate, cream, vanilla, blackberry and liquorice fruit. Weighty and structured. Most agreeable. Powerful finish. *Approach Trade*

Price	**£15–17/€19–22**
Region	**Ribera del Duero**
Grape	**Tempranillo**
Alc/vol	**13%**
Food	**Roasts, grilled meats**
Drink	**2001–3**

Faustino I Gran Reserva DOC Rioja **94** ✓

Striking nose of ripe black fruit, figs, cinnamon and spice, a touch of rubber tyre and leather. Delicious sweet strawberry and vanilla cream tart flavours. A smooth, unctuous palate with great length. A big wine in the mouth, it's still remarkably young. A fine Gran Reserva. *Gilbeys*

Price	**£15–17/€19–22**
Region	**Rioja**
Grape	**Rioja varieties**
Alc/vol	**13%**
Food	**Lamb, duck**
Drink	**2001–4**

Herencia Remondo Reserva DOC Rioja **95**

Nicely knit and stylish Rioja with cherry/redcurrant fruit aromas and flavours. Good example of traditional Rioja and best drunk with food. *IberExpo*

Price	**£15–17/€19–22**
Region	**Rioja**
Grape	**Rioja varieties**
Alc/vol	**13%**
Food	**Red meats**
Drink	**2001–3**

Les Terrasses DO Priorat **98**

Intense, multi-layered nose of ripe blackberries, blackcurrants, liquorice, walnuts and prunes. Plenty of character on the succulent, spicy palate of pure, juicy fruit, balanced by firm tannins. Lingering, tasty finish. *Approach Trade*

Price	£15–17/€19–22
Region	Priorat
Grape	Garnacha/Cariñena/ Cabernet Sauvignon
Alc/vol	13.7%
Food	Beef
Drink	2001–5

Pesquera Tinto DO Ribera del Duero **98** ✓

Well-rounded style, offering plenty of rich black fruit, mouthwatering acidity, supple tannins and a vanilla and spicy oak character. Lengthy, flavoursome finish. *Searsons*

Price	£15–17/€19–22
Region	Ribera del Duero
Grape	Tempranillo
Alc/vol	13%
Food	Couscous, stews
Drink	2001–4

PradoRey Crianza DO Ribera del Duero **97**

Full-bodied, rich and concentrated style. Meaty, with intense sweet plum and damson fruit, subtle and well knit, a good firm tannic grip and a lengthy finish. *J. S. Woods*

Price	£15–17/€19–22
Region	Ribera del Duero
Grape	Tempranillo
Alc/vol	13%
Food	Lamb tagine
Drink	2001–2

Viña Salceda Reserva DOC Rioja **95**

Lovely, complex nose of plummy and cherry-like fruit, fresh coffee and sweet, spicy oak. Velvety texture, with spicy cherry and plum fruit and the slight walnut and date characters of bottle age. *TDL*

Price	£15–17/€19–22
Region	Rioja
Grape	Tempranillo/ Graciano/Mazuelo
Alc/vol	13%
Food	Versatile
Drink	2001–2

£17–20/€22–25

Casa Castillo Las Gravas DO Jumilla **98**

You could spend a lot of time dissecting this nose—Christmas cake, liquorice, allspice, prunes and nuts. A big wine with lots of fruit, it needs time to open up. All the aromas carry on through the palate to a long, spicy, warm finish. *Approach Trade*

Price	£17–20/€22–25
Region	Jumilla
Grape	Monastrell/Cabernet Sauvignon
Alc/vol	14.5%
Food	Red meat
Drink	2001–4

Gran Caus DO Penedès **95**

Super. A developed style, with caramel and raisined fruit aromas, figs and prunes on the palate, good balancing acidity and supple tannins. The end result is a classic, complex wine that is drinking extremely well now. *Approach Trade*

Price	£17–20/€22–25
Region	Penedès
Grape	Merlot/Cab Sauv/ Cab Franc
Alc/vol	13%
Food	Lamb
Drink	2001–2

Marqués de Cáceres Gran Reserva DOC Rioja 90 ✓

Surprisingly youthful nose for a 90 wine. Figs,
dates, orange peel, vanilla, nutmeg and sandal-
wood intermingle. The weighty palate is just as
complex. More dates, figs, bitter chocolate and
spice appear. Flavours are very concentrated
and the finish is wonderful. It's all there in the
bottle—fruit, spice, creamy elegance. *Grants*

Price	**£17–20/€22–25**
Region	**Rioja**
Grape	**Rioja varieties**
Alc/vol	**13%**
Food	**Roast pork**
Drink	**2001–4**

Tinto Arroyo Reserva DO Ribera del Duero 95

Complex nose of cedar, spice and berry fruits.
Some attractive red and black fruit flavours with
a hint of spice. Firm acidity and tannins contribute to this wine's structure. It has a lovely
aftertaste, with something like rhubarb coming
through on the finish. *IberExpo*

Price	**£17–20/€22–25**
Region	**Ribera del Duero**
Grape	**Tempranillo**
Alc/vol	**13%**
Food	**Game**
Drink	**2001–2**

£20–25/€25–32

Casa Castillo Pie Franco DO Jumilla 98

Full-bodied, rich style of wine, full of smoky,
plummy fruit flavours, blackberries and spice.
Still young, but has the potential to develop
into a very arresting, heady number, complex
and rewarding. *Approach Trade*

Price	**£20–25/€25–32**
Region	**Jumilla**
Grape	**Monastrell**
Alc/vol	**14.5%**
Food	**Roasts**
Drink	**2001–3**

Chivite Colección 125 Gran Reserva DO Navarra 92

Layered nose—smoky, sweet vanilla, spicy/
earthy hints and developed black cherry and
plum fruit. Serious stuff—classy, complex wine,
with spicy, chewy plum, date and blackberry
flavours. *TDL*

Price	**£20–25/€25–32**
Region	**Navarra**
Grape	**Tempranillo**
Alc/vol	**12.5%**
Food	**Traditional**
Drink	**2001–5**

Faustino de Autor Reserva DOC Rioja 94

Lovely nose of plums, red cherries, figs and
dates. Dry and medium bodied with noticeable
tannins, this is an elegant wine with excellent
mouthfeel and plenty of plum and cherry fruit
backed by chocolatey, coffee bean and gamy
notes. Lingering finish. *Gilbeys*

Price	**£20–25/€25–32**
Region	**Rioja**
Grape	**Rioja varieties**
Alc/vol	**13%**
Food	**Turkey**
Drink	**2001–5**

Marqués de Riscal Gran Reserva DOC Rioja 94

Intense nose of ripe blackcurrants, blackberries,
boiled sweets and liquorice. Crisp acidity, firm
tannins and pure sweet blackcurrant fruit with
a vanilla backdrop make this an appealing wine
that will age well. *Findlaters*

Price	**£20–25/€25–32**
Region	**Rioja**
Grape	**Rioja varieties/**
	Cabernet Sauvignon
Alc/vol	**13%**
Food	**Roast duck**
Drink	**2001–6**

Palacio de Muruzabal Reserva DO Navarra **94**

Gorgeous savoury nose, reminiscent of beef pie fresh out of the oven. Though young, this wine has all the hallmarks of quality—a deeply flavoured palate of vanilla, blackberries, spice and liquorice, gripping tannins and powerful length. *Approach Trade*

Price	**£20–25/€25–32**
Region	**Navarra**
Grape	**Cabernet/Merlot/ Tempranillo**
Alc/vol	**13%**
Food	**Roasts, beef**
Drink	**2001–3**

Torres Mas La Plana DO Penedès **95**

A farmyardy nose, complex and vegetal with moist tobacco leaves. Initial burst of ripe fruit, with a gamy, spicy character and drying tannins. *Woodford Bourne*

Price	**£20–25/€25–32**
Region	**Penedès**
Grape	**Cabernet Sauvignon**
Alc/vol	**13.5%**
Food	**Red meat**
Drink	**2001–3**

Viña Ardanza Reserva DOC Rioja **95** ✓

There are layers upon layers of colour and depth to this wine, starting with aromas of toffee, burnt sugar, soft berries and coconut. The palate is dry, with soft berried fruit, vanilla, toffee and spice. Length is long, with fruit to the end and lashings of flavour. *Woodford Bourne*

Price	**£20–25/€25–32**
Region	**Rioja**
Grape	**Rioja varieties**
Alc/vol	**13%**
Food	**Pheasant**
Drink	**2001–2**

£25–30/€32–40

Herencia Remondo Gran Reserva DOC Rioja **94**

An ageing and developing Rioja, still with great colour and aromas of inky perfumed black plums and stewed tea. Tremendous layers of flavours—dried fruit compote and tobacco leaf with a fine cherry palate. The tannins are still grippy, so wait a few years if you can. *IberExpo*

Price	**£25–30/€32–40**
Region	**Rioja**
Grape	**Rioja varieties**
Alc/vol	**13%**
Food	**Lamb/roast turkey**
Drink	**2002–5**

Malleolus DO Ribera del Duero **98**

Perfumed nose of ripe blackberries, spice, liquorice, nutmeg and cream. Full bodied yet elegant. An enormous parcel of rich, sweet blackberries and plums is concentrated on the palate. A wine to keep and watch over. *Approach Trade*

Price	**£25–30/€32–40**
Region	**Ribera del Duero**
Grape	**Tempranillo**
Alc/vol	**14%**
Food	**Red meat**
Drink	**2001–5**

Sta Ma de la Piscina Gran Reserva DOC Rioja **94** ★

A wonderful classic style of Rioja, still very young. Aromatic nose of black fruit and spice. The tannins have lots of grip but strong blackcurrant fruit shows through with toasty vanilla. Very long length. A real treat. *IberExpo*

Price	**£25–30/€32–40**
Region	**Rioja**
Grape	**Rioja varieties**
Alc/vol	**12.5%**
Food	**Leg of lamb**
Drink	**2001–5**

Uruguay

Red

Under £7/Under €9

Don Pascual Cabernet Sauvignon 99 £/€ ✓

Good strong blackcurrant jam, violets and creamy vanilla. Nicely zippy, it tastes just like a handful of ripe blackcurrants and blackberries in the mouth, though there are some leather notes in the background. Very fruit driven with a lengthy, tasty finish. *Greenhills*

Price	**Under £7/Under €9**
Region	**Juanico**
Grape	**Cabernet Sauvignon**
Alc/vol	**12.5%**
Food	**Barbecued spare ribs**
Drink	**2001–2**

Don Pascual Merlot 99

Makes quite an impression with aromas—sweet and sour cherries. Very pleasant, with tobacco, spice and berries. Lots of minerals there too, quite complex with a vegetal twist and medium length. *Greenhills*

Price	**Under £7/Under €9**
Region	**Juanico**
Grape	**Merlot**
Alc/vol	**13%**
Food	**Beef goulash**
Drink	**2001–2**

Don Pascual Tannat 99 £/€

Earthy, rubbery nose, very vegetal. Acidity is quite crisp on the palate, but there are plenty of warm flavours of pleasant summer fruit berries, sweet peppers and violets, with a touch of tobacco leaf. Clean medium finish. Easy-drinking style, yet would suit food. *Greenhills*

Price	**Under £7/Under €9**
Region	**Juanico**
Grape	**Tannat**
Alc/vol	**12%**
Food	**Lamb**
Drink	**2001–2**

£7–9/€9–11.50

Don Pascual Tannat Roble 99

Black cherries and sweet peppers on the nose, with some cigar box and vanilla notes. An easy-drinking wine, it has sappy tannins and a velvety mouthfeel. The fruit is ripe and succulent, leading to a long, warm, spicy finish. *Greenhills*

Price	**£7–9/€9–11.50**
Region	**Juanico**
Grape	**Tannat**
Alc/vol	**12.5%**
Food	**Roasted Mediterranean vegetables**
Drink	**2001–3**

USA–California

'There are over 800 wineries in California, and though six or seven dozen are making world-class wine, several hundred insist on charging world-class prices.' So says Robert Parker in a review of Californian wines at the end of December 2000 in his magazine *The Wine Advocate*. It is certainly noticeable how much more expensive US wines are, which is only partly explained by the strength of the dollar. Perhaps it is because they have a ready-made market on their doorstep and the less expensive end of the market is dominated by the big brand names. 'At the top level California is exciting, as it is rewriting the definition for greatness of Cabernet Sauvignon, Chardonnay and Pinot Noir.' This is certainly true and there are lots of very good examples of these varieties this year, but perhaps the most exciting reds at the price were the Zinfandels, which are so distinctively Californian. Also good value and worthy of attention are wines made from Syrah and Sauvignon Blanc.

White

Under £7/Under €9

Nathanson Creek Chardonnay 98

Interesting nose of lychees, pears and apples with a slight floral touch. Smooth, peachy, rounded palate with some nutty flavours. *Barry & Fitzwilliam*

Price	Under £7/Under €9
Region	California
Grape	Chardonnay
Alc/vol	13%
Food	Mild chicken curry
Drink	2001–2

£7–9/€9–11.50

Talus Chardonnay 99

A wine for lovers of oaked Chardonnay. The wood is evident in the creamy vanilla/toffee aromas and flavours, which are well combined with tropical fruit. *Barry & Fitzwilliam*

Price	£7–9/€9–11.50
Region	California
Grape	Chardonnay
Alc/vol	13%
Food	Chicken pie
Drink	2001–2

£9–11/€11.50–14

Beringer Vineyards Sauvignon Blanc 98

Not typical Sauvignon Blanc—this is off-dry with intense, mouth-filling, sweet, ripe fruit with buttery vanilla flavours. The finish is long and very fruity, almost sweet and smooth. *Allied Drinks*

Price	£9–11/€11.50–14
Region	California
Grape	Sauvignon Blanc
Alc/vol	13.5%
Food	Oriental
Drink	2001–2

Fetzer North Coast Viognier 99 £/€

Intense aromas, honeyed tropical fruit, some lemon and orange peel. Dry, with rich mouth-feel and multi-layered peach, pear and honeyed tropical fruit flavours. There is good supporting acidity too. *Dillons*

Price	**£9–11/€11.50–14**
Region	**North Coast**
Grape	**Viognier**
Alc/vol	**13.5%**
Food	**Stir fries**
Drink	**2001–3**

Ironstone Vineyards Chardonnay 99

Toasty, nutty aromas, but some ripe fruit there as well—bananas and papayas. Quite a spicy palate of peaches and baked apples, backed by a bit of cinnamon and white pepper. Full-fla-voured, full-bodied wine. *Gilbeys*

Price	**£9–11/€11.50–14**
Region	**Sierra Foothills**
Grape	**Chardonnay**
Alc/vol	**13.5%**
Food	**Spicy**
Drink	**2001–3**

Stratford Chardonnay 99

Just like freshly pressed apple juice! This is a very enjoyable wine with its aromas and fla-vours of apples and lemons. Pleasantly long finish. *Barry & Fitzwilliam*

Price	**£9–11/€11.50–14**
Region	**California**
Grape	**Chardonnay**
Alc/vol	**13%**
Food	**Roast monkfish**
Drink	**2001–2**

£11–13/€14–16.50

Beringer Appellation Collection Fumé Blanc 99

Very pungent, oaky nose followed by a big, rich, alcoholic palate laden with oak. The palate has a buttery mouthfeel, sherbet sweetness and stewed gooseberries. *Allied Drinks*

Price	**£11–13/€14–16.50**
Region	**Napa Valley**
Grape	**Sauvignon Blanc**
Alc/vol	**13.5%**
Food	**Oriental**
Drink	**2001–3**

Clos du Bois Chardonnay 99 ✓

A classic style with excellent ripe, golden fruit on both nose and palate. Creamy and round with deep, ripe fruit flavours. Rich and unctu-ous and good with food. *Grants*

Price	**£11–13/€14–16.50**
Region	**Sonoma County**
Grape	**Chardonnay**
Alc/vol	**13.5%**
Food	**Fish with cream sauce**
Drink	**2002–4**

£13–15/€16.50–19

J. Lohr Riverstone Chardonnay 97 ✓

Not all Chardonnays taste the same. This one is almost savoury on the nose, with smoky nuances and distinctive tangerine/citrus aro-mas. On the palate there's a perfect balance of tangy orange and lemon flavours and restrained use of oak. Restrained toasty, bready, butter-scotch flavours complement the coconut and vanilla finish. Delicious! *TDL*

Price	**£13–15/€16.50–19**
Region	**Monterey**
Grape	**Chardonnay**
Alc/vol	**13%**
Food	**Pork**
Drink	**2001–3**

Murphy-Goode Sonoma County Barrel Fermented Chardonnay 98

The 98 vintage in California was quite cool and this comes through in the flavours of the wine, with its orchard/peach fruit and crispish acidity. There's a slight sweetness to the wine in a Californian fashion. *Wines Direct*

Price	**£13–15/€16.50–19**
Region	**Sonoma County**
Grape	**Chardonnay**
Alc/vol	**13.5%**
Food	**Mild chicken curry**
Drink	**2001–3**

£15–17/€19–22

Napa Vista Peter Mondavi Family Chardonnay 99

A wooded Chardonnay style, best with food. Apples and vanilla on both nose and palate, very smooth and full, but with balancing acidity to support the fruit. Nice lingering finish. *Findlaters*

Price	**£15–17/€19–22**
Region	**California**
Grape	**Chardonnay**
Alc/vol	**14%**
Food	**Lemon sole**
Drink	**2001–2**

Robert Mondavi Coastal Sauvignon Blanc 97

Inviting, rich nose of soft yellow plums, ripe melon and pineapple. Full and fat on the palate, with unctuous apple fruit balanced by enough acidity to keep it together. Strong oaky and toasty finish. *Febvre*

Price	**£15–17/€19–22**
Region	**Central Coast**
Grape	**Sauvignon Blanc**
Alc/vol	**12%**
Food	**Roast cod**
Drink	**2001–3**

£17–20/€22–25

Sequoia Grove Chardonnay 95

Rich aromas of lemon, melon, vanilla, butterscotch and toast. Lovely, full-bodied wine, packed with powerful and complex flavours, crisp acidity and a never-ending finish. Excellent food wine. *Findlaters*

Price	**£17–20/€22–25**
Region	**California**
Grape	**Chardonnay**
Alc/vol	**13%**
Food	**Chicken**
Drink	**2001–2**

£20–25/€25–32

Clos LaChance Chardonnay 98

Creamy vanilla aromas. The silky, soft palate has rounded nectarine, peach and passion fruit flavours. Oak is nicely integrated with fruit and there is a lovely toasted brioche finish. *Fields*

Price	**£20–25/€25–32**
Region	**Napa Valley**
Grape	**Chardonnay**
Alc/vol	**14.1%**
Food	**Turbot**
Drink	**2001–2**

Kendall-Jackson Grand Reserve Chardonnay 97

Plenty of soft tropical fruit on the smoky nose. The palate is luscious, offering a big mouthful of melons, peaches, tropical fruit, toast, vanilla, butter and butterscotch. American Chardonnay with attitude! *Cassidy*

Price	£20–25/€25–32
Region	California
Grape	Chardonnay
Alc/vol	14%
Food	Versatile
Drink	2001–3

Red

Under £7/Under €9

Diamond Grove Merlot 99

Very sweet, ripe, plummy aromas. Dry and slightly slaty, with plum and cherry fruit and a good bite. Light in style, with a warming touch of alcohol. *Dunnes Stores*

Price	Under £7/Under €9
Region	California
Grape	Merlot
Alc/vol	12.5%
Food	Grills
Drink	2001–2

> Originally from Italy, where it is called the Primitivo, **Zinfandel** has been grown in California since the early 19th century. The wines tend to be dry, sturdy and unsubtle with wild blackberry flavours and chewy, robust textures. The alcohol can be quite fiery.

Diamond Grove Zinfandel 99 £/€

Refreshingly different. Minty aromas, with stewed, jammy plum and cherry fruit. The generous baked red berry flavours are ably backed by a warm alcoholic touch and firm tannins. A classy structure. *Dunnes Stores*

Price	Under £7/Under €9
Region	California
Grape	Zinfandel
Alc/vol	13%
Food	Pizza
Drink	2001–3

Nathanson Creek Cabernet Sauvignon 97

Complex farmyard aromas, tea leaves, wet leather and vegetable nuances. The palate offers ripe blackcurrant fruit with Ribena and cream. Tannins are ripe and yielding; the wine has quite a seductive overall balance and a lengthy, spicy blackcurrant finish. *Barry & Fitzwilliam*

Price	Under £7/Under €9
Region	California
Grape	Cabernet Sauvignon
Alc/vol	13.5%
Food	Oriental
Drink	2001–2

Rocking Horse Zinfandel 98 £/€

Spicy cinnamon aromas mixed with bramble jam. Straightforward jammy blackcurrant fruit on the palate, with quite robust tannins, plenty of balancing acidity and a spicy, tasty finish. *Oddbins*

Price	Under £7/Under €9
Region	Napa Valley/Howell Mountain
Grape	Zinfandel
Alc/vol	15%
Food	Chinese beef with green peppers
Drink	2001–3

Vendange California Cabernet Sauvignon 98

Damsons, blackcurrants and stewed plums on the nose. The velvety palate has a moist tobacco leaf background with green peppers, blackcurrants and mineral/vegetal notes.
Barry & Fitzwilliam

Price	Under £7/Under €9
Region	California
Grape	Cabernet Sauvignon
Alc/vol	12%
Food	Beef casserole
Drink	2001–2

£7–9/€9–11.50

Ernest & Julio Gallo Sonoma County Zinfandel 95

Definitely not what you would expect from Zinfandel, more like Amarone, but whatever the content—amazing. Rich, fruity, meaty and savoury. More than subtle shades of the connection between Zinfandel and the Primitivo grape of Italy. *Irish Distillers*

Price	£7–9/€9–11.50
Region	Sonoma County
Grape	Zinfandel
Alc/vol	13.5%
Food	Chillin con carne
Drink	2001–2

Ernest & Julio Gallo Turning Leaf Merlot 97 £/€

Good example of a well-made commercial style of Californian Merlot. Very ripe, clean fruit, exuberant and enjoyable. Soft red fruit and plum aromas and flavours. Gentle tannins reveal the full force of the fruit. *Irish Distillers*

Price	£7–9/€9–11.50
Region	California
Grape	Merlot
Alc/vol	13.5%
Food	Picnic
Drink	2001–3

Pepperwood Grove Pinot Noir 97

A well-made, approachable and balanced Pinot Noir, where the balance of strawberry fruit, alcohol and body work well, resulting in an appealing, round mouthfeel. *Gleeson*

Price	£7–9/€9–11.50
Region	California
Grape	Pinot Noir
Alc/vol	13.5%
Food	Tuna steaks
Drink	2001–2

Pepperwood Grove Zinfandel 98

A fruity New World style but just a little bit different. Upfront, warm tinned strawberry aromas and flavours in abundance, coupled with hot spicy and smoky notes. Smooth tannins are well integrated and the finish is long. *Gleeson*

Price	£7–9/€9–11.50
Region	California
Grape	Zinfandel
Alc/vol	13.5%
Food	Steak with mustard
Drink	2001–3

Stratford Zinfandel 98 ✓

A toast, vanilla and squashed blackcurrant nose leads to a soft palate of brambles and sour cherries with coffee/mocha undertones. Easy drinking, warm, with a soft supple finish.
Barry & Fitzwilliam

Price	£7–9/€9–11.50
Region	California
Grape	Zinfandel
Alc/vol	13.5%
Food	Mexican
Drink	2001–2

Talus Cabernet Sauvignon 97

Vanilla, blackcurrant and tobacco leaf aromas. Blackcurrant fruit and toast dominate the palate, but there are also undertones of leather and spice with sweet peppers. *Barry & Fitzwilliam*

Price	**£7–9/€9–11.50**
Region	**California**
Grape	**Cabernet Sauvignon**
Alc/vol	**13%**
Food	**Pizza**
Drink	**2001–2**

£9–11/€11.50–14

Beringer Vineyards Zinfandel 98

Intense bouquet of tar and leather, stewed damsons and vanilla pods. Full bodied and spicy in the mouth; the gripping tannins don't hide the cherry and damson fruit. Very deep and dense wine, definitely a winter warmer. *Allied Drinks*

Price	**£9–11/€11.50–14**
Region	**California**
Grape	**Zinfandel**
Alc/vol	**13.5%**
Food	**Beef**
Drink	**2001–3**

CK Vineyards Wildwood Canyon Syrah 99 ★

Rich, inviting nose of roasted red peppers and savoury spices. Beautifully structured, with heaps of blockbusting flavours of raspberry, dark chocolate, plums and pepper, the palate shows incredible concentration. The firm tannins support the fruit and will allow the wine to age and mellow for a year or two. *Findlaters*

Price	**£9–11/€11.50–14**
Region	**California**
Grape	**Syrah**
Alc/vol	**14%**
Food	**Duck**
Drink	**2001–3**

CK Vineyards Wildwood Canyon Zinfandel 99

Appealing nose of juicy cherries and coffee beans. Mouth-filling, jammy cherry and plum flavours, with loads of spices and mocha, well able to handle the warm alcoholic feel. Great length. *Findlaters*

Price	**£9–11/€11.50–14**
Region	**California**
Grape	**Zinfandel**
Alc/vol	**14%**
Food	**Roast turkey**
Drink	**2001–4**

Fetzer Eagle Peak Merlot 99

This wine has character. Warm, fruity aromas—spice, fruit of the forest and plums. The palate has ripe, earthy, plummy flavours, with red and black berries, touches of spice and a long, creamy finish. Soft tannins make it easy to drink. *Dillons*

Price	**£9–11/€11.50–14**
Region	**California**
Grape	**Merlot**
Alc/vol	**13.5%**
Food	**Mediterranean**
Drink	**2001–3**

Ironstone Vineyards Merlot 96

This wine has ageing vegetal aromas among the strawberries and plums. The full-flavoured palate has generous plum and strawberry fruit with a hint of cherries and good length. Not a typical fruit-driven New World wine, this is restrained, almost in a traditional Mediterranean style. *Gilbeys*

Price	**£9–11/€11.50–14**
Region	**Sierra Foothills**
Grape	**Merlot**
Alc/vol	**12.5%**
Food	**Pasta with meat sauce**
Drink	**2001–2**

Ironstone Vineyards Shiraz 98

Tempting aromas of blueberry fruit, spicy and oaky with a hint of roses and rubber. This is a lovely full-bodied, juicy, fruity wine with lively acidity and firm tannins. A weighty mouthfeel of dark fruits—blueberries, cherries, black-currants. A rich floral element and a long creamy finish. *Gilbeys*

Price	£9–11/€11.50–14
Region	Sierra Foothills
Grape	Shiraz
Alc/vol	13.5%
Food	Grilled meats, tomato sauce
Drink	2002–4

£11–13/€14–16.50

Beringer Appellation Collection Zinfandel 97

Deep, dense, vegetal nose—brambles and Christmas cake. The palate is broadly structured with layers of red fruit. A serious and meaty contender. Very full bodied and savoury with a long, spicy finish. *Allied Drinks*

Price	£11–13/€14–16.50
Region	North Coast
Grape	Zinfandel
Alc/vol	13.5%
Food	Game
Drink	2001–2

Bonterra Cabernet Sauvignon 97 🌿

Elegant nose with berry fruits and vanilla. Lovely depth of flavour, with soft berries, cherries and cranberries. Cigar box and vanilla in there as well, with a smooth, creamy, chocolate lushness. Fantastic finish. *Dillons*

Price	£11–13/€14–16.50
Region	North Coast
Grape	Cabernet Sauvignon
Alc/vol	13.5%
Food	Roast lamb
Drink	2001–4

Bonterra Zinfandel 98 🌿

Sweet, smoky aromas, with cherry and plum fruit. A wine of highs. Alcohol is high and holds together the concentrated, spicy layers of warm bramble, cherry and plum fruits and firm, asser-tive tannins. *Dillons*

Price	£11–13/€14–16.50
Region	Mendocino
Grape	Zinfandel
Alc/vol	14.5%
Food	Pork and mushrooms
Drink	2001–4

Cypress Lodi Zinfandel 97

Concentrated and rich, an unusual style of Zin-fandel, displaying more softness than might be expected. Attractive aromas of walnuts, tea leaves and blackberries carry through to the rich palate. A very satisfying bottle for a winter's evening. *TDL*

Price	£11–13/€14–16.50
Region	Lodi
Grape	Zinfandel
Alc/vol	13%
Food	Versatile
Drink	2001–2

St George Cabernet Sauvignon 99

Ripe, warm blackcurrant fruit nose, with good firm tannic structure and a whopping great mouthful of pure blackcurrant fruit.
Peter Dalton

Price	£11–13/€14–16.50
Region	Sonoma County
Grape	Cabernet Sauvignon
Alc/vol	12.5%
Food	Pizza
Drink	2001–3

St George Merlot 99

Deep, inky nose, slightly muted, a little leafy.
Generous, rich black fruit with a good bite of
firm tannin on the palate. Concentrated fruit.
Needs food. *Peter Dalton*

Price	**£11–13/€14–16.50**
Region	**Sonoma County**
Grape	**Merlot**
Alc/vol	**12.5%**
Food	**Lamb**
Drink	**2001–4**

£13–15/€16.50–19

Kendall-Jackson Vintner's Reserve Pinot Noir 97

A fine, ripe, black fruit nose is followed by a
juicy, savoury, farmyardy palate with a big
structure. Gentle tannins and refreshing acidity
underpin cedar and moist tobacco leaf flavours,
with a heavy slash of steely minerals. Spicy,
long finish. At its best with food. *Cassidy*

Price	**£13–15/€16.50–19**
Region	**California**
Grape	**Pinot Noir**
Alc/vol	**13.5%**
Food	**Cold meats**
Drink	**2001–2**

£15–17/€19–22

Clos du Bois Merlot 97 ✓

A multi-layered nose of strawberries, fruit of the
forest and spice deepens into a rounded, structured, complex palate of ripe plums, cherries,
dried fruits, vanilla and spice. The mellow flavours carry right on through the flavoursome
finish. *Grants*

Price	**£15–17/€19–22**
Region	**Sonoma County**
Grape	**Merlot**
Alc/vol	**13.9%**
Food	**Lamb cutlets with rosemary**
Drink	**2002–4**

Clos du Bois Pinot Noir 99

Oaky vanilla, tomatoes and green peppers on
the nose. The palate is full of strawberry fruit.
Ripe, lush, appealing, commercial style, but still
with a firm bite of tannin. *Grants*

Price	**£15–17/€19–22**
Region	**Sonoma County**
Grape	**Pinot Noir**
Alc/vol	**13.8%**
Food	**Salmon**
Drink	**2001–2**

Clos du Val Zinfandel 96

The nose has very sweet, honeyed fruit with
some cedar wood and liquorice. It's a full-bodied wine with a nice dollop of ripe red fruit and
sweet/sour flavours of Morello cherries. This
wine has an extrovert character, but with a
creamy feel in the mouth. Tannins are noticeable, but don't overpower. Long, hot finish. *Fields*

Price	**£15–17/€19–22**
Region	**El Dorado/Napa Valley**
Grape	**Zinfandel**
Alc/vol	**14.3%**
Food	**Versatile**
Drink	**2001–3**

J. Lohr Seven Oaks Estates Paso Robles Cabernet Sauvignon 97

Intense fruity aromas of blackcurrants. With really ripe blackcurrant fruit on the palate, it's in a lovely New World style with a good structure of ripe tannins and sufficient acidity to prevent flabbiness. Great finish. *TDL*

Price	£15–17/€19–22
Region	Paso Robles
Grape	Cabernet Sauvignon
Alc/vol	12.5%
Food	Steak and kidney pie
Drink	2001–2

£17–20/€22–25

Beringer Appellation Collection Cabernet Sauvignon 96

Smoky, brambly nose. Plenty of intense blackcurrant and ripe red berry fruit on the palate, but well underpinned by firm tannins and well-judged acidity. Mineral and vegetal tones. Great balance of sweet fruit tannins, acidity and long, delicious length. *Allied Drinks*

Price	£17–20/€22–25
Region	Napa Valley
Grape	Cabernet Sauvignon
Alc/vol	13.5%
Food	Lamb
Drink	2001–4

Ernest & Julio Gallo Sonoma Frei Ranch Vineyard Zinfandel 96

Lots of concentration in this stylish wine. Autumn flavours of currants and blackberries alongside spice and walnuts. For this price and this vintage, you get style and elegance from Zinfandel. *Irish Distillers*

Price	£17–20/€22–25
Region	Sonoma County
Grape	Zinfandel
Alc/vol	14.5%
Food	Beef stir fry
Drink	2001–4

Robert Mondavi Coastal Pinot Noir 98

Attractive, smoky Pinot nose of oak, cream and strawberries. Juicy, fruity, well-made, rounded wine with a velvety mouthfeel and great length. Lovely on its own or with food. *Febvre*

Price	£17–20/€22–25
Region	Central Coast
Grape	Pinot Noir
Alc/vol	13%
Food	Milleens
Drink	2001–2

£20–25/€25–32

Ravenswood Merlot 97

Forget simple, juicy Merlot—here's a blockbuster of plumcake flavour. This is a wine that has been treated very seriously and it shows. Something different in the Merlot library. *Woodford Bourne*

Price	£20–25/€25–32
Region	Napa Valley
Grape	Merlot
Alc/vol	14.5%
Food	Lamb chops
Drink	2001–3

Ravenswood Zinfandel 97 ✓

Delightful fig and blackcurrant aromas promise sweet fruit on the palate. Soft, gentle flavours reveal layers of cassis, brambles, liquorice and figs. Tannins are firm, acidity is balanced and length is spicy and long. Drink it now if you like firm tannins or keep it for a year or two and have it mellow. *Woodford Bourne*

Price	**£20–25/€25–32**
Region	**Napa Valley**
Grape	**Zinfandel**
Alc/vol	**14.5%**
Food	**Osso buco**
Drink	**2001–2**

Sequoia Grove Cabernet Sauvignon 98 ✓

A big, serious wine in every sense. Deep and inky, it has aromas of cherries, meat and truffles. The powerful palate has concentrated ripe forest fruit, blackcurrant and Black Forest gâteau flavours and well-integrated oak. *Findlaters*

Price	**£20–25/€25–32**
Region	**Napa Valley**
Grape	**Cabernet Sauvignon**
Food	**Beef casserole**
Drink	**2001–5**

£25–30/€32–40

Robert Mondavi Zinfandel 98

Refined and elegant, with great complexity. Concentrated and pure fruits of the forest, plums and cherries are followed by smoke and spice. Alcohol is almost masked by the complexity of the fruit. Very rich and ripe, with soft tannins and massive extract and fruit, but still balanced, and will develop. *Febvre*

Price	**£25–30/€32–40**
Region	**Napa Valley**
Grape	**Zinfandel**
Alc/vol	**14.6%**
Food	**Rack of lamb**
Drink	**2001–5**

USA–Washington

White

Ch. Ste Michelle Chardonnay 99

Quite a distinctive, unusual wine. Savoury, smoky, ripe, almost toffee-like flavours combine with a ripe fruit underlay of pineapple and papaya. Oakiness adds to the complexity and the finish goes on and on. It's quite rich, so should be drunk with food. *United Beverages*

Price	**£11–13/€14–16.50**
Region	**Columbia Valley**
Grape	**Chardonnay**
Alc/vol	**13.5%**
Food	**Monkfish kebabs**
Drink	**2001–3**

Red

Ch. Ste Michelle Cabernet Sauvignon 97

Wonderful nose of blackcurrants and green peppers. Nice integration of leather and fruit flavours on the palate, which shows some complexity and a decent finish. Definitely one for traditional grub. *United Beverages*

Price	**£13–15/€16.50–19**
Region	**Columbia Valley**
Grape	**Cabernet Sauvignon**
Alc/vol	**13.5%**
Food	**Irish stew**
Drink	**2001–2**

Washington State *is a distant second to California in US wine production.*

Ch. Ste Michelle Canoe Ridge Estate Vineyards Merlot 98

This is a highly aromatic wine with intense notes of mulberry, cinnamon and toasty oak. Ripe plum fruit, herbs, spices, smoke and chocolate play on the palate. Tannins are firm but yielding. This is a youthful, concentrated New World wine that has the potential to evolve. *United Beverages*

Price	**£20–25/€25–32**
Region	**Columbia Valley**
Grape	**Merlot**
Alc/vol	**13.5%**
Food	**Beef**
Drink	**2001–4**

Rosé

The majority of the rosés featured this year are from France and Spain, two countries that take the production and consumption of rosé seriously. Rosés are particularly appropriate for warmer climates, where they are a good alternative to red and white wines. They can be especially good with food and shouldn't necessarily be reserved for sunshine.

Under £7/Under €9

Alma Garnacha DO Navarra 00 (Spain)

A well-made light wine, full of red berry fruit flavours—strawberries and raspberries. Very refreshing and with enough backbone to be enjoyed with food. *Approach Trade*

Price	**Under £7/Under €9**
Grape	**Garnacha**
Alc/vol	**12.5%**
Food	**Salmon**
Drink	**2001–2**

Antu Mapu Rosé 99 (Chile) ★

A rare find—a rosé with class and style. It's a perfect vibrant pink and is full bodied with minty aromas and flavours of wild strawberries and herbs. Smooth and balanced, it's a star all the way. *Barry & Fitzwilliam*

Price	**Under £7/Under €9**
Grape	**Cabernet Sauvignon**
Alc/vol	**12.5%**
Food	**Salads, shellfish**
Drink	**2001–2**

Marqués de Cáceres DOC Rioja 99 (Spain)

This fruity rose-pink rosado is full of red summer berry fruits—strawberries and redcurrants. It has nice grip, good structure and lovely acidity. *Grants*

Price	**Under £7/Under €9**
Grape	**Garnacha**
Alc/vol	**12.5%**
Food	**Shellfish, paella**
Drink	**2001–2**

Nathanson Creek White Zinfandel 99 (USA/California)

A medium-dry blush from California—ideal for those who like their wine fruity and off-dry, easy drinking and chilled on a summer's day. *Barry & Fitzwilliam*

Price	**Under £7/Under €9**
Grape	**Zinfandel**
Alc/vol	**11%**
Food	**Aperitif**
Drink	**2001–2**

£7–9/€9–11.50

Albet i Noya Pinot Noir Merlot DO Penedès 99 (Spain) £/€ ☙

A sturdy dry rosé with a fairly complex nose of red berries and gooseberries. Good zippy palate of cherries and summer fruits, with cherries lingering on the finish. *Mary Pawle Wines*

Price	**£7–9/€9–11.50**
Grape	**Pinot Noir/Merlot**
Alc/vol	**12.5%**
Food	**Prawns**
Drink	**2001–2**

Bergerie de l'Hortus Pic St Loup Rosé de Saignée
AC Coteaux du Languedoc **00 (France/South)**

A warm, full-bodied rosé with good balance of
fruit and acidity and slight bite of tannin. It has
good length with a little spice on the finish.
Wines Direct

Price	**£7–9/€9–11.50**
Grape	**Syrah/Mourvèdre**
Alc/vol	**12.5%**
Food	**Picnic, barbecue**
Drink	**2001–2**

Ch. Lacroix Merlot Saignée Rosé AC Bordeaux Rosé **00 (France/Bordeaux)**

A light wine full of red berry fruit. Interesting
nose of summer red berries, slightly underripe
plums and cream. Dry and refreshing with
intense strawberry and raspberry flavours and a
long finish. *Findlaters*

Price	**£7–9/€9–11.50**
Grape	**Merlot**
Alc/vol	**12.5%**
Food	**Charcuterie**
Drink	**2001–2**

> **Saignée** translates as 'bled'. In this winemaking technique, juice from black
> grapes is run off from the vat and used to make **rosé**. The remaining juice, or
> 'must', which makes red wine, is more concentrated as a result.

Ch. Thieuley AC Bordeaux-Clairet **00 (France/Bordeaux)** ★

A dry, fruity Bordeaux rosé, beautifully made.
Vibrant blackcurrant and plum flavours finish
with creamy hints of vanilla. Balanced and very
elegant, it brings rosé into a different league.
Wines Direct

Price	**£7–9/€9–11.50**
Grape	**Merlot/Cab Franc/ Cab Sauv**
Alc/vol	**12%**
Food	**Antipasti**
Drink	**2001–2**

Guigal AC Côtes du Rhône **00 (France/Rhône)**

Very good, warm vinous rosé from the south.
Ripe red fruit with a dash of pepper on the nose
and intense flavours of strawberries and cherries. It's a serious wine, with decent style and
structure, delivering power and warmth. Best
with food. *Barry & Fitzwilliam*

Price	**£7–9/€9–11.50**
Grape	**Grenache/Camarèse/ Cinsault/Carignan**
Alc/vol	**13%**
Food	**Grilled salmon steak**
Drink	**2001–2**

Marquis de Chasse AC Bordeaux Rosé **99 (France/Bordeaux)**

Light strawberry fruits on the nose and a tasty
palate of ripe berry fruits with some boiled
sweets. Dry, with a good streak of balancing
acidity and a flavoursome finish. *Bacchus*

Price	**£7–9/€9–11.50**
Grape	**Merlot blend**
Alc/vol	**12%**
Food	**Cold chicken**
Drink	**2001–2**

£11–13/€14–16.50

Ch. de Sours AC Bordeaux Rosé 00 (France/Bordeaux)

A serious, complex and stylish wine. It has a good sturdy nose with some character, quite intense blackcurrant/herby aromas and ripe fruit flavours balanced with good intrinsic acidity. *Woodford Bourne*

Price	**£11–13/€14–16.50**
Grape	**Merlot blend**
Alc/vol	**13%**
Food	**Cod**
Drink	**2001–3**

Gran Caus Rosado DO Penedès 99 (Spain)

Dry, deeply coloured wine full of lush Ribena and ripe blackcurrant aromas, which follow through beautifully on the peppery, spicy blackcurrant palate. An unusually full-bodied rosé with flavours that go on and on. *Approach Trade*

Price	**£11–13/€14–16.50**
Grape	**Merlot**
Alc/vol	**13%**
Food	**Tapas**
Drink	**2001–2**

Sparkling

Champagne comes in many styles—light, fruity and lemony, rich and biscuity, floral and fragrant or nutty and aged. The style partly depends on which grapes are used and where they come from in the Champagne region. Three different varieties are permitted—Chardonnay, Pinot Noir and Pinot Meunier. Blanc de blancs styles are made wholly from Chardonnay grapes and produce paler wines with apple and citrus flavours, which make perfect aperitifs. Blanc de noirs, from black Pinot Noir and/or Pinot Meunier grapes, have a more golden colour with richer red fruit flavours. Most Champagnes, however, are blends of the three varieties and the proportions used by each Champagne house can be very different. The use of oak is another influence in Champagne styles.

So do sparkling wines made elsewhere taste like Champagne? It depends on how they're made. Many inexpensive sparkling wines are not made by the traditional method (see panel) but undergo a second fermentation in a large pressurised tank. The ratio of yeast to wine contact is very different and fermentation time is usually shorter. Bubbles produced by the tank method are larger and more assertive than the finer mousse (bubbles) achieved by the traditional method.

Where sparkling wines are made by the traditional method, they can come close to Champagne. Of course different grape varieties and soils as well as shorter lees contact result in different tastes. Many Champagne houses have expanded into operations in the USA, Australia and New Zealand and are producing excellent sparkling wines. But it doesn't have to come from a Champagne house to be good. Some New World sparkling wines, Pelorus for example, have established a serious reputation for quality.

Sparkling wines made by the traditional method include French Crémants, Spanish Cavas and South African Méthode Cap Classique wines. When buying Australian, US or New Zealand sparkling wines, look for 'Traditional method' or 'Fermented in this bottle' on the label.

Champagne

£17–20€22–25

Henri Harlin Brut nv

Good 'everyday Champagne'—if there is such a thing. Spicy apple and citrus aromas have some complexity and the palate has almost overpowering citrus and spice flavours. At the price, this is good quality and quite attractively fruity with well-integrated acidity and lively bubbles.
Oddbins

Price	**£17–20/€22–25**
Grape	**Pinot Noir/ Chardonnay/ Pinot Meunier**
Alc/vol	**12%**
Food	**Oriental**
Drink	**On purchase**

*The recommendation to drink **on purchase** has been given for most non-vintage (nv) Champagnes, which are generally ready to drink on release. In practice, nv Champagne is usually drunk shortly after purchase.*

J. Dumangin Fils Brut nv £/€

Yeast and sourdough nose. Dry, with easy acidity, flavoursome apples and some pears. Elegant for a non-vintage Champagne. *River Wines*

Price	**£17–20/€22–25**
Grape	**Chardonnay/Pinot Noir/Pinot Meunier**
Alc/vol	**12%**
Food	**Aperitif**
Drink	**On purchase**

Tesco 1er Cru nv

Attractive light bubbles. Elegant, fresh, yeasty lemon and lime aromas and a slight biscuity character with underlying rose petals. Tangy citrus fruit with crisp acidity, fair length. *Tesco*

Price	**£17–20/€22–25**
Alc/vol	**12%**
Food	**Aperitif**
Drink	**On purchase**

£20–25/€25–32

Canard-Duchêne Brut nv £/€

Classic bready nose, crisp on the palate and full of lemon and toast Champagne flavours. Easy to drink, with a smooth finish. *TDL*

Price	**£20–25/€25–32**
Grape	**Pinot Noir**
Alc/vol	**12%**
Food	**Aperitif, strawberries**
Drink	**On purchase**

De Venoge Cordon Bleu Brut Sélect nv

Subtle nose of ripe pears with tropical notes. Dry, with refreshing acidity, good mousse and quite a complex palate of hazelnuts and apple fruit. Long finish. *Bacchus*

Price	**£20–25/€25–32**
Grape	**Chardonnay/Pinot Noir/Pinot Meunier**
Alc/vol	**12%**
Food	**Aperitif, smoked salmon**
Drink	**On purchase**

Gallimard Cuvée Réserve Brut nv

Fresh apple aromas. Quite a green and crisp style of Champagne, fruity rather than yeasty. Well rounded, with a clean, refreshing finish. *Bubble Brothers*

Price	**£20–25/€25–32**
Grape	**Pinot Noir**
Alc/vol	**12%**
Food	**Aperitif, first courses**
Drink	**On purchase**

J. Charpentier Brut Prestige nv £/€

Good mousse on pouring. Complex nose, quite minerally, with plenty of toasty, ripe apple fruit and floral hints. The palate is fresh, toasty with citrus and soft red fruit flavours. Very ripe and forward, this is a crowd-pleasing Champagne. *Wines Direct*

Price	**£20–25/€25–32**
Grape	**Pinot Noir/Chardonnay/Pinot Meunier**
Alc/vol	**12%**
Food	**Aperitif**
Drink	**On purchase**

Jacquart Brut Mosaïque nv

Tangy green apple and yeast aromas. This is crisp and fresh Champagne, with green apple, lime and grapefruit flavours. Very elegant. *Gleeson*

Price	£20–25/€25–32
Grape	Chardonnay/Pinot Noir/Pinot Meunier
Alc/vol	12.5%
Food	Aperitif, shrimps
Drink	On purchase

Jean-Claude Vallois Assemblage Noble Blanc de Blancs Brut nv

Very persistent bubbles. Developed nose of ripe, mature melon with buttery tones. Dry, with crisp acidity and appetising green apple fruit. Good flavour and length. *Bubble Brothers*

Price	£20–25/€25–32
Grape	Chardonnay
Alc/vol	12%
Food	Aperitif, olive tapenade
Drink	On purchase

£25–30/€32–40

SPARKLING WINE OF THE YEAR

Bernard Gentil Brut Réserve nv

Would that more Champagnes were as balanced as this one! Lovely complex aromas of warm brioche and honeyed melon with some citrus. The palate is beautifully smooth and integrated, with a creamy texture. Rich and supple, it has a fine mousse, lively acidity and a long, well-rounded finish. It will be delicious for a year or two. *Bubble Brothers*

Price	£25–30/€32–40
Grape	Pinot Noir
Alc/vol	12%
Food	Aperitif, versatile
Drink	2001–2

---

*Champagne styles: **Extra Dry** is actually an off-dry style. **Brut** is drier. **Extra Brut** or **Brut Nature** are even drier styles.*

Laurent-Perrier Brut nv

This Chardonnay-dominated Champagne has an excellent lively mousse and a pronounced nose of toasted sesame seeds with honey and floral notes. The palate is dry, weighty and honeyed, with apple drops and toasty lemon/lime flavours. The crisp acidity on the palate cuts through the fine fruit character. Good length. *Gilbeys*

Price	£25–30/€32–40
Grape	Chardonnay/Pinot Noir/Pinot Meunier
Alc/vol	12%
Food	Aperitif, crab salad
Drink	2001–2

Louis Roederer Brut Premier nv

Subtle aromas of lemons, yeast and baked biscuits. The very stylish palate has concentrated apple and lemon/lime fruit and a satisfying finish. *Searsons*

Price	£25–30/€32–40
Grape	Chardonnay/Pinot Noir/Pinot Meunier
Alc/vol	12%
Food	Aperitif
Drink	2001–2

Nicolas Feuillatte 1er Cru Brut Réserve Particulière nv

Nose of freshly baked apples with toasted almonds carries through to a full and gutsy palate with apple fruit and some ginger and cinnamon spice. A lovely delicate balance of all the component parts. *Febvre*

Price	£25–30/€32–40
Grape	Chardonnay/ Pinot Noir
Alc/vol	12%
Food	Aperitif, Indian
Drink	2001–2

Pol Roger Extra Dry White Foil nv ★

A full-bodied, lively wine with vibrant, fresh aromas of hazelnuts, brioche and apricots. Lovely defined ripe nectarine fruit on the palate, powerful and lingering, sustained by elegant acidity and vigorous mousse. Long finish. A beauty—more like a vintage style than nonvintage. *Barry & Fitzwilliam*

Price	£25–30/€32–40
Grape	Chardonnay/Pinot Noir/Pinot Meunier
Alc/vol	12%
Food	Aperitif, versatile
Drink	2001–2

Pommery Brut Royal nv

This Champagne has an attractive, lasting mousse and very delicate floral and complex green fruit aromas. Lovely fresh acidity complements the apple and citrus fruit on the palate. Good length. *Grants*

Price	£25–30/€32–40
Grape	Chardonnay/Pinot Noir/Pinot Meunier
Alc/vol	12.5%
Food	Aperitif, first courses
Drink	2001–2

Ruinart Brut nv £/€

Biscuity, ripe apple and pineapple nose with a mousse that stays the distance. The dry, nutty palate is complex, with tropical green fruit and citrus flavours. It has lovely balance and finesse—classy Champagne. *Taserra*

Price	£25–30/€32–40
Grape	Chardonnay/Pinot Noir/Pinot Meunier
Alc/vol	12%
Food	Aperitif, versatile
Drink	2001–2

Veuve Clicquot Ponsardin Brut nv

Just what one would expect from a bottle of Champagne. Fragrant nose of toast, nuts, cream, limes, apples and brioche. Very fine mousse, with a palate of wonderful freshness displaying a great weight of brioche and apple fruit. A very elegant and completeChampagne with tremendous class and style. *Findlaters*

Price	£25–30/€32–40
Grape	Chardonnay/Pinot Noir/Pinot Meunier
Alc/vol	12%
Food	Aperitif, caviar
Drink	2001–2

Over £30/Over €40

Bollinger Special Cuvée nv ✓

Champagne in a classic style—balanced, elegant and fruity. Crisp, floral, citrus nose and an elegant, smooth, silky texture with concentrated flavours of melon, butter, honey and Brie. Long, lingering, clean finish. *Woodford Bourne*

Price	Over £30/Over €40
Grape	Pinot Noir/ Chardonnay/Pinot Meunier
Alc/vol	12%
Food	Aperitif, oysters
Drink	2002–4

*The innovative house of Charles Heidsieck was the first to label their bottles with the year in which the blend and second fermentation took place and the bottles were laid down in the cellar for ageing—**mis en cave**.*

Charles Heidsieck Réserve Charlie Brut Mis en Cave 1990 nv ✓

Wonderfully integrated, complex, multi-layered aromas of butter, biscuits, mocha and honey follow through on the palate, giving a full-flavoured, elegant, silky, smooth-textured wine. It has classic elegance and style with a lively vibrant mousse that lasts all the way through its very long length. A touch of creamy caramel on the finish. *Maxxium*

Price	Over £30/Over €40
Grape	Chardonnay/ Pinot Noir
Alc/vol	12%
Food	Aperitif, versatile
Drink	2001–4

De Venoge Brut Blanc de Blancs 90

Mature aromas of toasted brioche. Concentrated and complex palate of fruit, nuts, toast—integrated and harmonious. Splendid length. It just goes on and on. Mature and should be drunk soon. *Bacchus*

Price	Over £30/Over €40
Grape	Chardonnay
Alc/vol	12%
Food	Aperitif, smoked salmon
Drink	2001–2

Deutz Brut Classic nv

Enticing aromas of peaches, caramel and toast. The wine has a delicious palate of strawberries and summer fruit with toast and nuts—almost like strawberry shortcake. Great length. *Febvre*

Price	Over £30/Over €40
Grape	Chardonnay/Pinot Noir/Pinot Meunier
Alc/vol	12%
Food	Aperitif, prawns
Drink	2001–2

*The Champagne method, called the **traditional method**, is the most expensive, time-consuming and labour-intensive method of producing a sparkling wine. After the normal first fermentation, the wine is bottled and yeast is added to each bottle, which causes a second fermentation to take place. The wine may be left in contact with the yeast for 15 months to 3 years, or even longer, where it will develop aromas and flavours of biscuits or bread. The yeast is removed from the bottle by a process called 'disgorgement' and the wine is then topped up with a mixture of wine and sugar. Depending on the amount of sugar added at this point, the Champagne will be anything from bone dry to sweet.*

Joseph Perrier Cuvée Royale Brut Vintage 90 £/€

Yummy nose of fresh-baked bread, toast, lime, lemon, apple and biscuit. A lovely round wine, full of flavours of green apples, citrus, toast and nuts. Very smooth, with a finish that goes on and on. Rare to find a Champagne of this age at this price. *United Beverages*

Price	**Over £30/Over €40**
Grape	**Chardonnay/Pinot Noir/Pinot Meunier**
Alc/vol	**12%**
Food	**Aperitif**
Drink	**2001–2**

*The rare wine produced from a single year owes its first allegiance to the characteristics of that particular year. **Vintage Champagnes** can benefit from ageing. The vintages of 88, 89 and 90 were wonderful, but very little remains on the shelves. The 91 vintage was poor and only a few Champagne houses made vintage wines in the years 92 to 94; 95 was a really good year and 96 looks set to be a great year.*

Louis Roederer Brut Vintage 93

Toasty, nutty aromas are followed by rich, ripe pineapple and nut flavours. Lovely, complex finish. Still developing. *Searsons*

Price	**Over £30/Over €40**
Grape	**Chardonnay/Pinot Noir/Pinot Meunier**
Alc/vol	**12%**
Food	**Aperitif, celebration**
Drink	**2001–4**

Taittinger Brut Réserve nv

Biscuity and toasty, with lemon/lime peel and nutty flavours. Rich yet elegant, powerful yet delicate, with that lovely concentrated cut that one expects from Champagne. *Febvre*

Price	**Over £30/Over €40**
Grape	**Chardonnay/Pinot Noir/Pinot Meunier**
Alc/vol	**12%**
Food	**Aperitif, foie gras**
Drink	**2001–2**

Rosé

*Pink or rosé **Champagne** is made by either the maceration or the addition method. The **maceration method** leaves the skins of the crushed black grapes in contact with the fermenting grape juice for a few days to stain the juice pink. This method gives the winemaker very little control over the consistency of colour. Using the **addition method**, a small amount of still red wine from the Champagne region, AC Coteaux Champenois, is added during the blending before the second fermentation in bottle. Demand for pink fizz moves in cycles—it seems to gain in popularity during times of prosperity.*

£25–30/€32–40

Montaudon Grand Brut Rosé nv £/€

Elegant nose of rose petals. Soft, fruity palate—strawberries and summer fruits—goes on to a lovely dry, fruity finish. *Mitchells*

Price	**£20–25/€32–40**
Grape	**Chard/Pinot Noir**
Alc/vol	**12%**
Food	**Aperitif**
Drink	**2001–2**

Over £30/Over €40

Laurent-Perrier Brut Rosé nv ★

The fragrant nose shows finesse, with its strawberry and raspberry aromas and yeasty notes. The palate is beautifully structured, with fine acidity subtle red fruit flavours. Delicious, with all the best attributes of fine Champagne—finesse, elegance, firm fruit, intrinsic balancing acidity and fabulous length. *Gilbeys*

Price	**Over £30/Over €40**
Grape	**Pinot Noir**
Alc/vol	**12%**
Food	**Aperitif, versatile**
Drink	**2001–3**

Moët et Chandon Brut Imperial Rosé 93

Lovely Turkish Delight aromas with apples and lemons. The palate has flavours of summer fruits, toasted almonds and biscuity chocolate, with a refreshing bite of acidity and a crisp finish. *Dillons*

Price	**Over £30/Over €40**
Grape	**Chardonnay/Pinot Noir/Pinot Meunier**
Alc/vol	**12.5%**
Food	**Aperitif, salmon**
Drink	**2001–2**

Taittinger Prestige Brut Rosé nv

Summery, toasty, biscuity nose of red fruits and strawberries. On the palate there is a delicious mélange of strawberries, red fruits and a hint of vanilla. Acidity is quite marked and the finish is long. *Febvre*

Price	**Over £30/Over €40**
Grape	**Pinot Noir/Pinot Meunier**
Alc/vol	**12%**
Food	**Aperitif, lobster**
Drink	**2001–2**

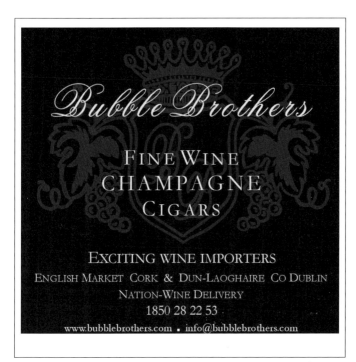

Sparkling

> **Cava** is Spain's traditional sparkling wine. It is made using the traditional, or Champagne, method, with the second fermentation in bottle. The DO rules specify that only the first portion of free-run juice (the finest-quality juice when the grapes are pressed) may be used. Non-vintage wines must rest on their lees in bottle for at least nine months (as opposed to fifteen months in Champagne). Vintage Cava must be aged on the lees for three years.

£7–9/€9–11.50

Gala DO Cava nv (Spain)

This sparkler has real charm. It has aromas of lemon and citrus fruits together with some nuts and yeastiness. The palate is very refreshing and quite dry, with lemon and bread flavours. *SuperValu-Centra*

Price	**£7–9/€9–11.50**
Grape	**Macabeo/Xarel-lo/ Parallada**
Alc/vol	**11.5%**
Food	**Aperitif, guacamole**
Drink	**On purchase**

£9–11/€11.50–14

Chevalier de France Chardonnay Brut nv

Nice tiny bubbles, apple and some bready aromas. Full of crisp, light fruit. A good, easy-drinking bubbly. *TDL*

Price	**£9–11/€11.50–14**
Grape	**Chardonnay**
Alc/vol	**11.5%**
Food	**Aperitif, terrine**
Drink	**On purchase**

Jacob's Creek Chardonnay Pinot Noir Special Cuvée Selected Reserve nv (Australia)

Very pleasant aromas of strawberries, peaches and melons. On the palate, acidity is high and flavours are of stoned fruit, apples and limes. *Irish Distillers*

Price	**£9–11/€11.50–14**
Grape	**Chardonnay/Pinot Noir**
Alc/vol	**12%**
Food	**Aperitif**
Drink	**On purchase**

> Italy's popular sparkler **Asti Spumante** is made by suppressing and filtering out the yeast half-way through the first fermentation. The natural carbon dioxide gas is trapped and the remaining unfermented sugars add sweetness to the wine. The Muscat grape contributes a perfumed and grapey character.

Mondoro Asti DOCG Asti nv (Italy)

Asti Spumante should always be drunk as young as possible, as it soon loses its delicate aromas and flavours. It is traditionally drunk with panettone at Christmas. This Asti has inviting aromas of citrus peel and grapes. The medium-sweet palate is fresh, floral and grapey with citrus notes. Fun and very low in alcohol! *Grants*

Price	**£9–11/€11.50–14**
Grape	**Moscato**
Alc/vol	**7.5%**
Food	**Christmas cake**
Drink	**On purchase**

Paul Cheneau Blanc de Blancs Brut DO Cava nv (Spain)

Delicious almond biscotti nose and a broad palate of toasted nut flavours. Refreshing and a traditional Cava style without Chardonnay. *Bacchus*

Price	£9–11/€11.50–14
Grape	Macabeo/Xarel-lo/ Parellada
Alc/vol	12%
Food	Dessert
Drink	On purchase

£11–13/€14–16.50

Codorníu Cuvée Raventós Brut DO Cava nv (Spain)

Cava isn't traditionally made with Chardonnay, but the Spanish firm of Codorníu makes this Chardonnay-based Cava to appeal to international tastes. It's a stylish, fruity sparkler with biscuit flavours and some structure. Good long-lasting bubbles and clean-cut Chardonnay fruit. Crisp, clean finish. *Grants*

Price	£11–13/€14–16.50
Grape	Chardonnay, Macabeo/Xarel-lo
Alc/vol	12%
Food	Aperitif, smoked salmon
Drink	On purchase

Freixenet Cordon Negro DO Cava nv (Spain)

Characterful nose with aromas of apples, citrus and some biscuit—not unlike lemon sherbet. A dry style with very crisp acidity, it has a little creaminess but is predominantly citric in flavour, like a good lemon tart. *Woodford Bourne*

Price	£11–13/€14–16.50
Grape	Macabeo/Xarel-lo/ Parellada
Alc/vol	11.5%
Food	Aperitif, fish
Drink	On purchase

Graham Beck Brut WO Robertson nv (South Africa)

Two Champagne grapes are used to make this yeasty, fruity sparkler. Very dry, with quite toasty, minerally flavours, this is a sturdy wine with broad fruit carrying plenty of punch. It would suit food very well. *Cassidy*

Price	£11–13/€14–16.50
Grape	Chardonnay/Pinot Noir
Alc/vol	11.5%
Food	Aperitif, Chinese
Drink	On purchase

Gratien & Meyer Brut AC Saumur nv (France–Loire)

Beautifully made fruity Saumur. There's a hint of sweetness, but only a hint, making it even more drinkable. Strawberry and apple aromas are followed by rich, ripe fruit on the palate and a lingering finish. *Gilbeys*

Price	£11–13/€14–16.50
Grape	Mainly Chenin Blanc
Alc/vol	12.5%
Food	Aperitif
Drink	On purchase

Hardys Nottage Hill Chardonnay Brut 99 (Australia)

Tropical fruit aromas. This sparkler has a rich, creamy mousse and is quite full in body and flavour. The melon and peach flavours together with some toastiness make this very pleasing. *Allied Drinks*

Price	£11–13/€14–16.50
Grape	Chardonnay
Alc/vol	11.5%
Food	Aperitif, spicy food
Drink	2001–2

Lindauer Brut nv (New Zealand) £/€

Honest, fruity, fun. The mousse is explosive and soft. Acidity is high, but the fruit compensates. Citrus touches—very fresh. *Grants*

Price	£11–13/€14–16.50
Grape	Mainly Chardonnay/ Pinot Noir
Alc/vol	12%
Food	Aperitif
Drink	On purchase

René Barbier Mediterranean Cava DO Cava nv (Spain) £/€

A tasty aperitif in the traditional style at a good price. Appealing nose of apples and limes, nicely rounded and moussy with refreshing, acidity. *Febvre*

Price	£11–13/€14–16.50
Grape	Macabeo/Xarel-lo/ Parellada
Alc/vol	11.5%
Food	Aperitif, shellfish
Drink	On purchase

Seppelt Salinger Brut 93 (Australia)

Small, fine bubbles. A crisp style, with plenty of lemon peel and apple flavours. Its slightly tart style would make it a good foil for rich dishes or stir fries. *Dunnes Stores*

Price	£11–13/€14–16.50
Grape	Chardonnay/Pinot Noir
Alc/vol	12.5%
Food	Aperitif, Chinese
Drink	2001–2

£13–15/€16.50–19

Masia Sagué Gran Reserva Brut Nature Cava
DO Cava **nv (Spain) £/€**

This sparkler is in the traditional style, also has earthy, yeasty influences. Good concentration of toasty apple fruit flavours. Very complex for the money. *Nectar Wines*

Price	**£13–15/€16.50–19**
Grape	**Macabeo/Xarel-lo/ Parellada**
Alc/vol	**11.5%**
Food	**Aperitif, olives**
Drink	**On purchase**

> **Prosecco** *is the name of the grape variety and of a style of sparkling wine from the Veneto region in north-east Italy. The sparkle generally comes from a second fermentation of the wine in tank and not the traditional method where the second fermentation occurs in bottle.*

Musaragno Vino Spumante Brut
DOC Prosecco di Valdobbiadene **nv (Italy)**

Attractive floral aromas with good mousse. This sparkler is fresh and lively on the palate, with lots of zippy melons and pears. *Select Wines*

Price	**£13–15/€16.50–19**
Grape	**Prosecco**
Alc/vol	**11%**
Food	**Aperitif, parma ham**
Drink	**On purchase**

Seaview Pinot Noir Chardonnay Brut 95 (Australia)

A nutty and sourdough nose with bready and baked apple flavours on the palate. Acidity quite marked. A very nice sparkler, fruity yet complex. *Findlaters*

Price	**£13–15/€16.50–19**
Grape	**Pinot Noir/Chard**
Alc/vol	**12%**
Food	**Aperitif, oysters**
Drink	**2001–2**

£15–17/€19–22

Bouvet Saphir Brut AC Saumur 98 (France–Loire)

This is a real dessert wine, made in an off-dry style. Quite a pungent honeysuckle nose with some vegetal notes. The palate has intense pear fruit and crisp acidity, which acts as a counter-balance to the sweetness. *Le Caveau*

Price	**£15–17/€19–22**
Grape	**Mainly Chenin Blanc**
Alc/vol	**12.5%**
Food	**Dessert, fruit**
Drink	**2001–2**

Ch. Tour Grise Brut AC Saumur nv (France–Loire) 🌿

Toasted almonds on the nose lead into a palate of marmalade—lemon and Seville oranges. Clean and fresh, there is good grape extract and a dry finish. *Mary Pawle Wines*

Price	**£15–17/€19–22**
Grape	**Mainly Chenin Blanc**
Alc/vol	**12%**
Food	**Aperitif, Waldorf salad**
Drink	**On purchase**

Dopff au Moulin Cuvée Julien AC Crémant d'Alsace **nv** (France–Alsace)

This sparkling wine has assertive fizziness. Flavours are of apples, pears, red apple skins and floral elements with some toastiness. Just a little bit different. *Woodford Bourne*

Price	**£15–17/€19–22**
Grape	**Pinot Blanc**
Alc/vol	**12%**
Food	**Aperitif**
Drink	**On purchase**

Gran Caus Extra Brut Reserva DO Cava 98 (Spain)

Promising nose of summer nectarines, but the palate is quite different—buttered toast, nuts and peach/apricot fruit. The finish is long and dry. *Approach Trade*

Price	**£15–17/€19–22**
Grape	**Xarel-lo/Chardonnay/ Macabeo**
Alc/vol	**12.5%**
Food	**Aperitif, prawns**
Drink	**2001–2**

Mumm Cuvée Napa Brut nv (USA–California)

Clean, fruity, easy fizz that can be knocked back very easily. It has apple freshness on the palate, a good slow mousse and a flavoursome finish. *Barry & Fitzwilliam*

Price	**£15–17/€19–22**
Grape	**Chardonnay/Pinot Noir/Pinot Meunier**
Alc/vol	**12.5%**
Food	**Aperitif**
Drink	**On purchase**

> *Méthode Cap Classique* on a South African sparkling wine label indicates that it has been made in the same way as Champagne, with the second fermentation taking place in the bottle.

Pongrácz Méthode Cap Classique **nv (South Africa)**

Ripe red apples from the Cape on the nose of this wine, with pears, honey and nuts. Though dry, it's in a rich, nutty style, filled with pears, green apples and honey. Lingering finish. Partner with food. *Febvre*

Price	**£15–17/€19–22**
Grape	**Pinot Noir/ Chardonnay**
Alc/vol	**11.5%**
Food	**Aperitif, salmon**
Drink	**On purchase**

£17–20/€22–25

Albet i Noya 21 Brut DO Cava 98 (Spain) ✓ 🌿

An elegant Cava. It has a savoury nose of overbaked sugar biscuits and a palate of apricots and shortbread. Crisp acidity, lasting mousse, good length. *Mary Pawle Wines*

Price	**£17–20/€22–25**
Grape	**Macabeo/Xarel-lo/ Parellada**
Alc/vol	**12%**
Food	**Cakes, desserts**
Drink	**2001–3**

> The combination of a cool climate and mineral-rich volcanic soils in **New Zealand** gives it the potential to produce sparkling wines with elegance and concentration of flavour, especially when the two classic Champagne grapes Pinot Noir and Chardonnay are used.

Huia Marlborough Brut nv (New Zealand) ★

A rich style, with a fine balance between the fizz and the toasty fruit character. Warm golden colour, pronounced and inviting nose of nuts, yeast and lemon tart. Gorgeous palate with apple and lemon flavours, brioche and nuts. Could I ever tire of this? No. *Searsons*

Price	£17–20/€22–25
Grape	Chardonnay/Pinot Noir
Alc/vol	12.5%
Food	Aperitif
Drink	On purchase

£20–25/€25–32

Cloudy Bay Pelorus 96 (New Zealand)

Warm gold colour, developed style, flavours of honey, brioche and some floral notes, delicate. A bottle-aged style showing a mellow balance between bubbles and fruit. This wine will stand up well to food, even lightly smoked dishes. *Findlaters*

Price	£20–25/€25–32
Grape	Pinot Noir/ Chardonnay
Alc/vol	13%
Food	Aperitif, smoked chicken
Drink	2001–2

Rosé

£15–17/€19–22

Mumm Cuvée Napa Rosé nv (USA–California)

Pale pink with red fruit aromas and some yeasty notes. Good mousse. The off-dry palate yields slightly toasted flavours and strawberry fruit. Acidity is crisp and the overall result is a fruity, easy-drinking, fun bubbly. *Barry & Fitzwilliam*

Price	£15–17/€19–22
Grape	Pinot Noir/ Chardonnay
Alc/vol	12.5%
Food	Aperitif, brunch
Drink	On purchase

Gran Caus Rosado Extra Brut DO Cava 98 (Spain) ✓

A big, powerful raspberry nose is followed by a palate chock full of raspberry fruit. There is a touch of brioche too. With its fresh acidity and dry finish, this is an excellent pink Cava. *Approach Trade*

Price	£17–20/€19–22
Grape	Pinot Noir
Alc/vol	12.5%
Food	Cakes, desserts
Drink	2001–2

Sweet

This year's sweet wines come from six different countries and from many different grape varieties. Most sweet wines are white, but there are also a number of interesting reds. Sweet wines may be made in a variety of ways. Some, like Sauternes, are made from late-harvested grapes affected by a fungus known as noble rot (*Botrytis cinerea*). Others, such as Vin Santo, are made from dried grapes, which have concentrated sugar. A very different method is used to produce *vin doux naturel*. Alcohol is added to stop the fermentation process, preserving the sweetness of the wine. Sweet wines are often enjoyed at the end of a meal with cheese or dessert, but may also be served as an aperitif or matched with spicy dishes or rich, savoury foods such as pâté de foie gras. Prices are for a full bottle unless otherwise indicated.

Under £7/Under €9

Achaia Clauss Imperial Mavrodaphne of Patras
AO Mavrodaphne de Patras **nv (Greece) £/€**

The Greek answer to port is made from Mavro-daphne ('black laurel') grapes. It has treacle, Christmas cake and candied fruit aromas. The palate is sweet, with good acidity and prune, toasted nut, coffee bean, honey and lemon flavours. It's unusual and very pleasant. *Taserra*

Price	**Under £7/Under €9**
Grape	**Mavrodaphne**
Alc/vol	**15%**
Food	**Chocolate desserts**
Drink	**On purchase**

Achaia Clauss Muscat de Patras
AO Muscat de Patras **nv (Greece)**

Prune juice, honey and sultana nose. Honey, lime zest and apricots come together on the rich palate. Perfect wine for desserts. *Taserra*

Price	**Under £7/Under €9**
Grape	**Muscat Blanc à Petits Grains**
Alc/vol	**15%**
Food	**Baklava**
Drink	**On purchase**

Miranda The Pioneers Raisined Muscat 00 (Australia)

Tasty stickie with warm, creamy orange tart flavours. Very easy on the palate. Balanced and finishes nicely. *Taserra*

Price	**Under £7/Under €9**
Bottle	**37.5 cl**
Alc/vol	**11.5%**
Food	**Ice cream**
Drink	**2001–4**

£7–9/€9–11.50

Bernkasteler Alte Badstube am Doktorberg Riesling Auslese QmP Auslese **90 (Germany) £/€**

A classic petrol nose. Light, elegant, fresh and appealing palate of lemon sherbet, honey, blood orange and green apples. The balance between fruit and acidity is perfect. Very youthful for a 90 wine. *Karwig Wines*

Price	**£7–9/€9–11.50**
Bottle	**50 cl**
Grape	**Riesling**
Alc/vol	**8%**
Food	**Apple tart**
Drink	**2001–3**

Maculun Dindarello IGT Veneto **00 (Italy)**

The nose is light and grapey, but the flavours are rich, with lots of sweet fruit, rich marmalade and honey. The finish is very pleasant. *Oddbins*

Price	**£7–9/€9–11.50**
Bottle	**37.5 cl**
Grape	**Moscato**
Alc/vol	**13%**
Food	**Desserts**
Drink	**2001–4**

£9–11/€11.50–14

Baumard AC Coteaux du Layon **99 (France)** ✓

With its inviting bright lemon colour, all glint-ing jewels, this is an elegant and classic Loire wine. It has honey and sweet grapefruit aromas. The beautifully balanced palate, sweet but not overpowering, has light honey and marmalade flavours with sweet apricots. *J. S. Woods*

Price	**£9–11/€11.50–14**
Bottle	**37.5 cl**
Grape	**Chenin Blanc**
Alc/vol	**12%**
Food	**Flans, poached pears**
Drink	**2001–5**

> **Muscat de Beaumes-de-Venise** *is made exclusively from Muscat Blanc à Petits Grains. Domaine de Durban, one of the most noted producers, makes a concentrated and aromatic style. Lighter than the Muscats from further south in France, it is drunk as an aperitif or with desserts.*

Dom. de Durban AC Muscat de Beaumes-de-Venise **99 (France–Southern Rhône)**

Very fresh, with floral and grapey aromas. Exemplary of the Mediterranean fruit flavours of Muscat—peaches, pears, lemons, citrus. Deli-cious with fruit salad, fruit flans or indeed as an alternative aperitif. *United Beverages*

Price	**£9–11/€11.50–14**
Bottle	**37.5 cl**
Grape	**Muscat Blanc à Petits Grains**
Alc/vol	**15%**
Food	**Aperitif, desserts**
Drink	**2001–5**

Lamole di Lamole DOC Vin Santo del Chianti Classico **95 (Italy)**

Vin Santo wines are concentrated, nutty and sweet. There is plenty of honeyed and candied fruit and an oxidative orange twist on the fin-ish. *Select Wines*

Price	**£9–11/€11.50–14**
Bottle	**37.5 cl**
Grape	**Trebbiano/Malvasia/ Canaiolo Nero**
Alc/vol	**16%**
Food	**Pecorino, Cantucci**
Drink	**2001–5**

Les Vignerons de Septimanie
AC Muscat de St Jean de Minervois **nv (France–South) £/€**

Good-value dessert style. Aromas and flavours of butterscotch and honey and a clean finish, without cloying sweetness. *Searsons*

Price	**£9–11/€11.50–14**
Grape	**Muscat Blanc à Petits Grains**
Alc/vol	**15%**
Food	**Fruit-based desserts**
Drink	**Within 2 years of purchase**

Miranda Golden Botrytis 93 (Australia) £/€

An unusual blend of 65% Semillon (the grape used for Sauternes) and 35% Riesling. Decadent nose of sultanas, figs and sticky toffee. The broad, rich palate is layered with delectable orange peel, stewed fruit, honey, marmalade and raisins. Finishes with a roast coffee bean flavour. *Taserra*

Price	**£9–11/€11.50–14**
Bottle	**37.5 cl**
Grape	**Semillon/Riesling**
Alc/vol	**10%**
Food	**Rich desserts**
Drink	**2001–4**

Mitchell's Gold AC Graves Supérieures 97 (France–Bordeaux)

A good introduction to an affordable Bordeaux sweet style. Fruity and fresh, lemony and hon-eyed, with a long, satisfying finish. *Mitchells*

Price	**£9–11/€11.50–14**
Grape	**Sauv Blanc/Sémillon**
Alc/vol	**12.5%**
Food	**Desserts, Roquefort**
Drink	**2001–4**

Peter Lehmann The Barossa Botrytis Semillon 97 (Australia)

Very elegant, with aromas of citrus, ripe peaches, pear-like fruit, honey and floral hints. Fresh and quite zingy, it has nice rounded trop-ical fruit on the palate. *United Beverages*

Price	**£9–11/€11.50–14**
Bottle	**37.5 cl**
Grape	**Semillon**
Alc/vol	**13%**
Food	**Blue cheese**
Drink	**2001–5**

*Some of the world's finest dessert wines come from the **Tokaji-Hegyalja** region in the extreme north-eastern part of Hungary. Two grape varieties make up the blend. The Furmint, the dominant grape, has very high acidity and high alcohol levels with a susceptibility to noble rot. The Hárslevelú ('lime leaf') is an aromatic and spicy grape. The number of 'puttonyos' denotes the level of sweetness. The higher the number of 'putts', the sweeter the wine.*

Royal Tokaji Tokaji Aszú 5 Puttonyos 96 (Hungary)

Tangy, slightly oxidised nose of burnt citrus and caramel. Very concentrated orange/citrus peel palate with good balancing acidity. A great introduction to Tokaji, not too sweet nor con-centrated, yet very balanced. *Findlaters*

Price	**£9–11/€11.50–14**
Bottle	**50 cl**
Grape	**Furmint/Hárslevelú**
Alc/vol	**10.5%**
Food	**Christmas pudding**
Drink	**2001–5**

Yalumba Eden Valley Botrytis Semillon 99 (Australia) £/€

The nose is pure grapefruit. On the palate there's a crisp acidity that's very lively in the mouth. This wine will mellow, improving the already yummy flavours of honeyed citrus fruit, apricots and raisins. Elegant and concentrated, with good mouthfeel, this is a sweet wine that's not cloying. *Cassidy*

Price	**£9–11/€11.50–14**
Bottle	**37.5 cl**
Grape	**Semillon**
Alc/vol	**13%**
Food	**Crème brûlée**
Drink	**2001–5**

Prices are for a full bottle unless otherwise indicated.

Monbazillac is a sweet wine appellation within the Bergerac area, close to Bordeaux. It is made from the same grape varieties as the more famous Sauternes—Sémillon, Sauvignon Blanc and Muscadelle. The grapes must be affected by noble rot (Botrytis cinerea), a fungus that appears at harvest time in vineyards with high humidity due to their proximity to water, in this case the River Dordogne.

£11–13/€14–16.50

Ch. Haute-Fonrousse AC Monbazillac 95 (France–South-West) £/€

Pronounced nose of sultanas, roses, apples and honey. Flavours on the palate are fresh and fruity—honey, raisins, stewed fruit, toffee pudding—with balancing acidity to give the wine freshness. *Waterford Wine Vault*

Price	**£11–13/€14–16.50**
Grape	**Sémillon/Sauvignon Blanc/Muscadelle**
Alc/vol	**13.5%**
Food	**Lemon tart**
Drink	**2001–5**

Kracher Beerenauslese Cuvée Prädikatswein 99 (Austria)

Nicely balanced butterscotch/honey fruit and refreshing acidity, with a honeyed, sweet, but not cloying, aftertaste. An opportunity to taste the rich dessert style Austria is famous for. *Searsons*

Price	**£11–13/€14–16.50**
Bottle	**37.5 cl**
Grape	**Varies**
Alc/vol	**13%**
Food	**Apple strudel**
Drink	**2001–4**

£13–15/€16.50–19

d'Arenberg The Noble Riesling 97 (Australia)

There's a little bit of petrol on the nose, along with honey, marmalade, spice, figs and a touch of citrus. An appealing, flavoursome palate combines honey, lemon and marmalade. It's a big wine, but not overpowering, with a lovely citrus finish. *Taserra*

Price	**£13–15/€16.50–19**
Bottle	**37.5 cl**
Grape	**Riesling**
Alc/vol	**12.5%**
Food	**Apple tart**
Drink	**2001–4**

Muscat de Rivesaltes is a vin doux naturel, one of the most important in France in terms of production. It may be made from the Muscat of Alexandria grape as well as the finer Muscat Blanc à Petits Grains. It should be drunk chilled and as young as possible.

Mas Amiel Muscat AC Muscat de Rivesaltes 00 (France–South) £/€

Very fresh on the nose, floral with ripe citrus fruit, tropical fruit and some honeyed hints. A relatively concentrated Muscat with lots of peach and pear supported by balanced acidity and alcohol. *Bubble Brothers*

Price	**£13–15/€16.50–19**
Grape	**Muscat Blanc à Petits Grains/Muscat of Alexandria**
Alc/vol	**15.5%**
Food	**Aperitif, fruit desserts**
Drink	**2001–2**

£15–17/€19–22

Mas Amiel AC Maury 98 (France–South) £/€

Maury is a red *vin doux naturel* from Roussillon, which benefits from being aged in bottle. This one has a slightly spicy, peppery nose with prunes, walnuts and cherry/kirsch hints. Very powerful palate—spicy, strong damson and black fruit, chocolate, good and chewy.
Bubble Brothers

Price	**£15–17/€19–22**
Grape	**Grenache**
Alc/vol	**15.5%**
Food	**Cheese, chocolate desserts**
Drink	**2001–5**

Paul Jaboulet AC Muscat de Beaumes-de-Venise 99 (France–Southern Rhône)

A honeysuckle nose opens into a palate of more honey, stem ginger and apricot. Light and fresh, the wine has flavours of candied peel, honey, raisins and prune juice, all coming in layer after layer. A streak of zesty lemon sherbet lightens the wine and gives it life. *Gilbeys*

Price	**£15–17/€19–22**
Grape	**Muscat Blanc à Petits Grains**
Alc/vol	**15%**
Food	**Mince pies, desserts**
Drink	**2001–2**

£20–25/€25–32

Oremus Tokaji Aszú 5 Puttonyos 94 (Hungary) ✓

Delicate and fragrant aromas of marmalade and butterscotch lead to a palate of honeyed, luscious fruit flavours perfectly balanced by crisp acidity. Extremely long finish on this classic sweet wine. *Searsons*

Price	**£20–25/€25–32**
Bottle	**50 cl**
Grape	**Furmint/Hárslevelú**
Alc/vol	**11%**
Food	**Foie gras, desserts**
Drink	**2001–4**

> *Eiswein translates as 'ice wine'. Frozen grapes are picked late in the year, even sometimes in the New Year, though the wine is still given the previous year's vintage. Once pressed, the water separates, leaving a very sweet concentrate. Eiswein, which should not be drunk young, is capable of many years' ageing in bottle.*

Over £30/Over €40

Kreuznacher Narrenkappe Ehrenfelser QmP Eiswein 99 (Germany)

Fresh, with floral aromas, very ripe citrus, peach and apricot aromas. Apricot fruit on the palate with good balancing acidity—this one will last and last. Though it's drinking very enjoyably now, it will go on maturing and developing complexity for years to come. *The Wine Seller*

Price	**Over £30/Over €40**
Bottle	**37.5 cl**
Grape	**Ehrenfelser**
Alc/vol	**7%**
Food	**Fruit puddings**
Drink	**Can leave in cellar**

Prices are for a full bottle unless otherwise indicated.

Tasters' choices

We once again invited the members of our tasting panel to recommend favourite wines (from firms other than their own, if they work in the wine trade) and these are what they came up with. There was no limit to the price and the tasters were encouraged to select wines other than those they had blind-tasted for the main section of the book. The tasters who responded came up with a remarkable selection for you to explore.

Argentina

Red

David Lonergan
Santa Julia Bonarda 99 £7–9/€9–11.50

If you're looking for an inexpensive, everyday wine with some character, this wine is slightly different from the norm. Every time I try it, I'm impressed by its character and concentration. It's made from a grape variety originally from north-west Italy, also grown widely in Argentina. Dry and medium bodied, it's a silky wine with sweet and sour flavours, tons of ripe black-cherry-like fruit and enough tannins to give it good structure. Pleasant on its own, it's also very good with antipasto, tomato-based dishes or pizza. *Taserra*

Liam Campbell
Alta Vista Malbec 99 £9–11/€11.50–14

Made by Jean-Michel Arcaute, superstar Bordeaux winemaker, from thirty-year-old Malbec vines, a variety often hailed as Argentina's most interesting. The aromas are reserved, with sweet fruits infused with herbs and spices. However, the palate demonstrates a more dramatic style of Malbec. Gripping tannins are drenched with juicy blackberry and cherry fruit over a layer of vanilla and chocolate. The long finish is dry and oaky. Invite it to a summer barbecue. *Mitchells*

Mary O'Callaghan
Simonassi Gran Reserva San Rafael 98 £9–11/€11.50–14

Intense, glossy, deep, dark ruby wine with black cherry hues and a pinkish rim. The well-developed bouquet has a warm, mellow, spicy aromas of ripe black cherries and freshly roasted coffee beans with evolving layers of cigar-box smokiness and spicy earthiness. The palate is very well structured, with excellent acidity and firm, smooth, well-rounded tannins balancing an abundance of very ripe black cherry and freshly roasted coffee bean flavours, with underlying dark truffle and herb flavours. A mocha, creamy, silky-smooth refined texture with huge concentration and intensity of very defined flavours. The long length finishes with a subtle herbal twist of rosemary. This very well-made wine has a strong personality while being refined and of a classic style that is beautifully integrated and subtle. Still very young, it will improve for several more years and will last up to ten. Serve with seriously large roasts on the bone. *Gleeson*

Australia

White

Colm Conaty
Bethany Barossa Riesling 00 £7–9/€9–11.50
Pale yellow in colour with a hint of green. A lovely nose with hints of lime and citrus. The palate is packed with lots of the same citrus fruits and crisp acidity, giving a long, clean finish. Terrific value. *O'Briens*

Barbara Boyle
Leeuwin Estate Siblings £11–13/€14–16.50

Leeuwin Estate makes some great wines—its Art Series 00 Chardonnays and Cabernet Sauvignons are collectors' items. At the more basic level are wines such as Siblings, which is a blend of Sauvignon Blanc and Semillon. Very much in a Bordeaux style, it has harmonious flavours of honey with apple and green fruit. Wonderful texture and concentration, but with refreshing, crisp acidity. *Searsons*

Red

Niamh Boylan
Brown Brothers Nebbiolo 96 £13–15/€16.50–19

Cruising the wine shelves can often just throw up a lot of samey stuff, so Brown Brothers Nebbiolo certainly stood out as something different. This one is a gorgeous wine—a rich, inky purple colour with an appealing nose of alpine straw-berries and Morello cherries. The palate has true Nebbiolo flavours, roasted coffee beans, liquorice and a lick of tar. It was sumptuous, quite aristocratic with non-invasive tan-nins, and proved a welcome warmer with a Sunday roast duck. Like its Italian cousin Barolo, this Nebbiolo would be a terrific partner for game dishes. *Woodford Bourne*

Sergio Furno
Pipers Brook Pellion Pinot Noir 98 £15–17/€19–22

This is a wonderfully smooth and fruity red wine all the way from Tasmania. Clearly inspired by Burgundy, it would give any Burgundian wine at double the price a run for its money. When young, it is a wine that is full of strawberry and crushed raspberry flavours. It is medium bodied with crisp acidity balanced by a wonderful use of oak, which helps to give the wine a very long and creamy finish. If you can bear to wait a few years, this is a wine that ages beautifully, developing wonderful vegetal and earthy notes. Cabbage and stewed lettuce are just two flavours that spring to mind, along with a lovely black pepper spiciness. So drink this now or wait for five years—whichever you decide, you're on a winner. *Irish Distillers*

Ben Mason
Irvine Eden Crest Vineyards Merlot 99 £17–20/€22–25

James Irvine is known as the Merlot magician and the chances are that if you have drunk a stunning Australian Merlot recently, Irvine had a hand in it. This wine is sensational; deep purple in colour, it has massive aromas of sweet plum, earth, spice and oak. On the palate this density translates into a rich and silkily structured wine, with plenty of fine-grained tannins. The finish seems to last forever. It is hard enough to find, so buy it if you can find it. *Wineknows*

Ciaran Newman
Peter Lehmann The Barossa Mentor 93 £20–25/€25–32

Peter Lehmann is a great supporter of the Barossa and produces some stunning wines that are considered a reflection of his showman character. Barossa reds are more subtle than most other big Aussie reds and this one is no exception. It's a dense, garnet-coloured wine with a pronounced liquorice and toffee nose opening up to display a 'pencil shavings' character. The wine is matured in both French and American oak hogshead barrels for two years and bottle matured for a further two years before release. This gives the palate a velvety refined elegance with subtle tannins and a hint of spice. Cellaring for ten years will be rewarded and this is definitely one for those cold winter nights. *United Beverages*

France

White

Julie Martin
Champy AC Mâcon-Uchizy 99 £9–11/€11.50–14

Uchizy is one of the top three of 43 Mâcon villages, where 90 per cent of wines are co-op made. Whispers of the Mediterranean start beyond this point. Pierre Meurgeuy is the winemaker and co-owns Maison Champy with his brother Henri. They also have a wine brokerage, Diva, which deals in top Burgundy houses. The Chardonnay vines for Mâcon-Uchizy are over ten years old. True old-style Burgundy, the wine is mellow and fragrant, exuding rich fruit and buttery tones with a mineral zing and nutty nuances. It's talented enough to partner many dishes, but one of my favourites is fried prawns in butter with chopped parsley and potato purée. *Allied Drinks*

Pat Carroll
Dom. Guillemot-Michel Quintaine AC Mâcon-Clessé 99
£11–13/€14–16.50

This wine is so healthy it has to be good for you. There's no added sugar, acidity or sulphur dioxide and it's unfined and unfiltered. Pierrette and Marc Guillemot-Michel follow biodynamic methods, carrying out vineyard work according to the phases of the moon and stars. Different phases are thought to favour the growth of leaves, roots, flowers or fruit. No pesticides are used and the soil is manured to make it as healthy as possible. It takes ten years of avoiding chemicals before a vineyard can be declared biodynamic. The grapes for this wine were left to ripen three to four weeks longer than those in neighbouring vineyards, making them ultra-ripe. No oak is used. And do these methods work? Judging by this wine, they certainly do. On the nose there are pure, rich melon and pineapple aromas. The palate has concentrated ripe fruit—more pineapples, plus some grapefruit. There's a smoky background, lovely textured mouthfeel, lots of flavour and a lingering finish. This is a wine of quality and character—and it's very good value. *Burgundy Direct*

Mary O'Callaghan
Sipp Mack Rosacker Grand Cru AC Alsace Riesling **98**
£13–15/€16.50–19
This wine is an intensely bright, deep lemon colour, with lime hues and excellent viscosity. The bouquet is very distinguished and complex— exquisitely floral, with intriguing mineral nuances expressive of *terroir*. The wine is dry, with crisp, refreshing and vigorous acidity, balancing vibrant and intense green apple and white peach fruit flavours. Underneath there are characteristic peppery notes that have begun to round out as it develops to reveal the more mineral flavours of the vineyard's calcareous/marl soils. Finely structured, the elegant, smooth and full texture reflects much style and finesse that remain through the long, clean finish. It will age particularly well and will develop even more complex aromas and powerful body, together with that famous 'old Riesling' taste. Enjoy it with fish and shellfish in cream or wine sauces. *Mitchells*

Ciaran Newman
Domaine de Nalys AC Châteauneuf-du-Pape **96** **£15–17/€19–22**
On a trip to the Rhône in 98 I found myself intrigued with superlative whites, including those of Châteauneuf-du-Pape. Domaine de Nalys is a devotee of traditional Rhône winemaking and uses all thirteen permitted varieties in their red Châteauneuf-du-Pape. The white is made from up to six varieties, which are vinified separately and then blended to create a wine of great character. The developed nose of the 96 reminds me of *miel aux noisettes* (honey with nuts), with hints of baked bananas and melon wedges, all well integrated with wood. On the palate it is full flavoured with an oily texture and hints of tropical fruits and lychees, ending with a long finish. A wine to have with Christmas dinner. *TDL*

Niamh Boylan
Blanc de Lynch-Bages AC Bordeaux **96** Over £30/Over €40
How do you astound and excite the palates of a group of wine-mad friends? Château Lynch-Bages is Ireland's best-known Bordeaux red wine, loved and enjoyed by many. Its current price is a bit beyond us ordinary mortals, but wait! How about a bottle of Lynch-Bages white? With the first sniff we were hooked. But first of all the colour—golden daffodil with a rich sheen. The bouquet was powerfully perfumed with ripe quince and mirabelle fruit and the smooth, concentrated palate was layered with flavour. This was a beautifully balanced wine with a luscious lemon peel acidity. I suspect it has quite a bit of Sémillon—it's a big wine but not overpowering. We drank it with gravlax and warm dill potatoes. Delicious. *Superquinn*

Red

Sarah Grubb
L'Ermitage Vignes des Deux Soleils VdP d'Oc 99
£9–11/€11.50–14

A delicious wine representative of the ever-increasing quality available at all price levels from the South of France. It's medium/full bodied with blackberries, damsons, spice and currants in smooth, rich layers supported by lively yet not sharp acidity. L'Ermitage is a blend of three grape varieties—two classic Bordeaux varieties, Cabernet Sauvignon and Merlot, and one Rhône star, Syrah. Matured for six months in French barriques, it  retains a firm regional identity while drawing on the characteristics of Bordeaux's St Émilion and the Rhône's Gigondas in terms of structure and food-oriented style. A delicious alternative to Bordeaux or Rioja, it should be served with classic roast lamb or with a hearty bean casserole or a north African tagine of lamb, prunes and roast almonds. *Findlaters*

Colm Conaty
Clos de Cuminaille AC St Joseph 99 £15–17/€19–22

On the nose aromas of rich, dark fruit with a hint of spice. A complex palate with layers of spice, fruit and chocolate. Firm tannins give great structure to this wine, which is still quite young and will benefit from decanting. *Terroirs*

David Lonergan
Dom. Besancenot-Mathouillet AC Beaune 1er Cru Les Bressandes 91 £25–30/€32–40

Trying this silky, complex, voluptuous wine reminds me how excellent good Burgundy is, and what it is all about. It is made from Pinot Noir, and when done properly in Burgundy no Pinot Noir from anywhere else can touch it. It has a mature and developed nose of spices and earthy hints with complex, smoky aromas of black cherry and raspberry fruits. On the palate it is medium bodied, with elegant, spicy and smoky cherry-like fruits, mature tannins and a good backbone of acidity, giving lovely balance and structure. A classic food wine and an ideal accompaniment to game dishes. This Burgundy is ready to drink now. *Burgundy Direct*

Anne Mullin
Ch. Yon-Figeac AC St Émilion Grand Cru Classé 96 £25–30/€32–40

This is one of the truly classic, elegant wines of St Émilion, made with an unusually high proportion of Cabernet Sauvignon. The wine is matured in 100 per cent new oak for 18 to 20 months. There are wonderful aromas of spicy, warm bramble fruits, Christmas cake and a hint of old cigar box aromas. On the palate it is intensely rich with great structure. Laden with ripe blackcurrant fruits and with a lovely warm vanilla mouthfeel, it is rich, ripe and robust and beautifully balanced. A superb wine, drinking beautifully now, soft, elegant and velvety, yet capable of ageing for years to come. *Febvre*

Ciaran Newman
Ch. Phélan-Ségur AC St Estèphe 95 Over £30/Over €40

A favourite with Irish consumers, given that the founder was Bernard Phelan, one of the original Wine Geese, who left his native Clonmel to seek his fortune in France. St Estèphe is the most northerly of the Médoc's famous four appellations and it has an abundance of high-quality Cru Bourgeois wines. The 95 is one of the better vintages of the 90s and this shows. Beautiful ruby colour, still showing signs of youth. The nose yields abundant fruit reminiscent of rich Christmas cake and dark chocolate with mellow cigar-box nuances underneath. The fruit resurges on the palate in the classic Bordeaux form of ripe blackberries with beautifully integrated wood flavourings and sufficient tannins to reward those who can lay down this wine for a few more years to come. *Grants*

Germany

White

Gerry Gunnigan

Weingut Ludwig Thannisch Brauenberger Juffer Riesling Trocken QmP Auslese **96**

£11–13/€14–16.50

This is without doubt one of the best German wines I have ever tasted. It is unusual in that it is a dry Auslese from the Mosel; most Ausleses here tend to be light and quite sweet. This is more akin to a Pfalz Riesling or an Alsace Grand Cru. It has delicious mineral fruit, terrific structure and a finish that keeps going on. Also it's a 96 and as fresh as a daisy. This is a wine I would happily keep for a few years. *Octavius Fine Wines*

Italy

White

Liam Campbell

San Vincenzo IGT Veneto **99** **£9–11/€11.50–14**

The aromas of the 99 San Vincenzo are highly aromatic and perfumed with freshly ground almonds and notes of flint. The taste is dry but without austerity. This is a full-bodied wine with an ample weight of almond nuttiness and lemony zestiness throughout the palate. The flavours finish long with a marzipan flourish. The San Vincenzo, like the best of friends, is rich, warm and generous. Serve cold rather than chilled with baked chicken and broccoli in a cream sauce thickened with ground almonds and presented on a square pillow of basmati rice. *James Nicholson*

Red

Willie Dardis

Barbaglio IGT Rosso del Salento **96** **£7–9/€9–11.50**

This wine comes from the winery of Santa Barbra in the town of San Petro Vernatico, which provides perfect grow- ing conditions for the Negroamaro and Primitivo grapes used in this fine wine. The wine itself is a big, sturdy blockbuster, full of the warmth of the south. Bitter cherries, figs, plums and smoky leather tantalise the nose, while the palate is enveloped by a big mouthful of damsons, figs, raisins and a jammy spiciness aided by a soothing velvety, chocolate edge.

All this with a long, long finish make it a perfect food wine—hearty casseroles and spicy, peppery dishes would complement it beautifully. *Findlaters*

Barry Walsh
Candido DOC Salice Salentino Riserva **97** £7–9/€9–11.50

Medium/full bodied red wine, lots of ripe fruit and a lovely rustic, hot sunny edge. From the heel of Italy, this wine brings back memories of Mediterranean warmth and blue seas. Lovely with pasta and spaghetti dishes; it's also the wine I look out for in a Greek restaurant. *Findlaters*

Des Drumm
Villa Dorato DOC Eloro Pachino **97** £11–13/€14–16.50

I am a late convert to Sicily, but this wine would win anyone over instantly. Made from 100 per cent Nero d'Avola, it comes from Pachino, a sub-zone of DOC Eloro. It's a vibrant dark ruby with purple tinges. The nose lifts with a whoosh of over-ripe bramble fruit and the palate hits you with a smack—sweet fruit, rich and sunny with dark flavours of plums and prunes with that over-ripe feel—almost port-like. All this is wrapped in soft tannins and good acids. A great value-for-money wine for easy drinking, but with a touch of quality too. One to watch in the future. *Findlaters*

Gerry Gunnigan
Lamole di Lamole DOCG Chianti Classico **98** £13–15/€16.50–19

Chianti doesn't come much more Classico than this. Lamole is a full-bodied style with a lot of character. It has delicious brooding black fruit, with excellent structure and a long finish. For an extra-special treat, try Lamole's single-vineyard Chianti Classico Vigneto di Campolunga. *Select Wines*

Liam Campbell
Pio Cesare Fides DOC Barbera d'Alba **98** £20–25/€25–32

This single-vineyard wine epitomises the quest for quality over the pleasures of profit. Fides is a beautifully smooth wine—rich, seductive and round. The ripe red and black berry fruits owe their deep concentration to the old vines in the vineyard. The wine spent two years in cask, 90 per cent in new French oak and the remainder in Yugoslavian oak. This rare wine is produced in minute quantities, 500 cases from the 1.5 hectares (just over 4 acres). Partner it with rich red meats or a strong, hard Italian cheese. *Cassidy*

Sergio Furno
Sorano DOCG Barolo **97** £20–25/€25–32

Ascheri is quite a small producer in the village of Morra, Piedmont, producing both new- and old-style Barolos. The new-style wine is more approachable when young and is aged in new French oak barriques, which impart a vanilla flavouring. In less expert hands than Ascheri's this can overpower the delicate flavours of the Nebbiolo grape. This wine, however, is an old-style Barolo and one that shows off the true potential of Nebbiolo. Like Pinot Noir, this is a delicate grape that is hard to grow and has high acidity with subtle flavours. And, like Pinot Noir, it responds well to old oak treatment, in Nebbiolo's case Slovenian. As for the wine itself, it has a very light appearance (due to Nebbiolo's thin skin) and on the nose it is full of strawberries, raspberries, cherries, violets, roses and oak. These characteristics follow through to the palate, where they are accompanied by high acidity and lots of tannins. As 97 was considered one of the best vintages of the last century, this is a wine with the potential to age for 15–20 years and, if the conditions are right, even longer. With age, the fruity tones to this wine will fade and the floral tones will become more prominent and the oak influence will change into a slightly bitter spiciness, giving the 'roses and tar' for which Barolos are famous. *Findlaters*

Des Drumm
Ornellaia VdT **97** Over £30/Over €40

The most complete wine I have tasted this year, this is in the Supertuscan mould, using Cabernet Sauvignon and Merlot with a touch of Cabernet Franc and aged in barriques—half new, half one year old. It is made in Bolgheri, near where Sassicaia is made. Even looking at it you can detect quality—dark, intense, brooding, textured. Heady aromas develop quickly; for such a young wine it is awash with dark fruit aromas and spices. It has voluptuous fruit of rich, ripe blackcurrant and plum and a spice and vanilla finish. Unbelievably forward, yet it has enormous depth and power. This is close to perfection. The price (over £80) reflects this. *Woodford Bourne*

Des Drumm
Tignanello IGT Toscano **97** Over £30/Over €40

The wine that started a revolution still shows that it is at the head of the van. Piero Antinori and Giacomo Tachis add Cabernet Sauvignon to their Sangiovese-based wine and use barriques to smooth it down. It's a wine of real class. I was lucky enough to taste the 95, 96 and 97 vintages this year. Lucky, because it has always been one of my real favourites, because I was not paying (and Tignanello does not come cheap—or easily) and because all three were superb. 95 was very good indeed, 96 superb, but the 97 was stupendous. Everything about it says class—the soft cedary smell, the unctuous blackcurrant and dark cherry pie fruit and the long, creamy finish. Good for many years to come. *Grants*

Portugal

Red

Julie Martin
Atlantic Vines (CURB) VR Beiras Baga **98**
Under £7/Under €9

The Baga grape, or Tinta Bairrada as it's known locally, thrives on the Jurassic-clay-based soils in the centre and south of the Bairrada region. It makes dry rosé in the Ribatejo, but my favourite red is this version, made by Peter Bright, a native of Australia who came to settle in Portugal about eighteen years ago. He started a super-modern adega (winery) at João Pires in Pinhal Navo 30 km west of Lisbon at Setúbal. The grapes are fermented without the stalks to yield a softer, easier-drinking style. This wine is hugely rustic with an earthy character. I find it distinct and very affordable. Partner with grilled fresh sardines. *Superquinn*

Barbara Boyle
Luis Pato Vinha Barossa Vinha Velha DOC Barraida 96
£20–25/€25–32

Luis Pato's wines take time to mature and the 96 is drinking perfectly now, but is still very youthful and lively. The colour is rich, red velvet Burgundian. The aromas are of plums and chocolate with a cool palate of mellow coffee and dates with leathery, savoury and vegetal flavours and smooth, ripe tannins. Luis Pato describes it as being in a Burgundian style, but while there are violets and perfume, this is unmistakably wonderful Portuguese wine. His initial efforts with the Baga grape were unoaked, but he has since mastered the use of oak using old barrels initially with a few months in new oak before release (very unusual). *Karwigs Wines*

South Africa

White

Willie Dardis
De Wetshof Bon Vallon Chardonnay 00 £7–9/€9–11.50

Danie de Wet, winemaker and owner of the De Wetshof estate in Robertson, has won many awards worldwide for his Chardonnays. My favourite is the Bon Vallon Chardonnay. This wine has gorgeous peach blossom aromas and hints of walnut and melon. A great juicy mouthful, almost sweet with a balancing acid tweak, surprisingly rich and complex for an unwooded wine. It has a warm and seductive finish and is excellent with fish or pasta. *Findlaters*

Red

Kate Barrett
Graceland Cabernet Sauvignon 99 £11–13/€14–16.50

From a small family-run property in the heart of Stellenbosch comes this new-style South African Cabernet Sauvignon. Despite the name, the wine in the bottle is delicious. A wonderfully ripe nose full of violets with hints of spice leads to a velvety, rich palate with well-balanced tannin and heaps of dark berried fruit laced with cocoa. This is a real winter warmer that would be great with a venison stew or a good hearty lamb casserole. *James Nicholson*

Pat Carroll
Middelvlei Shiraz 96 £11–13/€14–16.50

South Africa makes excellent Shiraz. This one is made by the Momberg family, who aim for a style that falls between the Old World and the New World, putting some backbone behind the ripe fruit. The spicy nose offers black fruits, coffee beans and cloves and the palate is full of damsons, blackberries, black pepper, cloves and spices. Tannins are soft and the medium finish is spicy and warm. *Papillon*

Spain

Red

Colm Conaty

Beronia DOC Rioja Gran Reserva **87** £15–17/€19–22

On the nose this wine has wonderful aromas of leather, spice and cedar. The palate is dry, with lovely notes of vanilla and strawberry fruits. It's all held together with firm but well-rounded tannins and balanced by crisp acidity, giving a long, clean, elegant finish. *Barry & Fitzwilliam*

Gerry Gunnigan

Salguero VdM de Castillo y Leon **98** £15–17/€19–22

This wine comes from a producer in the Ribera del Duero region. Salguero is 100 per cent Cabernet Sauvignon and is medium bodied in style. It has good ripe cassis fruit and is well balanced. To taste it at its best, it needs some food. *J. S. Woods*

USA–California

White

Anne Mullin

Beringer Napa Valley Appellation Collection Fumé Blanc 99 £11–13/€14–16.50

Sauvignon Blanc has always been one of my favourite white grapes. When grown in a warmer climate, (where it is often referred to as Fumé Blanc), it takes on numerous characteristics not found when grown in a cooler climate. This wine is very aromatic on the nose with lovely rich, spicy tropical fruit aromas and a subtle hint of new oak. On the palate it is dry, with an excellent weight of intensely rich tropical fruits, pineapples, mangoes and apricots all well integrated, some citrus fruit flavours and a hint of ginger and new oak. It is a delicious wine, gloriously fresh and crisp with great length and a long finish. *Allied Drinks*

Red

John Quinn

Ravenswood Vintners Blend Zinfandel 98 £13–15/€16.50–19

Originating as I do from the land of baseball, hot dogs and Zinfandel, I'd be remiss if I didn't mention the US's most popular red grape. It's a versatile grape, capable of making anything from 'blush'-style medium-dry wines to port-style fortified wines. Ravenswood, whose slogan is 'No Wimpy Wines', makes this one in the middle-of-the-road style. The grapes are sourced from over fifty different vineyards throughout California so that they produce a  consistent style year to year with the emphasis on freshness. This wine has a lovely nose and palate of ripe blackcurrants and other summer fruits, with a hint of pepper and spice. It would go well with tomato-sauce-based dishes such as pasta Bolognese, spicy sausages or pizza. *Woodford Bourne*

Anne Mullin

De Loach Vineyards Russian River Valley Pinot Noir 99
£20–25/€25–32

This wine has lots of upfront, ripe, perfumed aromas of spicy, soft strawberry fruits with a hint of vanilla. On the palate it is dry, with an excellent weight of juicy summer berries—raspberries, strawberries and redcurrants, all well integrated with new oak. This is a delicious wine, well balanced, drinking beautifully, elegant and with great finesse. It has a long finish and great length. An excellent example of a Pinot Noir grown outside Burgundy. *TDL*

Champagne

Barbara Boyle

Pol Roger Cuvée Winston Churchill AC Champagne 90
Over £30/Over €40

This is a prestige Champagne originally made by the Pol Roger family to honour their great friend Winston Churchill. When it was first made, it was available only to members of Churchill's family and the British royal family. The style is quite robust and full bodied, as Churchill liked his Champagnes, and the blend is a closely guarded secret, although it is thought to be heavily based on Pinot Noir. When I tried this in April 2001, it was a rich golden colour, with aromas of oranges, figs and a light smattering of nuts. The palate is intense and memorable, with spice, nuts, super fruitiness and a wonderful length of flavour. It was youthful and will be drinking well and developing further over the next decade. Expect to pay between £80 and £85. *Barry & Fitzwilliam*

Sergio Furno

Bollinger AC Champagne nv Over £30/Over €40

A full, rich wine. The nose is intriguing and so full of varying scents that it is hard to pinpoint any precisely. However, after having forced myself to taste this wonderful wine repeatedly, this is what I came up with: lemon, green apples, cream, digestive biscuits and a very delicious hint of underripe raspberry (due to the fact that this Champagne is made in the main from the black grape Pinot Noir). The palate is very similar to the nose. The sharpness of the lemon, green apple and underripe raspberries accompanied by a slight greenness reminiscent of grass. All this is deliciously balanced by the biscuity/yeasty flavours derived from the second fermentation and a wonderful use of oak that helps give this wine a lovely, smooth, seductive and lingering finish. Definitely one of the best Champagnes available on the market and luckily for you it can be found at most off-licences. *Woodford Bourne*

Rosé

Niamh Boylan

Prestige Rosé Brut Taittinger AC Champagne nv
Over £30/Over €40

Rosé Champagne comes in many shades, but for my money the vibrant creamy raspberry of Taittinger Rosé does the business. Wonderful aromas of fresh redcurrants and strawberries jump from the glass. This is a highly aromatic style of Champagne with an elegant palateful of flavours—fresh and full at the same time with a fine persistent mousse, always a sign of real class. The perfect aperitif or celebratory drink, it was absolutely delicious with some sea trout which was cooked very simply. Salmon or some light sushi dishes would also work very well. *Febvre*

David Lonergan
Dom Ruinart Rosé AC Champagne **86** Over £30/Over €40
From the oldest Champagne house, founded in 1729, comes this most complex and classic wine. It is made mainly from Chardonnay (around 80 per cent, which is an unusually high percentage for a rosé), to which a small proportion of Pinot Noir is added. All the grapes are sourced from Grand Cru vineyards. The wine is pale orange-yellow with a slightly copperish tint and has profuse, long-lasting bubbles. The complex nose has oily minerals with grapefruit and strawberries. On the palate it is oily and toasty, with tropical and pineapple fruit, butterscotch and burnt citrus. Classy stuff, it costs £85. This is food Champagne and would be a real treat with caramel-ised poached citrus and red fruits for dessert, or maybe a first course of lobster, richly sauced. *Taserra*

Sparkling

Willie Dardis
Pongrácz Méthode Cap Classique **nv** £15–17/€19–22
Pongrácz Cap Classique—what a refreshing alternative to Champagne! Made by the leading house of South Africa's sparkling wine sector, this wine has won many awards in its homeland, including double gold at the prestigious 1998 Veritas awards. Made using the traditional Champagne method, the grapes used are 60 per cent Pinot Noir and 40 per cent Chardonnay. The characteristics are a complex nose, with a lovely scent of baked apples and warm toast. It has a mature palate of full fruit, toast and mushrooms. Dry and full bodied, this wine is crisp, clean and generous. Its elegance guarantees a smooth, rewarding finish. A value-for-money spar-kler that will go with light dishes and seafood. *Febvre*

Sarah Grubb
Cloudy Bay Pelorus nv £20–25/€25–32
Cloudy Bay's Pelorus non-vintage rates as my favourite New World sparkler. Indeed I would go as far as to say that it can beat the socks off many a non-vintage bottle of Champagne retailing at up to £10 more a bottle. First produced in 95, Pelorus is a multi-vintage blend based on Chardonnay, produced by the same traditional method as Champagne and aged for two years on the lees. Similar to a *blanc de blancs* in style, the wine is fresh, clean and elegant, serving as an ideal summer bubbly. Citrus and apple fruit predominate in a lively yet balanced palate, supported by persistent small bubbles and delicious underlying creamy, structured yeastiness. Ideal on its own or as an accompaniment to a simple plate of fresh oysters or shellfish. *Findlaters*

Sweet

John Quinn
Bonny Doon Muscat Vin de Glacière 99 £13–15/€16.50–19 (37.5 cl)

The normal way to make this style of wine, known as Eiswein, is to allow the grapes to remain on the vine long after the harvest—sometimes into the New Year in Germany and Austria. When the temperature drops to –8°C, the frozen grapes are gathered, pressed and fermented. As a result, the wine is highly concentrated and sweet. That's the 'normal' way. However, Bonny Doon's winemaker, Randall Grahm, is anything but normal. Rather than waiting for the advent of another Ice Age in California, he harvests the grapes (Muscat and Malvasia Bianca) and puts them into a freezer. Hence the name, which means 'Wine of the Icebox'! The result is a lovely dessert wine with a nose and palate of pineapples and orange marmalade and a very long, luscious finish. It's a perfect match for fruit-based desserts such as tarts, puddings or (especially) apple pie. *James Nicholson*

Mary O'Callaghan
Ch. de Fesles AC Bonnezeaux 97 Over £30/Over €40 (50 cl)

In last year's book I featured Ch. de Fesles Bonnezeaux 97 as my all-time favourite dessert wine. This still holds true. I have since tasted a rare and very special Coteaux du Layon 43. It could not be called 'Bonnezeaux', as the appellation did not exist then. It was a stunning wine—still fresh and vibrant with layers of honeyed apricot, white peach, honeysuckle and beeswax and an underlying development of nuttiness. It was refined and elegant and had a cool, silky-smooth texture that was almost ethereal. This was a brilliant example of the ageing potential of well-made Chenin Blanc. These wines are extraordinarily good value and can be a very worthwhile investment. Buy as much as you can and watch or, better still, taste the transformation through the years. However, the 43 is not available at any price! *Febvre*

Vin de liqueur

Julie Martin
Pierre Ferrand AC Pineau des Charentes nv
£20–25/€25–32 (Selection), £25–30/€32–40 (Reserve)

For this wine, Ugni Blanc grapes from the Grande Champagne region are pressed and made into grape spirit (Cognac) then mixed with three parts fresh grape must. The Selection is aged in oak casks for 5 years and the Reserve is aged for 15 years in Cognac casks. The Reserve is structured and gold in colour. It has a light and delicate nose full of raisin-like fruit with a rich, dulcet, complex flavour with hints of flowers, oranges and vanilla. Serve chilled in small sherry glasses as an aperitif. It also goes very well in and with Christmas cake and plum pudding. *McCabes*

Where to buy the recommended wines

Wine is imported into Ireland by over a hundred separate importers, ranging from multi-million pound businesses to one-person operations. For most of these importers wine sold through restaurants (the 'on-trade') is as important as that sold retail (the 'off-trade')—most wine is, after all, designed to be consumed with food. As a result, some wines are deliberately given a low retail profile because they are popular in restaurants, and restaurant proprietors prefer that their customers shouldn't find it too easy to calculate the mark-up.

The picture is further complicated by the fact that for some wines—the so-called 'trophy' or 'allocation' wines—the producers may make only a few dozen cases of that vintage available to the importers, which naturally go to favoured outlets. These are just the wines that receive rave reviews from wine writers. Then again, popular wines styles such as Rioja, Chianti, Australian Chardonnay and Bordeaux are much more widely distributed than less well-known styles.

Perhaps three-quarters of the wine sold in Ireland comes through the top five importers. Much of this is branded wine such as Pedrotti, Blossom Hill and Jacob's Creek. As well as the high-volume brands, all the larger importers also carry a range of fine wines, which is less widely available. So a single importer might have some wines that are available in most convenience stores, and others that can be bought only from a handful of specialist shops. The commonly used term 'widely available' is quite inadequate to describe this situation.

A group of twenty middle-sized importers accounts for a further 20 per cent of the market, with the small operators the remaining 5 per cent. Naturally the coverage of the country varies widely from organisation to organisation. As a result some of the wines listed in this book are readily available across the country, others at a few select outlets, others again in only one outlet, or solely by direct mail.

The key to buying wine in Ireland, however, in every type of outlet is a manager/proprietor who is sufficiently interested in wine to respond to and stimulate local demand. Luckily, there are lots of them around.

Importers sell into seven broad categories of retailer, each with different characteristics. We have confined the use of the term 'widely available' to wines that are stocked in at least five of the seven categories listed.

1. *Multiple stores: Dunnes, Roches Stores (which is owned by Musgraves), Superquinn, Tesco:* The multiples usually import their own wine as well as selling wine from other importers. Their own wines are available only through their branches. Because of their enormous buying power, they can provide great value for money, but. because they need the volume, they tend not to have the most exclusive wines, though the larger Dunnes and Tescos have an impressive range.

2. *SuperValu/Centra* (owned by Musgraves) Particular managers can make an enormous difference to the range carried. The combination of this chain and Roches make Musgraves a powerful influence in the market.

3. *Symbol groups: e.g. Londis, Mace, Spar.* These shops generally stock a smallish range of basic wine. Once again, a particular manager with an interest in wine can make a substantial difference.

4. *Pub–off-licence groups: Cheers and Next Door* Until these two chains got going, pub off-licences had a dismal reputation. The two chains are run by the Licensed Vintners' Association (Dublin) and the Vintners' Federation (rest of the country) respectively and are changing the image dramatically with the aid of wine consultant Mary O'Callaghan. Both chains are growing rapidly—at the time of going to press Cheers had twenty-three stores and Next Door thirty.

5. *NOffLA members* There are over three hundred members of the National Off-licence Association who have the triple licence (beer, wine and spirits). Members are encouraged to display the NOffLA logo on the door. NOffLA run an annual awards scheme in conjunction with Gilbeys to encourage exoertise and to raise standards. From the winelover's point of view the best NOffLA stores have several hundred wines in stock, as well as interesting beers and spirits, and will have time and interest to help you personally. They will often be able to order specific wines from the importer.

6. *Off-licence groups* NOffLA also includes a number of chains of off-licences. Some trade observers believe that this is the way the Irish trade will go, following the British example. Irish examples of this growing sector include O'Donovans (Cork), Galvins (Cork), Fine Wines of Limerick, Molloys (Dublin), O'Briens (Dublin), and of course Oddbins, the one British chain in the south.

7. *Specialists* A few stores, like the wine merchants of old, sell nothing but wine and wine accessories. Typical examples are Mitchells, Searsons and Berry Brothers & Rudd. They tend also to import and sell their own wines elsewhere, as well as selling wine imported by others.

Importers' contact details

Allied Drinks
- JFK Road, JFK Industrial Estate, Dublin 12. Tel (01) 450 9777, Fax (01) 450 9699, e-mail anne@allieddrinks.ie.
- Windsor Hill House, Glounthaune, Co. Cork. Tel (021) 435 3438, Fax (021) 435 4362, e-mail info@allieddrinks.ie.

Wines are widely available. In case of difficulty in finding a particular wine, e-mail anne@allieddrinks.ie.

Approach Trade Ireland
- South Quay, Carrick-on-Suir, Co. Tipperary. Tel (051) 640 164, Fax (051) 641 580.

Wines are available direct and in Dublin from Mitchell & Son, On the Grapevine (Dalkey), O'Briens off-licences, Michael's Wines (Mount Merrion), Layden Fine Wines (Middle Abbey Street); in Wicklow from the Wicklow Wine Co. Wicklow and Murtagah's (Enniskerry); in Co. Clare from Egan's (Liscannor) and Miles Creek (Kilkee); in Cork from Karwig Wines; in Galway from McCambridge's.

Henry J. Archer & Sons
- White Walls, Ballymoney, Gorey, Co. Wexford. Tel (055) 25176, Fax (055) 25842, e-mail paul.dubsky@oceanfree.net.

Wines are available in Dublin from Redmond's (Ranelagh) and Terroirs (Donnybrook); in Co. Wexford from Cullen's (Ballymoney) and Next Door at Kavanagh's (Enniscorthy).

Bacchus Wine & Spirit Merchants
- T28 Rowan Avenue, Stillorgan Industrial Park, Stillorgan, Co. Dublin. Tel (01) 294 1466, Fax (01) 295 7375
- Bacchus Munster, Gurrane, Upton, Innishannon, Co. Cork. Tel (021) 487 4164, Fax (021) 487 4307, e-mail bacchuswines@eircom.net.

Wines are available from Roches Stores, SuperValu-Centra, Cheers, Molloy's and a few individual off-licences.

Barry & Fitzwilliam
- Ballycurreen Industrial Estate, Airport Road, Cork. Tel (021) 432 0900, Fax (021) 432 0910.
- 50 Dartmouth Square, Dublin 6. Tel (01) 667 1755/660 6984, Fax (01) 660 0479, e-mail sinead@barryfit.iol.ie.

Some ranges, such as Michel Lynch, Guigal, McGuigan, Antu Mapu, Chapel Hill, Vendange and Yaldara are widely available. Specialist stores such as O'Donovans (Cork), Redmonds (Ranelagh), DeVine Wine (Castleknock) and On the Grapevine (Dalkey) stock most of the list.

Bubble Brothers
- 43 Upper John Street, Cork. Tel/Fax (021) 455 2252.
- 116A Lower Georges Street, Dun Laoghaire, Co. Dublin. Tel (01) 230 4117, e-mail info@bubblebrothers.com, web site www.bubblebrothers.com.

Wines are available direct and from off-licences and wine merchants.

Cassidy Wines

- 1B Birch Avenue, Stillorgan Industrial Estate, Stillorgan, Co. Dublin.
Tel (01) 295 4157/4632, Fax (01) 295 4477.

Wines are widely available.

Le Caveau

- Market Yard, Kilkenny. Tel (056) 52166, Fax (056) 52101,
e-mail lecaveau@eircom.net, web site www.lecaveau.ie.

Wines are available direct.

Peter A. Dalton Food & Wine

- Loch Grein, Ballybetagh, Kilternan, Co. Dublin. Tel/Fax (01) 295 4945,
e-mail padwines@indigo.ie, web site www.daltonwines.com.

*Wines are available in some SuperValu-Centra stores, some symbols, some
Cheers (Co. Dublin, Roscommon), Deveneys (Dublin), DeVine Wine
(Castleknock), Ashford Food & Wine (Wicklow), Cana (Mullingar) and
Cuisine de Vendange (Naas).*

Edward Dillon & Company

- 25 Mountjoy Square East, Dublin 1. Tel (01) 819 3300,
Fax (01) 855 5852.

Most wines are widely available but some only from specialist outlets.

Dunnes Stores

- Head Office, 67 Upper Stephen Street, Dublin 8. Tel (01) 475 1111,
Fax (01) 475 1441, web site www.dunnes-stores.com.

Wines are available only from branches of Dunnes Stores.

Febvre & Co.

- 15–17 Maple Avenue, Stillorgan Industrial Park, Stillorgan, Co. Dublin.
Tel (01) 295 9030, Fax (01) 295 9036.

Most wines are widely available but some only from specialist outlets.

Fields Wine Merchants

- 1B Birch Avenue, Stillorgan Industrial Park, Stillorgan, Co. Dublin.
Tel (01) 295 4422, Fax (01) 295 4452.

*Fields is the wholesale branch of Berry Brothers & Rudd; Berry Brothers'
own-label wines are available only through the shop, while others are available
through NOffLA specialists.*

Findlater Wine Merchants

- Magna Drive, Citywest Business Campus, Dublin 24. Tel (01) 452 9112/
452 9116, Fax (01) 452 9120, e-mail sales@findlaters.com, web site
www.findlaters.com.

*Most of the wines are widely available through Superquinn, Pettitts, SuperValu-
Centra, Cheers, Next Door, O'Donovans (Cork), Molloy's and the top
individual independents and specialists. The Ironstone range may be harder
to find.*

Gilbeys of Ireland

- Nangor House, Nangor Road, Western Estate, Dublin 12.
Tel (01) 419 4040, Fax (01) 419 4041, e-mail gilbeys.info@udv.com.

*Some wines are widely available, others only through NOffLA outlets,
independent specialists, Superquinn and other wine-focused supermarket
off-licences.*

M. & J. Gleeson & Co.
- 15 Cherry Orchard Estate, Ballyfermot, Dublin 10. Tel (01) 626 9787, Fax (01) 626 0652.
- Greenlawn, Borrisoleigh, Co. Tipperary. Tel (0504) 51113, Fax (0504) 51480.

  Most of the wines are available through independents and specialists and through wine-oriented symbols and SuperValu-Centras.

Grants of Ireland
- Kilcarberry Industrial Park, Nangor Road, Clondalkin, Dublin 22. Tel (01) 630 4156/630 4157/630 4121, Fax (01) 630 4124.
- Annerville, Clonmel, Co. Tipperary. Tel (052) 72174/72175/72135, Fax (052) 72255, e-mail grants@cantrell.ie, web site grantsofireland.ie.

  Wines are all distributed through the multiples; they are also available from O'Briens off-licences and specialists such as McCabes (Blackrock) and Redmonds (Ranelagh).

Greenhills Wines & Spirits
- Aisling House, Shanowen Road, Santry, Dublin 9. Tel (01) 842 2188, Fax (01) 842 2455.

  Wines are widely available. Try Mace, Spar and Superquinn.

IberExpo
- Kinsale Road, Cork. Tel (021) 496 1031, Fax (021) 496 1405, e-mail iberexpo@aio.ie, web site www.wine-ireland.com.

  Wines are available direct or from specialist outlets.

Irish Distillers Group
- 11–12 Bow Street, Dublin 7. Tel (01) 872 5566, Fax (01) 872 3109, e-mail info@idl.ie, web site www.jameson.ie.

  Most wines are widely available and others only from specialist outlets.

Jenkinson Wines
- 97 Butterfield Park, Rathfarnham, Dublin 14. Tel (01) 493 3480, Fax (01) 493 3480.

  Wines are available from SuperValu-Centra, Spar and independent retailers.

Karwig Wines
- Kilnagleary, Carrigaline, Co. Cork. Tel/Fax (021) 437 2864/437 4159/437 3710, e-mail info@karwig-wines.ie, web site www.karwig-wines.ie.

  Wines are available direct or through the Internet and from Molloy's and some SuperValu-Centra stores.

Koala Wines
- 25 Seatown, Dundalk, Co. Louth. Tel (048) 4175 2804, Fax (048) 4175 2943, e-mail koalawines@ireland1.fsbusiness.co.uk.

  Wines are available from Roches Stores, Superquinn, SuperValu-Centra, Londis, Musgrave's, Spar, Cheers, Next Door, Pettits, O'Donovans (Cork), most NOffLA independents and Mansans CK Wine Shops.

B. MacCormaic Vintners
- 116A Terenure Road North, Dublin 6W. Tel (01) 490 7928, Fax (01) 490 7930, e-mail maccormaicvintners@eircom.net.

  Wines are available from SuperValu-Centra and symbols.

Maxxium
- Rembrandt House, 1 Longford Terrace, Monkstown, Co. Dublin.
  Tel (01) 280 4341, Fax (01) 280 1805, web site www.maxxium.com.

  Wines are widely available. Try Roches Stores, Londis, SuperValu-Centra and O'Briens off-licences.

Mitchell & Son
- 21 Kildare Street, Dublin 2. Tel (01) 676 0766, Fax (01) 661 1509.
- 54 Glasthule Road, Sandycove, Co. Dublin. Tel (01) 230 2301,
  Fax (01) 230 2305, e-mail wines@mitchellandson.com, web site
  www.mitchellandson.com.

  Wines are available from Mitchell & Son wine shops or through the Internet at mitchellandson.com.

Molloy's Group
- Head Office, Block 2, Village Green, Tallaght, Dublin 24.
  Tel (01) 451 5544, Fax (01) 451 5658, e-mail molloys@indigo.ie,
  web site www.molloys.com.

  Wines are available from branches of Molloy's or through the Internet at www.liquorstore.ie.

Musgrave SuperValu-Centra
- Tramore Road, Cork. Tel (021) 480 3000, Fax (021) 431 3621,
  e-mail msvc@musgrave.ie, web site www.musgrave.ie.

  Wines are available from SuperValu-Centra shops.

Nectar Wines
- 53 The Millrace, Chapelizod, Dublin 20. Tel/Fax (01) 623 3846,
  e-mail sales@nectarwines.com, web site www.nectarwines.com.

  Wines are available from off-licences and wine shops. Check web site for details.

O'Briens Wine Off Licence Group
- Head Office, Unit 33, Spruce Avenue, Stillorgan Industrial Park, Stillorgan, Co. Dublin. Tel (1850) 269 777/(01) 269 3139, Fax (01) 269 7480,
  e-mail info@obriensgroup.ie.

  Wines are available from branches of O'Briens.

Oddbins
- 31–33 Weir Road, Wimbledon, London SW19 8UG. Tel (0208) 944 4400,
  Fax (0208) 944 4411, web site www.oddbins.com.

  Wines are available from branches of Oddbins.

On the Case
- 2 St James Terrace, South Circular Road, Dublin 8. Tel/Fax (01) 473 0156,
  e-mail info@onthecase.ie, web site www.onthecase.ie.

  Wines are available direct and also in Dublin from McCabes (Blackrock), Laydens (Middle Abbey Street), Claudio's (Georges Street Arcade), On the Grapevine (Dalkey), For Goodness Sake (Skerries), Morton's (Ranelagh), Bird Flanagan (SCR), Swiss Delicatessen (Rathfarnham) and Quinns (Drumcondra); in Co. Meath from The Barrow (Ashbourne).

Papillon Wines (Vaughan Johnson)

◾ 56 North Strand, Fairview, Dublin 3. Tel (01) 856 1339,
Fax (01) 855 4740, e-mail greg.grouse@oysterinfo.com.

*Wines are available from specialist outlets or from the Vaughan Johnson shop,
11 East Essex Street, Temple Bar, Dublin 2. Tel (01) 671 5355.*

Mary Pawle Wines

◾ Gortamullen, Kenmare, Co. Kerry. Tel/Fax (064) 41443,
e-mail marypawlewines@oceanfree.net.

Wines are available from specialist outlets and Superquinn shops.

River Wines

◾ Sandpit House, Termonfeckin, Co. Louth. Tel (1850) 794 637,
Fax (041) 982 2820, mobile (087) 207 5970, e-mail rvrwines@indigo.ie.

Wines are available by mail order.

Searsons Wine Merchants

◾ Monkstown Crescent, Blackrock, Co. Dublin. Tel (01) 280 0405,
Fax (01) 280 4771, e-mail sales@searsons.com.

*Wines are available direct from Searsons; individual wines are also stocked in
Dublin by DeVine Wine (Castleknock), On the Grapevine (Dalkey), McCabes
(Blackrock), The Vintry (Rathgar), Michael's Wines (Mount Merrion),
Redmonds (Ranelagh), Layden Fine Wines (Middle Abbey Street); outside
Dublin by the Wine Centre (Kilkenny), the Wicklow Wine Co. (Wicklow),
Murtagh's (Enniskerry), The Old Stand (Mullingar), O'Donovans (Cork) and
The Vineyard (Galway).*

Select Wines from Italy

◾ 13 Grattan Court, Gorey, Co. Wexford. Tel (055) 80955,
Fax (055) 80958, e-mail info@select.ie, web site www.select.ie.

*Most of the wines are available from Mitchell & Son; individual wines are
available from independent wine shops nation-wide.*

SuperValu-Centra *see* **Musgrave SuperValu-Centra**

Taserra Wine Merchants

◾ 17 Rathfarnham Road, Terenure, Dublin 6W. Tel (01) 490 4047,
Fax (01) 490 4052.

Wines are widely available.

TDL Distributors

◾ Naas Road, Clondalkin, Dublin 22. Tel (01) 413 0100, Fax (01) 413 0123,
e-mail tdl@tdl.ie.

Wines are widely available.

Tesco Ireland

◾ Gresham House, Marine Road, Dun Laoghaire, Co. Dublin.
Tel (01) 280 8441, Fax (01) 215 2116, web site www.tesco.ie.

Wines are available only from branches of Tesco.

United Beverages

◾ Finches Industrial Park, Long Mile Road, Dublin 12. Tel (01) 450 2000,
Fax (01) 450 9004.

Wines are widely available.

Waterford Wine Vault

High Street, Waterford. Tel/Fax (051) 853 444,
e-mail wineshop@waterfordwinevault.com,
web site www.waterfordwinevault.com.

Wines are available direct.

Wicklow Wine Company

Main Street, Wicklow. Tel (0404) 66767, Fax (0404) 66769.

*Wines are available direct and in Dublin from On the Grapevine (Dalkey),
Michael's Wines (Mount Merrion); in Wicklow from Murtagh's (Enniskerry);
in Galway from The Vineyard.*

The Wine Seller

5 Seapoint Road, Bray, Co. Wicklow. Tel (01) 276 5323, Fax (01) 276
1899, e-mail info@the-wine-seller.com,
web site www.the-wine-seller.com.

Wines are available direct.

WineOnline

Unit 4B, Santry Hall Industrial Estate, Santry, Dublin 9. Tel (01) 886
7717, Fax (01) 842 3829, e-mail anne@wineonline, sales@wineonline.ie,
web site www.wineonline.ie.

Wines are available through the Internet.

Wines Direct

Lisamate, Irishtown, Mullingar, Co. Westmeath. Tel (1800) 579 579,
Fax (044) 40015, e-mail info@wines-direct.com,
web site www.wines-direct.com.

Wines are available by mail order.

Woodford Bourne

79 Broomhill Road, Tallaght, Dublin 24. Tel (01) 404 7300,
Fax (01) 459 9342.

Wines are widely available.

J. S. Woods

6 Sandford Road, Dublin 6. Tel (01) 497 4041, Fax (01) 496 5299,
e-mail radichio@eircom.net.

Wines are available from specialist outlets.

Glossary

AC: Appellation Contrôlée, a French wine classification system that certifies a wine as coming from a particular area. The geographical area may be as large as a region (e.g. AC Bordeaux) or as small as a vineyard (e.g. AC Montrachet). Rules of inclusion differ from AC to AC, but they may prescribe any or all of the following over and above the wine's place of origin—grape varieties, density of planting, yield, alcohol level. Wines must be analysed and tasted before being admitted to the AC.

acidity: all wines contain acids of various kinds, including malic, lactic, tartaric, citric (fixed acids) and acetic (the acid found in vinegar). The fixed acids give wines a crispness to the taste and contribute to the ageing process.

American oak: see ***oak***.

aroma: a somewhat imprecise term, sometimes applied to the entire ***nose***, sometimes only to specific easily distinguishable smells.

balance: a term of praise when applied to a wine, indicating that the wine's ***tannins***, ***acidity*** and alcohol blend well and complement each other, without any individual element dominating.

barrique: an ***oak*** barrel with a capacity of 225 litres.

big wine: a full-bodied wine with an exceptionally rich flavour.

black fruits: tasters' term used to refer to dark berry ***fruits*** such as blackberries, blackcurrants, black cherries, blueberries, etc.

blend: a wine made from more than one grape variety, as opposed to a ***varietal***.

blind tasting: a tasting in which the identities of the wines are unknown to the taster until after tasting notes have been made and scores assigned. All competitive tastings are blind, as are all tastings for this guide.

body: the combination of ***fruit*** extract and alcoholic strength that gives the impression of weight in the mouth.

Botrytis: properly *Botrytis cinerea* (noble rot), a fungus that attacks grapes on vines. Depending on weather conditions and the ripeness of the grapes, it will either spoil the harvest completely (in which case it is known as grey rot) or concentrate the sugars in the ***fruit*** to produce a high-quality, sweet, very long-lived wine.

bottle: the standard bottle size is 75 centilitres. A magnum contains two bottles or 1.5 litres. See also ***maturation***.

bouquet: strictly speaking, this refers only to those mature aromas that develop as the wine ages in the ***bottle***, but it is often used to refer to all characteristics of the grape variety on the ***nose***.

buttery: a rich, fat and delicious character found in some Chardonnay wines, particularly if produced in a good ***vintage*** or warm climate.

carbonic maceration: see ***maceration***.

claret: an English term for a red Bordeaux wine. It comes from the French 'clairet', a wine between a dark rosé and a light red.

classic: word used by wine tasters to indicate that a wine is of high quality, showing the correct characteristics for its type and origin, and possesses great style.

corked: a wine is corked when it has been spoiled by contact with a contaminated cork. This is the most common cause of wine spoilage and can be identified by the wine's stale, woody, mould smell.

cru: literally means 'growth', but on a French wine label refers to the status of the vineyard in which the vines were cultivated; the cru classification is in addition to the *AC*. The system is rather complicated and varies from region to region. In the Médoc region of Bordeaux, there are five *grand cru classé* divisions, beginning with *premier cru* (1st growth), *deuxième cru* (2nd growth), and so on down to the *cinquième cru* (5th growth). In St Émilion, there are three levels—*premier grand cru classé* at the top, then *grand cru classé* and *grand cru.* In Burgundy the top vineyards are *grands crus; premiers crus* come below them. *Grand cru* is also used in Alsace and Champagne to distinguish particularly good vineyard sites.

crust: sediment that forms in bottle-aged port.

Deutscher Tafelwein: lowest level of wine classification in Germany.

DO: Denominación de Origen (designation of origin) is the main quality classification in Spain, similar to the *AC* category in France.

DOC: (1) Denominazione di Origine Controllata (controlled denomination of origin) is the main Italian quality category and is broadly similar to the French *AC.* (2) In Portugal Denominação de Origem Controlada (demarcated region) is the highest quality category. (3) Denominación de Origen Calificada (qualified designation of origin) (sometimes DOCa) is the highest quality category in Spain, currently awarded only to Rioja.

DOCG: Denominazione di Origine Controllata e Garantita (controlled and guaranteed denomination of origin) is the highest Italian quality category.

fermentation: the chemical process whereby the sugar in grapes is converted into alcohol.

fining: the process of adding substances such as egg whites, gelatine or clay to a wine, which causes microscopic suspended solids to fall to the bottom, so that after being racked (transferred to another barrel) or bottled, there will be a minimum of *sediment* or cloudiness in the wine.

finish: the last flavours a wine leaves in the mouth, especially after being swallowed or (in a tasting) spat out.

French oak: see *oak.*

fruit: the fruity flavour of a wine.

grip: word applied to describe red wines with firm tannins, which are sensed on the teeth and gums.

IGT: Indicazione Geografica Tipica (indication of regional typicity) is an Italian quality category similar to the French *VdP.*

IPR: Indicação de Proveniência Regulamentada (indication of origin) (also known as *VQPRD*) is a Portuguese category similar to the French *VDQS* and the Italian *IGT.*

large oak: see *oak.*

lees: sediment that falls to the bottom of a vat of wine after *fermentation* and *maturation.* Most wines are transferred to another container when the lees form; others, especially Muscadet and sparkling wines, are aged on the lees (*sur lie*).

length: the length of time a wine's flavours linger in the mouth after sipping. Long length is one of the markers of a quality wine.

maceration: the period of *fermentation* of a red wine during which the *must* has contact with grape skins. It is during this process that red wines derive their colour and *tannin.* Rosé wines undergo a very short maceration period of one or two days. Red wines intended to be drunk young sometimes undergo carbonic maceration, in which uncrushed grapes are fermented under a layer of carbon dioxide. This results in a wine light in colour and low in tannin, but high in *fruit* and *aroma.*

malolactic fermentation: see *fermentation*.

maturation: the ageing process by which wines develop character and complexity. Maturation is good only up to a point, beyond which the wine will start to decline, but that point differs for each type of wine. A Beaujolais Nouveau will spend only a few months maturing, while tawny port may be aged in *oak* for as long as twenty years. The larger the *bottle*, the slower the maturation—half-bottles of wine mature and decline more quickly than whole bottles.

mousse: the bubbles in a sparkling wine. Ideally these should be very small and long lasting.

mouthfeel: specifically refers to the texture of a wine, as opposed to the *palate*, which also refers to the flavour.

must: unfermented grape juice.

noble rot: see *botrytis*.

nose: the combined smells of a wine's grape varieties' *aromas* and *bottle*-matured *bouquet*.

oak: maturation in new oak adds flavours to wine—the smaller the barrel, the greater the effect. Old oak does not have this effect, but it does allow for controlled *oxidation*. Other oak treatments include adding oak chips or oak staves. See also *barrique*.

oxidation: a chemical reaction that takes place when wine is exposed to air. Barrel *maturation* allows for slow, controlled oxidation, improving the flavour of the wine. However, if this happens too fast or if the process is allowed to go too far, it transforms the alcohol into acetic acid. Wine that is too oxidised tastes unpleasant and may look brown and smell of vinegar.

palate: the flavour and texture of the wine in the mouth; see also *mouth-feel*.

QbA: Qualitätswein bestimmter Anbaugebiete (quality wine from a specified region) is the second-highest quality category in Germany.

QmP: Qualitätswein mit Prädikat (quality wine with special attributes) is the highest classification for German wines. The classifications, which depend on the sugar levels in the grapes, are Kabinett, Spätlese, Auslese, Beerenauslese, Trockenbeerenauslese and Eiswein.

Reserve: in Italy, Portugal, Spain and Bulgaria, a wine labelled 'Riserva' or 'Reserva' must by law be of very high quality and, in the case of Italy and Spain, have undergone a certain minimum ageing, with at least some of it in *oak* barrels. Anywhere else, the word 'Reserve' or 'Réserve' just means that the winemakers think it is one of their best.

sediment: solid debris that falls to the bottom of a wine barrel or, in the case of an unfiltered wine, the *bottle*. Wines undergo *fining* or filtration to reduce the amount of sediment left after bottling.

small oak: see *oak*.

stainless steel vats: vessels used in *fermentation*. The use of stainless steel vats, rather than wood or concrete, makes it easier to control the wine's fermentation temperature.

structure: the sum of the component parts that shape a wine, including *fruit*, *alcohol* and *acidity*, and, in reds, *tannin*.

sur lie: see *lees*.

tannin: a chemical substance found in grape skins and hence in red wines but not whites. The ability of a red wine to improve as it matures depends very much on its tannins, but a wine that is too tannic will taste dry and hard; red wines intended to be drunk young will sometimes be put through a process called carbonic *maceration*, which minimises tannin. Tannins can also be derived from *oak*, stalks and pips. Tannin from pips is the harshest of all.

terroir: the complete growing environment of soil, aspect, altitude, climate and any other factor that may affect the life of the vine.

vanilla: often used to describe the *nose* and sometimes the *palate* of an *oak*-aged wine, especially a Rioja.

varietal: a wine made entirely, or almost entirely, from a single grape variety, as opposed to a *blend*.

VdlT: Vino de la Tierra (wine of the land) is a Spanish classification for country wines similar to the *VdP* category in France.

VdM: (1) Vino de Mesa (table wine) is the lowest quality category in Spain. Wines are basic and are often a blend of wines from different regions. This category is also used by progressive producers to make wines that don't conform to *DO* rules. (2) Vinho de Mesa (table wine) is the lowest quality category in Portugal.

VdP: Vin de Pays (country wine) is the third-highest quality classification of French wine.

VDQS: Vin Délimité de Qualité Supérieure (delimited wine of superior quality) is the second-highest classification for French wines, just below *AC*.

VdT: (1) Vin de Table (table wine) is the lowest quality category in France. No region or vintage may be stated on the label and the wine is likely to be of basic quality. (2) Vino da Tavola (table wine) is the basic table wine classification in Italy, but is also used by makers of fine wines that do not conform to *DOC* regulations.

VQPRD: see *IPR*.

VR: Vinho Regional (regional wine) is the equivalent of French *VdP*.

vintage: the year the grapes were harvested. Wines differ from year to year, depending on weather conditions during the vine's growing seasons. Champagnes and sparkling wines, unlike still reds and whites, are more often than not made from *blends* of grapes harvested in different years ('non-vintage'). A vintage Champagne—one made from grapes harvested in a single season—is rare and expensive.

Index of wines

Wines of the year are indicated in **bold** type.